Philipp Robinson Rössner

Scottish Trade with German Ports 1700–1770

Studien zur Gewerbe- und Handelsgeschichte der vorindustriellen Zeit

Vormals Göttinger Beiträge
zur Wirtschafts- und Sozialgeschichte

Begründet von
Wilhelm Abel und Karl Heinrich Kaufhold

Herausgegeben von
Karl Heinrich Kaufhold und Markus A. Denzel

Redaktion:
Hans-Jürgen Gerhard

Nr. 28

Philipp Robinson Rössner

Scottish Trade with German Ports 1700–1770

A Sketch of the North Sea Trades and the Atlantic Economy on Ground Level

Franz Steiner Verlag Stuttgart 2008

Bibliografische Information der Deutschen Nationalbibliothek
Die Deutsche Nationalbibliothek verzeichnet diese Publikation in der Deutschen Nationalbibliografie; detaillierte bibliografische Daten sind im Internet über <http://dnb.d-nb.de> abrufbar.

ISBN: 978-3-515-09215-9

Gedruckt auf säurefreiem, alterungsbeständigem Papier.
Druck: Printservice Decker & Bokor, München
Printed in Germany

To

Ailidh Johanna

* 17/12/2007

TABLE OF CONTENTS

PREFACE

The present study contributes to three fields: comparative or European economic history; German, as well as Scottish economic history. It does so by deliberately picking out two of the smaller players in eighteenth-century European or even world trade, in order to show how intrinsically-linked their trades were with the larger, pan-European, Atlantic, or even "global" economic patterns. Monitoring two comparatively small trading partners – Germany's North Sea (and to a small extent, Baltic) and Britain's northern (Scottish) ports in the eighteenth century – provides, due to the exceptionally good source material, a good opportunity of studying the workings of the global patterns in a very detailed way. Mostly this is due to the near-complete preservation of the eighteenth-century Scottish customs accounts since Christmas quarter 1742. These records are the most detailed and comprehensive of their kind, as they – contrary to similar files of other contemporaneous trading nations – afford detailed information as to all commodities shipped into or out of Scotland at any one time, regardless whether these were liable to taxation or not. They are therefore unique and provide the best starting point for studies in bi-lateral and even multilateral trade on a macro- or aggregate pattern (import-export statistics) involving Scottish trade with countries x, y and z, as well as a micro-level (individual merchants involved in the trades).

This will serve as an apology for the thematic approach. Some explanation by ways of another apology, regarding the scope of the present work, may also be made. The monograph is a side-project of a larger study on Scotland's eighteenth-century trade, which has already been published as P. R. RÖSSNER, Scottish Trade in the Wake of Union (1700–1760). The Rise of a Warehouse Economy (*Vierteljahrschrift für Sozial- und Wirtschaftsgeschichte-Beihefte Nr. 198*), Stuttgart 2008. As a consequence there are some similarities here and there. But as the present book has existed for a longer time – it was conceived and large parts of it written and accepted for publication in 2005, whilst the other one was written-up in 2006 and accepted for publication in 2007 –, it has the "right of way" so to speak. I therefore kept some of these similarities in, so as to retain the original structure of the work. Nevertheless I chose to leave out chapter five, a study on three Scottish merchants involved in trade with Germany, which would have been identical to chapter 8 in my larger work mentioned above. That chapter – I hope – drives home the "multi-lateral" facets of Scottish trade with Germany, and I consider it part of and intrinsically-linked to the argument put forward within the present work. Therefore the following monograph is to be understood as an addition to and "thematic enlargement" of my *Scottish Trade in the Wake of Union* – in fact the two belong to each other. The resulting and consequential third apology has to go to the publisher, Franz Steiner Verlag, as well as the editors of the *Studien zur Gewerbe- und Handelsgeschichte der vorindustriellen Zeit* (SGHVZ) monograph series, for such a long delay between acceptation and submission of the manuscript.

During the process of writing this study I have collected a great deal of intellectual and other debts from scholars and colleagues. I should like to express my gratitude above all to Professor emeritus Ian Blanchard (Edinburgh) who has proved an admirable academic teacher and companion. Without him the present work could neither have been conceived nor written. I should further like to extend my thanks to my other colleagues in the subject areas of Economic and Social History and Scottish History at the University of Edinburgh, as well as colleagues and friends Dr Andrew MacKillop (Aberdeen), Professor Leos Müller (Uppsala), Professor T. Christopher Smout (Anstruther / St Andrews), and Professor Christopher A. Whatley (Dundee).

I am also much indebted to Professor emeritus Karl Heinrich Kaufhold (Göttingen) for supporting the inclusion of this study in the *Studien zur Gewerbe- und Handelsgeschichte der vorindustriellen Zeit*. My greatest debt in the academic department, however, has – without question – been incurred to my mentor and teacher, Professor Dr. Markus A. Denzel (Göttingen, now Leipzig). Professor Denzel constantly inspired, supported and actively encouraged my work from its earliest stages onwards. His honours classes on European expansion overseas, the Fuggers and the development of trade-fairs, banks and stock exchanges since the Middle Ages, which he taught at the University of Göttingen during the 1998-2000 academic diet, have to a considerable degree influenced and shaped my way of thinking of the subject. *Vielen Dank, Herr Professor Denzel!*

Last but not least, I should like to dedicate this to the nuclear family of mine. Words cannot adequately describe what you mean to me.

Leipzig, April 2008 Philipp Robinson Rössner

I. THE ANALYTICAL FRAMEWORK

As demonstrated elsewhere[1], Scotland and her foreign trade – part of British trade – after 1707 underwent some formidable changes, so as to become a "warehouse economy". Between 1730 and 1760 – the last three decades of Scotland's pre-industrial period, trade levels began to expand significantly, probably matching or surpassing all growth rates realized during previous decades, if not centuries. Scotland underwent her own "commercial revolution", yet on terms decidedly different from England. Overseas trade levels tripled between 1700 and 1760. But trade levels remained small, both in comparison to England, as well as in relation to Scotland's national income. Trade was furthermore biased towards the importation and re-exportation of colonial foodstuffs, particularly tobacco. This peculiar Scottish trading pattern was conditioned by the structure of the domestic economy and the inclusion of Scottish ports and merchants into the English commercial empire, institutionally framed by the Navigation Acts and subsequent parliamentary legislative efforts related to the former. Scotland's manufacturing base was weak – the domestic economy neither exported particularly large amounts and shares of her production, nor was it heavily reliant upon imports from overseas. Accordingly, average imports of tobacco, sugar and rum from the Americas far outpaced yearly average domestic exports of linen, woollen, leather and other manufactures to that region. On the other hand the commercial regulations covered under the English restoration customs system provided for some beneficial aspects that encouraged and stimulated the re-export trades in colonial non-essentials. Scots traders thus made use of the commercial opportunities afforded by the Union 1707, by the profitable entrepôt trades in American foodstuffs to continental destinations which expanded at an exponential rate after the mid-1730s. These tropical and sub-tropical non-essentials could be sold on continental European markets with a generous profit mark-up, especially since they could draw back up to 100 per cent of customs duties paid upon import. Germany was part of these markets and in some ways intrinsically linked to the cyclical upswing characteristic of Britain's – both Scotland's, as well as England's – foreign trade during the eighteenth century.

1 P. R. RÖSSNER, Scottish Trade in the Wake of Union (1700–1760). The Rise of a Warehouse Economy, Stuttgart 2008.

1. THE "EMBEDDEDNESS" OF EIGHTEENTH-CENTURY SCOTTISH-GERMAN TRADE (I): THE HISTORICAL CONTEXT

On September 1st in 1716, John Steuart, a Scottish fish and grain merchant based at Inverness, wrote to his correspondent Alexander Andrew, merchant banker in Amsterdam. He was concerned about money due to him at various places across north-western Europe. At that date he had credit in the Netherlands, in Spain, and not least in Germany: "I hope to Balance what I am Due you by the proceeds of hering I am Just shepping for Hamburg."[2] These balances were the result of commodity sales on Steuart's account all across the northern European sea ports, stretching from the Baltic to the North Sea. Steuart's fellow merchant, Alexander Mackintosh, likewise dealt in herring; the proceeds of his sales on the Hamburg market were remitted by bill of exchange drawn on a London merchant banker, Nathaniel Cambridge, whom both Mackintosh, as well as his Hamburg correspondent, Bartholomew Bludworth, had an account with.[3] At that time the exchange rate for bills Hamburg on London stood below par (12.46 Mark Banko per £Sterling) – a scenario which had obtained for virtually the entire first half of the eighteenth century.[4] Thus Mark Banko, the local Hamburg bank money, stood at a premium, Sterling was available at an attractive price. This situation corresponded to a glutted fish market in Hamburg. In 1715–1717, Scots herring dispatched to Hamburg generally came "to a Very bad Markett. [...] Our fishmongers are so very much overstocked [...] if they bidd any price at all [...] t'will be a very poor one. [...]".[5] Even early in the eighteenth century, therefore, Scottish-German trade was contingent upon generally prevailing European commodity and financial market conditions – conditions and spatial frameworks that went far beyond either Scotland or Germany.

This was by no means different later on in the century or confined to a particular group of merchants. Whenever the large Glasgow tobacco firm of BUCHANAN & SIMSON sent over tobacco, sugar or coffee to Hamburg and Bremen, they usually sent out letters to their German factors first, enquiring about the current market conditions.[6] What they normally had to bear in mind, other than the German market, or the current exchange rate between the £Sterling and Mark Banko in correctly determining their anticipated profits, were factors such as French demand for tobacco in Britain, or French supply of sugar and coffee from the French Antilles to Hamburg, because the

2 W. MACKAY (ed.), The Letter-Book of Baillie John Steuart of Inverness 1715–1752, Edinburgh 1915, pp. 24s. (1 September 1716).

3 NAS, GD23/6/33/6, e.g. 29 May 1716, 5 October 1717, Bartholomew Bludworth to Alexander Mackintosh.

4 J. SCHNEIDER / O. SCHWARZER / F. ZELLFELDER / M. A. DENZEL (eds.), Währungen der Welt, VI: Geld und Währungen in Europa im 18. Jahrhundert, Stuttgart 1992, pp. 45–47 (par exchange rate); 200-203 (bill rate). W. Reiss, Historical Exchange Rates, in: W. FISCHER / R. MARVIN MCINNIS / J. SCHNEIDER (eds.), The Emergence of a World Economy 1500–1914, Pt. I.: 1500–1850, Wiesbaden 1986, pp. 171–190, at p. 189 / Fig. 5.

5 Bludworth (factor resident in Hamburg) to Mackintosh. NAS, GD23/6/33/2, GD23/6/33/8 (copy), identical wording but different dates (29 November 1715, 10 December 1716).

6 RÖSSNER, In the Wake, ch. 8, esp. p. 277f.

French usually offered colonial products at very attractive prices.[7] With regard to the tobacco available in Glasgow for re-export to Germany, BUCHANAN & SIMSON also monitored the purchasing patterns of the French tobacco buying agents in London, Glasgow and Edinburgh. If the French agents bought too much or made a bulk purchase earlier than expected, there would be no cargo available in Glasgow to be shipped to the German market.[8]

The preceding remarks provide some first hints as to the "degree of embeddedness" of Scottish-German trade in the eighteenth century in its various contexts: contemporary economy and society, as well as historiography – past and present. First, regardless the type of transactions and scale of business involved, early modern European trade was hardly ever truly bilateral, as the ceteris paribus conditions of the various trade models in international economics would have it. This applies to market conditions and payments alike. Market conditions in Germany for products traded by Scots were, apart from German demand for and Scottish supply of these products and depending on the type of commodity under consideration, frequently also contingent for instance upon the Amsterdam bill market, or determined by preceding French purchases and sales and so on. If neutral shipping was required, the size of the Scottish-German trade volume was partly contingent upon the availability or supply of Hamburg and Bremen shipping.[9] Therefore Scottish-German trade took place within a pan-European economic matrix. Secondly, many transactions involved a multilateral system of payments. As commodity flows, which can be captured statistically (chapter four; financial flows are normally elusive), were almost never balanced, they usually required further financial streams in the opposite direction. But was that really the opposite direction? Assume that a Scots merchant sent over tobacco and rice to Bremen, did he always receive back *Osnaburghs* (Osnabrück linen cloth) and other German cloth from Bremen directly in return to roughly the same value? – Hardly. Such transactions usually involved locations and time frameworks different from those obtaining in the commodity trades, even though it is impossible to prove that point quantitatively. Preciously few private papers and records have survived on either the Scottish or German side, but those examples that have, seem to suggest that even comparatively small merchants whose business operations did – in comparison to some English Atlantic traders – not require particularly impressive outlays of circulating capital, nevertheless used the recently developed multilateral payments mechanism with its foci Amsterdam and London as a matter-of-course. This aspect has been fully developed in chapter 8 of *Scottish Trade in the Wake of Union 1700–1760. The Rise of a Warehouse Economy.*[10] In terms of the argument the reader should consider it the consequential collateral to the statistical analysis of chapters two to four of the present book.

---

7 M. A. DENZEL, Zur Geschäftspraxis eines Nanteser Handelshauses: Der Preiskurant von Pelloutier & Cie (1763–1793), in: J. HOOCK / W. REININGHAUS (eds.), Kaufleute in Europa. Handelshäuser und ihre Überlieferung in vor- und frühindustrieller Zeit, Dortmund 1997, pp. 61–87, at p. 78.

8 NAS, CS96/507, Buchanan & Simson Letter Book, 12 January, 25 February, 29 February, 26 May 1760.

9 NAS, CS96/507, 28 December 1759, 25 February 1760.

10 RÖSSNER, In the Wake, ch. 8.

Thus, regardless whether the "top-down" (statistical analysis) or "bottom-up" (individual merchants) approach is chosen, the same pattern occurs: trade was usually multilateral. Scottish-German trade was furthermore firmly integrated into what scholars have variously called the "Atlantic economy" (Price)[11], or the "European-centred world trading system" (Sperling).[12] Its corollary in accounting terms was the north-west European financial network and system of cashless payments, studied in-depth by Denzel.[13] In this way, Scottish-German trade during the eighteenth century was a phenomenon of truly European dimensions.

11 J. J. MCCUSKER / K. MORGAN (eds.), The Early Modern Atlantic Economy, Cambridge 2000.

12 J. SPERLING, The International Payments Mechanism in the Seventeenth and Eighteenth Centuries, in: Economic History Review, Second Series, XIV (1961–2), pp. 446–68.

13 M. A. DENZEL, 'La Practica della Cambiatura'. Europäischer Zahlungsverkehr vom 14. bis zum 17. Jahrhundert, Stuttgart 1994.

2. THE "EMBEDDEDNESS" OF EIGHTEENTH-CENTURY SCOTTISH-GERMAN TRADE (II): HISTORIOGRAPHY

How is the present study to be placed in historiography? A brief survey of the available literature on the topic under consideration might best commence with the remark that new territory is being claimed. Whilst sound and general studies on British and German overseas trade as such do exist, especially in the British tradition of writing economic history, as Britain has the best historical statistics of her time and those statistics were usually concerned with trade and taxation, very few and truly comparative studies, defined here as cross-country or bi-lateral studies of overseas commerce, exist for early modern Europe. The present study is a first step into this direction. Accordingly it will have to remain synoptic to a certain extent, linking different views and traditions of economic history, in order to achieve a comparative and more detailed perspective on eighteenth-century European trade.

Scottish-German relations have not received detailed treatment ever since Fischer's ground-breaking yet anecdotal studies. Fischer first raised awareness of the presence of Scots, in particular small traders, but also larger merchants, in considerable numbers in the larger German and quasi-German cities such as Stralsund[14], Danzig and other cities in the Baltic[15], and the German empire in general.[16] Recently, Zickermann has worked on Scots resident in Hamburg in the seventeenth century.[17] Neither these, nor Ditchburn's study, however, which includes Germany, but does not go beyond the Middle Ages[18], have an economic focus. This represents a considerable scholarly gap, in particular since German ports such as Hamburg and Bremen were amongst the closest destinations for Scottish sea-borne traffic outside the British Isles, and trade – much more than politics – was one of the most obvious reasons for Scots to engage in relations with Germany and vice versa.

The same deficiency still applies to eighteenth century German overseas trade in general. In 1964 Kellenbenz remarked pitifully that there was not a single comprehensive study on Germany's overseas trade available for any period in the eighteenth century.[19] Unfortunately, this statement has remained valid to-day. True, Germany had no commercial statistics comparable to those famous English, Irish (both 1696s.), and later on Scottish (1755s.) sources. These *Ledgers of Imports and Exports*, which for the first time in the history of statistical recording covered *all* imports and exports, regardless whether these were liable to duty or not (thus drawing up a balance of trade), really were unique. But at least for the larger German North Sea ports of Ham-

14 T. FISCHER, The Scots in Sweden, Edinburgh 1907, p. 90.

15 ID., The Scots in Eastern and Western Prussia, Edinburgh 1903, ch. 1.

16 ID., The Scots in Germany, Edinburgh 1902.

17 K. ZICKERMANN, 'Briteannia ist mein patria'. Scotsmen and the 'British' Community in Hamburg, in: A. GROSJEAN / S. MURDOCH (eds.), Scottish Communities Abroad in the Early Modern Period, Leiden / Boston 2005, pp. 249–273.

18 D. DITCHBURN, Scotland and Europe: The Medieval Kingdom and its Contacts with Christendom, c.1215–1545, Vol. 1: Religion, Culture and Commerce, East Linton 2000.

19 H. KELLENBENZ, Der deutsche Außenhandel gegen Ausgang des 18. Jahrhunderts, in: F. LÜTGE (ed.), Die wirtschaftliche Situation in Deutschland und Österreich um die Wende vom 18. zum 19. Jahrhundert, Stuttgart 1964, pp. 4–60, at p. 5.

burg, Bremen and Emden quite a good set of import statistics can be derived from those ports' customs records. The Hamburg *Admiralitätszoll- und Convoygeldeinnahmebücher,* Bremen's *Schlachteangabebücher,* and Emden's *Licenteinnahmebücher* have all been preserved from at least the mid-eighteenth century onwards, for Hamburg even earlier.[20] Yet only the Hamburg records were – fairly recently – edited as a statistical manual useable by historians, and no comprehensive study on their trade has hitherto been produced.[21] To an extent this deficiency is not only due to the absence of financially viable and manageable computerized databases prior to the 1980s, but also to the fact that "German overseas trade" is a non-operational tool. Kellenbenz and Kaufhold[22] pointed out the theoretical as well as technical difficulties of constructing "German" aggregates or even time series of imports and exports. They also elaborated on the potential pit-falls of proposing the analytical concept of "Germany's foreign trade" as a topic for discussion for the period under consideration.

One consequence of this was the emergence of a peculiarly "German" academic tradition of focusing on particular ports, rather than attempting the big synopsis. Very obviously this approach was chosen mostly for reasons of analytical safety and robustness of the conclusions (and perhaps, prior to the 1980s/1990s the absence of affordable and manageable spreadsheet and database programs). On the other hand, these studies have not usually reached beyond the article level and have thus been severely limited in terms of scale and analytical scope. Exemplary, but frequently outdated, studies are available for Emden[23], Bremen[24], Hamburg[25], Lübeck[26] and Flens-

---

20 K. NEWMAN, Hamburg in the European Economy, 1660–1750, in: Journal of European Economic History, XIV, 1 (1985), pp. 57–93.

21 J. SCHNEIDER / O.-E. KRAWEHL / M. A. DENZEL (eds.), Statistik des Hamburger seewärtigen Einfuhrhandels im 18. Jahrhundert. Nach den Admiralitätszoll- und Convoygeld-Einnahmebüchern, St Katharinen 2001.

22 K. H. KAUFHOLD, Deutschland 1650–1850, in: W. FISCHER / J. A. VAN HOUTTE / H. KELLENBENZ / I. MIECK / F. VITTINGHOFF (eds.), Handbuch der Europäischen Wirtschafts- und Sozialgeschichte, Vol. 4: Von der Mitte des 17. zur Mitte des 19. Jahrhunderts, Stuttgart 1993, pp. 530–588, at pp. 571–573.

23 K. H. BOKELOH, Emder Wirtschaftsgeschichte 1744–1806. Preußischer Absolutismus der zweiten Hälfte des 18. Jahrhunderts in einer Randprovinz, University of Tübingen PhD Thesis, Tübingen 1984. A. MÜLLER, Emdens Seeschifffahrt und Seehandel von der Besitzergreifung Ostfrieslands durch Preußen bis zur Eröffnung des Dortmund-Ems-Kanals 1744–1899, Hansische Geschichtsblätter, LV (1930).

24 H.-J. VON WITZENDORF, Beiträge zur Bremischen Handelsgeschichte in der zweiten Hälfte des 18. Jahrhunderts, Bremisches Jahrbuch, XLIII (1951), pp. 342–394; ID., Bremens Handel im 16. und 17. Jahrhundert, Bremisches Jahrbuch, XLIV (1955), pp. 128–174.

25 E. BAASCH, Zur Statistik des Ein- und Ausfuhrhandels Hamburgs Anfang des 18. Jahrhunderts, Hansische Geschichtsblätter, LIV (1929).

26 C. MEYER-STOLL, Die lübeckische Kaufmannschaft des 17. Jahrhunderts unter wirtschafts- und sozialgeschichtlichen Aspekten, Frankfurt-am-Main / Bern / New York / Paris 1989, has focused on the later seventeenth century, based on the Lübeck Zulagebücher. E. HARDER (-GERSDORFF), Seehandel zwischen Lübeck und Rußland im 17./18. Jahrhundert nach Zollbüchern der Novgorodfahrer, Pt. I, Zeitschrift des Vereins für Lübeckische Geschichte und Altertumskunde, LXI (1961), pp. 43–114, and E. HARDER-GERSDORFF, Handelskonjunkturen und Warenbilanzen im lübeckischrussischen Seeverkehr des 18. Jahrhunderts, Vierteljahrschrift für Sozial- und Wirtschaftsgeschichte, LVII (1970), pp. 15–45, focus on Lübeck's trade with "Russia" (but mainly Riga, Nerva, and Reval). ID., Mitteleuropäische Gewerbezonen und ostbaltischer Handel im 18. Jahrhundert, in: K.

burg[27] (the latter being a Danish port at that time).[28] Editions of primary sources or databases derived from information contained in customs accounts are virtually non-existent. Hamburg represents the exception; recent rediscoveries of earlier volumes of the *Admiralty Toll Accounts* have initiated a fresh research initiative with a source whose value had been discovered long ago.[29] The main obvious downfall of all these works, however, is that their analysis, by normally relying on the local set of quantitative sources only, tends to be unilateral and its focus accordingly biased. True cross-country or comparative studies, in which the number of sets of sources used is equal to the number of trade links examined, are rare, not only for British-German trade, but for eighteenth century European trade in general. Partly this outcome is an inevitable one, as none of the contemporary nations or ports are as well endowed with statistical material in the eighteenth century as Scotland – not even England, where the eighteenth century port books equivalent to the Scottish series, have been destroyed by several fires in the London Customhouse.

But contrary to the situation of a comparatively excellent source endowment, Scottish historiography has not advanced particularly far, either. There is only one cross-country study, on Scottish trade with Ireland, which is based on both Scottish, as well as Irish records.[30] But even regarding trends, structure and fluctuations in Scotland's trade in the eighteenth century, the situation is in fact similar to the one prevailing for Germany. Existing studies have focused on particular commodities, ports, or countries Scotland traded with. The big synopsis is an issue scholars have largely evaded to-day.[31] General surveys on Scotland's eighteenth-century trade have not reached beyond the article or chapter level: remarkable but heavily out of date is the

---

FRIEDLAND / F. IRSIGLER (eds.), Seehandel und Wirtschaftswege Nordeuropas im 17. und 18. Jahrhundert, Ostfildern 1981, pp. 26–37. R. HAMMEL-KIESOW, Hansischer Seehandel und wirtschaftliche Wechsellagen. Der Umsatz im Lübecker Hafen in der zweiten Hälfte des 14. Jahrhunderts, 1492–6 und 1680–2, in: S. JENKS / M. NORTH (eds.), Der Hansische Sonderweg? Beiträge zur Sozial- und Wirtschaftsgeschichte der Hanse, Cologne / Weimar / Vienna 1993, pp. 77–93 tentatively yet briefly discusses trade in relation to Lübeck's economic development in the longer run.

27 T. LINK, Flensburgs Überseehandel von 1755 bis 1807. Seine wirtschaftliche und politische Bedeutung im Rahmen des Dänisch-Norwegischen Seehandels, Neumünster 1959.

28 Further references to literature up to 1964 can be found in KELLENBENZ, Außenhandel.

29 SCHNEIDER et al. (eds.), *Statistik.*

30 L. E. COCHRAN, Scottish Trade with Ireland in the Eighteenth Century, Edinburgh 1985; ID., Scottish Trade with Ireland in the Eighteenth Century, Unpubl. University of Stirling PhD thesis, 2 Vols. Stirling 1980; ID, Scottish-Irish Trade in the Eighteenth Century, in: T. M. DEVINE / D. DICKSON (eds.), Ireland and Scotland 1600–1850. Parallels and Contrast in Economic and Social Development, Edinburgh 1983, pp. 151–162.

31 For earlier centuries this deficiency has been partly compensated for by recent studies: M. RORKE, Scottish Overseas Trade 1275/86–1597, Unpubl. Univ. of Edinburgh PhD thesis, 2 Vols., Edinburgh 2001; I. BLANCHARD, Northern Wools and Netherlands Markets at the Close of the Middle Ages, in: G. G. SIMPSON (ed.), Scotland and the Low Countries 1124–1994, East Linton 1996, pp. 76–88; D. DITCHBURN, Trade with Northern Europe, 1297–1540, in: M. LYNCH / R. M. SPEARMAN / G. STELL (eds.), The Scottish Medieval Town, Edinburgh 1988, pp. 161–179; Sections on Trade in P. G. B. MCNEILL / H. L. MACQUEEN (eds.), Atlas of Scottish History to 1707, Edinburgh 1996, pp. 238–283; A. STEVENSON, Trade with the South, 1070–1513, in: LYNCH / SPEARMAN / STELL (eds), Medieval Town, pp. 180-206.

first general discussion in two chapters by Hamilton.[32] Unfortunately, the instructive accounts on trade by Lynch and Stevenson in the *Atlas of Scottish History*[33] finish their analysis in 1700. The accounts on trade in the generalist but rather outdated economic history textbooks on eighteenth century Scotland are limited in scale and scope, which is apparent from the works of Butt and Lythe[34], Campbell[35], Lenman[36] and Whyte.[37] The most recent textbook on Scottish economic history, which is largely a reprint of articles written in the 1970s and 1980s, contains no systematic discussion of the commercial sector of the economy in eighteenth-century Scotland.[38]

It should be noted that until very recently, earlier centuries had not been served well either. Model studies for the mediaeval period by Rorke[39] and for the early seventeenth century by Watson[40] came in the wake of a handful of rather pioneering articles in the 1980s, which for the first time used quantitative evidence (customs accounts) for their analysis.[41] These studies were overdue, as by that time the pioneer edition of England's customs accounts was already old and out-dated.[42] Generally speaking, trade as a sub-sector of the inhomogeneous tertiary or service sector of the economy, should ideally be dealt with in a macro-economic perspective. Without doubt in that regard the 1960s appear as a watershed, as English economic historiography became quantitative since that date, more interested in pinpointing the overall and long-term quantitative framework (trends and fluctuations), rather than discussing trade purely on the basis of institutional aspects and non-quantitative accounts. Unfortunately, this tendency never reached north of the English Border. Exemplary English exercises in the field, such as the classical works by Davis[43] and Schlote[44], are either

---

32 H. HAMILTON, An Economic History of Scotland in the Eighteenth Century, Oxford 1963, chs. IX, X.

33 MCNEILL / MACQUEEN, Atlas.

34 S. G. E. LYTHE / J. BUTT, An Economic History of Scotland, 1100–1939, Glasgow / London 1975, ch. IX.

35 R. H. CAMPBELL, Scotland since 1707. The Rise of an Industrial Society, Edinburgh, 2nd revised ed., 1985, ch. III.

36 B. LENMAN, An Economic and Social History of Modern Scotland 1660–1976, London 1975.

37 I. D. WHYTE, Scotland before the Industrial Revolution. An Economic and Social History c1050 – c1750, London / New York 1995, esp. pp. 301–307; ID., Scotland's Society and Economy in Transition, c.1500–c.1760, Basingstoke / London / New York 1997.

38 T. M. DEVINE / C. L. LEE / G. C. PEDEN (eds.), The Transformation of Scotland. The Economy Since 1700, Edinburgh 2005.

39 RORKE, Scottish Overseas Trade; ID., English and Scottish Overseas Trade, 1300–1600, in: Economic History Review, Second Series, LIX, 2 (2006), pp. 265–288.

40 J. C. WATSON, Scottish Overseas Trade, 1597–1645, 2 Vols., Unpubl. University of Edinburgh PhD Thesis, Edinburgh 2005.

41 BLANCHARD, Northern Wools; DITCHBURN, Trade; MCNEILL / MACQUEEN (eds.), Atlas, pp. 238–283; STEVENSON, Trade.

42 E. M. CARUS-WILSON / O. COLEMAN, England's Export Trade 1275–1547, Oxford 1963.

43 R. DAVIS, English Foreign Trade, 1660–1700, in: Economic History Review, Second Series, VI (1954), pp. 150–166; ID., English Foreign Trade, 1700–1774, in: Economic History Review, Second Series, XV (1962), pp. 285–303.

absent or exist, but do not quite match the analytical level of the studies available for England.[45] And at their time pioneering editions of information contained in English customs accounts and contemporary trade statistics have not yet been repeated for Scotland.[46] Instead, scholars previously working on Scotland have chosen to pursue a particularistic approach, sometimes in a way very similar to Germany, by focusing on specific commodities, countries, ports and merchants. The most prominent examples, which have been discussed elsewhere, are tobacco[47], the ports of Aberdeen[48], Dundee[49], Glasgow[50] and Montrose.[51] Coherent geographical areas (regional economies) and their trade have also been studied, for instance Shetland[52] and "the West" of Scotland.[53] Another framework of trade in a historical perspective is represented by studies on particular merchants or companies or partnerships of merchants. With the exception of tobacco, such studies are almost completely absent. There is only one study on a small merchant active in the early decades in Leith, who clearly was a minor player

---

44 W. SCHLOTE, Entwicklung und Strukturwandlungen des englischen Aussenhandels von 1700 bis zur Gegenwart, Jena 1938. Engl. translation: British Overseas Trade. From 1700 to the 1930s, Oxford 1952.

45 HAMILTON, Economic History, chs. IX, X is an exception, as in a way is T. C. SMOUT, Where Had the Scottish Economy got to by the Third Quarter of the Eighteenth Century?, in: I. HONT / M. IGNATIEFF (eds.), Wealth and Virtue. The Shaping of Political Economy in the Scottish Enlightenment, Cambridge 1983, pp. 45–72.

46 CARUS-WILSON / COLEMAN, England's Export Trade; E. B. SCHUMPETER, English Overseas Trade Statistics, 1697–1808, Oxford 1960. "Guides" to the immensely rich (and in the eighteenth century richer than England) Scottish statistical materials have likewise not been produced. G. N. CLARK, Guide to English Commercial Statistics 1696–1782, London 1938.

47 J. M. PRICE, The Rise of Glasgow in the Chesapeake Tobacco Trade, 1707–1775, in: William and Mary Quarterly, II (1954), pp. 179–199; as well as his article collections: ID., The Atlantic Frontier of the Thirteen American Colonies and States. Essays in Eighteenth Century Commercial and Social History, Aldershot 1996; ID., Tobacco in Atlantic Trade. The Chesapeake, London and Glasgow 1675–1775, Aldershot 1995; ID., Overseas Trade and Traders. Essays on Some Commercial, Financial and Political Challenges Facing British Atlantic Merchants, 1660–1775, Aldershot 1996; T. M. DEVINE, The Tobacco Lords. A Study of the Tobacco Merchants of Glasgow and their Trading Activities 1740–1790, Edinburgh 1975; I. W. STEVENSON, Some Aspects of the Geography of the Clyde Tobacco Trade in the Eighteenth Century, in: The Scottish Geographical Magazine, LXXXIX (1973), pp. 19–35.

48 G. JACKSON, The Economy: Aberdeen and the Sea, in: E. P. DENNISON / D. DITCHBURN / M. LYNCH (eds.), Aberdeen Before 1800. A New History, East Linton 2002, pp. 159–180.

49 C. A. WHATLEY / D. SWINFEN / A. M. SMITH, The Life and Times of Dundee, Edinburgh 1993.

50 G. JACKSON, Glasgow in Transition, c.1660 to c. 1740, in: T. M. DEVINE / G. JACKSON (eds.), Glasgow, Vol. 1: Beginnings to 1830, Manchester / New York 1995, pp. 63–105; and T. M. DEVINE, The Golden Age of Tobacco, in: ibid, pp. 139–183.

51 G. JACKSON / S. G. E. LYTHE (eds.), The Port of Montrose: A History of its Harbour, Trade and Shipping, Tayport 1993; therein: I. D. WHYTE, 'All Kynds of Graine': the Trade in Victual c. 1680–1825 (pp. 115–124); D. G. ADAMS, Trade in the Eighteenth and Nineteenth Centuries (pp. 125–149.

52 H. D. SMITH, Shetland Life and Trade, 1550–1914, Edinburgh 1984.

53 A. SLAVEN, The Development of the West of Scotland 1750–1960, London 1976.

in the game.[54] Jackson's study of the Edinburgh whale fishing company remains an interesting starting point for the larger companies.[55] With regard to firms or partnerships active in the Atlantic trades, Price's article on Buchanan & Simson is still fairly much the starting and the ending point.[56]

54 T. MCALOON, A Minor Scottish Merchant in General Trade: The Case of Edward Burd 1728–39, in: J. BUTT / J. T. WARD (eds.), Scottish Themes. Essays in Honour of S. G. E. Lythe, Edinburgh 1976, pp. 17–27.

55 G. JACKSON, Government Bounties and the Establishment of the Scottish Whaling Trade, 1750–1800, in: BUTT / WARD (eds.), Scottish Themes, pp. 46–66.

56 J. M. PRICE, Buchanan & Simson, 1759–1763: A Different Kind of Glasgow Firm Trading to the Chesapeake, in: William and Mary Quarterly, XL (1983), pp. 3–41.

3. OBJECTIVES AND SUBJECTS OF STUDY

Considering the aforementioned deficiencies in historiography, particularly of eighteenth-century Scottish trade, the present study is intended to bridge, if not close, the gap. This will be done using a statistical or top-down viewpoint – for the individual merchants involved in trade with Germany on the Scottish side, or the micro-economic / bottom-up aspect so to speak, the reader is referred to chapter 8 of the above-mentioned *Scottish Trade in the Wake of Union*. A thesis on *Scottish Foreign Trade towards the End of the Pre-industrial Period, 1700–1760* formed the initial starting-point for both.[57] It is hoped that the present book serves a heuristic purpose on its own, being a model study of how eighteenth-century intra-European trade worked as part of a larger historical context which might be labelled an "Atlantic economy". It is intended to tease out the more subtle patterns of the commodity trades, as they appear from contemporary quantitative, as well as narrative sources, but moreover to suggest directions for future research into European trade and economy in a comparative framework.

The analysis will focus on eighteenth-century Scotland, drawing on the under-explored Scottish customs accounts which have been preserved nearly in entirety after 1742. The Scottish records are unique. Not only are British customs accounts generally the most detailed of their kind available for early modern Europe. But the loss of the London port books, covering about 80 per cent of England's foreign trade in the period, also places Scotland into pole position for a historical analysis of commercial fluctuations within a European dimension. This is because the basic difference of British accounts to most other available material for European ports in the period is that, inasmuch as foreign or overseas trade was concerned, all commodities imported or exported were recorded, regardless whether they were liable to duty or not. Thus, whilst the limitation on Scotland on the one and northern Germany on the other hand is to an extent a choice of academic convenience, it will nevertheless facilitate conclusions that reach far beyond this merely geographic limitation, but in fact apply to early modern European or "world" trade in general. Much of the following will show characteristic signs of "suggestions for further research" rather than "textbook evidence". And even though Scottish-German trade was firmly embedded into the eighteenth-century Atlantic economy without any apparent or significant deviance in the general patterns, some explanation is necessary nonetheless, chiefly for the choice of eighteenth century Scotland and Germany as the objects of study. There is, of course, the problem that neither of the two were "countries" in the full modern sense.

As of Mayday 1707, Scotland and England were joined together into one United Kingdom, which cost the Scots their parliament and political sovereignty (the Scottish Parliament was only re-established in 1997–1999). In economic terms the Union 1707 created a customs union between Scotland and England, furthermore allowing Scotland legal access to the tradable products of the English colonies overseas. By abolishing customs duties on Scottish-English trade, Scotland's two main domestic exports, cattle and linen, now had free entry into their largest foreign market. Furthermore, the

57 P. R. RÖSSNER, Scottish Foreign Trade towards the End of the Pre-industrial Period, 1700–1760, Unpubl. University of Edinburgh PhD Thesis, Edinburgh 2007.

inclusion of Scots traders into the protection of the English Navigation Acts (including the protection of Scottish merchant shipping by the English Navy) now allowed for certain colonial goods previously reserved to English traders, such as tobacco and sugar, to be legally imported into Scottish ports. These "enumerated commodities" subsequently laid the foundation stone for a thriving re-export business, enjoying the highest growth rates in eighteenth-century Atlantic trade. The Union 1707 therefore positively affected Scotland's future chances for economic growth, even though the time framework, as well as the precise causal nexus, is open to debate.[58] But as will be shown below overseas trade levels remained small, both in relation to total economic activity, as well as in comparison to England. The Union of 1707 generally failed to make a large impact on Scottish economic and commercial performance until late. The administrative grip of the "British" state, as well as the ability of British institutions to penetrate Scottish economic and social life remained rather weak until well after the middle of the century. Suffice it to cite just a few relevant aspects.

During the first half of the century, government in Scotland took place informally via the Scottish "viceroy", the Duke of Argyll and his system of nepotism and patronage.[59] Twenty years after the Union, he commented that in Scotland "by a long series of no administration, the mere letter of the law has little or no weight with the people" – there had been no real political administration at all prior to that date.[60] Throughout the eighteenth century the £Scots, Scotland's pre-Union currency, remained in use as a money of account, especially when it came to rents and related transfer payments, as well as certain forms of taxation.[61] A further outright violation of the stipulations and spirit of the Treaty of Union was the retaining of the old Scottish measures of length and capacity, which differed from parish to parish. Apart from standardized measures to be used in customs and excise procedures, the old Scottish pre-Union measures continued to be used well into the nineteenth century.[62] But most importantly, pre-industrial Scottish society and economy were marked by a high propensity to tax evasion. Partly this was a result of the very weak and in many ways rather informal administrative grip of the state.

---

58 Ibid., ch. 6.

59 C. A. WHATLEY, Bought and Sold for English Gold? Explaining the Union 1707, East Linton 2nd ed. 2001; L. Paterson, The Autonomy of Modern Scotland, Edinburgh 1994, esp. p. 24, pp. 31–34. M. Lynch, Scotland. A New History, Edinburgh 8th ed. 1997, chs. 18–19, esp. pp. 315–319, 323–326.

60 J. S. SHAW, The Management of Scottish Society 1707–1764. Power, Nobles, Lawyers, Edinburgh Agents and English Influences, Edinburgh 1983, p. 86.

61 In the years preceding the Union, the £Scots exchanged at 1/12 £Sterling. This rate was retained after 1707 for accounting purposes. NAS, Trinity House Records, GD 226/7/1, Crown Money Book, passim; GD 226/18/250, GD 229/13/36, Tables of Shore Dues, Leith (3rd June 1761 – January 1775, 29th May 1776 – 10th May 1780, January 1788 – 18 January 1827). See also R. SAVILE, Bank of Scotland. A History 1695–1995, Edinburgh 1996, p. 78 and n. 14.

62 A. D. CONNOR / A. D. C. SIMPSON, Weights and Measures in Scotland: A European Perspective, East Linton 2004; R. E. ZUPKO, The Weights and Measures of Scotland before the Union, in: Scottish Historical Review, LVI, 2, Nr. 162 (1977), pp. 119–145; I. LEVITT / (T.) C. SMOUT, Some Weights and Measures in Scotland, 1843, in: Scottish Historical Review, LVI, 2, Nr. 162 (1977), pp. 146–152, esp. pp. 146s., p. 151; J. M. HENDERSON, Scottish Reckoning of Time, Money, Weights and Measures (no date / place of publication indicated), pp. 5s. A. BALD, The Farmer and Corn-Dealer's Assistant, Edinburgh 1780.

Prior to 1746, when the last Jacobite uprising was finally subdued and roads suited for long-distance travel, reaching far into the Highlands were constructed, the arm of the British state (in the shape of customs and excise taxation) did not effectively extend to the Highland region of Scotland at all. There were no permanent customs precincts north-west of Loch Ness or the line spanning the two customs precincts of Inverness and Fort William (The Scottish Highlands and Islands). To contemporary "Lowlanders", members of the educated urban Scottish and English elites, this was where civilization ended and an entirely different, even alien, tribal society and economy began. The customs precinct of *Lochbroom* with its head- or outport Ullapool in the northwest of Scotland, which in theory covered virtually the entire Highland area north-west of Loch Ness, was closed in 1747. This closure followed a period of four years of complete inactivity during which the resident customs collector had recorded no taxable incoming or outgoing waterborne traffic whatsoever. Partly this was due to the Jacobite uprising in 1745/6, when the customs collector left his post for good on the grounds that as a British official he feared for his life in an environment that was thoroughly Jacobite. But the fact that no economic activity had been recorded since 1742 is a telling example of the generally very weak grip of the central or "British" state – chiefly the Treasury and Exchequer based in London – in this area of Great Britain. It does not mean that nothing had been traded or produced in the vicinity of Ullapool and the North-western Highlands, but the locals clearly were in formidable opposition to British taxes and duties.[63] But it was by no means the Highlands region alone that frequently and successfully evaded taxation. The level of smuggling in Scotland's overseas trades was remarkable, as will be seen below, but it was particularly high in the south-western tobacco ports of Glasgow, Ayr, Irvine, Dumfries and Kirkcudbright. A similar situation applied with regard to the *excise*, a duty charged at the point of production on selected essentials, such as beer, ale, malt, skins, hides, candles, and certain types of linens. Thus a considerable yet unquantifiable share of Scottish economic activity was neither taxed nor recorded during the eighteenth century. Net remits of taxation yields from Edinburgh to London remained tiny, especially in the Customs, during the first half of the eighteenth century.[64] British government institutions concerned with economic administration, such as the Treasury or the Board of Trade, showed little interest in Scotland in anything that went further than revenue accounting. These aspects had a considerable effect on the amount and coverage of economic statistics that were compiled for Scotland.[65] Trade statistics, which for Ireland and England had been compiled since 1696, were not produced for Scotland prior to 1755, and no "British" aggregate trade statistics were kept, either after 1707.[66] Those statistics available for Scotland prior to 1755 were mainly concerned

63 NAS, E504/23/1, Customs Accounts Lochbroom (Ullapool), esp. signatures of collector in permanente absentia.

64 R. H. CAMPBELL, The Anglo-Scottish Union of 1707.II. The Economic Consequences, in: Economic History Review, Second Series, XVI, 3 (1964), pp. 468–477; J. M. PRICE, Glasgow, the Tobacco Trade, and the Scottish Customs, 1707–1730, in: Scottish Historical Review, LXIII (1984), pp. 1–36, at p. 7.

65 See ch. 2 below.

66 The English "ledgers of imports and exports" continued to record only English overseas trade after 1707. See ch. 2 below.

with tobacco, wine and grain. These were commodities in which the state had a slightly higher interest than usual, as their trade was either highly regulated (as was the case with grain[67]), or taxed at above-average rates of duty, such as wine and tobacco. With the exception of such commodities, Scottish commercial and economic fluctuations are therefore difficult to establish *ex post* for the first half of the eighteenth century. (These problems will be addressed in more detail in chapter two of the present work.)

Then there was – or still is – the "index number problem". Given the relatively small levels of Scottish economic activity compared to the larger British neighbour to the south – England – one obvious question is: how valuable or worthwhile would be a separate analysis of Scottish-German, rather than British-German, trade in the eighteenth century? Even an analysis of eighteenth-century Scottish trade patterns on their own needs to face the obvious question: why examining Scotland at all, since as of Mayday 1707, there existed a United Kingdom of Great Britain after all? – On purely arithmetic grounds, quantitative studies of eighteenth-century *Scotland* alter almost nothing in terms of *British* commercial fluctuations or the British macro-economic trajectory after 1707: the growth rates of British overseas trade for instance, about 95 per cent of which was English and 5 per cent Scottish trade c.1700–1760, can be approximated using English evidence exclusively. And even if Scottish-German trade patterns were radically different from British-German trade patterns, 1700–1770, British-German trade could probably be usefully approximated using English statistics and accounts of English-German trade. To this the answer is: even though scholars frequently speak of "British" commercial and macro-economic fluctuations after 1707[68], it can be demonstrated that this is a generalization which, although neither totally impracticable nor entirely meaningless, in terms of its historical value is a rather unhelpful analytical tool. It is fairly valuable and rewarding to examine the eighteenth-century Scottish trade pattern on its own terms, not least because it was England, and neither "Britain" nor Scotland, which was the first country to industrialize. Over the period under consideration incomes, living standards and thus "Rostovian"[69] stage of development were higher in England than in Scotland. In and around 1760 the Scottish economy was still more similar to Norway, Sweden, France and Central Germany than to her southern neighbour. Scottish overseas trade also exhibited some peculiarities in terms of scope and scale, which made it very different from the English pattern in the period of discussion (chapter 3, section 3.1). Therefore, the "British" view, if it is approximated using English evidence, considerably distorts

67 Grain imports were prohibited by the Corn Laws. These, however could – on the shire level and by an official decree of the Sheriff Court – be waived temporarily in times of dearth when the domestic grain prices (prevailing in the respective shires) surpassed certain thresholds. Depending upon the domestic price, a gliding import tariff became then applicable on grain imports. Grain exports could obtain bounties.

68 W. SCHLOTE, British Overseas Trade. From 1700 to the 1930s, Oxford 1952; P. DEANE / W. A. COLE, British Economic Growth 1688–1959. Trends and Structure, Cambridge, 2nd ed. 1967, p. 43, n. 1; N. F. R. CRAFTS, British Economic Growth during the Industrial Revolution, Oxford 1985.

69 W. W. ROSTOW, The Process of Economic Growth, New York, 2nd ed. 1962; ID.(ed.), The Economics of Take-off into Sustained Growth, London / Basingstoke 1963; ID., Stages of Economic Growth, Cambridge, 2nd ed. 1971.

the historical picture and seriously hampers a balanced understanding of differential patterns of economic development.

Thus, for reasons of her considerable differences from England in economic, cultural, social, even political terms after 1707, Scotland can safely be treated as a separate country. Even the application of trade theory, based on national economies as the basic economic actors, is therefore possible, yielding meaningful results, even though Scotland was no independent country any more. Scottish-German trade in the eighteenth century therefore is a valid and – due to the near complete availability of all Scottish customs accounts 1743–1770 – highly operational topic, at least from the (contemporary) Scottish viewpoint. With regard to Germany – in the period under consideration roughly equal to the "Holy Roman Empire" in its 1648 boundaries established by the Treaty of Westphalia – the problem is somewhat similar. As an analytical tool, "German foreign trade" is virtually non-operational prior to the unification of 1871 (even the *Zollverein* excluded significant chunks of "German" trading activity) – it is notoriously difficult to quantify and hard to define in conceptual terms. At the Peace and Treaty of Westphalia (1648), which set the political-administrative framework that remained valid until late in the eighteenth century the Holy Roman Empire consisted of about 1,800 separate political entities. There were some 300 independent states and 1,500 Imperial Knighthoods, each of which enjoyed virtually complete political sovereignty. Discarding the Knighthoods, the more than 300 remaining states in the proper sense not only usually operated their own import (and less frequently export) customs, but usually also charged a variety of internal and transit tolls.[70] Arguably, then, "German foreign trade in the eighteenth century" could mean two things. It could either be the sum total of each of these 300 sovereign entities' (disregarding the Knighthoods) exports from and imports to any place within and outside the Empire, that lay outside the boundaries of the entity under consideration. But it could also mean exports from or imports into any place within the *Empire* to (or from) any place outside the Empire, thus disregarding commerce *within* the Empire as domestic. Very obviously the first concept is non-operational, due to the absence or inadequacy of available sources. The number of variables to be examined and sources to be consulted, such as separate states, customs posts and tolls, would go into the tens or even hundreds of thousands, apart from the fact that mostly these records do not exist (any more). Thus, whereas none of these two concepts has got its particular virtues, the second one has to be the obvious choice for the historian, derived from the need to reduce the topic to a manageable and meaningful basis for discussion. In the following therefore, German foreign trade will be defined as imports into and exports from the Holy Roman Empire, disregarding mutual trade between the sovereign states that made up the Empire.

This concept is, however, also fraught with considerable practical, as well as theoretical difficulties, which should be addressed prior to the analysis. First, to pursue this approach means to include more than one might have bargained for: especially those parts of the Empire that were under the rule of foreign sovereigns, such as Danish Holstein (Altona) or Swedish Pomerania (former Hansa towns of Wismar, Rostock

70 KELLENBENZ, Außenhandel, p. 7. S. C. OGILVIE, Proto-Industrialization in Germany, in: ID. and M. CERMAN (eds.), European Proto-industrialization (Cambridge, 1996), pp. 118–136, esp. at pp. 121–125.

and Stralsund) become ambiguous.[71] As they were located within the Empire yet subject to foreign rule, they could arguably be assigned to the either Denmark-Norway's and Sweden's foreign trade on the one, or to German foreign trade on the other hand. In the following analysis all ports within the Holy Roman Empire in its 1648 boundaries will be considered German, without any further ideological-political implications. Only those ports which lay outside the Empire, but which could arguably be considered "German" in socio-economic (and, of course, cultural) terms, such as *Königsberg* in Prussia or *Danzig* in Poland, will be left out from the discussion.[72] Secondly, a considerable amount of German imports and exports overseas was consigned overland, for instance from the Leipzig fairs, which could mean that it was not always recorded at the large German sea-ports. A contemporary source quoted Leipzig's share in total exports from Germany to England in 1763 at 75 per cent.[73] A third aspect is directly related to the preceding comment. For obvious reasons the present analysis will focus on sea-borne trade. If trade with the large German sea-ports is considered, however, a distinction between transit and trade originating (ending) in these ports is impossible. As Hamburg and Bremen were entrepôts, their markets reached far into west-central and eastern Germany.[74] Fourthly, the discussion will focus on the North Sea ports of the German Empire, mainly Hamburg and Bremen, as Scottish trade with the Baltic German (Lübeck, Neustadt) or quasi-German (Stralsund, Wismar, Rostock) ports was overall irrelevant during the period under consideration. Whilst in the sixteenth and seventeenth centuries, the share of the Baltic ports would have been considerable, not only in terms of Scottish-German trade, but German trade in general, in the eighteenth century Hamburg and Bremen were not only the largest and most important German sea-ports[75], but also the most important German ports Scotland had trading relations

71 W. DOTZAUER, Die Deutschen Reichskreise in der Verfassung des Alten Reiches und ihr Eigenleben (1500–1806), Darmstadt 1989, ch. 3.10. The legal implications of these "ambiguous" places and their varying degree of affiliation to the Empire in administrative terms are discussed in: N. JÖRN / M. NORTH (eds.), Die Integration des südlichen Ostseeraumes in das Alte Reich, Cologne / Weimar / Vienna 2000, in particular: M. NORTH, Integration im Ostseeraum und im Heiligen Römischen Reich (ibid., pp. 1–11); O. MÖRKE, Holstein und Schwedisch-Pommern im Alten Reich: Integrationsmuster und Politische Identitäten in Grenzregionen (ibid., pp. 425–472).

72 In the following a historically correct German spelling and nomenclature have been adopted throughout (thus Königsberg instead of Kaliningrad, Danzig rather than Gdansk etc.). This is only for historical reasons, without any further implications. Only when a German place name has been anglicized, the English term has been preferred (thus Cologne rather than Köln, Vienna rather than Wien, Hanover rather than Hannover etc.).

73 KELLENBENZ, Außenhandel, pp. 19s. Cf. N. BRÜBACH, Die Reichsmessen von Frankfurt am Main, Leipzig und Braunschweig (14. –18. Jahrhundert), Stuttgart 1994.

74 Hamburg: Silesia, Moravia, Bohemia, Saxony, Thuringia, Brandenburg. Bremen's commercial hinterland is said to have included the Duchy of Brunswick and Oldenburg. F.-W. HENNING, Handbuch der Wirtschafts- und Sozialgeschichte Deutschlands, Vol. 1: Deutsche Wirtschafts- und Sozialgeschichte im Mittelalter und in der Frühen Neuzeit, Paderborn 1991, pp. 858s., p. 863.

75 W. ZORN, Gewerbe und Handel, 1648–1800, in: H. AUBIN / W. ZORN (eds.), Handbuch der Deutschen Wirtschafts- und Sozialgeschichte, Vol. 1: Von der Frühzeit bis zum Ende des 18. Jahrhunderts, Stuttgart 1971, pp. 531–573; at pp. 561s. F.-W. HENNING, Das Vorindustrielle Deutschland 800–1800, Paderborn / Munich / Vienna / Zurich, 5th ed., 1994, p. 267; ID., Handbuch, Vol. I, pp. 858s., p. 863; KAUFHOLD, Deutschland 1650–1850, at pp. 571–573; H. BECHTEL, Wirtschaftsgeschichte Deutschlands. Vom Beginn des 16. zum Ende des 18. Jahrhunderts, Munich 1952, p. 299, pp. 332–4.

with. Therefore, a focus on Bremen and Hamburg is likely to capture a significantly large share of Germany's total foreign exports and imports, as well as imports from and exports to Scotland in the eighteenth century. Fortuitous circumstances have resulted in the preservation of comparatively good quantitative sources for both ports. These records allow at least a tentative reconstruction of structure and fluctuations in these ports' trade volume and thus provide valuable insights into the commercial position of North-West Germany. A fifth and last cautionary remark needs to be made with regard to sea-borne German trade that took place via the Netherlands. Of the three large West German rivers Rhine, Weser, and Elbe, which run into the North Sea, only two have their estuaries within Germany. Products that had originated in the Rhineland therefore were sometimes imported into Britain via the Netherlands, especially Rhenish wine and German linens.[76] It was not always indicated in British statistics, whether Dutch imports had really originated in the Netherlands, or elsewhere. But these trades can be discarded, for reasons of their low overall significance.[77]

The preceding remarks demonstrate that the decision relating to the object of study needs to a certain extent remain an arbitrary one, apart from the fact that economic historians are in agreement that the volume of European *seaborne* trade was usually dwarfed by the intra-European *overland* trades. (A similar case may be made for the relation of domestic trade, or domestic consumption, to foreign imports and exports[78]). On the other hand it is obvious that, disregarding Scottish-German trade that went via England[79], all recorded trade between Scotland and German ports was in fact trade overseas, due to the fact that a sea barrier had to be crossed in either case. Trade between Scotland and Germany was most likely to be recorded at some point in one of the larger ports, at least in Scotland, as British administrative practice required that all traffic entering or leaving a British port was recorded, regardless whether or not the commodities under consideration were liable to duty. This is what makes the British sources so invaluable and German-Scottish trade so operational ("measurable"), compared to other topics in early modern European economic history. It is an historical phenomenon that can be captured most accurately from contemporary statistical materials.

---

76 Davenant made the case for German or "Rhenish" wines. C. D'AVENANT, A Report to the Honourable The Commissioners For putting in Execution the Act, intitled An Act, for the Taking, Examining, and Stating the Publick Accounts of the Kingdom, London 1712, p. 43.

77 The discrepancy between total imports of Narrow German linens and imports of Narrow German linens from Germany for instance, which can be explained through trade via the Netherlands, was normally a small one (less than five per cent).

78 I. BLANCHARD, 'Russia's Age of Silver'. Precious Metal Production and Economic Growth in the Eighteenth Century, London 1989.

79 In the eighteenth century a considerable amount of German linens to be re-exported from Scottish ports were obtained from London.

1.4 WORKING HYPOTHESES

The central working hypotheses of the current work may then be formulated as follows. In the 1750s and 1760s, the share of German ports in Scotland's total imports and exports did not usually exceed about five per cent (volumetric £Sterling values in the Scottish trade statistics, 1755 valuations. Prior to that date conclusions become difficult and unreliable due to the absence of trade statistics). Nevertheless, trade in some particular commodities significantly exceeded these values. Scotland for instance sent up to 13 per cent of her total tobacco re-exports, up to 71 per cent of total re-exports of rice, up to 81 per cent of total exports of domestic salt and (briefly) up to 99 per cent of her vitriol oil exports to Germany. As these values far exceeded the average or "expected value", i.e. their share in total Scottish exports at the time being, one can detect some patterns of considerable significance in terms of the German market for the Scottish economy, and, as will be discussed below, vice versa – at least in the case of salt. Tobacco and rice linked the German market to the British Atlantic economy. With regard to imports from Germany on the other hand, imports that were dominated by what the British Customs administration called *Narrow German* linens, the trans-Atlantic link of Scotland's eighteenth century trades becomes even more apparent – these items were not used in Scotland, but usually re-exported to the British colonies in America. Therefore, Germany (or better: Hamburg and Bremen) in the eighteenth century represented an important component of Scotland's total trade in two ways: First, the German market represented an intrinsic component of Scotland's traditional trades with continental Europe ("the European lifeline"[80]). But secondly, it also became integrated into the only recently fully developed Atlantic trades via re-exports of rice and tobacco and imports of Narrow and other German linens.

There are several ways of explaining such particular trade flows (such as the trade in one particular commodity or between two particular countries, as opposed to the balance on current account which captures gross total trade). Trade theory would explain trade flows using comparative advantage, resulting from differential factor endowment (labour, land) and resulting productivity and production cost differentials. In a two-countries-two-goods world of theory, trade lowers the relative price of both goods, and thus benefits either of the two trading partners or countries. As this is a mere expression of a ceteris paribus condition, this theory, whether it relates to labour or capital endowment, purports to apply in general to trade in a multi-goods and multilateral trading reality. In fact, the present study will demonstrate that this approach may have its weaknesses in explaining multilateralism in the forms and shapes observable in eighteenth century overseas commerce.

Scottish merchants handling the larger share of Scottish-German trade were essentially operating in a wider, multilateral sphere of trade and payments. Their consignments to or from German ports usually represented only a small fraction of their total volume of transactions and more often than not merely one link within a chain of transactions. Frequently their ventures connected Scotland with Germany (for barrel staves and other timber items), London (banking services), the Netherlands (banking

80 T. C. SMOUT, The European Lifeline, in: G. MENZIES (ed.), In Search of Scotland, Edinburgh 2001, pp. 112–135.

services, manufactures), Africa (slaves), the West Indies (market for slaves, supply of sugar, coffee etc.) and North America (tobacco). From the Scottish side (Scots merchants) the purpose of trading with Germany could be subordinate to the requirements of keeping in motion a much larger, circular business. Therefore, the micro-level of individual merchants and firms becomes as important in the explanation of the origin, nature and composition of the Scottish-German trade volume, as trade theory and its empirical basis would suggest. Therefore, private merchants' records are pivotal in explaining the macro-picture of trade between Scotland and Germany. Singling out bilateral trade flows without modification therefore creates a biased picture of early modern European trade. This hypothesis will be explored further in chapter five, but the present work should also be understood as a caution against general or tautological models of trade – be they historical or economic.

Note on the time framework (1700–1770). Unfortunately, scholars are not normally in complete agreement as to the precise landmarks or turning-points in Scotland's eighteenth-century economic development, of which trade was only a minor, yet historically more significant component than its mere share in Scottish economic activity would suggest.[81] Benchmark dates for pinpointing macro-economic change usually range from c.1740[82] to c.1780. If formulated emphatically, they coincide with what is regarded as the beginning of Scotland's "industrial revolution" and the commencement of "Rostovian" or "modern economic growth".[83] Another convenient date may be 1760, as on January 1st of the same year, the Carron Ironworks, Scotland's first modern iron production complex, lit their furnaces in Stirlingshire. For foreign trade the War of American Independence (1776–1783) represents an important caesura, when Scotland's overseas trade collapsed, due to its being dependent upon American tobacco imports. But taking 1776–1783 as a benchmark might mean to overemphasize the role the colonial trades played in Scotland's macro-economy. So for the present work the benchmark date of 1770 has been chosen fairly arbitrarily, and the Scottish customs accounts have been surveyed for the time between Christmas Quarter (October–December) 1742 (when they start) to January 1771 (when the Christmas Quarter 1769 ends).

A most commonly-used starting date for a historical discussion of the Scottish economy is, of course, the Union 1707. With the latter certain institutional aspects changed – in the overseas trades, the fisheries, woollen and linen production for instance – so as to alter the Scottish macro-economic production function fundamen-

81 RÖSSNER., In the Wake of Union, ch. 6.

82 As in T. M. DEVINE, The Modern Economy: Scotland and the Act of Union, in: ID. / C. H. LEE / G. C. PEDEN (eds.), The Transformation of Scotland. The Economy Since 1700, Edinburgh 2005, pp. 13–33, mainly using trends in linen output and the colonial trades which gathered momentum after the mid-1730s.

83 R. H. CAMPBELL, Scotland since 1707. The Rise of an Industrial Society, Oxford 1965, p. 29 and chs. I–IV in general. H. HAMILTON, An Economic History of Scotland in the Eighteenth Century, Oxford 1963, p. 1; C. A. WHATLEY, The Industrial Revolution in Scotland, Cambridge 1997, p. 20, p. 24. I. D. WHYTE, Scotland before the Industrial Revolution. An Economic and Social History c. 1050 – c. 1750, London / New York 1995, esp. pp. 328–333; ID., Scotland's Society and Economy in Transition, c. 1500–c. 1760, Basingstoke / London / New York 1997, esp. p. 165; S. G. E. LYTHE / J. BUTT, An Economic History of Scotland, 1100–1939, Glasgow / London 1975, pp. 102s., p. 162.

tally, at least in the very long run (1740s, 1750s, or 1760s onwards, depending upon different scholarly tendencies, see above). Recent studies, however, most importantly and recently by Whatley[84], have emphasized continuity rather than change in explaining Scottish political, social and economic history in the seventeenth and eighteenth centuries, suggesting that 1707 represented no immediate or radical turning point in Scottish economic and social history. Thus 1700 has been chosen – quite arbitrarily – as a starting point for the following discussion, somewhat underlining the fact that the year 1707 as such was a mere institutional caesura.

The existing macro-economic data is too sparse to allow constructing a neat and consistent time framework for a macro-economic analysis of eighteenth-century Germany.[85] Around 1740 growth rates for victual prices changed, so as to suggest a decline in average incomes and living standards in subsequent decades.[86] For German trade, the data is scantier, but extant Hamburg import figures (Hamburg being the largest German sea port at the time) show no significant upwards trend until the last two decades of the eighteenth century.[87] Sometimes the Seven Years' War is taken as a benchmark date, when certain economic indices at least changed, for instance due to war-induced changes in aggregate demand, supply and shifts in relative prices.[88] Future studies on the eighteenth-century German business cycle might reveal a totally different time framework. Thus, in Germany's case the 1700–1770 framework seems to be a consistent choice inasmuch as – thus far – it is about as good as any other.

84 C. A. WHATLEY (with D. PATRICK), The Scots and the Union, Edinburgh 2006.

85 R. METZ, Säkulare Trends der Deutschen Wirtschaft, in: M. NORTH (ed.), Deutsche Wirtschaftsgeschichte. Ein Jahrtausend im Überblick, Munich, 2nd ed. 2005, pp. 427–500.

86 W. ABEL, Agrarkrisen und Agrarkonjunktur in Mitteleuropa vom 13. bis zum 19. Jahrhundert, Berlin 1935; Hamburg / Berlin, 3rd ed. 1978.

87 Figures derived from O. SCHWARZER, Die Stellung 'Westeuropas' in der Weltwirtschaft 1750–1950, in: M. NORTH (ed.), Nordwesteuropa in der Weltwirtschaft 1750–1950 / Northwestern Europe in the World Economy 1750–1950, Stuttgart 1993, pp. 257–290.

88 M. A. DENZEL / H.-J. GERHARD, Inflationäre Prozesse in Nordwestdeutschland im 18. Jahrhundert, in: Vierteljahrsschrift für Sozial- und Wirtschaftsgeschichte, XC (2003), pp. 1–25, transl. as ID., Global and Local Aspects of Pre-Industrial Inflations: New Research on Inflationary Processes in XVIIIth-Century Central Europe, in: Journal of European Economic History, XXXIV, 1 (2005), pp. 149–185.

II. THE SOURCES

Trade statistics and customs accounts are amongst the best preserved quantitative records for eighteenth-century Europe. And without doubt, in terms of precision, coverage and design, British customs accounts and trade statistics were by far the most superior records of their time and class. But as the eighteenth-century London customs accounts, capturing at least 80 per cent of England's trade at the time, have been lost, the Scottish records occupy "pole position" for historical research relating to the period between 1700 and 1770. The following therefore is partly intended to highlight the uniqueness of the Scottish sources within the context of eighteenth-century intra-European trade – sources the value of which has been clearly under-appreciated by previous research on the eighteenth-century economy of Europe. This occasions a detailed analysis of the Scottish material, as well as a comparison with similar records on the German side, as the analytical value and historical relevance of each reach far beyond either Scotland or Germany.

On the German side, the discussion shall be limited to the Bremen and Hamburg customs materials, because during the eighteenth century Scottish-German trade, as well as German overseas trade in general, mainly went through these two sea ports.

1. SCOTLAND

The principal sources used on the Scottish side of the trades are the Scottish port books or *Customs Collectors' Quarterly Accounts*, commencing in Christmas Quarter (October–December) 1742.[1] They provide a complete set of disaggregate import and export declarations made by the importing and exporting merchants in each of the 28 or so Scottish outports[2] in the years under consideration. Prior to 1755 they are the only source containing particulars of all commodities shipped into and out of Scotland. After some statistical manipulation – basically the organization of single-entries into a database suitable for mathematical processing – these data can be rendered useful for a discussion of Scotland's trade balance with Germany.

After 1755 aggregates for total Scottish imports from and (re-)exports to Germany can be obtained from the Scottish *Inspector General's Ledgers of Imports and Exports*, contemporary trade statistics which resulted from an attempt to monitor Scot-

1 The accounting year used in the British Customs ran as follows: Ladyday: January–March; Midsummer: April–June; Michaelmas: July–September; Christmas: October–December. NAS, E504.

2 Outport: customs precinct, comprising the head port, after which the precinct was named, as well as its several member ports and creeks. A creek was no port in its own right, but only a place where ships might be unloaded or laden upon prior written application to the Customs.

land's commercial position on world markets.[3] These are, however, fraught with a variety of biases. One of the lesser disadvantages of this source is that trade is broken down by commodities and countries only, but not by ports (neither Scottish nor foreign ports). Furthermore, it is clear that severe frictions occurred in the precision of recording when it came to the transmission of outport data (port books etc.) to a superordinate level (inspector general, Board of Customs etc.). All these aspects need to be taken into account when it comes to the analysis of trade flows on the basis of these records. Sometimes under-recording or misreporting would be so severe as to cast serious doubt on the validity of these figures. On a more general level the problems to be addressed in the following also bear relevance as to the quality of contemporary economic accounting and statistical measuring. As most of the English materials have been lost, the Scottish sources provide a unique insight into how statistical recording worked in early modern Britain. In this way they also show how the transmission of statistical data was organized – from the original source (customs accounts) to the government departments needing it in its processed form (trade statistics) for fiscal and economic policy.

1.1 The Scottish Port Books

Port books or "customs accounts" are revenue accounts, supplemented by a detailed and comprehensive list of items assessed on import and export, including those cargoes that were imported or exported duty free. This practice of recording allowed for a variety of ex post arrangements and amendments. It enabled British customs officials to levy duties *ex post*, for example if it turned out that a particular cargo, which had not been taxed in the first instance, was subsequently found to be liable to duty. It could then be re-assessed and duties settled accordingly, sometimes years after the cargo had been shipped and the original declarations had been made. Such aspects render this type of accounts useful for a *comprehensive* analysis of trade flows ("balance of trade").

The Scottish port books are unique for at least two reasons. First, as mentioned in the introductory section to this chapter, their English equivalents have mostly been lost courtesy of several fires that wrought havoc to the nineteenth-century London customhouse. But more importantly, the basic difference of British accounts to most other available contemporary material is that, inasmuch as foreign trade was concerned, all traffic and all commodities imported or exported was recorded, regardless whether or not the goods under concern were liable to duty. Similar records of other nations or ports, as far as they have been traced yet[4], usually only exist in gaps. More-

3 The National Archives (of England and Wales, formerly Public Record Office / PRO), Customs 14. Henceforth referred to as TNA, Customs 14.

4 With regard to *German* ports see works cited in chapter 1, section 1.2 above. *Danzig* and *Stockholm* records: M. BOGUCKA, Handelsbeziehungen im Ostseeraum: Der Handel zwischen Danzig/Gdansk und Stockholm in der 1. Hälfte des 17. Jahrhunderts, in: K. FRIEDLAND / F. IRSIGLER (eds.), Seehandel und Wirtschaftswege Nordeuropas im 17. und 18. Jahrhundert, Ostfildern 1981, pp. 38–47; Riga and Tallinn/Reval, see: V. V. DOROSENKO, Quellen zur Geschichte des Rigaer Handels im 17. und 18. Jahrhundert und Probleme ihrer Erforschung, in: Ibid., pp. 3–25. Additio-

over they frequently cover imports only, as it was not particularly common to tax exports in eighteenth-century Europe. Furthermore, these records usually covered traffic from specified areas only. The Hamburg *Convoygeld- und Admiralitätszolleinnahmebücher* for instance only recorded European imports from ports eastwards of the River Scheldt and westwards of Cape Skagen.[5] But most importantly, apart from Scotland and England, eighteenth-century European customs accounts usually only covered commodities that were taxed, without recording traffic in duty-free goods (Hamburg *Convoygeld- und Admiralitätszolleinnahmebücher*, Bremen *Schlachteangabebücher*[6]). This is what makes the British records of the period the best of their class, and Scotland is in pole position for the historian of eighteenth-century European commerce, for reasons of the loss of the Port of London data.

By these standards the Scottish port books provide the unique opportunity of reconstructing the recorded or declared volume of trade in yearly series since Christmas Quarter 1742, when a Scottish Board of Customs that had been temporarily abolished in 1723, was re-established in Edinburgh. These customs accounts also provide the rare opportunity of reconstructing trade patterns on a micro-basis by tracing the transactions of particular merchants or firms, ports, commercial regions and the like. A standard entry of an import (export) declaration in the port books contained the following information (Fig. 1):

Figure 1: Content and Design of British Port Books

(a) Ship's name;
(b) its place of registration (optional);
(c) port(s) or country(countries) or region(s) of last calling (destination);
(d) master's name;
(e) merchant's name;
(f) name of supercargo or forwarding agent (if applicable);
(g) the *commodities* carried:
  I. specification of material identity according to the two Books of Rates;
  II. in standard commercial measures (Books of Rates);
  III. amount shipped;
(h) amount of customs duties levied.

This information resulted from a tedious and standardized British practice of customming incoming and outgoing cargoes at one of the 28 legal ports of Scotland (outports). If a merchant wanted to export a cargo, he either brought his goods to the pier, or took them out of the King's (Queen's) Warehouse at the respective port. The latter was often the case when re-exports were concerned. The merchant then entered the collector's office in the customhouse, in order to settle the applicable duties. The

nally on Riga: E. HARDER-GERSDORFF, Mitteleuropäische Gewerbezonen und ostbaltischer Handel im 18. Jahrhundert, in: Ibid., pp. 26–37.

5 O.-E. KRAWEHL, Die Admiralitätszoll- und Convoygeldeinnahmebücher als handelsstatistische Quelle, in: J. SCHNEIDER / O.-E. KRAWEHL / M. A. DENZEL (eds.), Statistik des Hamburger seewärtigen Einfuhrhandels im 18. Jahrhundert. Nach den Admiralitätszoll- und Convoygeld-Einnahmebüchern, St. Katharinen 2001, pp. 9–18; H. POHL, Die Beziehungen Hamburgs zu Spanien und dem Spanischen Amerika in der Zeit von 1740 bis 1806, Wiesbaden 1963, p. 311, n.1.

6 Staatsarchiv Bremen, 2–Ss.2.a.4.f.1 seq.

ship's captain or shipmaster had to follow a similar practice; i.e. he was also required to testify as to the nature and number of goods to be exported on his ship. After the master's and merchant's declaration of goods had been made, the collector issued a warrant containing the same information as the masters' and merchants' invoice for the use of the surveyor(s) and land-waiter(s), subordinate officials who were supposed to cross-check the information provided by shipmaster and merchant personally. The collector simultaneously produced a "coquet" (cargo certificate) for the merchant, stating that the duties had been paid, and that the merchant or proprietor of the respective cargo was now allowed to laden his cargo. This coquet had to contain the same information as on the backside of the merchants' invoice. It was then checked by the surveyor and the land-waiter upon ship's departure.[7] This essential double check inherent to the British customs system, which would either verify or falsify the information given by the merchant, was intended to prevent the fraudulent lading of the ship after the collector had issued the warrant, and the merchant had paid the duties. The surveyors then returned the coquets to the customhouse after they had inspected the outward-bound ship.[8] Finally, the ship's master had to testify upon oath to the true composition of freight and persons on board, after which an entry was made into the Book of Masters' Reports Outwards. Again the searchers or surveyors compared the master's information with the merchant's coquet and finally tested this information again by searching the ship a last time.[9] Now the basic process of loading the ship was over. After the collector had copied all the relevant information into his books, he handed the respective files, or "bills of entry", over to the comptroller.[10]

The procedure of entering a cargo inwards was similar to that of clearing outwards. As in the case of the outward entries the inward entries provided the basis for the Collector's Quarterly Accounts mentioned above ("port books"). The ship's cargo was then checked by the surveyor and/or land-waiter.[11] If part of the cargo was found to be damaged and thus unfit for sale, allowances for *damages* were given. Those allowances were made *after* the full declaration of the goods. Therefore the merchants' entries inwards indicated the gross or total amount of commodities shipped in, but they were provided with a comment on the margin as to the damage sustained and allowance given by the collector.[12] Likewise, if surveyor and land-waiter found that the merchant had paid duties on a higher quantity of goods than actually landed, the latter was entitled to a repayment of the duties "*overpaid*".[13] But if the check revealed that the merchant had declared *less* than actually imported – what in fact became a regular phenomenon particularly in the Glasgow tobacco and the East coast timber trades – he was given the opportunity to make a *post-entry*[14] without

7 NAS, CE 7/11., p. 7, App. Nr. 5, Nr. 6.

8 Ibid., p. 9, §§XXIX–XXX, App. Nr. C.

9 Ibid..

10 Ibid., p. 8.

11 Ibid., p. 14, §XVI.

12 As in the case of the regular entries inwards, a *Book of Damages* had to be kept by the collector in a shape identical to the Book(s) of Entries. NAS, CE 7/11, p. 14; §§XXIX–XL, App. Nr. 1/L–O, Nr. 33–36.

13 NAS, CE 7/11, p. 15; §§XLI–LI, App. Nr. 37, No K/P–S. The Book of Over-entries corresponded to the said Book(s) of Entries Inwards and Book(s) of Damages.

trades – he was given the opportunity to make a *post-entry*[14] without being charged with an outright offence that would have resulted in legal action (as potentially under-declarations could be made deliberately and thus have in most instances to be interpreted as a form of intended smuggling).

This is how the customs accounts or "port books" originated. Several problems obtain with these seemingly accurate records. First, it is not at all clear whether the declarations of origin or destination were always correct. Secondly, even the true amounts and nature of goods in these declarations could be critical, as evidence from private merchants' records demonstrates. Thirdly, merchants frequently made amendments to their declarations much later than the original declaration of the cargo – frequently for years to come.

1. One of the more obvious problems with the Scottish customs accounts is the question of how reliable the declarations of the ports of origin and the intended destinations for the ships' cargoes really were. Imports from and exports to places within the British Empire could be cross-checked against the original shipping papers – the so-called bills of lading, which had been issued by the port of origin. Since an identical (i.e. British or British Colonial) administration was concerned, this represented a fairly straightforward task for customs officials.[15] Furthermore, a special regulation applied to traffic in commodities "enumerated" in the English Navigation Acts. If a ship was bound for a British plantation in Africa, America or Asia, intending to pick up a cargo of tobacco, sugar, rum etc., the merchants involved had to provide bonded securities over £1,000, if the ship's capacity did not exceed 100 tons, and £2,000 Sterling respectively, if the ship's capacity exceeded 100 tons. These obligations were cancelled after the ship's voyage and unloading of the cargoes, provided the commodities were proven to have been shipped in conformity with the English Navigation Acts.[16] Much more difficult was the verification of origin or destination for cargoes that either came from or went to a foreign, i.e. neither British nor British Colonial port.

With regard to *imports* from outside the British dominions, customs officials usually tried to check the original bills of lading. With regard to *exports* to non-British ports it is clear that, unless confirmation could somehow be obtained by customs officials, merchants' fantasy would be set no boundaries in their declarations. In this instance the Customs could not care less about duty free exports. But they were, if at all, most concerned about re-exports, as re-exports usually drew back a substantial share of customs duties paid upon import, which made these products notoriously prone to re-landing within Britain. In the eighteenth century smugglers supplied the domestic market amply at duty-free prices. Any high-value cargoes declared as re-exports from a British port therefore were, at least from the viewpoint of Customs officials, *a priori*

14 Those post-entries were added into the Book of Merchants' Entries Inwards. NAS, CE 7/11, p. 17, §LXVII. Cf. also H. CROUCH, A Complete View of the British Customs [...], Part II, London 1728, p. 16.

15 NAS, CE7/11. These papers, like anything else, could be forged.

16 These bonds became void as soon as the ship returned, provided that a direct voyage from a colonial to a British port could be proven. NAS, CE7/11.

suspect of intended re-landing within British realms.[17] For the Customs it would have been desirable to check, whether ships carrying declared re-exports really went to the foreign ports or whether they rather – as they frequently did – discharged their cargoes at some obscure British smugglers' creek, at night time, supported by armed gangs of carriers and bodyguards, thus circumventing the British high tax regime on tobacco, sugar, tea, brandies and the like. In theory, British customs officials did have the option to do a cross-check at the declared foreign port of call. One example may be traced from Aberdeen customs correspondence dating from the late 1720s. The letter book kept by the said outport's collector, in which he filed his outgoing letters to the Board of Customs (Edinburgh/London), reveals that early in 1729, two customs officers were ordered to accompany a ship on its voyage from Aberdeen to Bergen (Norway). The officers returned shortly thereafter and gave testimony to the lawful discharge of the cargo in Norway. They had been ordered to attend the voyage to Bergen, as the Aberdeen Customs collector anticipated that the ship's cargo was intended to be re-landed within Scotland. It comprised inter alia 340 *ankers* spirits, 107 reams writing paper, 21 half-pieces Holland linen, four Muslins, two half-pieces *Cambrics*.[18] All of these commodities were either high-value or high-duty goods – popular items in the domestic smuggling trades.

Such cross-checks were costly, labour- and resource-intensive, and accordingly seldom. The preceding observations underline the large potential bias and high degree of unreliability of the seemingly accurate British customs accounts. This bias can be measured by cross-checks with materials similar to the Scottish customs accounts on the other end of the trading link. There is for example a remarkable discrepancy between cargoes declared as exports from Scotland to Hamburg and Bremen in the Scottish customs accounts on the one and the corresponding records on the German side, i.e. the Hamburg *Convoygeldeinnahmebücher* and Bremen *Schlachteangabebücher* (1747, 1754, 1755) on the other hand.[19] This difference can only partly be explained by the fact that the Hamburg and Bremen sources only recorded *taxed* commodities, as most commodities declared in Scotland for either Hamburg or Bremen were subject to duty in the latter two places as well. Eighteenth-century customs declarations were open to ample defrauding opportunities and the information contained in the customs records should be treated with an according degree of awareness.

2. But not only are port books and other customs accounts marred by a certain degree of distortion as to the places declared. Even those components of a declaration that could be counted and measured by Customs officials were critical. This can be demonstrated using a comparison of merchants' records (account books and ledgers) with the declarations those merchants had made at the port (customs accounts).[20] As complete sets of business records for particular firms have rarely survived, the follow-

17 As the cargoes under consideration would have drawn back all or part of the prohibitive import duties (which applied if the commodities under consideration were to be retained for domestic consumption). This aspect was particularly relevant for the emergence of a peculiar eighteenth-century Scottish trade pattern. See ch. 3, section 3.1 below.

18 NAS, CE87/1/1, *Aberdeen, Letters Collector to Board*, 29 January 1729, 10 April 1729.

19 Appendix, Table 2.

20 P. R. RÖSSNER, Scottish Trade in the Wake of Union (1700–1760). The Rise of a Warehouse Economy, Stuttgart 2008, pp. 102–105, and Appendix, Table 3–1 (p. 314f.).

ing remarks need to remain speculative and might not be statistically relevant. Nevertheless they point towards marked weaknesses in terms of the reliability of the customs materials.

The example used in the following has been drawn from evidence on the Glaswegian merchant company of BUCHANAN & SIMSON, who were active around 1759–1763. Coincidentally this partnership has left some of their business records, mainly relating to the British colonial trades, as well as re-exports of tobacco, sugar and rice to continental markets.[21] For the present purpose only cargoes declared as exports to German ports on account of this firm will be considered. Table 3 in the appendix contains a list of all consignments sent to Hamburg and Bremen on BUCHANAN & SIMSON's account during their period of activity (1759–1763), as apparent from this firm's business records in combination with information contained in the Greenock and Port Glasgow customs accounts for the same period. Although the list might be incomplete, and the composition of particular voyages uncertain, particularly as the quality of BUCHANAN & SIMSON's invoice books and the journals deteriorates after 1761, it is nevertheless apparent that more was indicated in the firm's records as having gone to Germany than recorded in the Greenock and Port Glasgow customs accounts, assuming that the firm used no other Scottish port. Furthermore there are striking deviations between the names of the exporting merchants as given in the customs accounts and the information regarding the ownership of the cargo, as given in BUCHANAN & SIMSON's business records. The whole is neither surprising per se – merchants cheated the Customs whenever the potential gains exceeded the risks, after all! – nor trivial. To the contrary: It provides at least a first hint of an explanation as to why information recorded in customs accounts may only be used as a very rough approximation of real trade flows.

Since the reconstruction of the itineraries in Appendix, Table 3.1 (firm's records) is somewhat conjectural, the difference between quantities and itineraries given compared to Table 3.2 (customs accounts) might not be crucial. Obviously, the customs declarations (port books) did not indicate the names "Buchanan" and/or "Simson" as the exporters' names in all cases indicated in BUCHANAN & SIMSON's set of records as exports that had taken place on the account of BUCHANAN & SIMSON themselves. Presumably, collective or lump-sum entries would be made in the customs accounts for large cargoes owned by several merchants or firms in joint company, without necessarily distinguishing the several components or shares of single merchants in the cargoes under consideration. Cargoes might also have been re-directed by BUCHANAN & SIMSON without indication in the customs accounts. A further potential source of a mismatch between private papers and customs declarations is that the "exporters" given in the port books were either the persons BUCHANAN & SIMSON had purchased their cargoes from initially (perhaps on credit?), or else BUCHANAN & SIMSON obtained the cargoes on consignment themselves. The latter would mean that technically the sellers to BUCHANAN & SIMSON remained owners of the tobacco until the final sale in Hamburg and Bremen. Suffice it to cite but two examples; the final outcome will be that our modern-day understanding of British port books could be weaker than hitherto acknowledged.

21 Ibid. pp. 274–283.

The first consignment to Germany on account of BUCHANAN & SIMSON, according to the firm's records, was *Voyage 1* in Appendix, Table 3.1 (ship: *Young / Jonge / Junge(r) Lucas*, Captain Gerrit Kooter, in March 1759, to Stephen Wolfenden, who was their consignee at Hamburg. According to BUCHANAN & SIMSON's business records, the cargo consisted of: 61 hhds (55,872 lbs) tobacco, bought from James Ritchie & Colin Dunlop (Glasgow), and 16 hhds tobacco, bought from Thomas Aitchison & William Miller. Neither the Greenock nor the Port Glasgow customs accounts, however, contain any indication as to this particular voyage having taken place on account of BUCHANAN & SIMSON. Instead all merchants indicated in BUCHANAN & SIMSON's business records as the persons which the tobacco had been bought from (Colin Dunlop, William Miller and Thomas Aitchison), appear in the Greenock and Port Glasgow customs accounts *as exporters on their own account* (or in company) via the *Young Lucas*, which cleared Greenock and Port Glasgow for Hamburg in Ladyday Quarter 1759. A further 137 cwt[22] of Muscovado sugar, which can be found in BUCHANAN & SIMSON's records as having gone to Hamburg in the same ship, are likewise not declared in the customs accounts on BUCHANAN & SIMSON's account, but rather on account of Alexander Houston and William Hyndman. BUCHANAN & SIMSON's journals, however, indicate Alexander Houston as the person who BUCHANAN & SIMSON had initially purchased the sugar from.[23] According to the customs accounts, this was the only export of sugar to Germany in the quarter and ship under consideration. Furthermore, the quantities are identical. Thus there is an apparent mismatch of names in the merchants' records compared to the customs declarations. Apparently – at least in BUCHANAN & SIMSON's case – the customs accounts seem to have deliberately recorded not the exporter's name, but the name of the persons which the exporters had bought the commodities from (in the space in the entry normally left for the exporting merchant's name). This seems to be more than a coincidence.

There is one further very immediate deviancy between the merchants' private records and their declarations in the customs accounts. According to their invoice books, BUCHANAN & SIMSON consigned 60 hhds of tobacco to Hamburg in March 1759 in a different ship (ship: *Young / Junge / Jonge Hendrick*, master: Roloff). In the Glasgow customs accounts however, only 35 hhds are indicated as having been exported on account of BUCHANAN & SIMSON themselves (Appendix, Table 3.2). The composition of the remaining 25 hhds was as follows (according to BUCHANAN & SIMSON's invoice books): 3 hhds bought from *Andrew Ramsay*; 2 hhds bought from *William Miller*; and 20 hhds from *Baird&Walker*. All of the latter re-appear as exporters of identical quantities in the customs accounts, yet in separate customs declarations/entries, again under their own names, rather than "BUCHANAN & SIMSON".[24] This list of examples could certainly be extended. The heuristic value of the preceding exercise, however, is immediately apparent. If the German trades, which were merely a small branch of Scotland's total trades, on account of one Scottish tobacco firm, that was only one amongst several firms active in the tobacco trades in the period, during a comparatively short period (1759–62) exhibit such a markedly different pattern of

22 In Customs practice the sugar hundredweight was assessed at 112 lbs.

23 NAS, CS96/504, p. 36, p. 111.

24 Appendix Table 3.1–2.

recording compared to the information contained in official government records (customs accounts), one unpleasant question is bound to arise: what exactly did the customs export declarations record? The exporting merchant? The consigning merchant? Obviously, the two might not always be identical. This question is particularly unpleasant, considering that a century's worth of preceding model studies on firm size, scope and scale of the Scottish tobacco trades were based on the Scottish customs accounts to a considerable extent, rather than on private records.[25] Obviously the customs accounts are not particularly reliable accounts for micro-economic analyses or studies of firm size in the eighteenth-century transatlantic trades. Business records, mainly invoice and letter books, journals, and to a lesser extent, ledgers, are a much more reliable source and clearly to be preferred over customs accounts. But, apart from a few exceptions, they are virtually absent. Thus the customs accounts will have to remain the starting point for any analysis of Scottish trade flows, whether micro- or macro-economic in terms of its scientific approach; but their limitations have to be acknowledged.

3. Another very obvious cause for a mismatch between declared and factually shipped amounts arises from under-recording of official or government sources. The first association that comes to mind in this context usually is smuggling, i.e. deliberate defrauding of the Customs, and true, the eighteenth century has received a particularly bad press for smuggling.[26] Possible scenarios out of which differences between true and declared amounts could arise are as follows[27]:

Figure 2: Possible Defrauding Scenarios ("Smuggling") in Eighteenth-Century British Overseas Trade

1. No declaration at all (landing / shipping the goods outside a legal port or creek without the payment of customs duties).
2. Fraudulent declaration of goods:
    a. declaration of less / more than actually imported / exported (legally shippable commodities);
    b. statement of a false (or incorrect) material identity;
    c. incorrect country (origin/destination) declaration, because
        i. the next destination (exports) or last port of calling (imports) might be (have been) merely a transit point, or
        ii. exports to / imports from particular destinations might be prohibited.

25 E. g. J. M. PRICE, Buchanan & Simson, 1759–1763: A Different Kind of Glasgow Firm Trading to the Chesapeake, in: William and Mary Quarterly, XL (1983), pp. 3–41. T. M. DEVINE, The Tobacco Lords. A Study of the Tobacco Merchants of Glasgow and their Trading Activities 1740–1790, Edinburgh 1975.

26 W. A. COLE, Trends in Eighteenth Century Smuggling, in: Economic History Review, Second Series, X (1957/58), pp. 359–410; R. C. NASH, The English and Scottish Tobacco Trades in the Seventeenth and Eighteenth Centuries: Legal and Illegal Trade, in: Economic History Review, Second Series, XXXV (1982), pp. 354–372.

27 G. N. CLARK, Guide to English Commercial Statistics 1696–1782, London 1938, pp. 15s.; pp. 34–38; E. E. HOON, The Organisation of the English Customs System 1696–1789, Newton Abbot, 2nd ed. 1968, pp. 260s.; W. SCHLOTE, British Overseas Trade. From 1700 to the 1930s, Oxford 1952, p. 7.

It needs to be kept in mind, however, that not all under-recordings were due to outright smuggling. Several other factors, such as human deficiencies in first counting, and many more rather than criminal intention could be the real underlying cause. Theoretically every commodity imported into or exported from a British port for instance, needed to be declared and recorded, regardless whether or not it was liable to the payment of duties. Any cargo that was not recorded but still shipped, was either shipped without consent or knowledge of the Customs, or re-directed. Most of the activities covered by the first component of the problem could be described as outright smuggling. There was, however, a certain degree of *legal* variance between merchants' declarations and factually shipped amounts, which could be made good for by the merchants ex post without the latter becoming the subject of a court case relating to a defrauding of the Customs (smuggling).

In the eighteenth century the English Customs System, which had become law in Scottish ports as of Mayday 1707, knew two commodity classification schedules (Books of Rates) according to which imported and exported commodities were "rated", i.e. assessed for taxation. The original list or "First" *Book of Rates* was attached to an Act of Parliament issued in 1660, commonly abbreviated as 12 Car. II. c. 4. It included a collection of statutes relating to the assessment of the cargoes, as well as an alphabetical list of each taxable commodity, together with its official value in 1660 and the duty payable on it. The "Second" Book of Rates, an Act of Parliament 11 Geo. I, c. 7, was a mere supplement containing rates on previously unrated goods. It did not contain new valuations or rates of duties on commodities that had already been listed in 12 Car. II c. 4 (1660).[28] This valuation and assessment schedule (1660) remained the basis for taxation in eighteenth-century Scotland. There was not much place for generous commodity differentiation within this schedule, and confusion was particularly great when this schedule was coupled with officials who were unfamiliar with the types of goods whose importation they had to supervise. With regard to the linen trades, for instance, contemporaries observed that

> *Cambricks* (a particular type of linen cloth, originally from the French town of Cambrai, P.R.) are imported under the denomination of *Silesia Lawns* and as such pay only a duty of 2½ d per yard instead of 6 d per yard formerly paid when legally imported. *Silesia Lawns* which ought to pay 3 ½ [d] per Ell are entered as narrow Germany and pay only 1 1/3 [d] per Ell. Osnaburg Linen which is rated so low as to pay only a duty of 1 12/20 d is entered as Narrow Germany and pays only 1 6/20 [d]. Dutch Hollands entered as such pay a duty of nigh 8 d per Ell but are commonly entered as broad Germany and pay only 3d per Ell.[29]

As a variety of differing grades and labels of cloth had to be discerned from each other, and protective import tariffs applied to certain types of cloth, linen import figures are particularly susceptible to a large error margin, not only with regard to the factual quantities shipped, but also their factual material identity.[30] A most extreme

---

28 P. R. ROESSNER, Scottish Foreign Trade towards the End of the Pre-industrial Period, 1700–1760, Unpubl. University of Edinburgh PhD Thesis, Edinburgh 2007, chapter 2 and Appendices.

29 NAS, RH2/5/11/23–24, *Memorandum on the Common Practice Used in Importing Foreign Linen etc.*

30 In the Scottish linen industry the stamp masters, responsible for the collection of Scottish linen produced for the market, were usually chosen from the ranks of professional weavers, as specialist

case was chemicals ("drugs"), with hundreds of different specimens listed in the Book of Rates.[31] A similar story unfolds with timber. Both Books of Rates allowed for a higher than average degree of differentiation, which by the same token conferred an imputed degree of expertise upon the examining customs officials which might not necessarily correspond to their factual level of training. Timber was inhomogeneous, often imported in large numbers of comparatively small pieces, which could in almost all cases be assigned to at least two different classifications employed in the Book of Rates. This inherent ambiguity frequently led to a particular phenomenon called *post-entries*.

Merchants and ship's captains were responsible for orderly declarations of their imported and exported cargoes, regardless whether or not these cargoes were imported (or exported) duty free. Nevertheless, the British Customs operated a thorough and dense system of cross-checks on such declarations, in order to curb the smuggling tendencies inherent to eighteenth-century British trade.[32] If a difference between declared and factually imported *amounts* or *type of commodity* was detected by the outport's collector and his staff (land-waiters, searchers, tidesmen) *ex post*, i.e. upon the second check after the original import declaration had been made, the merchant was ordered back to the customhouse in person, in order to "post-enter" the difference and pay duty accordingly. Post-entries would in fact sometimes be made, and differential duties settled accordingly, several years after the original cargo had been landed. They are a clear indication that there was a certain degree of tolerance on the part of the British Customs administration of what might be called a form of smuggling.[33]

Two different categories of post entries can then be distinguished. The first relates to the *amount* of a particular cargo which, upon cross-examination of the merchant's declaration by the surveyor and land-waiters, was found to be inaccurate. This type of post-entry is easy to interpret and to deal with in the statistical analysis. All one has to do is to add up the amounts to the original entry; the decision only becomes difficult if both fell into different years. Another category of post-entries applied, when the cross-examination of the searchers revealed that the original merchant's declaration as to the *material identity* of the cargo was at variance with the facts detected ex post. If the amounts remained the same (e.g. one ct of *middle masts* was to pass as one ct of *small masts* etc.), the tracking of the true amounts shipped is a straightforward task. But some of the later amendments relating to the nature of the commodities did not exactly specify the resulting new amounts, as a change in the material identity could result in a different applicable measure per unit.[34] Official evidence as to how to translate the

---

knowledge was required to adequately distinguish the several available types of linen. A. J. DURIE, The Scottish Linen Industry in the Eighteenth Century, Edinburgh 1979.

31 T. LANGHAM, The Neat Duties (All Discounts and Abatements deducted) of all Merchandize, Specified in the Book of Rates (London, 3rd ed., 1715).

32 Discussed in detail in ROESSNER, Foreign Trade, chs. 2, 3 and Appendices.

33 It is quite obvious that a post-entry could well be the result of a deliberately false declaration, either of an incorrect material identity, or, more commonly, incorrect quantity of goods shipped.

34 E.g. one *ct* (120) of *cut* Deals might upon cross examination become one quarter (0.1.0 ct) of *Norway deals*. Thus, if of, say, four hundred (480) "cuts of deals" imported some were detected later on to be "whole deals" but without a specification as to how many of the initial "cuts of deals" were whole deals in the corresponding post-entry, it is impossible to determine the factual amounts of both *cuts of deals* and *whole deals* shipped.

legal requirements into practice and re-compute amounts arising from those post-entries remains scarce and ambiguous.[35] Whilst most post-entries may be treated as regular import (or export) declarations, there remains ample scope for ambiguities when it comes to aggregate trade figures obtained from the customs accounts. Any database constructed on the basis of the customs accounts therefore needs to remain to a large extent the product of ad-hoc decisions by the compiler.

The preceding paragraphs are to be understood as a first glimpse on the complexity and error magnitude faced by any researcher working with this type of records. There always is a certain bias inherent to databases and spreadsheets constructed on the basis of information contained in the Scottish customs accounts or "port books". Sources for errors are legion and the degree of imprecision of these records is likely to have been enormous.[36] The same accordingly applies to contemporary statistics derived from these types of customs accounts (see below).

35 NAS, CE7/11, p. 17, §LXVII. H. CROUCH, A Complete View of the British Customs […], Part II, London 1728, p. 16.

36 Cf. also S. E. ÅSTRÖM, From Cloth to Iron. The Anglo-Baltic Trade in the Late Seventeenth Century, Pt. II: The Customs Accounts as Sources for the Study of the Trade, Helsingfors 1965, pp. 65s.

1.2 The Inspector General's Ledgers of Imports and Exports ("TNA, Customs 14")

From 1755 onwards, detailed trade statistics have survived, which break down Scotland's gross total trade by imports, exports and re-exports. The latter were distinguished by re-exports *in time*, if the goods under concern were re-exported within three years after their importation and re-exports *out of time*, on which no draw-back was granted, as the goods were either re-exported more than three years after their importation, or the import had been an unlawful one.[37] Re-exports in time would usually obtain a draw-back of customs duties paid on import, in tobacco's case in the order of 100 % (see chapter 3). The inspector general's ledgers were furthermore divided up by countries Scotland traded with, which makes them a handy tool for historically-minded economists and trade historians. These records were produced by the Scottish *Inspector General of Imports and Exports*, an office established by a Treasury warrant dated 13 December 1754.[38]

Aims and purposes of that office were laid out in a later memorial, drawn up by the Scottish Customs administration for the London-based British Treasury in 1765 thus:

> That in consequence of a Representation from the Lords Commissioners of Trade and Plantations, setting forth the Necessity of an Account being annually laid before them of the Exports and Imports from and to that part of Great Britain called Scotland, in order to enable them to examine into the true state of this Kingdom, the then Right Honourable Lords Commissioners of His Majestys Treasury were pleased to signify their Commands by the late Mr Hardinges Letter dated the 10th of April 1754, that the said Account should be prepared accordingly, and transmitted to the Lords Commissioners of Trade and Plantations. [...] [T]he Account of Exports and Imports, to be so annually transmitted from hence, might be similar in point of Method and Form to that made out in England; the Commissioners here applied to the Commissioners at London and obtained from them specimens of the Books kept in England of the Imports and Exports; of the Accounts thereof delivered to the Lords Commissioners of Trade & Plantations; and of the Accounts received Quarterly from the Ports as the foundation of the whole.[39]

The Scottish trade statistics were to be produced using English blueprints; they were based upon materials and accounts sent to the Scottish inspector general of imports and exports at Edinburgh from the circa 30 Scottish outports on a quarterly basis. Presumably the main task of re-grouping the information contained in the customs accounts – in the customs accounts commodities were aggregated chronologically by day and ship calling – by imports/exports, commodities and countries was already done by the collectors of the customs in the outports.[40] This is suggested by a letter

---

37 "Out of time" generally meant that no draw-back of import duties was granted. This could be a result of the fact that either the commodities under consideration were re-exported more than three years after importation; or the re-exported goods under consideration had been seized (i.e. had been smuggled before). The latter could draw-back no import duties and were thus labelled "out of time" in the *lingua franca* of the Customs and Treasury administration.

38 NAS, CE1/8, 31 December 1754. TNA, T1/447/242–243, *Memorial of the Commissioners for Managing His Majesty's Customs in Scotland.*

39 TNA, T1/447/242–243, 21 February 1765.

40 ROESSNER, Foreign Trade, p. 97s.

written by Archibald Campbell, the first Scottish inspector general, who held office between 1755 and 1763, in which he instructed the customs collector at Montrose that

> I have sent You Inclosed a Copy of the Speciemen transmittd. to me from the Office of the Inspector Generall of Exports & Imports at London, which Speciemen You are Exactly to Follow, As the Method of Making up Your Accounts of all Goods Exported and Imported. Which Accounts You are to transmitt to me Quarterly, in Order to furnish me with Materialls for makeing Up the Generall Account to be transmitted by me Yearly To the Right Honourable the Lords of the Treasury and the Hon[oura]ble Commissioners of Trade and Plantations. Youre Accounts are to Commence from the 5th January 1755.[41]

The first year for which trade balance sheets were drawn up was 1755; at that time the English and Irish offices of the same denomination and operational range had been in existence for sixty years.[42] Naturally these ledgers have aroused more scholarly interest than any other source, in particular as they conform to the range of data used in international economics and historical studies of foreign trade. With regard to their usability for monitoring Scotland's balance of trade with Germany, there would be three guiding questions. First, how much of Scotland's factual trade with German was recorded? This discussion is best to be carried out with regard to the customs accounts (port books), as these were the primary source for the ledgers. Accordingly, the problems of smuggling and under-recording have been addressed in the previous sections on the port books. Secondly, how much of what was recorded on the outport level (and written down in the local customs accounts) actually found its way into the ledgers? Thirdly, how reliable are the country classifications (here: "Germany") used in this source?

The second question highlights the critical heuristic value of the *monetary* figures contained in the ledgers. The first and foremost character of these statistics is that they provide aggregates for Scotland's total imports and exports in yearly series, valued at what contemporaries held to be reliable proxies for the current value of all goods covered in these aggregates. In other words, one of the foremost aims of these statistics was to calculate Scotland's balance of trade. The problem of the "current" values employed in these statistics has attracted considerable attention in the past, chiefly from economists, and mainly with regard to the English customs ledgers.[43] It will therefore be dealt with only very briefly here, as there is no need to re-iterate the conclusions drawn on the basis of the English materials, as these were identical to the Scottish source in terms of their design. But – and this is the crucial point scholars have over-

---

41 Dundee City Archives, NAS, CE53/2/6, Board to Collector (Montrose), 22 May 1755.

42 The English and Irish Inspectors General of Imports and Exports were inaugurated in 1696.

43 S. D. SMITH, Prices and the Value of English Exports in the Eighteenth Century: Evidence from the North American Colonial Trade, in: Economic History Review, Second Series, LXVIII, 3 (1995), pp. 575–590; J. J. MCCUSKER, The Current Value of English Exports, 1697 to 1800, in: William and Mary Quarterly, XVII (1971), pp. 607–28; P. DEANE / W. A. COLE, British Economic Growth 1688–1959. Trends and Structure, Cambridge, 2nd ed. 1967, pp. 40–50, pp. 315–322 (App. 1). SCHLOTE, Trade, pp. 3–38; CLARK, Guide, pp. 1–42; T. S. ASHTON, Introduction, in: E. B. SCHUMPETER, English Overseas Trade Statistics, 1697–1808, Oxford 1960, pp. 1–14; W. E. MITCHINTON, Introduction, in: ID. (ed.), The Growth of English Overseas Trade in the Seventeenth and Eighteenth Centuries, London 1969, pp. 1–63; esp. pp. 52–57; B. R. MITCHELL, British Historical Statistics, Cambridge 1988.

looked so far – to discuss *ceteris paribus* the possibility of re-computing the aggregate figures contained in the ledgers into current values[44], means to beg the central question of whether the *quantities* of commodities shipped, as recorded in these ledgers, were at all correct.

With regard to England, scholars have been justified begging the question. As mentioned previously, the eighteenth century English customs accounts, which would allow a comparison between the material quantities stated therein and the inspector general's ledgers, are largely lost. For Scotland, they are preserved in full series since Christmas quarter 1742, which allows a rare detailed insight into what these statistics actually cover. The following remarks should therefore be seen in a "British" rather than narrowly Scottish perspective, as the possible implications regarding the administrative practice and the resulting reliability of the economic statistics reach far beyond Scotland.

As mentioned above, the inspector general's ledgers of imports and exports[45] were specifically developed in order to determine Scotland's balance of trade in yearly series. They were designed accordingly (Figure 3).

Figure 3: Information contained in the post-1755 Scottish Trade Statistics

(a) country of origin (imports) / destination (exports);
(b) specification of commodities carried;
(c) quantities in British ships, or
(d) quantities in foreign ships;
(e) valuation (interval);
(f) total value (quantities in (c) and (d) multiplied by the arithmetic medium of starting and ending point of the interval in (e)).

Import and export tables were similar, but there were three different types of export tables, one each for domestic exports, re-exports in time (i.e. normally three years) and re-exports out of time. If commodities were re-exported "in time", they were entitled to drawback of part of or all customs duties paid upon import; the goods' valuations were adjusted accordingly.

Taken at face value, therefore, these ledgers appear to be a particularly useful aggregate of trade fluctuations, organized by countries and commodities. In terms of the information required it is superficially obvious that they needed to be based on information contained in the customs accounts. There is, however, a remarkable incongruence between these two sources for 1755 (the year for which both have been examined en detail) in terms of the aggregate trade figures. The most important issue to be discussed therefore is the question of how precisely the transmission of information between outports and inspector general worked in practice. For this purpose a re-appraisal of the port books (II.1.1) is necessary. Scholars using the port books in the past have frequently been tempted to believe that the customs accounts were factual accounts of imports and exports.[46] This, however, overlooks the basic fact that port books were mere accounts of customs duties paid. They did not usually contain information regarding warehoused goods, i.e. goods which had been imported already, but

44 E.g. McCusker, Current Value.

45 TNA, Customs 14.

on which duties were still pending. Unfortunately they are also largely elusive on re-directed traffic. Thus differences between them and the super-ordinate trade statistics can be expected *a priori*.

The crucial aspect in this regard is the problem of transmission, which can be formulated thus: "which commodities that can be found in the port books in a particular year will have to be omitted from an import-export account for the entire country (Scotland) in this year, and for which reasons?" A comprehensive examination of the full set of Scottish customs accounts, which are completely preserved for 1755, with the likewise complete trade statistics of the inspector general for the same year suggests the following.[47] Firstly, there were cargoes entered into the customs accounts which were excluded *deliberately* from the inspector general's ledgers of imports and exports. Secondly, some cargoes were included in the trade statistics, which for some reasons cannot be re-traced in the customs accounts. Such ambiguities could arise mainly from traffic into / ex warehouse, as well as post-entered cargoes – both particularities to the contemporary English and since 1707 British, Customs System.

The late seventeenth-century English Customs system provided warehouses at every outport for storing incoming cargo that was unclaimed, or for which a purchaser had not been found yet, or for which a final decision, as to whether it was to be imported (=retained for domestic consumption) or re-exported, was still pending. As customs duties on commodities that were imported but warehoused normally varied, and their payment could often be split, both depending upon whether and when the cargo was to be re-exported or released for domestic consumption[48], it was common practice to record the cargo in the port books only once. This was at the point when a final decision had been made, and the duties were computed definitively. Naturally this could only be the delivery *ex* warehouse.[49] It is obvious that in those cases in which delivery into and ex warehouse fell not only into different quarters, but also different years, the customs accounts "over-state" trade for the year in which the cargo was taken out of the warehouse and "understate" trade for the year in which the cargo had been dis-

46 S.-E. ÅSTRÖM, North European Timber Exports to Great Britain, 1760–1810, in: P. L. COTTRELL / D. H. ALDCROFT (eds.), Shipping, Trade and Commerce. Essays in Memory of Ralph Davis, Leicester 1981, pp. 81–98, at pp. 82s. The issue of how the port books and TNA, Customs 14 can be linked in a logical way has been briefly yet inconclusively addressed only by Price and Cochran. J. M. PRICE, New Time Series for Scotland's and Britain's Trade with the Thirteen Colonies and States, 1740 to 1791, in: William and Mary Quarterly, XXXII (1975), pp. 307–325; L. E. COCHRAN, Scottish Trade with Ireland in the Eighteenth Century, Unpubl. University of Stirling PhD thesis, 2 Vols., Stirling 1980, pp. 24s.

47 ROESSNER, Foreign Trade,3.2.4.

48 I.e. only part of the duty became due immediately, and the rest after it had been decided whether the cargo would be re-exported or retained for domestic consumption.

49 Accordingly, in the majority of Scottish customs accounts examined by the present author, an initial entry notifying the discharge and delivery of goods *into the warehouse* is lacking; but a full entry, including the ship's, master's and merchant's names, as well as the specification of the port or country of origin, was made upon delivery *ex warehouse* instead, within the section for standard entries of goods inwards ("General Goods Imported"). This procedure represents one serious source bias, as an *ex warehouse* entry not necessarily specified *when* the cargo had actually been landed (and sometimes years would pass between delivery into and ex warehouse).

charged from the ship. The actual problem arising is that the method of how exactly the inspector general dealt with such "inter-annual cargoes" remains ambiguous.[50]

A similar problem unfolds with regard to post-entries. As noted above[51], a post-entry was no import (or, much less frequently, export) declaration as such, but represented only a later amendment of a cargo's amount or material identity. When post-entries were made, the cargoes under concern had usually been discharged already, but it was then found that they had been declared and taxed incorrectly, either in terms of amount or material identity. In the present context – an examination of the validity of contemporary British trade statistics that were based on information contained in the customs accounts – the main questions are: how and to what extent were changes in the material identity or quantity of cargoes declared ex post captured in the contemporary trade statistics? Did the inspector general consider a post-entry (import), which was made in a year different from the year of importation, as an import he was to include in his calculations for the earlier (year of import) or the later year (year the post entry was made)? From a complete cross-examination of the Scottish customs accounts and ledgers of imports and exports carried out by the present author for 1755 (Scotland's total trade[52]), it appears as though the inspector general included virtually all post-entered cargoes into his 1755 ledger, mainly because the bulk of those entries still made in 1755 related to initial entries made in the same year, usually even in the same quarter. But, in the same way as with the ex warehouse entries mentioned above, post entries frequently fell into years different from the ones in which the original cargo had been entered or the ship had called. No definite statement can be made as to whether or to what extent such post-entries were included into or excluded from the inspector general's 1755 ledger. But a broader examination of the problem with regard to Scotland's total overseas trade in the year 1755, using a larger set of data, has shown that there could be a large deviance between the customs accounts / port books on the one and the inspector general's trade statistics on the other hand.[53]

A last item of relevance for the present purpose is the country classifications employed in contemporary British trade statistics. As these could be highly incongruent and ambiguous at times, they present a serious bias when it comes to the examination of partial trade flows, such as "Scottish-German trade", as opposed to "Scottish total foreign trade". Unless one went through all Scottish customs accounts – meaning that about 28 sets of customs records would have to be examined and searched for each year – naturally each analysis of Scotland's foreign trade will have to start with the inspector general's ledgers. But these post-1755 Scottish trade statistics are highly inconsistent in the country labelling employed (and so probably are the English ledgers). Therefore the following again needs to be seen in a pan-British perspective. The problem can be illustrated immediately using an example from 1755.

The customs accounts for instance indicate that a total of 3084 cwt (circa 27.5 metric tons) of rice were re-exported from Kirkwall, the head port of the Orkney Is-

---

50 Discussed at length in ROESSNER, Foreign Trade.

51 Section II.1.1 above.

52 The methodology and data set are discussed at length in ROESSNER, Foreign Trade, ch. 3 and appendices.

53 Ibid.

lands, to the German port of Bremen in 1755.[54] But no entry of rice exports to Germany can be found in the ledgers of imports and exports of the same year. Instead, an identical quantity of 3084.16 cwt occurs under re-exports to "Sweden". There are two possible explanations. Either the shipment had been re-directed to an unknown Swedish destination; the fact that the Bremen *Schlachteangabebücher* for 1755[55] contain no reference to an import of rice from Scotland, lends this possibility some support. The other option is that Bremen in that year was incorrectly thought to be a Swedish port. This is somewhat excusable, as the Duchy of Bremen had been Swedish territory until 1720, and the British Customs occasionally continued to assign trade with Bremen to Sweden after 1720.[56]

But there were also more deliberate biases, based on conscious decisions of the economic administrators who were in charge of designing and compiling the statistics under consideration. The general and super-ordinate principle of the inspector general's trade statistics was a country labelling based on political entities, such as "France", "Russia", "Sweden", "Denmark and Norway" etc. Nevertheless, and in particular due to the territorial and political fragmentations occurring in the early modern period, country classifications were sometimes bound to be ambiguous. In fact the somewhat odd entity of the Holy Roman Empire presents a good case in point. In general, the classification "Germany", as employed in the post-1755 trade statistics, represented the Empire. It therefore included those parts of *Prussia* that were part of the Empire, but excluded Ducal Prussia (mainly Königsberg), for which the separate heading "Prussia" was employed. But the political fragmentation of the pre-modern Holy Roman Empire as such had repercussions on British statistical recording as well, which led to several ambiguities. Consider *Altona* for instance, a Danish port close to Hamburg, whose trade thrived in the eighteenth century. Located at that time about 10 kilometres from Hamburg down the River Elbe (today it is part of Hamburg City), Altona was situated within the German Empire, but stood under Danish rule. As far as political administration on the highest level was concerned, Danish Holstein was an imperial district (*Reichskreis*), and the Danish-Norwegian king in this regard was an imperial prince (*Reichsfürst*).[57] The Scottish customs collectors in their post-1742 quarterly accounts, as well as the Scottish inspector general in his post-1755 ledgers of imports and exports, however, chose to include trade with Altona under "Denmark & Norway". In this they were not wrong per se – as Altona's rulers were no Germans, but an earlier order by the Scottish Board of Customs in 1722 had ruled – in quite the same right – that Altona was to be considered a *German* port, as far as the Customs were concerned.[58]

The old Hansa town of *Stralsund*, located within Hither Pomerania, represents a similar case, as it lay within the Roman Empire but was, as Hither Pomerania in general, under Swedish rule since 1648. At present it is impossible to determine whether

54 NAS, E504/26/3, Customs Accounts Orkney, Midsummer Quarter (April–June) 1755, Entries Outwards Nr. 3; Industry of Leith, Master: Andrew Cowan; Exporters: Clerk & Co.

55 *Staatsarchiv Bremen, 2–Ss.2.a.4.f.1.*

56 W. DOTZAUER, Die Deutschen Reichskreise in der Verfassung des Alten Reiches und ihr Eigenleben (1500–1806), Darmstadt 1989, p. 324f, p. 331.

57 Ibid.

58 NAS, CE57/2/251, *Index of Board's Orders*, p. 31.

trade with Stralsund in the British statistics was usually covered under "Sweden" or "Germany". Therefore the inspector general's ledgers of imports and exports are to be viewed critically with regard to the country classifications employed. Some of Scotland's trade with the Holy Roman Empire might not be covered under the heading "Germany" in the contemporary British trade statistics; some of Scottish trade with Sweden and Denmark-Norway, as listed in contemporary statistics, might in fact have been trade that took place with Altona, Stralsund, Rostock or Wismar – rather than with, say, Stockholm, Gothenburg or Copenhagen. Of this the reader, as well as future researchers, should be aware. Only a simultaneous and complete evaluation of the port books for each year covered by the ledgers (TNA, Customs 14) would yield a more detailed picture.

The analysis might be drawn to a close by a comparison of quantities declared as Scottish-German trade as they appear from the contemporary Scottish port books and the figures stated in the trade statistics for 1755. For operational reasons only the first year in the series (1755) was examined. From this exercise it appears as though the trade statistics (Scottish Inspector General's Ledgers of Imports and Exports, TNA, Customs 14) under-recorded trade – at least in 1755. This is not at all surprising, given the transmission difficulties between the customs collectors in the outports and the inspector general in Edinburgh, which have been hinted at in the previous sections. From this set of data, trade with Germany can be isolated in the following way.

Scottish imports from German ports, including those located in Danish Holstein and Swedish / Hither Pomerania, were recorded fairly accurately. The main item of concern, "Narrow German" linen, representing 94 per cent of the £Sterling totals in 1755, can be found in literally identical quantities in both sets of sources (Table 1 below).

Table 1: 1755 Quantities Given in the Port Books and TNA, Customs 14 (i): Imports

		E504		Cust 14		Difference E504-Cust14	
Commodity	**Measure**	**Amount Shipped**	**Value**	**Amount Shipped**	**Value**	**Amounts**	**Value**
Narrow German	ct ells	3,814.98	£20,982.35	3,814.75	£20,981.13	0.23	£1.22
Remaining			£1,289.95		£1,288.57		£1.39
Total			£22,272.30		£22,269.69		£2.61
Coverage			94%		94%		

Exports are more critical. With regard to domestic exports, worsted stockings were clearly under-recorded in the trade statistics (TNA, Customs 14), which covered only about one-sixth of the exported amounts declared in the port books. Likewise, whilst no lead exports were recorded in TNA, Customs 14, it is evident from the port books that lead was in fact exported to Germany in 1755 (Table 2).

Table 2: 1755 Quantities Given in the Port Books and Customs 14 (ii): Domestic Exports

		E504		Cust 14		Difference E504-Cust14	
Commodity	**Measure**	**Amount Shipped**	**Value**	**Amount Shipped**	**Value**	**Amounts**	**Value**
Stockings	dz pairs	6,383.33	£6,064.17	1,100.00	£1,045.00	5,283.33	£5,019.17
Barley	quarters	390.00	£273.00			390.00	£273.00
Bere (Bigg)	quarters			73.88	£44.33	-73.88	-£44.33
Malt	quarters	465.75	£465.75	465.75	£465.75	0.00	£0.00
Lead	tons	109.60	£1,808.40			109.60	£1,808.40
Scots Salt	weys	338.13	£281.77	319.60	£266.33	18.53	£15.44
Coal (great)	tons	2,285.00	£571.25	2,190.00	£547.50	95.00	£23.75
Coal (small)	chalders	133.00	£133.00	133.00	£133.00	0.00	£0.00
Vitriol Oil	lbs	39,391.00	£984.78	39,391.00	£984.78	0.00	£0.00
Cod, Ling	cwt	3,850.50	£1,925.25	3,384.50	£1,692.25	466.00	£233.00
Herring		3,142.00	£2,513.60	3,061.00	£2,448.80	81.00	£64.80
Selection covered as % of total given			£0.94		£0.89		
Total			£15,955.39		£8,588.17		£7,367.22

It may be noted that the number of stockings exported to Germany in subsequent years, as given in TNA, Customs 14, was lower on average than the pre-1755 port book figures. Although this phenomenon cannot be explained at present, it seems as though this was no random element.

Re-exports are slightly less critical. If the 1,656 lbs of cut tobacco (port books) are added to the recorded amount of 212,677 lbs of "unmanufactured" tobacco (Table 3), the customs accounts and inspector general's ledgers feature identical sums of tobacco re-exports to Germany in 1755. Obviously the inspector general assigned those 1,656.5 lbs of manufactured or "cut" tobacco with a valuation of 15d per lb to his column for "unmanufactured" tobacco, which had a lower valuation of 5d per lb (re-exported).

Table 3: 1755 Quantities given in the Port Books and TNA, Customs 14 (iii): Re-exports

		E504		Cust 14		Difference E504-Cust14	
Commodity	**Measure**	**Amount Shipped**	**Value**	**Amount Shipped**	**Value**	**Amounts**	**Value**
Tobacco	lbs	212,677.00	£4,430.77	214,333.00	£4,465.27	-1,656.00	-£34.50
Tobacco / cut	lbs	1,656.50	£103.53			1,656.50	£103.53
Tea	lbs	1,122.50	£449.00			1,122.50	£449.00
French Cambrics	halfpieces	284.00	£656.75	283.00	£654.44	1.00	£2.31
Foreign Salt	weys	16.10	£21.13	16.10	£21.13	0.00	£0.00
Rice	cwt	3,084.16	£1,464.98	0.00	£0.00	3,084.16	£1,464.98
Selection covered as % of total given			99%		100%	0.00	-£0.01
Total			£7,220.89		£5,140.84	0.00	£2,080.05

In the case of re-exports, the mismatch is obviously largely due to tea and rice, which were completely omitted from the Scottish trade statistics, although entries relating to these commodities can be found in the customs accounts for that year.[59]

The conclusion to the present section needs to remain speculative, mainly because no administrative records of the Scottish inspector general of imports and exports have

59 As shown above, TNA, Customs 14, however, includes an identical amount of 3,084.16 lbs of rice within re-exports to *Sweden* in 1755 (probably due to a misallocation of this accounting item).

survived. Such evidence would be needed, in order to determine why a considerable amount of 1755 traffic, indicated in the customs accounts as regular traffic that had taken place in 1755, was omitted from the trade statistics relating to that year, and why some traffic that could not be found in the complete set of port books would nonetheless be given in this year's trade statistics. Generally the most obvious explanation is to be sought in the fact that the inspector general did not have the customs accounts at hand, but relied on aggregate accounts sent to him by the various Scottish outports' collectors instead. As the latter obviously had a large degree of individual freedom in aggregating their individual data, the main source of error or bias would have arisen from the work of the customs collectors.

The last item on the agenda is the valuations employed in the inspector general's ledgers. Trade statistics require current values, lest the balance of trade or the balance on current account to be drawn up become meaningless figures. But especially in premodern times, the finding of suitable prices to be applied as valuations or goods' multipliers in a yearly series, was too costly and difficult a task to be carried out for more than a few consecutive years. The English inspector general stopped to enquire current prices after 1708, a mere 11 years after his office had been established (1696). Thereafter the English foreign trade valuations remained constant until the end of the eighteenth century. The Scottish valuations were virtually entirely fixed as early as 1755 and kept constant thereafter, as the Scottish office of inspector general was a comparatively small and minor one within the Scottish customs administration. But even finding a suitable panel of set prices for more than 700 commodities to be recorded in the Scottish trade statistics in 1755 and subsequent years would have been a considerable task, as the value of cargoes exported or imported was not normally recorded into the port books unless unrated goods were concerned.[60]

No records pertaining to the administration of the Scottish inspector general of imports and exports and the design and pricing employed in the Scottish ledgers of imports and exports could be traced so far. Thus our understanding of this source needs to remain rudimentary at best, and chiefly based on the much better documented English precedent. A thorough examination of the Scottish sources by the present author has suggested that imports were valued *free on board* or *ex works* in the exporting country, as were exports ("estimate of the first cost or value in Scotland").[61] Reexports were valued *free on board* as well ("estimate of the value in Scotland after the duties are drawn back"), but as the export of a previously imported product was concerned, this equalled *cost, insurance, freight* upon import plus the share of customs duties that could not be drawn back upon re-export. It possibly included a profit markup, but certainly excluded the costs of re-shipping these goods from Britain (transport and insurance). The valuations as such technically were no discrete values but *price intervals* were given instead, accounting for a range of differing prices and accordingly quality differentials of the products covered under each heading. The valua-

60 Then a statement of the goods' current value was made by the importer upon oath, and duties were levied *ad valorem*.

61 Although Ashton – without qualification – maintained (with regard to the English ledgers) that "the figures of exports were supposed to represent values of the goods when delivered at the foreign ports" (thus c.i.f.). T. S. ASHTON, An Economic History of England: The Eighteenth Century, London 1955, p. 151.

tion used in the end for multiplying the physical amounts of cargoes, however, was the arithmetic mean of the starting and the ending point of the price interval. Invisibles[62] were neither recorded, nor were estimates included in the trade statistics. Likewise, bullion transfers and flows of precious metals, which were recorded into the English ledgers, were not recorded in the Scottish ledgers.

The majority of valuations were kept unaltered after 1755, resulting in a quasi-volumetric series.[63] It was therefore not the intention to inquire current values on a yearly basis; presumably the financial resources of the office did not permit such an ambitious task. If the 1755 relative prices that were employed correspond to reality, this volumetric schedule would represent a useful tool for the analysis of real (or commodity) fluctuations, being a ready-made physical index for the weighing of commodities that entered the trades in different measures, which otherwise would have to be computed using an extremely tedious procedure. This particular volumetric schedule, however, had both virtues, as well as disadvantages. A volumetric series using constant instead of current valuations, whilst useful as a commodity index for real fluctuations, obviously neither captures fluctuations in *current*, nor changes in *relative prices*. There is always the possibility for instance that trade statistics employing fixed valuations at some point in time either over- or understate the real value of particular imports (exports) to the economy. This is especially likely if trade is biased towards a few significant commodities the prices of which were either highly volatile, such as grain prices, or rapidly declining in the longer run, such as tobacco prices in Scotland's case.[64]

Therefore, in the following discussion the method has been to value aggregates obtained from the customs accounts (1743–1755) at 1755 valuations found in the inspector general's trade statistics (TNA, Customs 14), bearing in mind all biases and disadvantages. Furthermore TNA, Customs 14 has been re-computed into a fully volumetric series, employing 1755 valuations throughout. Corrections were made in those rare instances in which the inspector general subsequently re-valued some commodities. This yields the opportunity of employing a comprehensive aggregate index that monitors real fluctuations over time of the entire set of traded commodities that were measured in different units of weight and capacity. The index measure for the quantitative discussion in chapters three and four is therefore £Sterling, without any further implications as to the *current* value of the trade flows under concern.

The discussion will now turn to a brief analysis of the quantitative source material available for German ports. It shall be limited to sources similar to the Scottish (British) port books, as trade statistics, such as the inspector general's ledgers, could and would not be compiled for Germany in the period under consideration. It is therefore

62 Net shipping earnings, profits, interest, dividends, insurance, brokerage commissions etc. F. N. BURTON, Contemporary Trade, Oxford 1984, ch. 2.

63 "Quasi-volumetric" because some valuations were altered in subsequent years. The English customs ledgers applied current prices as official values until 1709, after which date the prices were never adjusted again until the middle of the nineteenth century. MITCHELL, Statistics, pp. 551s. Ashton, "Introduction," p. 4. DEANE / COLE, British Economic Growth, pp. 42s. Cf. also CLARK, Guide, pp. 10s.; A. MAIZELS, Oversea Trade, in: M. G. KENDALL / A. BRADFORD HILL (eds.), The Sources and Nature of the Statistics of the United Kingdom, Vol. 1, London / Edinburgh 1952, pp. 17–31, esp. at p. 21.

64 L. E. COCHRAN, Scottish Trade with Ireland in the Eighteenth Century, Edinburgh 1985, p. 77.

mainly accounts relating to a particular duty in a particular port that provide some information as to cargoes shipped. With regard to contents and design, these sources were far from standardized and differed from port to port. Some apparent similarities amongst them, as well as in comparison to the Scottish port books, can be detected nevertheless.

2. SOURCES FOR GERMAN PORTS

As mentioned in the introduction to this chapter, the Scottish and the now lost English port books ranked amongst – they probably were – Europe's most sophisticated, most detailed and, in terms of commodities covered, most comprehensive sets of contemporary sources, indicating the *complete* yearly trade flows for each port within British realms. They were followed in historical significance by similar records produced in the two largest German sea ports: the Hamburg *Admiralitätszoll- and Convoygeldeinnahmebücher* (Admiralty Toll and Convoy Money Accounts) and the Bremen *Schlachteangabebücher* (Schlachte Toll Accounts). Other ports produced similar records; Lübeck for instance has the *Zulagebücher*[65], as did most other large German and "quasi-German" ports in the Baltic (Stralsund, Danzig, Königsberg, Riga and Nerva). These, however, covered only certain, narrowly defined branches of these ports' total commercial activity. This is their basic difference to British accounts.

2.1 Hamburg

Due to a wide variety of tolls and customs duties charged on incoming sea-borne traffic into the port of Hamburg, one might assume that in the eighteenth century the number and scope of accounts produced in Hamburg would have been similar to any British port. Apparently, this was not the case, but the most significant and for an economic analysis most valuable accounts have survived (*Admiralitätszoll und Convoygeldeinnahmebücher*). They contain details relating to particular incoming cargoes declared in the Port of Hamburg, which renders them useful for studying the long-term trends in Hamburg's import trades.[66]

The procedure of declaring a cargo inwards into the Port of Hamburg was remotely similar to declaring a cargo inwards into a British port. As soon as a ship had called in, the importer, the supercargo, or the forwarding agent had to declare the amount, origin and value of the imported cargo according to a book of rates in Mark Banko, the local money of account, in order for the applicable customs duties (or, in this particular case, an 0.5–1 per cent *ad valorem* toll charged towards meeting the

65 C. MEYER-STOLL, Die lübeckische Kaufmannschaft des 17. Jahrhunderts unter wirtschafts- und sozialgeschichtlichen Aspekten, Frankfurt-on-the-Main / Bern / New York / Paris 1989, p. 13.

66 W. VOGEL, Handelskonjunkturen und Wirtschaftskrisen in ihrer Auswirkung auf den Seehandel der Hansestädte 1560–1806, in: Hansische Geschichtsblätter, LXXIV (1956), pp. 50–64, esp. pp. 57s.; POHL, Beziehungen, p. 311, n. 1.

expenses for maintaining a convoy fleet guarding foreign freighters into the Port of Hamburg) to be levied. Thus an import declaration in the Hamburg *Admiralitätszoll- und Convoygeldeinnahmebücher* contained the following information:

Figure 4: Information contained in the Hamburg Admiralty Toll Accounts

(a) the date of declaration;
(b) the shipmaster's name;
(c) the port or country of origin;
(d) the unit and number of units of measure;
(e) the commodities' material identity;
(f) the value of the cargo in Mark Banko according to fixed rates;
(g) the *Admiralty Toll* levied.

O.-E. KRAWEHL, Quellen zur Hamburger Handelsstatistik im 18. Jahrhundert, in: W. FISCHER / A. KUNZ (eds.), Grundlagen der Historischen Statistik von Deutschland. Quellen, Methoden, Forschungsziele, Opladen 1991, pp. 47–69; ID., Die Admiralitätszoll- und Convoygeldeinnahmebücher als handelsstatistische Quelle, in: J. SCHNEIDER / O.-E. KRAWEHL / M. A. DENZEL (eds.), Statistik des Hamburger seewärtigen Einfuhrhandels im 18. Jahrhundert. Nach den Admiralitätszoll- und Convoygeld-Einnahmebüchern, St. Katharinen 2001, pp. 9–18.

Especially with regard to information covered under (d) and (e), a high degree of imprecision results from the basic fact that most commodity labels were frequently aggregates or lump sum headings (such as "manufactures") and thus unspecific as to the precise material identity of the imported commodities.[67] In this way the *Admiralitätszoll- und Convoygeldeinnahmebücher* were similar to the British customs accounts which frequently employed lump sum headings, too.[68] The main difference to British customs accounts, however, was that – as was the case with the Bremen Schlachte Toll Accounts to be discussed below – only cargoes liable to duty were recorded. This led to the exclusion of a significant share of Hamburg's total import and export trades in any given year.

Certain geographical areas were generally exempt from taxation, for instance any North Sea port east of the Scheldt River and westwards of Cape Skagen, as well Baltic ports in general. Trade with Holland and Flanders, which included some of the largest contemporary sea ports at that time, such as Rotterdam, Amsterdam and Ostend, as well as German Atlantic ports such as Emden and Bremen, and all Danish ports (including those in Danish Holstein), was therefore not recorded. Furthermore, some products were generally exempt from taxation, mainly coals and grain (for which separate accounts were kept in some cases). Transit traffic, private (non-commercial) imports, as well as imports by the English Merchant Adventurers were also duty free, and thus not recorded. These aspects render the admiralty toll books unsuitable for a reconstruction of a yearly balance of trade, a possibility which, as shown above, is theoretically provided by the eighteenth century Scottish port books. Lastly, recent research which has led to a first publication of the statistical information found in these books by commodities and countries of origin[69], has failed to explain the pricing

67 KRAWEHL, Quellen, pp. 63–65.

68 ROESSNER, Foreign Trade, ch. 3, section 3.1.6.

69 KRAWEHL, Admiralitätszoll- und Convoygeldeinnahmebücher, pp. 9–14.

schedule of the declared values required for assessing the cargoes and levying the toll duties. It would for instance be desirable to know, whether declared values in Mark Banko were given in *c.i.f.* or *f.o.b.* prices.

It is obvious that, for reasons of geography, and due to the composition of the volume of Scottish exports to Germany to be discussed below (chapter three), with a dominance of salt, coal, fish and vitriol oil, all of which were taxable in Hamburg, most cargoes declared in Scotland as exports to Hamburg should have reappeared as imports in the Hamburg records. A comparison of the Scottish customs accounts with the aggregates for Hamburg imports from Scotland for 1747 and 1755, however, suggests that there are some considerable differences in the recorded amounts.[70] As all cargoes declared on the Scottish side as exports to Hamburg were liable to Admiralty Toll, they should be expected to turn up in the *Admiralitätszoll- und Convoygeldeinnahmebücher*. Strikingly, it was only lead, vitriol oil and herrings, that were recorded as imports from Scotland in the Hamburg records for the two years that have been examined (1747, 1755). Furthermore, it is clear that the Hamburg valuations were far too low. At the par exchange rate of 12.46 Mark Banko/£Sterling, imports into Hamburg valued at 1,450 Marks Banko in 1747 and 600 Marks Banko in 1755, would have worked out at somewhere near £116 7s 5d (1747) and £48 3s Sterling (1755), compared to hypothetical total f.o.b. values for Scottish exports from Leith to Hamburg in the order of £4,158 17s 9d 2 *farthing* (1747) and £3,543 15s 7d 1 *farthing* Sterling (1755), as apparent from the Scottish records.[71] In this context it is irrelevant whether or not the Hamburg imports were declared in c.i.f. or f.o.b. values, as they are obviously too low in either case, even allowing for possible differences in the 1755 Scottish price structure, compared to relative prices prevailing in Hamburg in 1747, and possibly different exchange rate mechanisms.[72] The Hamburg figures therefore are clearly too low.[73]

Principally this might be due to a bundle of reasons, which could have operated singularly or in varying combinations, viz.: (a) Only certain commodities were liable to *Admiralitätszoll* and *Convoygeld* and only those that were liable were actually recorded. As has been discussed above, this possibility can be ruled out as an explanation, as those commodities not recorded as imports from Scotland in either 1747 or 1755 were in fact liable to *Admiralitätszoll* (and would be recorded in other years).[74] (b) Lax recording or documentation of traffic and taxation yields on the Hamburg side might be another option, for instance because the tolls were farmed and the farmers might have applied as large a degree of imprecision in their official documentation

---

70 See Appendix, Tables 2.1–2. I should like to thank Mr Frank Schulenburg for providing an excel file with the Scottish data via email attachment.

71 J. SCHNEIDER / O. SCHWARZER / F. ZELLFELDER / M. A. DENZEL (eds.), Währungen der Welt VI: Geld und Währungen in Europa im 18. Jahrhundert, Stuttgart 1992, pp. 45–47. Scottish exports have been valued at 1755 f.o.b. prices, obtained from TNA, Customs 14.

72 As the available literature on the Hamburg records unfortunately provides no evidence as to the price schedule employed in the *Convoygeldeinnahmebücher* (c.i.f. or f.o.b. prices?), conclusions need to remain tentative in that regard.

73 By valuing exports (and re-exports) f.o.b., the Scottish trade statistics (inspector general of imports and exports' ledgers) under-state the value of the cargoes arriving in Hamburg.

74 SCHNEIDER et al. (eds.), Statistik, passim.

(auditable accounts) as they possibly could. (c) Cargoes declared in Leith for Hamburg (or in any Scottish port for Germany) might not actually have been shipped to Hamburg but could have been redirected to a destination elsewhere. This, however, is only a theoretical possibility; on the basis of existing Scottish customs records it is impossible to determine whether or not all traffic indicated in the customs accounts actually took place according to the entries. (d) If the last-mentioned option represented a legal operation, another one would be the deliberately false statement as to the destination (smuggling). (e) A ship clearing a Scottish port outwards for Hamburg might have made a stop en route, for example at an English or Dutch port prior to its final calling in at Hamburg. (f) Also, in the Hamburg records "Leith" might have been handled loosely; perhaps due to imprecise geographical knowledge. According to the Scottish customs accounts for instance, the vitriol oil dispatched from Scotland to Hamburg in 1755 was shipped out from Kirkcaldy (2,023 lbs) and Prestonpans (37,368 lbs), but none from Leith (as the Hamburg records suggest). (g) A further mismatch could, of course, arise from the fact that the Scottish customs accounts for Christmas normally ended on January 5 of the following year, so that every year on the Scottish side was overlapping by five days into the following year. But for 1747 and 1755 this can be ruled out, as can be observed from Tables 2.1 and 2.2 (Appendix). (h) Differences might also arise from the duration of a voyage. Depending for example upon whether a ship sailed from the Shetlands or the Firth of Forth, and allowing for geographic particularities of the North Sea, a voyage between Scotland and Hamburg might last for up to four weeks. Moreover, the length and duration of an eighteenth-century ship's itinerary was not only contingent upon weather conditions. One of the central characteristic elements of eighteenth century shipping and customs procedures was that between a docking of a ship and the final declaration and discharge or loading of cargoes weeks and even months might pass. This depended on various factors, such as pending decisions as to whether goods were to be stored in warehouses or shipped right away. Sometimes cargoes would remain unclaimed, or disputes about the ownership of these cargoes would arise. All of these factors could cause delays in the ports on either side of the North Sea, as evident for instance from John Carmichael's case before the Scottish High Court of Admiralty in 1742.[75] In general, however, delays due to customs procedures and weather conditions may be ruled out as a main source of divergence between the Scottish and German customs and toll accounts in terms of amounts and type of commodities recorded, at least for the years examined here as an example. The last entry of a cargo made in Scotland (Leith) for Hamburg in 1746 was in October; and the last for 1747 again in October (28th). The same applies to the 1755 data set, where the first entry for Hamburg was made in April and the last in mid-October 1755, which again rules out a difference in recorded values due to time lags that might have carried a voyage into two adjacent accounting years.

For the two years under consideration, the difference between the export declarations made in the Scottish customs accounts and the import declarations traced in the Hamburg *Admiralitätszoll- und Convoygeldzolleinnahmebücher* can be distilled thus:

---

75 RÖSSNER, In the Wake, pp. 292–298.

Table 4: Relations given in Hamburg Records and Customs Accounts

NAS, E504. Hamburg: SCHNEIDER et al. (eds.), Statistik. Hamburg values given in Mark Banko. Amounts obtained from the Scottish customs accounts are valued at 1755 valuations.

	1753/1747	**1755/1753**
Hamburg (Admiralitätszoll- und Convoygeldeinnahmebücher)	3.13	.43
Scotland (Port Books)	2.53	.35

The match between the two does not appear to be very close. On the other hand it is not too far off the mark to be entirely dubious, given the expectable differences between the two sets of sources. For 1747, 1753 and 1755, the Hamburg records obviously under-record even those trades which they were supposed to cover in entirety. But as fraudulent declarations represented somewhat commonly recognized and acknowledged commercial practice, only a comprehensive cross-examination of customs accounts and merchant account books and ledgers over a longer time span would yield final clarity. This option, however, is only a theoretical one, as the German records exist in gaps, and even the best records available, the presently discussed *Admiralitätszoll- und Convoygeldzolleinnahmebücher*, are fragmentary, if compared to their British "peers", the post-1742 Scottish customs accounts.

2.2 Bremen

From 1738 onwards taxation and administration procedures required and produced records similar to the Hamburg *Admiralitätszolleinnahmebücher* for the port of Bremen. The *Schlachteangabebücher* (*Schlachte* Toll Accounts)[76], covering a select range of imports, originated from a tax on particular goods in ships about to enter the *Schlachte* pier. The latter was located in Bremen at a side-arm of the River *Weser*, where larger sea-going ships had to call in and trans-ship their cargoes on to lighter vessels (*Leichterschiffe*) suitable for inward traffic on the shallow Lower Weser.[77] For the period under consideration, the relevant *Schlachte* declaration books are preserved for 1738/1739 (covering only grain and salt), and to full extent from June 1754 onwards with minor gap years. In the case of the Bremen records similar restrictions as those discussed with regard to the Hamburg Admiralty Toll Accounts apply.

76 *StA Bremen*, 2–Ss.2.a.4.f.1 seq. I should like to express my gratitude to Dr Günter Garbrecht (University of Bremen) for pointing the *Schlachte* Toll Accounts out to me, as well as Dr Adolf Hofmeister, senior curator of documents, and other members of staff in the *Staatsarchiv* Bremen, for providing the records, microforms and some useful background information.

77 J. JOOST-KRÜGER, Der Weserkahn, in: H. RODER (ed.), Bremen: Handelsstadt am Fluß, Bremen 1995, pp. 304–5.

Only commodities subject to the Schlachte duty were recorded.[78] Exports were not taxed and thus went unrecorded. Entries of cargoes that were recorded were organized in chronological order, conveying the following information:

Figure 5: Information contained in the Bremen *Schlachte* Toll Account Books

(a) Date of entry;
(b) shipmaster's name;
(c) origin / port or country of departure;
(d) commodities;
(e) amounts;
(f) importing merchants.

Source: *StA Bremen*, 2–Ss.2.a.4.f.1 seq.

In most cases "Schottland" – rather than the name of a particular port – was given as the origin of the cargoes, with a few examples: in 1755 for instance imports of herring from Shetland were indicated as having come from South Wold and Lerwick.

Since the main commodities dispatched from Scotland to Bremen on a regular basis (according to the Scottish customs accounts), chiefly herring, salt, rice and tobacco, were in fact liable to the *Schlachte* levy, ships carrying these goods should be traceable in the *Schlachte* declaration books by the captain's names and commodities shipped, unless the goods were not declared, i.e. smuggled. Again, a comparison of the *Schlachte* Toll Account Books with the Scottish customs accounts in periods for which both are preserved (Appendix, Table 2.4) shows that this was not the case, but it appears that coverage was somewhat better than in the Hamburg records. First of all, smuggling was probably as endemic in Bremen as anywhere else in contemporary Europe. Cargoes would for instance be discharged up and down the River Weser, attempting to bypass the taxation point at the *Schlachte* pier.[79] Thus smuggling and non-recording of non-taxable goods may be seen as the major reasons for the mismatch between the Scottish and Bremen customs records. For the present purpose an examination of the years 1754 and 1755, for which records exist in both Scotland and Bremen, might suffice.

The *Schlachte* declaration book for 1754 is incomplete, as it starts in June. Nevertheless, none of the cargoes declared outwards for Bremen in Scottish ports between Midsummer and Christmas quarter (July–December), which can be expected to reappear in the Bremen records after June 1754, can be found on the Bremen side.[80] Instead, the only entry in the Bremen *Schlachte* Toll Accounts, referring to an import

---

78 Salt, grain, butter, cheese, herring, train oil, wine, brandy, linseed, ginger, rice, tobacco, tallow, tin, ox hides, sugar (incl. candy sugar, syrup, molasses), cotton textiles, raw cotton (cotton wool), coffee, pepper, raisins, and lead. *StA Bremen*, 2–Ss.2.a.4.f.1 seq. (1738/9, 1754–1755). H.-J. von Witzendorf, Beiträge zur Bremischen Handelsgeschichte in der zweiten Hälfte des 18. Jahrhunderts, in: Bremisches Jahrbuch, XLIII (1951), pp. 342–394, at p. 343.

79 H. Schwarzwälder, Geschichte der Freien Hansestadt Bremen, Vol. I: Von den Anfängen bis zur Franzosenzeit (1810), Bremen 1975, p. 428.

80 Two ships carrying salt from Bo'ness and Kirkcaldy that were declared for Bremen in Midsummer 1754 left too early to be traceable in the Bremen accounts.

from Scotland, indicates a ship and cargo that cannot be re-traced in the Scottish port books as an export (Appendix, Table 2.3).[81]

For 1755 the information is slightly better but still subject to a variety of explanations. Entries found in the Scottish customs accounts and in the *Schlachte* Toll Accounts have been juxtaposed in Table 2.4 in the appendix, for those cases where dates of declaration outwards (Scotland) and inwards (Bremen) were distant enough, allowing for four to five weeks of travel and customs procedures, and master's names identical or similar enough to suggest that the same ship and cargo were concerned. From this table it appears that what regards the material identity of the commodities, even in terms of their limited coverage, the *Schlachte* declarations correspond quite closely to the declarations made in Scottish ports. There were some deviations, however, which might be expected. It appears for example that more salt was actually declared for Bremen on 27 October 1755 at Bo'ness than imported into Bremen, even allowing for a certain degree of uncertainty as to the physical extent of the Bremen salt *last*.[82] The cargo of herrings landed on 29 September 1755 in Bremen, on the other hand, was initially declared for Hamburg (in the Shetland customs accounts). Perhaps part of the cargo – 28 ½ bbl herrings – had been shipped to and sold in Hamburg, but the rest, perhaps for want of a feasible price, might have remained unsold, and was then shipped on to Bremen.[83]

Out of the range of commodities that should be potentially re-traceable – if the Scottish customs declarations were correct and not marred by defrauding – it is only *rice* which, although liable to the *Schlachte* duty, cannot be found at all in the two *Schlachte* accounts that have been surveyed. According to the Scottish port books, 3,084.16 cwt of Carolina rice was re-exported in Midsummer 1755 in the *Industry of Leith* from Orkney to Bremen.[84] There are two possible explanations for their absence from the *Schlachte* Toll Accounts. First, as noted above, the Scottish inspector general's ledger of imports and exports for 1755 assigned precisely the same quantity indicated in the Orkney Midsummer port book to re-exports to "Sweden", for reasons that are elusive.[85] As the trade statistics for 1755 were drawn up in 1756, the inspector general might have had some *ex post* evidence for a re-direction of the cargo to a Swedish port after its initial declaration for Bremen in Orkney in Midsummer 1755. The other possibility is human error. Perhaps British customs officials confused the Free Imperial City of Bremen with the Duchy of Bremen, which – until 1720 – had been Swedish territory. Rice was not normally re-exported to Swedish destinations,

---

81 *StA Bremen*, 2–Ss.2.a.4.f.1 (1738/9, 1754–1755). 9 July 1754, Joseph Martin(i), captain from "Schottland", 187 *tonnen* herring; importer: Elter (Alderman) Duising & Sons. One Joseph Martin, however, cleared Shetland on 22 August in the same year. His ship was bound for Hamburg, carrying a cargo of 450 bbl herring. NAS, E504/32/2, III/1754, Goods Exported. Whereas the coals and vitriol oil could not possibly reappear in the *Schlachte* books (as they were not liable to the Schlachte duty), the herrings and whale oil should have re-appeared. Possible reasons as to why this was not the case are the same as those listed above (Hamburg).

82 See below.

83 Normally the number of *tonnen* imported at Bremen corresponded to the number of herring *bbl* in declared in Scotland.

84 NAS, E504/26/3, Customs Accounts Orkney, II/1755, Entries Outwards Nr. 3.

85 Sweden included Stralsund, see chapter I.

but rather, apart from the Netherlands, mostly to German North Sea ports. And if that was the case, rice was usually shipped exclusively to Hamburg or Bremen. Therefore, it seems more likely that the inclusion of this cargo under "Sweden" in 1755 was a simple mistake, possibly due to a defective "intermediary" account sent by the Orkney collector to the inspector general in Edinburgh and thus deficient geographical knowledge on account of the Orkney collector.

In conclusion, then, it can be said that the *Schlachte* Toll Accounts cannot be linked to a degree of 100 per cent to the Scottish customs accounts. This is mainly due to their limited coverage (deliberate and definitional bias), an unknown degree of efficiency of the Bremen customs collectors (the *Schlachteschreiber*) in capturing all taxable commodities (non-deliberate bias), as well as an unknown degree of tax evasion in Scotland and Bremen.

In very general terms it should be noted that a mismatch between customs accounts of several countries in terms of export declarations in, say, country (port) a for country (port) b deviating from import declarations in country (port) b indicating country (or port) a as country (port) of origin and vice versa, are somewhat expectable for eighteenth-century Europe.[86] Of all available sources in a northern European context, the Scottish customs accounts are clearly the best bet. They are, however, only superficially the most detailed and precise type of available material, and thus ought to be treated with the same reservations as any other available quantitative source of their time. They are contemporary estimates of the *intended* trade flows at best, rather than accounts of the factual amounts traded. Merchants could and would conceal, redirect and under-, or sometimes even over-, state the factual size and direction of trade flows, wherever they thought it appropriate, feasible or worth the potential cost. But in terms of trade theory or the heuristic value of the present book it makes no great difference whether some cargoes were only intended to be shipped without the final implementation of the intention, or whether they were shipped in reality as intended, as it was the *a priori* consideration of price differentials resulting from productivity and labour cost differentials prevailing in the two trading countries, which led to a particular structure of the trade volume between the two *in the longer run*. The Scottish customs accounts are therefore quite indicative of general trends and structures in the Scottish-German trades in the period under consideration. Furthermore, all imprecision and uncertainties apart, they are much more detailed and reliable than comparative records on the other side of the North Sea (Hamburg, Bremen). Any analysis of bi- or multilateral trade flows therefore has to start with British records. Having thus demonstrated the potential, as well as the pitfalls of the available source material on either side, the analysis will now proceed with a discussion of fluctuations, trends and structure in Scotland's gross total trade with Germany.

---

86 Discrepancies between the English port books and Gothenburg customs accounts in the seventeenth century have been discussed in Åström, Customs Accounts, pp. 65s. For trade between Riga and Lübeck in the eighteenth century, see Harder-Gersdorff, Mitteleuropäische Gewerbezonen, pp. 27–32, Table 1–3, pp. 29–31.

III. COMMERCIAL PATTERNS, GENERAL TRENDS AND FLUCTUATIONS

The present chapter provides a comparison of the Scottish (III.1) and German (III.2) trading patterns in the period under consideration, as far as the available sources allow this. A further section will discuss the Scottish-German trade volume in terms of fluctuations (1743–1770), composition (commodities), as well as distribution across Scottish ports (3.3). Due to the unique nature of British sources – here: Scottish customs accounts from 1743 onwards (chapter two) – such a precise analysis can only be carried out from a British angle or viewpoint, as the German sources are too sparse and non-standardized to allow precise quantitative studies that go beyond establishing the broad trends in some import trades. As mentioned in the introduction, a comprehensive analysis of Germany's overseas trade in the eighteenth century is still wanting. For Scotland on the other hand the present author has already contributed new evidence. In combination with Scotland's "comparative advantage" in quantitative source endowment (chapters one and two), this aspect accounts for the fact that statements regarding the Scottish trade pattern can be made in much more specific and precise terms than with regard to the German commercial patterns.

1. THE SCOTTISH PATTERN OF TRADE, C.1700–1760/70

As developed en detail elsewhere[1], Scotland's trade after 1700 rested upon three pillars, which at select points in time attained similar dimensions in value terms. First, there were the colonial or re-export trades, which expanded since 1736. Secondly, the "traditional" trades with England, in particular exports of Scots cattle and linens down south, continued long after 1707 and expanded at similar rates. In 1760 these trades still surpassed the colonial trades in value terms. Finally there came the smuggling trades, mainly in tobacco and tea. All three branches of commerce attained similar dimensions in value terms in the 1750s still, even though it is only the first component – the legal and recorded overseas trades of Scotland – that were recorded regularly (in yearly series) and comparatively reliably. As Scottish-German trade belongs to this first category, the latter two will be discarded in the present analysis.

During the period Scotland's *overseas* trade was an entrepôt trade, marked by a ratio of re-exports to total exports well in excess of 50 per cent, and accordingly a small ratio of retained imports to total imports. Re-exports in turn were dominated by

---

1 P. R. RÖSSNER, Scottish Foreign Trade in the Wake of Union, 1700–1760. The Rise of a Warehouse Economy, Stuttgart 2008, in particular ch. 4 and 5, section 5.2.2.

tobacco. The rise of an entrepôt trade as such was no peculiarly Scottish phenomenon. With regard to the precedent England, Wilson has remarked:

> In the [16]60s, re-exports accounted for less than a quarter of the export totals. By 1700, they represented about 30 per cent and much of this trade was provided by the import of cargoes of raw materials, foods and textiles from the colonies and tropical areas – America, the West Indies, India and the East. These areas were supplying about a third of our total imports by 1700. [...] Profound change was overtaking the whole economy. England was becoming a world entrepôt [...].[2]

To a considerable extent this was due to the 1660s Customs System and Navigation Acts, which, according to Wilson, "by automatically restricting imports, [...] paid tribute to the conception of the balance of trade. By eliminating the cost of foreign freight charges and replacing invisible imports by invisible exports in the shape of English shipping earnings, it recognized the same principle. By canalizing a large volume of English trade with the outside world in English ships and making England its focus, it aimed to create, by legislative compulsion backed by naval force, an entrepôt system such as the Dutch had created by spontaneous effort."[3]

1. A similar, yet still very peculiar pattern of trade obtained in Scotland after 1700. As comprehensive trade statistics do not commence prior to 1755, and the customs accounts, which would allow a re-construction of the Scottish balance of trade between 1743 and 1755 (and thereafter), have not been fully examined yet, observations regarding the scale and scope of Scotland's trade volume need to remain somewhat conjectural for most of the period under consideration. The overall trend, however, is fairly clear – commercial expansion occurred since the middle of the 1730s (Fig. 1).

2 C. Wilson, England's Apprenticeship 1603-1763, London 1965, p. 161.

3 Ibid., p. 164.

Figure 1: Scottish Overseas Trade, 1708–1783
Source: TNA, Customs 14; NLS, Ms 60; NAS, E501/1–76, money and bonds.

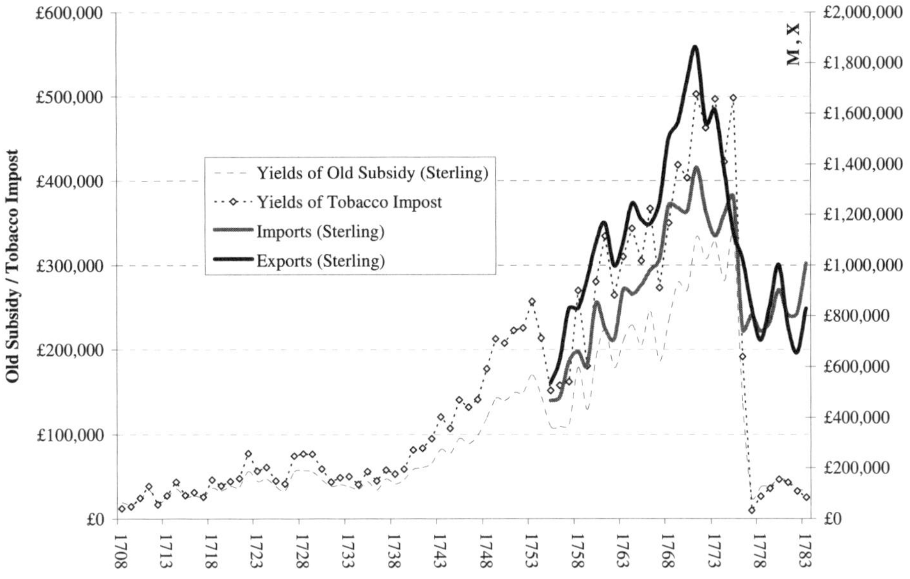

A short comment on the use of customs yields figures as a proxy for real fluctuations in the overseas trade volume might be in order prior to proceeding with the analysis of secular fluctuations, as a new methodology developed by the present author is proposed here.[4] Yields of "Customs" / *Old Subsidy* have been derived from the *General Accounts* of the Scottish Customs, accounting sheets stating the yearly balance of income accruing to the British state from customs duties levied in Scotland and the purpose they were assigned to (expense).[5] They exclusively relate to the import trades. Although the *Customs* (12 Car. II c. 4, 1660) in theory also covered the *Additional Duty, Petty Custom* and *One Per Cent Inwards*, these duties were not listed separately in the Scottish accounts. *Old Subsidy* was payable on all imported commodities that were not generally exempt from the payment of customs duties, normally at a rate of five per cent of the cargo's value as of the Acts of Parliament 12 Car. II c. 4 and II Geo. I c. 7.[6] As neither the rates nor modalities of levying the Old Subsidy changed in the period, it has been assumed that the yields of this duty

4 RÖSSNER, In the Wake, pp. 128–131.

5 NAS, E501/1–53 (1707/8–1760).

6 Commonly referred to as *Book(s) of Rates*. The second Book of Rates (II Geo. I. c.7) only contained valuations of and the rates of duty on those goods that had not been rated in 12 Car. II (1660) and that had been previously assessed *ad valorem* (value sworn upon oath by the importer upon unloading). Most of the commodities imported into Scotland in the eighteenth century were therefore rated and taxed according to an obsolete valuation schedule dating back to the 1660s. In the 1750s for instance, tobacco was taxed at its 1660 valuation of 20d per lb, whilst its official value f.o.b. at that time (1755) was given at 2d 2 farthings (2.5 d) per lb, only one-eighth of the value according to which it was taxed. Thus, the effective tax rate on retained imports of tobacco in 1755 amounted to c. 240 per cent of its f.o.b. price.

represent a volumetric index for fluctuations in the import trades, and by ways of basic trade theory and factual post-1755 evidence, the volume of trade in general (imports + exports + re-exports).

The logic for this runs as follows: It was a particularity of the English (and after 1707 British) political superstructure that customs and excise duties were generally fixed with regard to the rates levied and the period of duration. The overall level of taxation could only be increased by the application of two tools which had to be used simultaneously: (1) An existing duty had to be renewed (labelled "continuation" in contemporary usage) and, (2) simultaneously, a new or supplementary "top-up" duty, relating to the same commodity, had to be established by Act of Parliament, as parliamentary practice did not normally permit to simply raise the rates of existing duties. British customs and Excise accounting practice implemented this principle by keeping separate accounts for each duty and parliamentary period. Therefore, by restricting oneself to the original ("old duties" as they are often called), and disregarding all subsequent top-up duties, time series can be obtained from customs and excise accounts which are roughly volumetric, as they are deflated of purely fiscal effects resulting from an increase (or decrease) in the level of taxation. Whereas they should by no means be mistaken for an entirely accurate index, they nevertheless turn out to be a reliable proxy for the general secular fluctuations in the Scottish volume of trade, c. 1708-1783. (Table 1).

Table 1: Coefficient of Correlation, Yields of "Customs" (Old Subsidy), Scotland (x) with various other parameters (y)

Source: As Graph 1.

y	R
Imports (Scotland); 1755-1783	0.69
Imports (Scotland); 1755-1771	0.91
Imports (Scotland); 1773-1783	0.84
Imports (Scotland); 1776-1783	-0.34
Trade Volume (Scotland); 1755-1783	0.80
Trade Volume (England); 1708-1783	0.81
Impost on Tobacco (1708-1783)	**+1**

A correlation coefficient of R= .80 for *Old Subsidy* yields and Scotland's gross total trade (1755-1783), of R= .69 for *Old Subsidy* yields and imports (1755-1783), and of .91 for Old Subsidy and imports (1755-1771), support the notion that the yields of the *Old Subsidy* can indeed be interpreted as a rough volumetric index for overseas trade fluctuations over the entire period, especially for the time before Scottish trade statistics become available. Furthermore, a value of R= .81 for the Scottish yields of Old Subsidy and English gross total trade (1707-1783) points towards a fairly uniform movement of Scotland's and England's overseas trade during the period, although a more precise assessment is impossible, due to the absence of Scottish trade statistics prior to 1755 (Fig. 2).[7]

7 Changes in the level of taxation can be calculated from information contained in two (and if Saxby is counted as a separate item, three) major contemporary handbooks for Customs officials: H. CROUCH, A Complete View of the British Customs, Pt. I, London, first ed. 1725, Pt. II, London 1728, further, updated editions in 1731, 1738, 1745, 1755; H. SAXBY, The British Customs

Figure 2: The British View: Scotland's and England's Overseas Trade Compared, 1708/1755-1783 (£Sterling*1000)

Sources: as Graph 1.

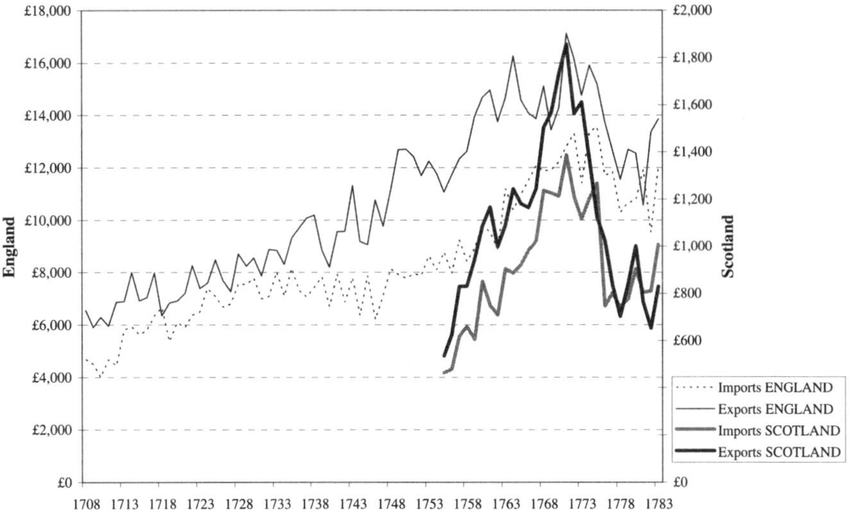

The Scottish volume of trade probably tripled between c. 1700 and 1755 and more than doubled between 1755 and 1771. This would, even on conservative terms, suggest an increase by a factor of about six for imports and exports over the entire period (c. 1700-1770), which is in line with the findings on English overseas trade in the period (see also Fig. 2 above).[8] Whereas in the first three decades, Scotland's overseas trade apparently neither showed a significant trend nor did it take place on a large level, the situation changed around the middle of the 1730s. In about 1734 or 1736, the long eighteenth century Scottish overseas trade cycle (1734/6-1776) commenced, which would be characteristic of the subsequent overseas trade pattern. Visible from the post-1755 trade statistics which are not fully indicative of this cycle, as they commence in a temporary, yet considerable slump, in less than 20 years (1755-1771) a leap was made, which, in mere terms of speed, matched any development previously or simultaneously experienced by the English. This cycle came to an end in

(London, 1757) is a corrective re-issue of CROUCH (1755); S. BALDWIN, A Survey of the British Customs [...], London 1770. Cf. also R. HARRIS, Government and the Economy, in: R. FLOUD / P. JOHNSON (eds.), The Cambridge Economic History of Modern Britain, Vol. I: Industrialisation, 1700–1860, Cambridge 2004, pp. 204–237, esp. pp. 214–225; P. K. O'BRIEN, The Political economy of British Taxation, 1660-1815, in Economic History Review, XLI (1988), pp. 1–32.

8 R. Davis, "English Foreign Trade, 1660-1700", in: *EcHR*, Vol. VI (1954), pp. 150-166; Id., "English Foreign Trade, 1700-1774", in: *EcHR*, Vol. XV (1962), pp. 285-303; N. Zahedieh, "Overseas Expansion and Trade in the Seventeenth Century", in: N. Canny (ed.), *The Oxford History of the British Empire, Vol. I: The Origins of Empire. British Overseas Enterprise to the Close of the Seventeenth Century* (Oxford, 1998), pp. 398-421.

the 1770s, with an abrupt decline in the volume of trade by about 55 per cent between 1771 and 1776.[9]

2. What can be said about the scope of Scotland's trade, i.e. the structure of her overseas trade volume in terms of (a) commodities, (b) the distribution of imports and exports across Scotland's trading partners, and (c) Scottish ports? Towards the end of the 1750s, when reliable trade statistics providing aggregate figures for Scotland's total exports and imports overseas, valued at 1755 current prices, become available (chapter 2), Scottish *domestic exports* overseas amounted to about £346,000 Sterling on average per year; re-exports to about £408,000 and imports to £567,943 Sterling per year (average figures, 1755–59). Of the latter about £180,000 Sterling or 31 per cent was tobacco, with values reaching 40 per cent and more in some years. On the export side, tobacco absolutely dominated, accounting for 78 per cent of Scotland's re-exports and 42 per cent of total exports. Scottish domestic exports were dominated by textile manufactures (mainly linen), bar lead and fish. They were outpaced, however, by re-exports, which accounted for 54 per cent of total exports. This was due chiefly to tobacco. With tobacco attaining a share of roughly 80 per cent of re-exports and therefore 42 per cent of total exports overseas, a characteristic pattern emerged. Both the patterns of supply and demand for this commodity were determined by and geared towards foreign markets, and thus, in terms of structure and composition, the Scottish import volume was largely a reflection of Scotland's (re-)export account. Unprocessed tobacco and sugar, as well as foreign linens to be re-exported to the British colonies in the Americas made up 52 per cent of Scotland's imports in 1755/59 – a relation similar to these products' share in total Scottish exports. This was a classical "entrepôt trading pattern."[10]

Two brief remarks should be added with regard to the geographical composition of the Scottish trade volume, in terms of Scottish ports, as well as countries Scotland traded with. Research on the distribution of the Scottish trade volume throughout Scotland has first been carried out by the present author.[11] Obtaining results on the basis of the Scottish customs accounts, however, is an extremely tedious and time-consuming process. For these reasons, only the year 1755 could be examined, even though this year might not necessarily have been very representative in the medium- to long run. Average figures of at least three years would clearly be preferable, given that much of the trade volume consisted of re-exports and a full or near-full refund of customs duties on previously imported commodities could be obtained for most goods for up to three years after their importation. Given these limitations, the distribution of gross total trade throughout Scotland was as follows:

9 The obvious discrepancy in the decline of gross total trade and customs yields 1771-1778 can be explained by the near complete collapse of tobacco imports 1774-1776, and the fact that many commodities important to the expanding textile industry, imported mainly through the East coast ports, came in duty free (flax, linseed, madder).

10 RÖSSNER, In the Wake, ch. 5.

11 Ibid., pp. 200–204, and ID., Scottish Foreign Trade towards the End of the Pre-industrial Period, 1700–1760 (=University of Edinburgh PhD thesis), 2 Vols., Edinburgh 2007, Appendices B_14 and B_15 on attached CD-Rom.

Figure 3: Rank Distribution of the Scottish Outports by Gross Total Trade, 1755 (£Sterling)

Source: Full set of Scottish Customs Accounts, 1755. NAS, E504.

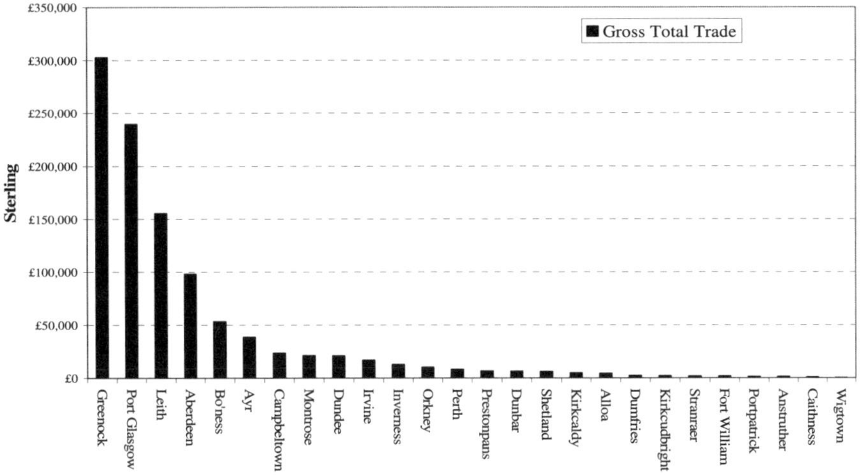

Two distinct economic areas emerge from these figures. The Glasgow outports dominated the picture unfolding with regard to the Western region, with a total of 52 per cent of gross total trade handled (87 per cent of the Western GTT). Theirs was an entrepôt business, centred on the importation and re-exportation of tobacco and sugar (together accounting for 78 per cent of total imports and 88 per cent of their total re-exports, 59 per cent of their total exports in 1755) and some other enumerated commodities. The markets faced for both supply and demand were abroad. Leith was the third-biggest port, and slightly more representative of economic activity in the Eastern region. This characteristic eighteenth-century dual pattern is likely to have evolved sometime between 1707 and 1740, causally linked to the commencing of the characteristic eighteenth century Scottish trade cycle. It was fully developed by 1755.[12]

If the evidence cited in the preceding paragraph as to the dualistic trade pattern of the two regions (East/West) is accurate, it would also imply a likewise clear-cut *geographical structure* of the trade volume in terms of countries Scotland traded with. In fact, the pattern is repeated. The ports in the West were geared towards the Americas and Ireland, as well as their continental re-export markets for tobacco. And, it may be added, the region was part of a larger integrated economic area, including the South-West of Scotland, North-Eastern Ireland, and the Isle of Man. In terms of countries Leith and the East traded with, the independent Netherlands dominated the picture, accounting for 57 per cent of Leith's gross total trade, followed by the Americas (12 per cent), Russia (7 per cent), and Sweden (6 per cent). Aggregated for

12 The question "When did the Glasgow ports overtake the ports in the East in terms of GTT handled?" cannot be answered in precise quantitative terms, as the main relevant source (port books) only dates back to 1742 (at that time the pattern was already established).

Scotland as a whole, thus doing violence to the fact that "there were many Scotlands"[13], the following picture emerges:

Table 2: The Geographical Distribution of Scotland's Overseas Trade Volume, 1755-1759

	Imports	Exports (total)	GTT
America	47%	31%	38%
Holland / Flanders	13%	35%	25%
Ireland	12%	12%	12%
Scandinavia	7%	3%	5%
Germany	4%	6%	5%
Russia	10%	0%	4%
Other	7%	13%	10%

TNA, Customs 14. Figures are averages for five years. GTT: gross total trade = imports+exports+re-exports.
"Germany": excluding Swedish Pomerania (Wismar, Stralsund), Flanders and those parts of Prussia which were not part of the Empire. "Russia": incl. Livonia (mainly Riga). Scandinavia: Denmark, Norway, Sweden, Swedish Pomerania. Other: "Africa", France, Greenland, Guernsey, Isle of Man, Italy, Poland (Danzig), Portugal (incl. Madeira), Prussia, Spain (incl. Canary Islands, Gibraltar).

Again the emergence and firm establishment of a second, new eighteenth century trade pattern alongside a strong and traditional, pre-1700 trade pattern can be observed quite clearly. Although the Americas represented the largest single item, taken together, North Western Europe, and especially the Netherlands (and, one has to add: England), remained the focus of Scotland's total commercial activity well into the 1760s and beyond.

3. But now an explanation of the strong bias towards tobacco, with a share of roughly 80 per cent of re-exports and therefore 42 per cent of total Scottish exports overseas (1755–59) should be attempted. Tobacco was an absolute transit commodity, as more than 90 per cent of the imported tobaccos were usually re-exported again, chiefly to French, Dutch, Irish and German destinations.[14] There hardly seems to have been any other country in contemporary world trade that exhibited a similarly biased trading pattern[15] – even though a strong bias towards re-exporting as such was a mere

13 T. M. Devine, "The Modern Economy: Scotland and the Act of Union", in: Id. / C. L. Lee / G. C. Peden (eds.), *The Transformation of Scotland. The Economy Since 1700* (Edinburgh, 2005), pp. 13-33, p. 14.

14 As far as the available statistics allow precise conclusions – especially in the tobacco trades merchants often forged their bills of loading in terms of the true extent or destination of the cargoes.

15 See for instance L. MÜLLER, Kolonialprodukter i Sveriges handel och konsumtionskultur, 1700–1800, in: Historisk Tidskrift, 2/2004, pp. 225–248, especially pp. 237s.; pp. 240–242, Tab. 1 (p. 241); ID., The Merchant Houses of Stockholm, c. 1640–1800. A Comparative Study of Early-Modern Entrepreneurial Behaviour, Uppsala 1998, pp. 45s.; Y. KAUKIAINEN, Finland and the World Economy, in: M. NORTH (ed.), Nordwesteuropa in der Weltwirtschaft 1750–1950 / Northwestern Europe in the World Economy 1750–1950, Stuttgart 1993, pp. 59–78; P. BOJE, Denmark's Role in the World Economy, 1750–1950, in: NORTH (ed.), Nordwesteuropa, pp. 21–38, at pp. 21s.; F. HODNE, Norway's Role in the World Economy, 1750–1950, in: ibid., pp. 39–58, at pp. 43–48; France: P. LÉON, L'élan industriel et commercial, in : E. LABROUSSE / P. LÉON / P.

copy of the successful blueprint provided by the Dutch trading supremacy during their "golden age", 1600–1750, initially followed by the English around the mid-1600s and then obviously copied by the Scots, the Swedes, the Danes and others since the mid-1730s.[16]

In explaining this pattern scholars have underlined the geographical advantages of Glasgow over London and western ports of England, especially the comparatively short and safe passage across the Atlantic to the English tobacco colonies of Virginia and Maryland.[17] Furthermore Devine has, in his seminal studies, worked out how – through a sophisticated and innovative purchasing system – asymmetrical ("colonial") credit relationships developed, which enabled Glaswegian tobacco lords to control both the purchasing price of tobacco in America, as well as the prices charged for the domestic British manufactures they sold in the Americas in return.[18] In this way Scotland, or rather Glasgow, after the mid-1730s emerged as one of the larger northern-European tobacco entrepôts. But still this is only an explanation of successful business techniques – not a valid answer to the question: why tobacco? It is suggested here that this bias was a result of the new taxation framework applicable in Scotland from 1707 onwards[19], in particular the draw-back and bonding scheme operated by the Customs, combined with a weak resource base of the domestic economy. As seen in chapter one, the English customs system, which dated back from 1660, became applicable in Scottish ports from Mayday 1707 onwards. By applying a 1660 price structure (Book of Rates) as the assessment basis for taxing imports of commodities that were becoming progressively cheaper over time (1660–1770), this taxation system by 1750 – almost 100 years after its initial introduction in England, and 50 years after its implementation in Scotland – would have tended to discourage the domestic consumption of colonial imports such as rice, tobacco, sugar, tea, coffee and the like, as apparent from the table below.

GOUBERT / J. BOUVIER / C. CARRIÈRE / P. HARSIN (eds.), Histoire Économique et Sociale de la France, Vol. 2 : Des derniers temps de l'âge seigneurial aux préludes de l'âge industriel (1660–1789), Paris 1970, pp. 499–528, at p. 503 / Graph on p. 502; C. CARRIÈRE, Négociants marsellais au xviiie siècle, in: Institut historique de Provence, 1973, Vol, 1, pp. 375–388, pp. 462–464, reprinted in: M. MARGAIRAZ (ed.), Histoire Économique XVIIIe–XXe Siècle, Paris 1992, pp. 526–538, graph on p. 532. For general surveys see articles in W. FISCHER / J. A. VAN HOUTTE / H. KELLENBENZ / I. MIECK / F. VITTINGHOFF, F. (eds.), Handbuch der Europäischen Wirtschafts- und Sozialgeschichte, Vol. 4: Von der Mitte des 17. zur Mitte des 19. Jahrhunderts, Stuttgart 1993.

16 P. R. RÖSSNER, Close Encounters with the Dutch?, or: How did Scotland react on Dutch Economic Prominence During the "Long Seventeenth Century", 1600–1750?, unpubl. paper given at the *International Institute of Social History* (Leiden) Conference on "Close Encounters with the Dutch. The North Sea as Near-Core Region for a Nascent Modern World (1550–1750)", Roskilde (Denmark), 5–6 October 2007.

17 J. M. PRICE, The Rise of Glasgow in the Chesapeake Tobacco Trade, 1707–1775, in: William and Mary Quarterly, II (1954), pp. 179–199.

18 DEVINE, Tobacco Lords.

19 Developed en detail in ROESSNER, Foreign Trade, chs. 2 and 6.

Table 3: Net Tax Expressed as Percentage of the 1755 "Official" Import Valuation for Chosen Retained Imports

Goods valuations: TNA, Customs 14, 1755, "estimate of first cost or value" (=f.o.b.);
Duties: "net duties" tabulated in H. CROUCH, A Complete View of the British Customs [...], London, 5th ed. 1755.

Commodity	Measure	Net Duty as % of Official 1755 Valuation
Tobacco (British plantations)	lb	220%-244%
Muscovado (Brit. Plantations)	cwt	19%
Muscovado (foreign)	cwt	60%
Rum	gallon	15%
Flax	cwt (112lbs)	free
Narrow German / etc.	120 ells	16%
Plain Irish	120 ells	free
ordinary deals (< 20ft)	120	16%
Mahogany	ton	8%
Iron: bar iron	ton	24%
iron: old (bushel)	ton	10%
Salt: Spanish	wey	81%
Salt: French	wey	59%
Pitch / tar (Brit. Plant.)	last	6%
Ashes: pearl ashes	barrel	31%
Ashes: pot ashes	barrel	34%
Horses	head	26%
Cowhides	piece	3%
Calf skins	piece	4%
Whale fins	ton	19%

But in eighteenth-century English and Scottish overseas trade, effective rates of duty usually collapsed down to insignificant levels, if the commodities were declared for re-exporting. This was in parts a result of the fact that this taxation system and customs regulations of 1660, particularly the English Navigation Acts, had been designed as an antidote to Dutch naval primacy in world trade. One of the – at least implicit – goals of English Mercantilism after 1660 accordingly had been to draw an increasing share of world trade, by attracting the third party or entrepôt trades to Britain:

> The re-export trade implied that Britain should become the warehouse of the world. From the introduction of the Navigation Acts in the 1650s the tariff policy of the state was consistently designed to facilitate the diversion of trade through British ports. [...] An ever increasing number of "drawbacks" were written into customs regulations that allowed revenue on goods that were imported to be recovered if they were subsequently re-exported.[20]

In order to achieve this, the transit trades had to be relatively modestly taxed, and under the 1660 English (and since 1707 British) customs system, the more important colonial goods were only taxed very modestly, if they were re-exported from Britain within three years after their importation (Table 4).

20 R. PRICE, British Society, 1680–1880. Dynamism, Containment and Change, Cambridge et al. 1999, p. 61, p. 60 (quotation in this order).

Table 4: Refund of Customs Duties Upon Regular Re-export (in per cent of Totals Charged on Import)

	% of total Re-X	1708	1715	1725	1731	1738	1745	1755	1770
Tobacco (British Plantations)	79%	91%	99%	100%	100%	100%	100%	100%	100%
Muscovado (Brit. Plantations)	5%	78%	79%	79%	79%	79%	79%	85%	89%
Narrow German / Muscovy	5%	86%	86%	86%	86%	86%	86%	89%	82%
Rice	3%	88%	87%	87%	87%	87%	87%	90%	90%

Duties per lb / cwt, rates as if all customs duties were paid down by British denizens, commodities imported in British ships, sums paid in ready cash immediately after declaration. Share in total re-exports: based on 1755–59.
Calculated from T. LANGHAM, The Neat Duties (All Discounts and Abatements deducted) of all Merchandize Specify'd in the Book of Rates, 1st ed. London 1708; 3rd ed. London 1715; H. CROUCH, A Complete View of the British Customs [...], Part I, London 1725; ID., A Complete View of the British Customs [...], 2nd ed. London 1731; 3rd ed. London 1738; 4th ed. London 1745; 5th ed. London 1755; S. BALDWIN, A Survey of the British Customs [...], London 1770.

But it was only tobacco that – provided it had been imported legally – after 1723 could obtain a *full* refund or "draw-back" of customs duties paid upon import. Such an opportunity of factually duty-free shipment was enjoyed by no other eighteenth-century colonial commodity.

But tobacco was only effectively shipped duty free – not factually (but it was still the most profitable commodity). A second element came to work: Customs duties had to be paid down immediately after a ship's cargo had been declared as an import, regardless whether or not the cargo(es) of concern were to be re-exported from Britain subsequently. But merchants were free to choose whether or not to meet liabilities in cash. In general, the British customs system permitted parts of the duties due upon import to be "bonded" for up to 18 months. Being a promise to pay a certain amount of cash at a specified later day plus interest on the principal for the time specified, a bond represented a letter of credit issued by the Crown to a merchant upon importation of a certain cargo in lieu of cash payments towards the applicable customs duties. Upon re-export of the cargo, the sums stated on the bond were "refunded", i.e. set against the draw-back which the cargo was entitled to. Cash would only change hands for the remaining difference between the sums stated on the bond, plus interest that had accrued meanwhile on the one and the possible draw-back of customs duties on the other hand. As discounts were given on customs duties paid in cash, but draw-backs were calculated on the basis of nominal (pre-discount) liabilities, a positive difference of about 11 per cent remained in most cases, representing the net income of the state from this type of transaction.[21]

The implications of this become clearer, if the sums involved are set in relation to other economic data for the period. In the 1750s for instance, when the Glaswegian tobacco trades were fully developed, import declarations of tobacco cargoes totalling 50,000 lbs or more on one merchant's or firm's account were not uncommon. Larger

21 NAS, CE7/11, App. Nr. 29/2; see also Nr. L. E. E. HOON, The Organisation of the English Customs System 1696–1789, Newton Abbot, 2nd ed. 1968, pp. 256–264.

firms easily imported 100,000 lbs and more in one single ship.[22] A tobacco cargo of 50,000 lbs would in 1755 have been liable to a net duty of £1,145 16 s 8 d Sterling. Such amounts were extraordinary and likely to strain the cash reserves of most living contemporaries.[23] Especially in the colonial trades, which were dependent upon an intrinsically linked import and re-export business, the sums involved in import declarations would in fact have exceeded the liquidity of all but the richest contemporaries. The incentive to provide bonds in lieu of cash payments is therefore immediately evident; often it would have arisen out of pure necessity.

It is this dual possibility – a generous 100 per cent draw-back on tobacco duties, as well as the credit mechanism operated by the British customs (bonding scheme) – which not only accounted for a particularly large profit mark-up on colonial tobacco re-exported from Scotland (sometimes in the order of 100 per cent and more[24]), but also abolished cash payments, where they were either technically unnecessary, as sums paid were refundable later, or else represented a considerable drain on the liquidity reserves of the merchants involved.[25] Thus, from 1723 at latest – when the drawback on tobacco duties was increased to 100%[26] –, Scottish overseas merchants were literally drawn into the tobacco trades by what initially was a purely institutional and rather non-economic stimulus, a rather unintended side-effect of the new taxation regulations introduced in Scotland in 1707. They were especially drawn into the colonial trades, as the domestic economy had not many attractive products to be sold on world markets.

4. As neither reliable estimates of Scotland's national income in the first half of the eighteenth century, nor estimates on the value and share of industrial output in total income exist, one has to go on a speculative spree and plunder the available secondary studies on Scottish domestic production instead, particularly within the secondary sector. Whatley has assembled evidence on stagnating or declining export levels in select Scottish industries such as linens, woollens, coal, salt, paper, glass, candle and shoe making, brewing, as well as fishing, one important production branch of Scotland's primary sector until the end of the 1730s.[27] "Scotland was faced with grave economic difficulties at what was a critical time in the process of British political integration. The roots of the problem were poverty and the weakness of domestic manufacturing."[28] According to Saville, "the country produced few

---

22 NAS, E504/28 (Port Glasgow port books), NAS, E504/15 (Greenock port books). J. M. PRICE / P. G. E. CLEMENS, A Revolution of Scale in Overseas Trade: British Firms in the Chesapeake Trade, 1675–1775, Journal of Economic History, XLVII, 1 (1987), pp. 1–43, at pp. 31–33.

23 RÖSSNER, In the Wake of Union, p. 61s.

24 J. M. PRICE, Capital and Credit in British Overseas Trade: The View from the Chesapeake 1700–1776, Cambridge, Mass. / London 1980, Appendix.

25 Examined en detail in ROESSNER, Foreign Trade, ch. 2, sections 2.2.1–3.

26 J. M. PRICE, The Excise Affair Revisited. The Administrative and Colonial Dimensions of a Parliamentary Crisis, in ID., Overseas Trade and Traders. Essays on Some Commercial, Financial and Political Challenges Facing British Atlantic Merchants, 1660–1775, Aldershot 1996, pp. 257–321.

27 C. A. WHATLEY, Scottish Society. Beyond Jacobitism, Towards Industrialization, Manchester / New York 2000, pp. 65–61.

28 Ibid., p. 60.

handicrafts and manufactured goods of a standard acceptable in foreign markets and even, in some products, nothing at all. This record may be illustrated in various ways. Virtually no ocean-going shipping was built in Scotland; only small fishing smacks and rowing boats. Attempts to encourage shipbuilders to settle [...] came to nought. [...] Competition from Dutch and English shipyards, a want of good workmen and lack of sustained government support meant that there was no progress by the Union. When the Company of Scotland decided to buy ships, it went to Hamburg and Rotterdam and also went abroad for the sails, the cordage, most of the ironwork, even the lead for the bread ovens. [...] [T]here were only a handful of glassmakers, and all the better-quality glassware was imported. So too were most iron goods, copper pots and pans, and all the pewter and tin goods; even earthenware came in large quantities from England. [...] The statistics for imports [...] show a sorry tale where most of the new consumer demands of the later seventeenth century were supplied from outwith Scotland."[29] Foreign markets for Scots *coal* and *salt* had been lost to foreign competition as early as the 1680s. The huge salt markets in the Baltic in particular were lost to English competition since the later seventeenth century. The coal industry, organized in relatively small units of production, "was limited in its response to its market opportunities through primitive technology and an inadequate labour force composed partly of independent workers and partly of serf labour. As mines grew deeper in the eighteenth century the technical problems of drainage, haulage and ventilation limited expansion of output as never before."[30] First attempts at establishing a modern *iron* industry following English practice and production methods at Invergarry in Scotland in 1727/29 proved abortive in 1736, as the iron produced there upon English initiative – the Invergarry iron works was an offshoot of the Backbarrow Company, based in Lancashire / England – was "so inferior that, while Furness [= *Lancashire*, P. R.] iron sold at 8 per ton, it [*the Invergarry iron*, P. R.] sold at only 5 10s. a ton."[31] Scotch *woollens* were generally hardly competitive outside Scotland.[32] Thus by far the major share of Scottish industrial output after 1707 was absorbed by the home market. Woollen and linen textiles, cattle and fish were virtually the only commodities produced in Scotland which could be at least partly disposed of in foreign markets in significant quantities, but in linen's case – Scotland's most significant "industry" at the time – only with the help of a protective institutional framework which put heavy tariffs on retained imports of German linens whilst paying out bounties on the export of domestic cloth.[33]

Linen, by far the largest branch of Scotland's industrial sector 1700–1760, was proverbial, as were the woollen and salt industry. Although government measures aimed at direct intervention towards productivity increases, such as the creation of a *Board of Trustees for Fisheries and Manufactures* (1727) were implemented, the

29 R. SAVILLE, Bank of Scotland. A History 1695–1995, Edinburgh 1996, p. 63.

30 A. SLAVEN, The Development of the West of Scotland 1750–1960, London / Boston 1975, p. 111s.

31 R. H. CAMPBELL, Scotland since 1707. The Rise of an Industrial Society, Oxford 1971, p. 64.

32 T. C. SMOUT, The Anglo-Scottish Union of 1707.I. The Economic Background, in: Economic History Review, XVI (1964), pp. 455–467, at p. 458s.

33 ROESSNER, In the Wake of Union, ch. 4.

lion's share of Scottish *linen* output after 1727 still remained coarse linen; for finer items Ireland, Germany or the Netherlands still had to be consulted instead.[34] Scotch linens in fact faced stiff competition from German producers in its only foreign market of significance, the English colonies in the Americas.[35] The industry suffered from a variety of constraints. Even though in both absolute, (*yds*) as well as value terms, Scottish linen output expanded rapidly after 1727, these gains were mainly due to the coarser items, as many important upstream production processes, such as the growing, spinning, heckling and clutching of flax, as well as the bleaching of the finished items either could not be organized at all in Scotland, or only according to quality standards that fell far short of desired levels (Scotch linen was frequently sent to Ireland or Holland for bleaching).[36] Partly this was a "consequence of an industry linked closely to unimproved agriculture. The raw material was poor; flax was badly grown, and the difficult operations in preparation for spinning incompetently performed; at the other end of the process of production the cloth was often bleached badly or not at all."[37] It was as late as 1754 that the practice of sending over brown Scotch linen to Holland for bleaching, ceased.[38] During its times of existence a bounty on exports of Scottish linens lowered the price of the item at which Scots traders were willing to offer it to the colonial consumer, thus partly pricing the better German re-exports out of the colonial market. But the second upsurge of imports and re-exports of "narrow German" linens from Scottish ports, 1753–58, after withdrawal of the subsidy, was indicative of a still highly uncompetitive Scottish industry, which captured large export markets only within a framework of protection and subsidization.[39] The Scottish *woollen* industry appears to have fared even worse.[40] It was a constant subject of lament by contemporaries between 1700 and 1755, realizing the English advantage in the production of all but the very coarsest types.[41] Accordingly the industry was rather neglected by the Scottish *Board of Trustees*, which distributed £2,600 each (43 per cent) out of a total fund of £6,000 for the first year of activity to linen production and herring fishing respectively, and only a meagre £600 to woollen manufactures, rightly acknowledging the hopelessness of putting tax money into an uncompetitive industry.[42]

34 Ibid., p. 125s.

35 A. J. DURIE, The Markets for Scottish Linen, 1730-1775, in: Scottish Historical Review, LII, 1 (1973), pp. 30–49.

36 SLAVEN, Development of the West, pp. 79–86.

37 R. H. CAMPBELL, The Rise and Fall of Scottish Industry 1707–1939, Edinburgh 1980, p. 7.

38 Ibid., p. 8.

39 RÖSSNER, In the Wake of Union, pp. 261–266. DURIE, Markets, pp. 30-49, pp. 42-4.

40 Scottish production costs in the stockings industry seem to have about matched continental costs. F.-W. HENNING, Handbuch der Wirtschafts- und Sozialgeschichte Deutschlands, Vol. 1: Deutsche Wirtschafts- und Sozialgeschichte im Mittelalter und in der Frühen Neuzeit, Paderborn 1991, p. 839.

41 I. D. WHYTE, Scotland before the Industrial Revolution. An Economic and Social History c1050 – c1750, London / New York 1995, p. 286s.; B. LENMAN, An Economic and Social History of Modern Scotland 1660-1976, London 1975, p. 5.

42 CAMPBELL, Scottish Industry 1707–1939, p. 7.

The situation was reflected in *export shares*. Between 1700 and 1760 there was a rapid and continuous loss of export shares of *Scots salt* – another of Scotland's most prominent pre-industrial "industries" – on world markets, with export shares declining from levels as high as 60 per cent around 1700 down to zero in the later 1750s (see ch. 4 below).[43] Only two per cent of Scotland's yearly production of *coal* was exported, 1755–59.[44] *Linen* probably enjoyed the highest average export-to-output ratio of 20–30 per cent, which for Scotland was exceptional; for other northern European regions it was not (consider Silesia's linen production for instance, of which more than 70 per cent was usually exported to the Americas and elsewhere after the 1750s). A similar relation obtained for the share of linen manufactures in total Scottish exports overseas, c. 1760.[45]

Given the profits to be made on tobacco, due to access being limited to those in possession of colonies producing the item (Navigation Acts)[46], the choice of procuring the item and re-selling it to continental Europeans was, if not strictly logical, at least a feasible one in financial terms. Thus the domination of re-exports in Scottish exports could have represented a viable solution to a problem of a weak manufacturing base and a weak domestic export sector, 1700–1760. What could be done, if levels and structure of domestic economic activity in Scotland were neither sufficient to create a significant demand for foreign imports, nor were domestic products competitive on world markets? One way certainly was to focus on certain goods that could not be obtained – but nevertheless were high in demand – in contemporary Europe. These were, above all, colonial goods, tropical non-essentials, frequently bearing an addictive and stimulating character, such as tobacco, and to a much lesser extent sugar tea, coffee and chocolate and the like. Here England – with less a bias towards re-exporting due to a good domestic manufacturing base – had already built up a large and flourishing entrepôt trade since about 1660, somewhat following the successful example provided by the Dutch carrying trades after 1600, against which the English Navigation Acts, including the Restoration Customs System of 1660 seq. had been initially designed. Scotland, after 1707 part of the "imperial core" with access to the products of the English overseas plantations, merely picked up on what was (correctly) regarded as best practice in world trade at that time (prior to industrialization, which changed and re-shuffled trade patterns entirely). Germany became part of the system – as a market for Scottish re-exports such as tobacco, sugar and coffee, as well as a provider of imports (linens) to be re-exported to the place of origin of these colonial goods in the Americas.

---

43 P. R. ROESSNER, 'New Light on Whatley's Numbers'. The German Market for Scots Salt in the Eighteenth Century, in: Scottish Historical Review 87, 1 (2008).

44 ROESSNER, In the Wake of Union, p. 211.

45 Ibid., p. 213, 224s.

46 The full set of implications of, as well as the applicable price mechanism under of the English Navigation acts are summarized in S. L. ENGERMAN, Mercantilism and Overseas Trade, 1700–1860, in: R. FLOUD / MCCLOSKEY, D. (eds.), The Economic History of Britain since 1700, Vol. I: 1700–1860, Cambridge, 2nd ed. 1994, pp. 182–204, at pp. 196–203, esp. Fig. 8.2.

2. GERMAN OVERSEAS TRADE – FLUCTUATIONS, PORTS, COMMODITIES

For eighteenth-century Germany the evidence is much scantier and less reliable than in the Scottish case. Also, a comprehensive history of eighteenth-century German foreign trade has yet to be written. Partly, as mentioned in chapter one, these deficiencies are due to the peculiar geo-political texture of the Holy Roman Empire – Germany – in the early modern period. The fact that Britain is surrounded completely by water and has been a unified state using standardized central recording and fiscal accounting practices since 1707, makes both the conceptual definition and recording of British, English, or Scottish foreign or overseas trade fairly easy compared to a country like pre-modern Germany (apart from the fact that, as mentioned above, Anglo-Scottish trade could not be recorded after 1707 any more, as all customs posts on the Anglo-Scottish border were abolished in 1707). Early modern Germany had land borders to most of her neighbouring countries. Furthermore, she was inhomogeneous and fragmented in political, administrative, as well as geographical terms. This makes for a great incongruence of the available quantitative sources for the German sea ports in terms of design, comprehensiveness, coverage and degree of preservation. The conceptual problems of defining German overseas trade in operational terms, as well as distinguishing domestic traffic from foreign trade, have been discussed in chapter one above. The available literature has therefore tended to be extremely careful, with statements focusing on particular ports, for which some quantitative evidence is available. The following synopsis, obtained from the more reliable standard accounts, has to be viewed in this light.

A general decline in German economic activity, as well as gross total trade, caused by the Thirty Years' War[47] and the general late-seventeenth century agrarian depression, would have been made largely good for by the beginning of the eighteenth century, even though some regions never quite recovered from the combined effects of the Great War and the ongoing "seventeenth century crisis" until late.[48] After the war the long-term trend in German overseas trade commenced on a path of expansion.[49] The overall trade balance, as well as the particular balance of trade with Britain, however, was a negative one in most years.[50] According to Beutin this negative balance was partly settled using invisibles, such as the incomes accruing to some German princes, such as the Landgraves of Hesse-Kassel, from the subsidies

47 B. STIER / W. VON HIPPEL, War, Economy and Society, in: S. OGILVIE (ed.), Germany. A New Social and Economic History, Vol. II. 1630–1800, London / New York 1996, pp. 233–262.

48 R. GÖMMEL, Die Entwicklung der Wirtschaft im Zeitalter des Merkantilismus 1620–1800, Munich 1998, pp. 77s.; P. KRIEDTE, Peasants, Landlords and Merchant Capitalists. Europe and the World Economy, 1500–1800, Leamington Spa 1983, ch. 2.

49 P. KRIEDTE, Trade, in: S. OGILVIE (ed.), Germany. A New Social and Economic History, Vol. II: 1630–1800, London / New York 1996, pp. 100–133, at p. 122.

50 K. H. KAUFHOLD, Deutschland 1650–1850, in: W. FISCHER / J. A. VAN HOUTTE / H. KELLENBENZ / I. MIECK / F. VITTINGHOFF (eds.), Handbuch der Europäischen Wirtschafts- und Sozialgeschichte, Vol. 4: Von der Mitte des 17. zur Mitte des 19. Jahrhunderts, Stuttgart 1993, pp. 530–588, at p. 572; GÖMMEL, Wirtschaft, p. 82.

paid for soldiers supplied to Britain during the Seven Years' War.[51] Generally speaking, however, German overseas trading activity was not particularly large vis-à-vis the English, Dutch, and later French, Swedish and Danish trade volumes, especially in terms of the "new" colonial and Asian goods. The latter had acquired or would acquire colonies on a permanent basis and also developed the financial and legal institutions, such as large incorporated or chartered companies, stock and commodity exchanges, Navigation Acts etc., necessary in order to successfully maintain a commercial empire. In this regard Germany clearly failed in the eighteenth century.[52] On the other hand, given the geographic, political and economic structure of pre-modern Germany, it is likely that overland trade – domestic traffic and "quasi-foreign" trade, i.e. mutual commercial exchange between the German states – was more important for the German economy than sea-borne trade.

In the eighteenth century German *exports* overseas were dominated by primary products and commodities obtained in the extractive industries, such as timber, salt, copper, lead, and stone. Large quantities of grain were also exported from Baltic ports such as Stralsund, Wismar and Rostock, as well as the big Prussian ports further east, such as Stettin and Königsberg. German, in particular Silesian, linen manufactures were traded to markets as far away as the Americas. As with Scotland, Ireland and England, linen provided for some pre-industrial dynamics, to the extent that Prussia's export volume towards the end of the century consisted to up to 70 per cent of linen manufactures.[53] The structure of the German *import* volume on the other hand was dominated by iron, timber, grain and fish, which came largely from Scandinavia and Northern Europe. Coal came predominantly from England and Scotland; oranges, lemons, wine and oil were provided from Portugal and Spain. The absence of direct access to colonies resulted in the necessity to import those non-essentials that had become fashionable and high in demand recently, such as tobacco, sugar, tea, coffee, and spices from intermediaries. The main intermediary or supplier of colonial goods was France, followed by the Netherlands. British suppliers gained in importance considerably after 1740, but in particular after the end of the Seven Years' War (1763).[54] Thus, German overseas trade took place mainly with the immediately adjacent countries – the Low Countries, France (colonial goods), Britain, Poland (Danzig), and the Russian Empire, but in the latter case chiefly the Livonian ports of Riga, Nerva and Reval which had recently (1721) been annexed from Sweden.

Much more difficult than asserting Germany's main trading partners is an estimate of the distribution of German exports and imports across German sea ports. Given the conceptual difficulties discussed in chapter one, North has proposed the

---

51 L. BEUTIN, Der Deutsche Seehandel im Mittelmeergebiet bis zu den Napoleonischen Kriegen, Neumünster 1933, p. 77.

52 The Brandenburg-Prussian African Company, established in 1682, proved abortive. Its African "empire", mainly the trading post Great Fredericksburg, was sold to the Dutch in 1717. The Royal Prussian Asian Company, founded in 1750, was likewise unsuccessful. M. NORTH, Von der Atlantischen Handelsexpansion bis zu den Agrarreformen (1450–1815), in: ID. (ed.), Deutsche Wirtschaftsgeschichte. Ein Jahrtausend im Überblick, Munich, 2nd ed. 2005, pp. 112–196; GÖMMEL, Wirtschaft, p. 28.

53 NORTH, Von der Atlantischen Handelsexpansion bis zu den Agrarreformen, p.156; Table.

54 GÖMMEL, Wirtschaft, pp. 78s.

existence (as a heuristic concept) of four separate German trading zones, of which only the first based its commercial exchange activity mainly on sea-borne trade. This area consisted of Lower or Northern Germany facing the North Sea. Hamburg, Bremen, and to a much lesser extent Emden, were its main sea-ports or entrepôts, with a commercial hinterland that reached far into central-western and eastern Germany and beyond (Westphalia to Silesia).[55] It is this zone that will be of interest in the following discussion on overseas trade.

In terms of value, shipping capacities and therefore probably gross total trade as well, German overseas trade was firmly in Hamburg and Bremen's hands. The former was without doubt Germany's largest and most important sea port in the period, handling supposedly much of Bremen's, as well as Lübeck's business as an intermediary.[56] Depending upon which measure is chosen for comparison (number of ships calling in? tonnage of ships registered in one particular port? value of certain commodities the trade of which was recorded in each port? value of consignments?) it is uncertain whether Lübeck or Bremen came second place after Hamburg. The problem becomes compounded if it is considered that a large share of German foreign trade went overland first. In this regard it was the Leipzig and Frankfurt trade fairs in particular that were important focal points, attracting large shares of total German foreign trade. It has been assumed for instance that in terms of total value of transactions, Leipzig followed Hamburg in second place.[57] What is fairly clear, however, is that in terms of overseas trade, Bremen and Lübeck came after Hamburg and before any other German sea port in the period.

For reasons apparent from the discussion so far, a meaningful way of carrying further the analysis of Scottish-German trade on the German side needs to be based on particular ports. By any standards, an eighteenth century discussion has to start with Hamburg.

2.1 Hamburg

Hamburg was according to contemporaries, "with respect to GERMANY, what AMSTERDAM is to EUROPE, a magazine of the different produce, and merchandize of the trading world."[58] It was the largest port of the Empire in terms of incoming traffic, with around 2,000 ships calling in annually; followed by Lübeck, totalling up to 950 and Bremen, which recorded up to about 500 ships calling in per annum during the

55 For the other regions see NORTH, Von der Atlantischen Handelsexpansion bis zu den Agrarreformen, pp. 157–162; Id., Kommunikation, Handel, Geld und Banken in der frühen Neuzeit, Munich 2000, pp. 18–23.

56 F.-W. HENNING, Das Vorindustrielle Deutschland 800–1800, Paderborn / Munich / Vienna / Zurich, 5th ed. 1994, p. 268. M. NORTH, Hamburg: the 'Continent's Most English City', in: ID., From the North Sea to the Baltic: Essays in Commercial, Monetary and Agrarian History 1500–1800, Aldershot 1996, paper VI, pp. 1–23, p. 2, n. 3.

57 GÖMMEL, Wirtschaft, pp. 79s.

58 J. HANWAY, An Historical Account of the British Trade over the Caspian Sea. With the Author's Journal of Travels from England through Russia into Persia; and back through Russia, Germany and Holland, Vol. II, London, 2nd ed. 1754, p. 17.

second half of the eighteenth century.[59] Hamburg supplied large parts of Germany and continental Europe with colonial staples, such as tobacco, sugar, coffee, cocoa, tea and spices, which could or would not be produced there, nor be obtained directly, due to the lack of colonies.[60] Hamburg also appears to have provided neutral shipping, services happily resorted to by Glaswegian merchants during times when French privateers were active in the English Channel, which endangered the regular supply of British re-exports to continental markets. During the Seven Years' War for instance, many ships employed by Glaswegian re-exporters of American tobacco to continental destinations might have been German (or Dutch), according to the ships' names which were often given in Low German in the Scottish customs accounts.[61]

Its somewhat fortuitous location at the mouth of Germany's largest river in the north-west, as well as its status as a Free Imperial City, which remained neutral in the major European conflicts, *inter alia* made Hamburg the ideal German entrepôt. Its main markets reached from Westphalia (linen) in the north-west, as far south as Franconia (iron) and Bavaria, and to Thuringia in the South-east via the Brunswick fairs).[62] The Leipzig trade fairs, where Hamburg merchants usually ranged amongst the largest group of regular visitors, extended the Hamburg market area far into eastern and central-eastern Europe, into areas such as Silesia and Russia.[63] Accordingly Hamburg was until the 1750s the principal source of Prussia's sugar imports.[64] Sugar and coffee traded on the Brunswick fairs were usually consigned via Hamburg; of the enormous range of foreign commodities available in Hamburg, 50 per cent were usually quoted in the price currents in Brunswick as well.[65] Hamburg was even reported to be Austria's principal source of imports overseas, even though it was neither part of nor connected to the Austrian realms, supplying goods such as English manufactures and even Mediterranean goods more cheaply than the Mediterranean port of Trieste.[66]

---

59 F. KOPITZSCH, Zwischen Hauptrezeß und Franzosenzeit 1712–1806, in: W. JOCHMANN / H.-D. LOOSE (eds.), Hamburg: Geschichte der Stadt und ihrer Bewohner, Hamburg 1982, pp. 351–490, at p. 376.

60 H. KELLENBENZ, The Rise of the European Economy. An Economic History of Continental Europe from the Fifteenth to the Eighteenth Century, London 1976, pp. 285s.; NORTH, Kommunikation, p. 19; ID., Von der Atlantischen Handelsexpansion bis zu den Agrarreformen, p. 162.

61 RÖSSNER, In the Wake, ch. 8.

62 M. A. DENZEL, Die Braunschweiger Messen als regionaler und überregionaler Markt im norddeutschen Raum in der zweiten Hälfte des 18. und im beginnenden 19. Jahrhundert, in: Vierteljahrschrift für Sozial- und Wirtschaftsgeschichte, LXXXV (1998), pp. 40–93.

63 N. BRÜBACH, Die Reichsmessen von Frankfurt am Main, Leipzig und Braunschweig (14.–18. Jahrhundert), Stuttgart 1994, pp. 487–514. F. KOPITZSCH, Aufklärung in Hamburg. Grundzüge einer Sozialgeschichte der Aufklärung in Hamburg und Altona, Hamburg, 2nd ed. 1990, pp. 178–185; H. LIEBEL, Laissez-faire vs. Mercantilism: The Rise of Hamburg & The Hamburg Bourgeoisie vs. Frederick the Great in the Crisis of 1763, in: Vierteljahrschrift für Sozial- und Wirtschaftsgeschichte, LII (1965), pp. 207–238, at pp. 213–215.

64 T. KUSTER, 500 Jahre kolonialer Rohrzucker- 250 Jahre europäischer Rübenzucker, in: Vierteljahrschrift für Sozial- und Wirtschaftsgeschichte, LXXXV (1998), pp. 477–512, at p. 496.

65 DENZEL, Braunschweiger Messen, p. 46f; p. 68f, p. 89.

66 BEUTIN, Seehandel, pp. 61–69, 78–81.

Hamburg's foreign trade expanded during the eighteenth century, even though the nature of the available sources do not allow more than a rough statement on the general trend in total turnover in the port of Hamburg, mostly imports, as covered by the extant sources, the *Admiralitätszoll- und Convoygeldeinnahmebücher* (Figure 4).

Figure 4: Total Turnover (Imports) in Hamburg, 1733-1798 (Marks Banko)

Source: KRAWEHL et al. (eds.), Statistik.

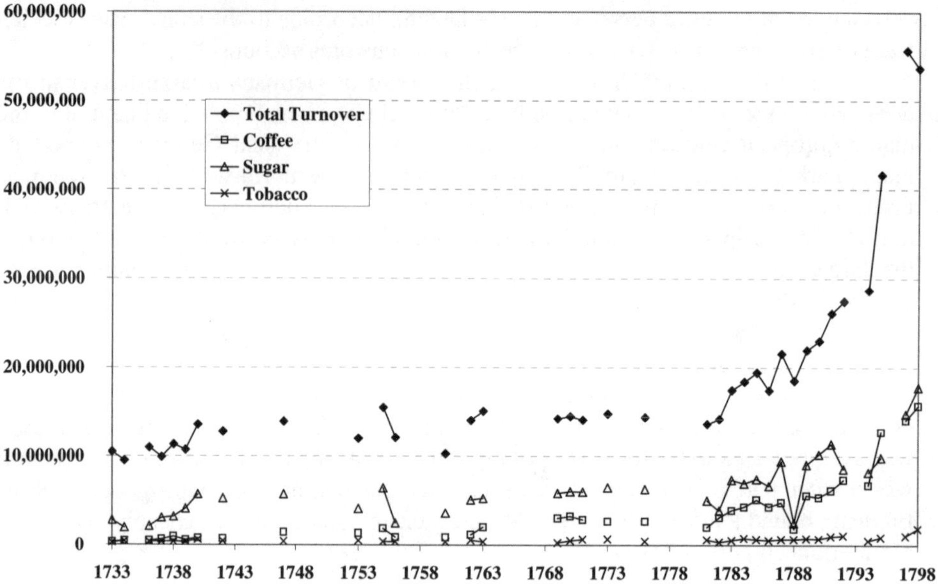

The recorded import trades were driven by coffee and sugar, much less so by tobacco; these three most important colonial goods, obtained chiefly from the French and British West Indies, thus to a large extent determined the cyclical pattern in Hamburg imports.

Whilst the period from 1680–1730 was marked by a depression in her commercial activity, partly mirroring the general European depression of the later seventeenth century, it was nevertheless during the first three decades of the eighteenth century that the foundations of the subsequent growth in Hamburg's trade volume (1730–1800) were laid. The volume of Hamburg's imports overseas increased according to North by a factor of at least six between 1713 and 1751; thereafter growth continued.[67] Whilst the real dynamics came long after the period under consideration – i.e. between 1780 and 1800, as the above graph suggests – there nevertheless was some growth in Hamburg imports between 1730 and 1760/1770, even though the long-run trend between 1730 and 1780 was fairly unspectacular, compared to the two decades after 1780 (Figure 4 above). Hamburg's long-term success was due to a well-designed institutional framework. A favourite inclination of Hamburg City Council towards "free" trade, including *inter alia* the application of comparatively moderate customs duties and fees, as well as more favourable legislation than elsewhere, coupled

67 NORTH, The 'Continent's Most English City', p. 5.

with neutrality in the numerous wars of the century, thus bore fruit since the early eighteenth century. In 1711, a treaty with Great Britain was signed which granted British subjects the same favourable conditions upon import for their fish as the Dutch: exemption from the *Admiralitätszoll* and *Convoygeld*. Effectively this meant duty-free access for British fish traders to the Hamburg fish market.[68] Especially the Shetland fisheries profited from this; Hamburg and Bremen were their largest foreign markets up to the 1750s (chapter four below). More beneficial legislation was to follow: in 1713, duties were abolished on transit commodities to be re-exported from Hamburg within six months. In 1727 duties on re-exports were waived in general – Hamburg became a free port in the proper sense.[69]

These aspects greatly stimulated Hamburg's commercial and economic development, 1700–1770. Hamburg's "trade began to increase at the expense even of Danzig and Amsterdam, especially in the boom years after the Seven Years' War had ended in 1763."[70] As seen above, Hamburg's imports overseas expanded considerably after the 1730s (in the long run, however, these figures were unimpressive vis-à-vis the commercial development in the 1770s, 1780s and beyond).[71] But the first half of the century witnessed some considerable changes, too. Whereas Britain had been Hamburg's largest supplier of imports roughly between the late 1670s and the early 1710s, some time after the later date France took over that role. In the 1750s Hamburg's largest trading partner in terms of imports, particularly of sugar and coffee, was France.[72] This pattern even applied vice versa: during the first half of the century about one quarter of total French colonial imports of sugar, coffee and others were sold on the Hamburg market.[73] This pattern, however, was to change again with the Seven Years' War, after which Britain re-gained market shares at the expense of the French. This was due to France cancelling a 1716 commercial treaty which from the French point of view treated Hamburg merchants as neutrals, as well as applying reduced customs duties on French imports.

Hamburg's *exports* were dominated by linen manufactures. Supply channels for this commodity reached far into central European production areas such as Silesia and

---

68 Hamburg, 31 January 1711. A copy of the treaty can be found in: NLS, Pamphlet Series, 1.22(96). Was this a compensation for the "expulsion" of Hamburg fish merchants from the Shetlands in and around 1700? See ch. 4 below.

69 E. WISKEMANN, Hamburg und die Welthandelspolitik von den Anfängen bis zur Gegenwart, Hamburg 1929, p. 112.

70 KELLENBENZ, Economy, p. 286; W. VOGEL, Handelskonjunkturen und Wirtschaftskrisen in ihrer Auswirkung auf den Seehandel der Hansestädte 1560–1806, in: Hansische Geschichtsblätter, LXXIV (1956), pp. 50–64, p. 62.

71 In fact, if the number of ships registered at the port of Hamburg can be taken as a reliable proxy for the long-term trend in this port's commercial activity (gross total trade), the period prior to the 1760s appears, in comparison to the last four decades of the century, as rather unspectacular. KRIEDTE, Trade, pp. 118–20, Fig. 4.1; ID., Peasants, Landlords and Merchant Capitalists, pp. 127s.

72 M. A. DENZEL / H. J. GERHARD, Global and Local Aspects of Pre-Industrial Inflations: New Research on Inflationary Processes in XVIIIth–Century Central Europe, in: Journal of European Economic History, XXXIV, 1 (2005), pp. 149–185, at pp. 157s.; NORTH, 'Continent's Most English City', pp. 7s., Tab. 3; ID., Von der Atlantischen Handelsexpansion bis zu den Agrarreformen, p. 155, Table; WISKEMANN, Hamburg, p. 118; LIEBEL, Rise, pp. 217s.

73 E. KLESSMANN, Geschichte der Stadt Hamburg, Hamburg 2002, pp. 226s.

Bohemia.[74] Some remarks may be included in the discussion on the development of the Hamburg money market. As cashless payments became the corollary of goods flows between the focal points of the north-west European "world" trading system since the 1690s[75], Hamburg, with its ever-increasing overseas trade volume, similarly to Amsterdam and London, also began to attract an ever-increasing amount of finance and cashless payments. It thus, alongside Amsterdam, London and Paris, became a banking centre of significance for northern Europe.[76] The Bank of Hamburg which had been founded in 1619, "issued" its own virtual currency or money of account (Mark Banko), thus providing a stable financial and institutional framework for the foreign trades which in the early modern period involved a multiplicity of currencies and trade imbalances.[77] Especially in financial market terms, Hamburg was at pole position, compared to the second-largest port on the German North Sea shore: Bremen.

2.2 Bremen

In the eighteenth century, Bremen was the second-largest German port in the North Sea, as well as the second- or third-largest German sea port in general.[78] Similar to Hamburg yet decidedly smaller, its chief commercial purpose was to be an entrepôt, catering for north-west Germany's appetite for tropical sugar, coffee, tobacco and rice. Bremen's markets not only extended to Eastern and Western Frisia, but also

74 WISKEMANN, Hamburg, p. 120.

75 M. A. DENZEL, 'La Practica della Cambiatura'. Europäischer Zahlungsverkehr vom 14. bis zum 17. Jahrhundert, Stuttgart 1994. See ch. 5, section 5.1 below.

76 ID., Die Integration Deutschlands in das internationale Zahlungsverkehrssystem im 17. und 18. Jahrhundert, in: E. SCHREMMER (ed.), Wirtschaftliche und soziale Integration in historischer Sicht, Stuttgart 1996, pp. 58–109, at pp. 76–80.

77 This money of account was fixed in terms of grams of silver and backed by precious metal deposits (silver ingots). In the eighteenth century it was stipulated that any commodity exchange transaction made by resident Hamburg merchants totalling 400 Marks Banko or more and any bill of exchange transaction above 400 Marks Lubish (current) Money, ought to be made or cleared via an account with the Bank of Hamburg. Whilst the Mark Banko in Hamburg was generally equal to 1/3 Imperial Dollars and 16 s (Schillinge) Lübeck Money, Mark Banko was available at an agio or premium compared to the Hamburg Mark current money. In the early eighteenth century, the agio usually stood at about 18%, i.e. about 85 Marks Banko bought 100 Marks current money. There was however, a considerable depreciation of Hamburg current money in the 1710s and 1720s. J. J. MCCUSKER, Money and Exchange in Europe and America, 1600–1775, Chapel Hill 1978, pp. 61–79 has the exchange rate Hamburg on London between 1657 and 1698. For the eighteenth century, the bill rate Hamburg on London is given in W. REISS, Historical Exchange Rates, in: W. FISCHER / R. MARVIN MCINNIS / J. SCHNEIDER (eds.), The Emergence of a World Economy 1500–1914, Pt. I. 1500–1850, Wiesbaden 1986, pp. 171–190, p. 189 / Fig. 5, and general remarks, pp. 171–177. Apart from the two works mentioned, vide etiam L. F. PETERS, Hamburger Bank, in: M. NORTH (ed.), Von Aktie bis Zoll. Ein Historisches Lexikon des Geldes, Munich 1995, pp. 154–5; M. A. DENZEL / O. SCHWARZER, Kurant, in: Ibid., pp. 210–12; DENZEL, Zahlungsverkehr, pp. 472–6.

78 KOPITZSCH, Zwischen Hauptrezeß und Franzosenzeit, p. 376.

penetrated deep into Hanoverian territory.[79] It drew its supplies of linen exports essentially from the same areas as Hamburg, i.e. regions like Westphalia, Hesse, Saxony and Silesia. (Her own production of linen and other goods for export was irrelevant in terms of her exports overseas.[80]) In general, however, there was scarcely a commodity that could be supplied more conveniently or more cheaply through Bremen than through Hamburg. Accordingly, Bremen never seriously took on Hamburg during the eighteenth century.

Naturally, Bremen's commercial links were strongest with the three biggest contemporary and adjacent colonial powers, of which the Netherlands and France, however were the most important. Whilst until about 1730 the Netherlands had been the largest supplier of foreign goods to Bremen, this role was subsequently taken over by France. Between 1730 and 1760, French imports, mainly products of the French Caribbean, far exceeded imports from the Netherlands.[81] In this way the pattern was very similar to the pattern of Hamburg's trade. After 1750, Bremen's trade with Baltic ports such as Danzig and Arkhangelsk expanded, too; and in the 1770s, direct trade with the Danish Caribbean, as well as with the now independent North American states, commenced.[82]

Located at the Weser, "the smallest of the large German rivers", Bremen was not as well suited for the export of domestic manufactures from the several German territories, as Hamburg (Elbe) and places located at the Rhine (then the German commodities were channelled through Dutch ports).[83] Nevertheless, the Weser, as a river without a spring (as it originates by the confluence of the two rivers Fulda and Werra at Münden) was navigable over its entire length and even had an extended navigable arm further inland, upstream along the Rivers Fulda and Werra. Thus the Bremen market radius potentially reached inland into central German territories as far south as the Hessian states.[84] As British exporters usually favoured Hamburg for their business with the German states[85] – due for instance to the preferential tariff agreement between Hamburg and British traders sealed with regard to herring in 1711, as well as a better financial infrastructure – Bremen merchants sought to counter this position with a commercial treaty with Britain, drafted in 1731. By this agreement, British

79 K. SCHWARZ, Die Lage der Handwerksgesellen in Bremen während des 18. Jahrhunderts, Bremen 1975, pp. 322s.

80 Ibid., p. 350.

81 In 1774–1777 for instance, the size of Bremen's total trade with France was twice the size of its total trade with Britain; Scotland would altogether have been of marginal commercial importance. G. FUHSE, Die Freie Hansestadt Bremen in Wirtschaftsgeschichtlicher Entwicklung, Bremen 1927, pp. 103s.; H.-J. VON WITZENDORF, Beiträge zur Bremischen Handelsgeschichte in der zweiten Hälfte des 18. Jahrhunderts, in: Bremisches Jahrbuch, XLIII (1951), pp. 342–394, at p. 345f; ID., Bremens Handel im 16. und 17. Jahrhundert, in: Bremisches Jahrbuch, XLIV (1955), pp. 128–174, at p. 146.

82 SCHWARZ, Lage, pp. 330s.; pp. 340–342; pp. 350–352.

83 VON WITZENDORF, Beiträge, p. 345.

84 K.-H. KAUFHOLD, Hauptrichtungen und wichtige Wege des binnenländischen Fernverkehrs in Niedersachsen in der frühen Neuzeit, in: U. BESTMANN / F. IRSIGLER / J. SCHNEIDER (eds.), Hochfinanz, Wirtschaftsräume, Innovationen. Festschrift für Wolfgang von Stromer, 3 Vols., Trier 1987, Vol. II, pp. 719–740, at pp. 726s.

85 Ibid., p. 353.

commodities shipped in Bremen vessels became exempt from payment of import duties in Bremen.[86] This, however – at least in terms of colonial re-exports – ran contrary to British Navigation Law. Therefore, the main branch of Scottish-Bremen trade receiving a commercial stimulus from the 1731 treaty would, according to the design of the Scottish-German trade volume, have been the fish trades (see chapter four and sections below). Notwithstanding these obvious attempts at drawing the colonial trades into German hands, Bremen remained an important, perhaps the most important, market for the supply of American tobacco to north-west Germany.[87] The number of tobacco manufactories in Bremen greatly expanded throughout the eighteenth century.[88] In this regard, Bremen would, alongside Hamburg, have been a favourite German port of calling for Scottish ships after 1707.

Bremen's trade, even though precise statements are impossible, appears to have expanded, following a cyclical pattern, c.1700-1770. Since the provisioning of English-Hanoverian troops employed in the Seven Years' War mainly went through Bremen, trade levels for instance increased in 1756–1763.[89] In the period following the war, the number of ships calling in declined from a peak of about 1,100 in 1757 and remained fairly stable through to the 1770s and 1780s, with the exception of the early 1770s, when a new all-time peak was reached (Figure 5 below). The largest number of ships came in from the North Sea Coast, thus representing mostly domestic trade, followed by Dutch vessels.[90] According to VON WITZENDORF, between 1696 and 1779 the value of linen exports through Bremen increased by a factor of at least four, or from one to 4–5 million Rix Dollars. Coffee imports rose by a factor of 14 between 1755 and 1796, sugar imports quintupled. Tobacco imports between 1700 and 1800 might have increased by 1,800 per cent.[91]

86 Ibid., pp. 353s.

87 It needs to be borne in mind, however, that since the later seventeenth century the Netherlands were Bremen's main supplier of tobacco; they remained in this position during the eighteenth century. L. BEUTIN, Drei Jahrhunderte Tabakhandel in Bremen, in: H. KELLENBENZ (ed.), Ludwig Beutin, Gesammelte Schriften zur Wirtschafts- und Sozialgeschichte, Cologne / Graz 1963, pp. 98–131, pp. 99s., pp. 104s.

88 From two in the middle of the seventeenth century, three in 1676 to 70 in 1770. A. HAUSER, Tabakstadt Bremen, in: H. RODER (ed.), Bremen: Handelsstadt am Fluß, Bremen 1995, pp. 239–246, at pp. 241s. H. SCHWARZWÄLDER, Geschichte der Freien Hansestadt Bremen, Vol. I. Von den Anfängen bis zur Franzosenzeit (1810), Bremen 1975, p. 426. Beutin quotes 59 tobacco manufactories in 1801. BEUTIN, Tabakhandel, p. 100.

89 SCHWARZ, Lage, p. 320f, pp. 330s., p. 342 (Table); VON WITZENDORF, Beiträge, p. 363.

90 VON WITZENDORF, Beiträge, Table on p. 387, and p. 359, 361seq. on the domestic and coastal trades.

91 VON WITZENDORF, Beiträge, p. 381, 384.

Figure 5: Number of Ships Calling in at the *Schlachte* Pier, Bremen

Source: VON WITZENDORF, Beiträge, Table on p. 387.
1764, 1766 incomplete

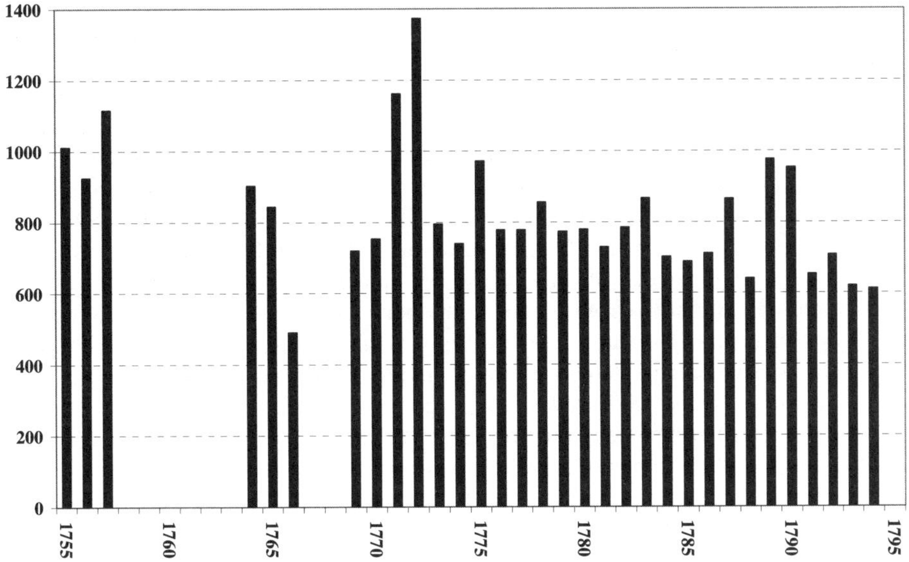

These stray observations may provide a rough glimpse on the commercial dynamics observable in Bremen during the period under consideration, which were in a way similar to Hamburg (see above). The post-1770 story on the other hand is a very different matter in terms of scale, patterns and scope, as several shifts and adjustment processes occurred, such as the commencement of direct trade with Caribbean and American ports, which greatly stimulated the trade in tropical non-essentials. Much more research into Bremen's overseas trade in the eighteenth century needs to be done, but it seems clear, though, that, even though the Hamburg and Bremen records are not strictly speaking comparable, Hamburg grew continuously and gained shares in total German overseas trade after the middle of the century, perhaps at the expense of Bremen's trade, which appears to have been stable, if not stagnant in the longer run.[92]

Both Hamburg and Bremen were chiefly transit or re-exporting ports.[93] They supplied the entire north, as well as central areas of Germany with colonial goods. Their linen supply areas likewise reached deep into central-western German production areas, in Hamburg's case certainly into East Prussian and Silesian production centres. This was facilitated by the existence of a relatively well developed river-canal system, connecting the Elbe and Oder, providing direct water-borne access between

92 KRIEDTE, Trade, p. 119, Fig. 4.2.

93 This section is largely based on P. KRIEDTE, Vom Großhändler zum Detaillisten. Der Handel mit Kolonialwaren im 17. und 18. Jahrhundert, in: Jahrbuch für Wirtschaftsgeschichte (1994/1), pp. 11–37, esp. pp. 33–35; NORTH, Von der Atlantischen Handelsexpansion bis zu den Agrarreformen, p. 171; BEUTIN, Tabakhandel, p. 99; HAUSER, Tabakstadt Bremen.

Hamburg and Silesia. Bremen's markets, in particular for tobacco and Scots salt, are thought to have comprised the states of Hanover, Brunswick and Oldenburg, the Weser area, Hesse and Westphalia. Hamburg has been labelled "Northern Germany's staple for raw sugar", and Bremen was called "tobacco city". These two ports therefore drew the lion's share of Germany's overseas trade in the period under consideration (1700–1770).

From these two entrepôts of the North foreign goods reached their customers via intermediaries, wholesalers in the smaller towns in central Germany, down to small retailers and peddlers, who supplied the rural areas. In 1744–6 for instance, several retailers and even peddlers dealing in "Bremen goods" – mainly sugar, coffee and the like – were mentioned in two smaller Hessian towns. The colonial goods were obtained mainly via the town of Münden, and only infrequently directly from Bremen. This suggests the existence of an already well-developed supply chain for colonial goods which ran smoothly from the large sea-ports to the consumer, penetrating into large areas of central Germany and involving a multiplicity of intermediaries other than the large Bremen and Hamburg foreign traders. Frequently the supply of colonial goods was linked to the *linen* trades in the opposite direction (chapter four). Bremen carters and haulage companies, often owned by the large Bremen overseas merchants, not only controlled the transportation of linen from Westphalia and adjacent areas to Bremen (for export to the Americas), but also supplied the central German producers with colonial goods in turn.[94] Hamburg's close ties with the Brunswick and Leipzig trade fairs also point towards a large and by the mid-eighteenth century highly integrated northern and north-eastern German market for colonial goods. Thus colonial goods permeated widely into northern German territories via the Bremen-Hamburg channel during the eighteenth century. The same channels were used in the opposite direction for Hessian and other linens exported to the Americas via Britain. In fact, smaller resident merchants frequently paid the larger wholesalers for their supplies of sugar, tea and coffee with linens which they had obtained locally. Therefore, even though evidence needs to remain non-quantitative, it is safe to assume that only a fraction of the commodities traded through Hamburg and Bremen was consumed there on the spot. If anything, food-processing industries, such as tobacco manufactories and sugar refineries were concentrated in Bremen and Hamburg, where the raw colonial materials were transformed prior to be sent on to their markets in west-central Germany.

2.3 Other Ports

It has been mentioned in chapter one that the Baltic German ports were, in terms of Scottish-German trade, largely irrelevant. It appears as though the German North Sea ports in the eighteenth century generally drew a larger business than the Baltic ports, although in absolute value and volume terms, both the North Sea, as well as the Baltic

94 J. G. KRÜNITZ (ed.), Oekonomische Encyklopaedie oder Allgemeines System der Land-, Haus- und Staatswirthschaft, 242 vols. Berlin 1773–1858, Vol. 107 (1799), entry: "Leinwandhandel".

trades probably increased.[95] Caution needs to be applied nonetheless. The possibility that much of the trade commissioned via the German North Sea littoral was actually destined for the Baltic makes a firm distinction of these two patterns and the determination of shifts in the commercial patterns during the eighteenth century extremely difficult.[96]

Notwithstanding these reservations, in the framework of Scottish-German trade, the Baltic, as well as all minor German ports in the North Sea, can safely be omitted from the analysis (chapter four) on the grounds of their statistical irrelevance. A few and brief comments on these ports will therefore suffice to get the picture right. The analysis, proceeding with the North Sea prior to discussing the Baltic, thus needs to move on to Altona, probably the third biggest German North Sea port in the period after Hamburg and Bremen.

2.3.1 Altona

As pointed out in chapter one, Altona needs to be included in an analysis of German trade, as it was part of the Danish-Norwegian dominions, yet located within the Holy Roman Empire (Germany). Situated close-by to Hamburg downstream (today it is part of Hamburg City), it was the second-biggest port on the River Elbe in the eighteenth century. It was, after Copenhagen, also the second-biggest port and city in the Danish realms.[97] After the Danish kings' first abortive attempts at establishing rival entrepôts to Hamburg on the River Elbe in Krempe and later on Glückstadt, these plans were finally crowned with some success since the later 1680s with the enlargement and forced economic development of what had initially been a modest village market a few kilometres away from Hamburg.[98] In the eighteenth century, Altona could in fact in many ways have developed into a serious competitor of Hamburg. It was located further down the Elbe, thus nearer towards the mouth of the river and the North Sea. Furthermore in the eighteenth century it boasted a good commercial and financial infrastructure, several banks and a stock exchange. Above all, no customs duties were levied on foreign traffic. Excise duties were moderate and fixed at lower rates than in Hamburg.

These aspects caused some commercial expansion and economic growth over the eighteenth century. Altona's population figures increased considerably: by 1720, it

---

95 GÖMMEL, Wirtschaft, pp. 80s.; NORTH, Kommunikation, pp. 19s.

96 Lübeck for instance is thought to have obtained most of its imports of colonial goods, with the exception of tobacco, via Hamburg. C. MEYER-STOLL, Die lübeckische Kaufmannschaft des 17. Jahrhunderts unter wirtschafts- und sozialgeschichtlichen Aspekten, Frankfurt-on-the-Main / Bern / New York / Paris 1989, p. 103, p. 214.

97 The classification employed by the British customs administration was not straightforward. In 1722, for example, the Scottish Board of Customs considered Altona "German", NAS, CE57/2/251, Index of Board's Orders, p. 31, whilst the inspector general's trade statistics obviously included trade with Altona under "Denmark & Norway".

98 H.-D. LOOSE, Das Zeitalter der Bürgerunruhen und der großen europäischen Kriege, in W. JOCHMANN / H.-D. LOOSE (eds.), Hamburg: Geschichte der Stadt und ihrer Bewohner, Hamburg 1982, pp. 259–350, at p. 293, p. 301.

counted about 12,000 inhabitants (Copenhagen: 60,000)[99]; in 1755 Altona was said to be larger than inner Vienna. With its stock exchange Altona was also an internationally recognized exchange market; exchange rates on Altona were quoted on a regular basis in some larger North-western European financial centres and stock exchanges.[100] In the later 1730s the Danish-Norwegian kings made Altona a free port by freeing foreign imports from customs duties and enhancing the capacity of shipbuilding facilities, as well as the number of commercial incorporations at that place.[101] Subsequently, but especially after the mid-1750s, Altona developed into a thriving entrepôt, channelling the full range of colonial staples obtained in or via the Danish West Indies.[102] Due to the moderate structure of applicable customs duties Altona was frequently resorted to as a port by Hamburg merchants.[103] It is also significant that, when the Habsburg East India Company in Ostende was dissolved (1729), and in reaction the Swedish (1731) and Danish (1732) East India Companies were founded in an obvious attempt at "interloping", i.e. bypassing the two monopolists of that time (the Dutch and English East India Companies), a first draft, dating from 1728/9, towards creating a Danish Asiatic Company, included the plan to set up a branch of this company at Altona.[104]

Whilst the preconditions for Altona to become a thriving entrepôt were clearly there in the eighteenth century, attempts at surpassing or even matching Hamburg remained unsuccessful. In 1754 a contemporary English traveller remarked – with proper English coolness and perhaps some understatement – that

---

99 H. RAMM, Altona, Wandsbek und die Südholsteinischen Randgebiete, in: E. VON LEHE / H. RAMM / D. KAUSCHE (eds.), Heimatchronik der Freien und Hansestadt Hamburg, Cologne, 2nd ed. 1967, pp. 263–354, at p. 295.

100 M. A. DENZEL (ed.), Währungen der Welt XI: Dänische und nordwestdeutsche Wechselkurse 1696–1914, Stuttgart 1999, pp. 77–106, esp. p. 77.

101 RAMM, Altona, p. 305; KELLENBENZ, Außenhandel, p. 26, p. 57.

102 Dansk Vestindien: St Croix, St Thomas and St John (since 1912: Virgin Islands, USA). Sugar production began to catch up in St Croix after 1733, based on the exploitation of slave labour and an Atlantic triangular trade following the Dutch and English pattern. S. DYRVIK / A. B. FOSSEN / T. GRØNLIE / E. HOVLAND / H. NORDVIK / S. TVEITE (eds.), Norsk Økonomisk Historie 1500–1970, Vol. 1. 1500–1850, Bergen / Oslo / Tromsø 1979, p. 110. B. N. THOMSEN / B. THOMAS, Dansk-Engelsk Samhandel. Et Historisk Rids 1661–1963, Arhus 1966, pp. 24s. O. FELDBÆK, Den lange fred 1700–1800: O. OLSEN (ed.), Gyldendal og Politikens Denmarkshistorie, Vol. 9, Copenhagen 1990, pp. 174–176. A. NIELSEN, Dänische Wirtschaftsgeschichte: Handbuch der Wirtschaftsgeschichte, Vol. 6, Jena 1933, pp. 296–8.

103 BEUTIN, Seehandel, p. 85.

104 K. GLAMANN, The Danish Asiatic Company, 1732–1772, in: Scandinavian Economic History Review, VIII, 1 (1960), pp. 109–149, at p. 109. L. MÜLLER, The Swedish East India Trade and International Markets: Re-exports of Teas 1731–1813, in: Scandinavian Economic History Review, LI, 3 (2003), pp. 28–44, esp. at pp. 31s., pp. 34s.; ID., Scottish and Irish Entrepreneurs in Eighteenth-Century Sweden. East India Trade and Iron, Unpubl. Paper, Uppsala 2003, pp. 3s. L. MAGNUSSON, An Economic History of Sweden, London / New York 2000, p. 88–90. T. FISCHER, The Scots in Sweden, Edinburgh 1907, pp. 16s.

> ALTONA has been long considered by the HAMBURGERS as an object of great jealousy; but there is not, I apprehend, so much cause to fear, as is suggested by many. ALTONA is a large place, but does not partake in the least of the pride of HAMBURG, with regard to its buildings; nor can it afford to pay any thing of consequence towards the revenues of DENMARK. It is an asylum for those who fly from the adjacent countries for debt, or worse crimes: the HAMBURGERS, whose fortunes reduce them to this extremity, take refuge there also. Except two or three houses of business, there is very little appearance of riches or plenty in ALTONA.[105]

According to the leading historian of Hamburg, Altona's failure to become a serious competitor of Hamburg may be attributed to two main reasons. First, Altona was under monarchic rule, whilst Hamburg as a free imperial city was governed by a proto-capitalist political oligarchy and commercial aristocracy. Secondly, an ancient tradition of trade and commerce in Hamburg had established informal structures and credit networks which it would have been impossible to create from scratch in Altona within only a few decades. Further to an excellent financial infrastructure, Hamburg was also griddled with canals that were bordered by the warehouses of the large overseas merchants. It was also considered to have better docking facilities for incoming ships and was thus generally favoured by geography, infrastructure and a long institutional history favouring trade and commerce.[106]

In terms of the present argument, Scottish-German trade, Altona was not important, either. In the period under consideration, Scots traders, as everyone else, clearly favoured Hamburg. And since Denmark had her own colonies, Scots, trading mainly tobacco, sugar and coffee to German ports, had not much to offer in Altona. They thus exclusively imported from Altona without exporting anything back to that place. – The main Scottish import from Altona was Portuguese and Spanish sea salt. It was the Shetland fisheries in particular, which received their main supplies of foreign salt for curing fish from Altona, rather than directly from Portugal or Spain.[107] In the eighteenth century, salt imports from Altona can be asserted as early as 1712, but it needs to be assumed that the pattern was much older than that.[108] This trading pattern can be explained fairly easily. As the curing of exported salt fish with domestic (Scots) salt was prohibited, and the Scottish product did not lend itself to that purpose very well anyway[109], the Scottish sea fisheries needed "white" (Spanish, Portuguese, or French) salt for curing their exported salt fish. For obvious reasons it was cheaper for the Shetland fish merchants to obtain the salt they needed en route from Hamburg, which happened to be their largest foreign market, thus stopping downriver at Altona, rather than to dispatch vessels directly to either Portugal, France or Spain.

105 HANWAY, Account, p. 19.

106 KOPITZSCH, Aufklärung, pp. 216–240.

107 Ch. 4, section 4.1.2 below.

108 Ibid.

109 Ibid.

2.3.2 Emden

Emden had been Germany's largest linen-exporting port in the sixteenth century, but subsequently lost that role to Hamburg, Bremen and Altona. Even though it remained the largest port in Eastern Frisia, its hey-days were over in the eighteenth century.[110] This is also reflected in Emden's weight in Scottish-German commerce, within which it was largely irrelevant, although some quantities of coal, salt and tobacco would be exported thence from Scotland in single years in the 1740s and 1750s.

2.3.3 Baltic Ports (i): Lübeck

Lübeck probably experienced a relative decline in her commercial activity during the eighteenth century, especially vis-à-vis the growing volume of transactions channelled through Hamburg and Bremen. The number of registered ships stagnated during the eighteenth century – when it occupied third place after Hamburg and Bremen – whilst Hamburg's shipping capacity expanded. Thus there was certainly some kind of loss of Lübeck at the expense of its two major North Sea rivals, perhaps in line with a general decline of the Baltic in terms of its share in world trade during the period under consideration, although conclusions need to remain entirely hypothetical.[111] Within the Baltic, however, Lübeck remained a large and important port during the eighteenth century, sometimes even matching Danzig's commercial activity.[112]

Being a virtually landlocked water system, only accessible from the West via the Øresund or the Great and Little Belt, the Baltic, by the excellent transport facilities geography provided, had been an integrating factor for the economies bordering this "big lake" in the North, East and South since Late Antiquity.[113] Scholars and contemporary policy makers accordingly, in their assessment of Britain's commercial position vis-à-vis this region, normally viewed this area as a coherent economic accounting item. Britain's foreign trade with "the Baltic" is thought to have been imbalanced in the seventeenth century, which, according to some scholars, caused some considerable balance of payments problems.[114] But the availability of colonial or tropical goods which were shipped in ever-increasing quantities eastwards through

---

110 GÖMMEL, Wirtschaft, p. 81. K. H. BOKELOH, Emder Wirtschaftsgeschichte 1744–1806. Preußischer Absolutismus der zweiten Hälfte des 18. Jahrhunderts in einer Randprovinz, University of Tübingen PhD Thesis, Tübingen 1984, pp. 113–115; KELLENBENZ, Außenhandel, p. 21; K. NEWMAN, Hamburg in the European Economy, 1660–1750, in: Journal of European Economic History, XIV, 1 (1985), pp. 57–93, at pp. 72s.

111 KRIEDTE, Trade, pp. 119s.

112 BEUTIN, Seehandel, p. 83.

113 E. C. SEMPLE, The Development of the Hanse Towns in Relation to Their Geographical Environment, in: Journal of the American Geographical Society of New York, XXXI, 3 (1899), pp. 236–255.

114 C. WILSON, Trade and Trade Balances: The Mercantilist Problem, in: Economic History Review, Second Series, II (1949), pp. 152–161; ID., Treasure and Trade Balances: Further Evidence, in: Economic History Review, Second Series, IV (1951), pp. 231–242; J. M. PRICE, Multilateralism and/or Bilateralism: The Settlement of British Trade Balances with 'The North', c. 1700, in: Economic History Review, Second Series, XIV, 2 (1961), pp. 254–274.

the Øresund from Britain, France and the Netherlands, especially after 1711/20[115], might, apart from the fact that outstanding balances were also settled via bills on Hamburg and Amsterdam, have made good for a considerable share of the former imbalance which seventeenth century Mercantilists had been so worried about.

If it is fair to view the Baltic as one highly integrated economic region, which figures for intra-Baltic trades strongly suggest to have been the case[116], thus assessing it as a whole, it needs to be acknowledged that any of the western European nations trading to it had as much incentive to take the long and – by means of the Sound Toll – taxing voyage overseas, as to avoid it and unload their goods in Hamburg instead, in order for the goods to be shipped on overland. Prior to the opening of the Eider canal connecting the North Sea with the Baltic in 1784, traffic between Hamburg and Lübeck had to resort to the overland route. But since the latter amounted to little more than 50 miles (~80 kilometres) as the crow flies, compared to the sea voyage through the Øresund, which took several hundred miles and on top of that was usually accompanied by payments of toll and accompanying delays, any Scots or English merchant anticipating a trading voyage to the Baltic, would have found an alternative itinerary via Hamburg almost always at least worth considering. He probably would have done so even in the case of commodities that had an extremely low value per unit, and even though transport on this route would have been liable to Danish customs and transit tolls in Holstein and Lauenburg.[117] The land route via Lübeck would have been a particularly attractive one after 1728, when Lübeck's staple legislation, i.e. the requirement that all imports into Lübeck had to be sold to Lübeck purchasers first, thus attempting to curb the overland transit trade via Hamburg into the Baltic, was waived.[118] Therefore, Kellenbenz's observation that Lübeck's overseas trade declined throughout the eighteenth century[119] needs to be viewed with a pinch of salt. It could be attributed to a general shift of commercial activity away from the Baltic to the Atlantic in the eighteenth century (which might have been the case), as much as to the fact that a lot of Lübeck's imports from the Atlantic and North Sea

115 N. STEENSGARD, The Growth and Composition of the Long-distance Trade of England and the Dutch Republic before 1750, in: J. D. TRACY (ed.), The Political Economy of Merchant Empires, New York 1991, pp. 102–52, at p. 105, Tab. 3.1.

116 M. BOGUCKA, Handelsbeziehungen im Ostseeraum: Der Handel zwischen Danzig/Gdansk und Stockholm in der 1. Hälfte des 17. Jahrhunderts, in: K. FRIEDLAND / F. IRSIGLER (eds.), Seehandel und Wirtschaftswege Nordeuropas im 17. und 18. Jahrhundert, Ostfildern 1981, pp. 38–47, at p. 38, n. 1.

117 R. BURMESTER, Lübecks Wirtschaft in den letzten 175 Jahren (1751–1926), in: A. REY (ed.), Lübeck seit Mitte des 18. Jahrhunderts (1751). Ein Jubiläumsbeitrag zur 700-Jahrfeier der Reichsfreiheit Lübecks, Lübeck 1926, pp. 39–52, at p. 41.

118 H. KELLENBENZ, Landverkehr, Fluss- und Seeschifffahrt im Europäischen Handel (Spätmittelalter bis Anfang des 19. Jahrhunderts), in: ID., Europa. Raum Wirtschaftlicher Begegnung: ID., Kleine Schriften, Vol. I, Stuttgart 1991, pp. 327–441. NEWMAN, Hamburg, p. 61, pp. 71s. E. HARDER (-GERSDORFF), Seehandel zwischen Lübeck und Rußland im 17./18. Jahrhundert nach Zollbüchern der Novgorodfahrer, Pt. I, in: Zeitschrift des Vereins für Lübeckische Geschichte und Altertumskunde, LXI (1961), pp. 43–114, at pp. 57s.

119 KELLENBENZ, Economy, p. 286.

(Britain, America) came in via and were declared in Hamburg.[120] Thus, the Scottish customs declarations outwards for or inwards from Lübeck might not necessarily be indicative of total declared Scottish trade with Lübeck.

The Scottish customs accounts suggest that to Lübeck, Scotland exported only salt directly on a more or less regular basis (yet on a small scale). This might have been commercially feasible due to salt's low bulk value – perhaps these salt cargoes were intended as ballast paying for its freight and thus the first link of a voyage that was primarily intended in order to pick up commodities in the Baltic, whilst Scotland herself had little to offer there. Between 1742 and 1751, the share of Lübeck in total exports of Scots salt ranged between three and 17 per cent (average 1743–1755: four per cent).[121] A similar relation might have obtained from the Lübeck side in the late seventeenth century. In the three incomplete years examined by Meyer-Stoll (1680–82), imports of salt from Scotland accounted for two per cent of total imports.[122] Between 1742 and 1755, tobacco was re-exported from Scottish ports to Lübeck only once (1746); flax and timber items were imported from this port only in 1750 and 1751 in tiny quantities.

2.3.4 Baltic Ports (ii): Swedish Pomerania

Hither Pomerania, located within the Holy Roman Empire but after 1648 officially under Swedish rule, had five main sea ports – Stralsund, Greifswald, Wismar, Wolgast and Barth. Of these only the first was of real significance, even though its heydays were over by the beginning of the eighteenth century. Once an important Hansa city, *Stralsund* had after 1648 declined into an appendix of the Swedish economy.[123] This was due to a mix of economic and institutional criteria.[124] Both resulted from the structure of the Swedish economy. Sweden, suffering from a permanent agrarian deficit but facing increasing needs for permanent armed forces and their supply with victuals, became reliant on grain imports since the later seventeenth century. Initially these were met by imports from Swedish Livonia. After the loss of Livonia to the Russian Empire in 1721, however, Hither Pomerania, Sweden's last remaining overseas possession in the Baltic, remained the only province yielding an agrarian surplus. The result was that grain was usually more expensive in Sweden proper than elsewhere. By furthermore freeing Pomeranian grain imports from Swedish import duties (1721), as well as retaining a price differential between Sweden proper and Swedish Pomerania, eighteenth-century Pomeranian grain was exported largely to

120 E. HARDER-GERSDORFF, Mitteleuropäische Gewerbezonen und ostbaltischer Handel im 18. Jahrhundert, in: FRIEDLAND / IRSIGLER (eds.), Seehandel und Wirtschaftswege, pp. 26–37, esp. at pp. 32s., remark in n. 5 (ibid., p. 35).

121 NAS, E504.

122 MEYER-STOLL, Kaufmannschaft, Tables, p. 247.

123 K.-F. OLECHNOWITZ, Handel und Seeschiffahrt der späten Hanse, Weimar 1965, pp. 140–150; HARDER (-GERSDORFF), Seehandel, pp. 58s.

124 The following, unless otherwise indicated, is based on W. BUCHHOLZ, Öffentliche Finanzen und Finanzverwaltung im entwickelten frühmodernen Staat. Landesherr und Landstände in Schwedisch-Pommern 1720–1806, Cologne / Weimar / Vienna 1992, pp. 99–116.

ports on the Swedish mainland.[125] Accordingly, between 30 and 50 per cent of Swedish grain imports usually came from Pomeranian ports, and Swedish destinations became more important for Pomerania's trade.[126] Under these circumstances the fact that both the 1721 Act freeing Pomeranian grain imports from Swedish import duties and the loss of Livonia to the Russian Empire fell into the same year is hardly a coincidence.

A further institutional component responsible for gearing the trade of Stralsund and other Hither Pomeranian ports largely towards the Swedish economy was due to the establishment of the Swedish Navigation Act (*Produktplakat*) in 1723. Modelled on the Dutch and English precedent, it forbade the importation of foreign products into Swedish ports from countries other than those which had produced these commodities. As Swedish Pomeranian ports in these acts were classified as foreign, the only produce they could legally export to Sweden was Pomeranian goods, the range of which, apart from urban industrial production, was largely limited to malt (accounting for about 62 per cent of exports), rye (28 per cent), as well as some oats, wheat and peas.[127] A third institutional component, however, was of equal importance: in times of grain shortage in Sweden, exports of grain from Pomerania to other than Swedish ports were prohibited.[128] This mix of mainly institutional constraints seems to have worked efficiently and in Sweden's favour. After 1738 and for the rest of the century, Sweden constantly imported more from Pomerania in value terms than it exported thence; with imports exceeding exports by three to five times.[129] In this way, the Swedish Pomeranian ports and their commercial hinterland differed from *Prussian* Pomeranian ports such as Stettin and Kolberg, inasmuch as the latter had a more diversified trade, most notably a flourishing timber exporting business.[130] Given the nature of the institutional and economic constraints for Pomerania's trade mentioned previously, one might not expect Stralsund and the other Hither Pomeranian ports to have been either a large destination for Scottish exports, or a significant source of imports into Scotland after circa 1720.

Scottish ports had been an important and regular source of seaborne imports of salt, coals and sea fish into the port of Stralsund since the middle of the fourteenth

---

125 RICE, Swedish Foreign Trade, pp. 88s. KELLENBENZ, Wirtschaftsgeschichte, Vol. I, p. 351; OLECHNOWITZ, Handel und Seeschiffahrt, p. 180.

126 The latter aspect, i.e. the use of price differentials by Pomeranian merchants, who were thus able to maximise their profit, argues against the thesis of "forced underdevelopment" of this region. But it is important to bear in mind that Pomeranian grain exports might have helped freeing Swedish surplus labour to be engaged in non-agrarian occupations and thus raised the stage of development and living standards in Swedish proper at the Pomeranian expense.

127 W. BUCHHOLZ, Das schwedische Pommern vom Westfälischen Frieden bis zum Wiener Kongress, in: ID. (ed.), Deutsche Geschichte im Osten Europas, Vol. 9. Pommern, Berlin 1999, pp. 237–305, at p. 271.

128 S.-E. ÅSTRÖM, The Swedish Economy and Sweden's Role as a Great Power, 1632–1697, in M. ROBERTS (ed.), Sweden's Age of Greatness 1632–1718, London / Basingstoke 1973, pp. 58–101, at p. 70.

129 E. F. HECKSCHER, Sveriges Ekonomiska Historia. Från Gustav Vasa, Vol. II, Pt. 2, Stockholm 1949, Appendix Tab. 24, 26, 28, 30.

130 D. LUCHT, Pommern: Geschichte, Kultur und Wirtschaft, Bielefeld 1996.

century.[131] Scottish salt exports to Stralsund had increased markedly towards the end of the sixteenth century; in 1595/99 the share of Scots salt imported into Stralsund through the Oresund amounted to 36 per cent of Stralsund's total imports. The Scots had thus increased their share in Stralsund's total salt imports by a factor of three over a period of just under 20 years, very obviously, as the Sound Toll Registers suggest, at the expense of Portuguese marine salt.[132] In fact, during the seventeenth century, Scotland, alongside Lübeck, was Stralsund's main source of foreign salt. Furthermore, as salt was one of Scotland's major industrial exports at the time, and Stralsund shipping was freed from paying duty at the Øresund, it is no wonder that Stralsund was one of the largest and most popular destinations for Scottish exports at the time.[133] At that time exports from Scotland to Stralsund on the Scottish side mainly went through Leith, but at least in the case of Scots salt, "Leith" might as well have been a lump sum declaration employed in the Sound Toll Registers for the "Firth of Forth".[134] Some of the Scots salt was further re-exported from Stralsund to other destinations in mainland Sweden.[135]

During the early seventeenth century Scotland thus occupied third place (after Bergen and the Netherlands) in Stralsund's seaborne imports, whilst England, a much more powerful country and larger economy, was of no relevance whatsoever as a trading partner for Stralsund.[136] This situation continued beyond the mid-1650s. During the Thirty Years' War, Scottish links with Stralsund were particularly strong and obviously related to geo-political contingencies. Recent research on Scots employed in Sweden's higher military service during the Thirty Years' War for instance has found that Scotsmen ranged amongst the largest non-Swedish ethnic groups from which higher officials servicing in the Swedish army were drawn. Scottish governors abounded in Swedish service all across the Swedish empire between 1629 and 1698.[137] Sadly this research has failed, however, to go further and ask whether this would also have led to an increase in trading connections between Scotland and those parts in the Swedish dominions that were governed by Scotsmen. Nevertheless, it seems at least worth noting that at precisely the same time in which Scotland appears to have occupied third place in Stralsund's seaborne imports and

---

131 J. SCHILDHAUER, Hansestädtischer Alltag. Untersuchungen auf der Grundlage der Stralsunder Bürgertestamente vom Anfang des 14. bis zum Ausgang des 16. Jahrhunderts, Weimar 1992, p. 83, pp. 85s. T. BRÜCK, Korporationen der Schiffer und Bootsleute. Untersuchungen zu ihrer Entwicklung in Seestädten an der Nord- und Ostseeküste vom Ende des 15. bis zum Ende des 17. Jahrhunderts, Weimar 1994, p. 89.

132 K.-P. ZOELLNER, Vom Strelasund zum Oslofjord. Untersuchungen zur Geschichte der Hanse und der Stadt Stralsund in der zweiten Hälfte des 16. Jahrhunderts, Weimar 1974, pp. 74–88, esp. at p. 75, 87; Appendix, Tab. 21b.

133 BUCHHOLZ, Pommern, p. 272; H. BRANIG, Geschichte Pommerns (ed. W. BUCHHOLZ), Pt. II. Von 1648 bis zum Ende des 18. Jahrhunderts, Cologne / Weimar / Vienna 2000, p. 125.

134 OLECHNOWITZ, Handel, p. 110.

135 Ibid., p. 113.

136 H. LANGER, Stralsund 1600–1630. Eine Hansestadt in der Krise und im Europäischen Konflikt, Weimar 1970, pp. 119s., p. 125, p. 128, p. 133.

137 A. GROSJEAN, A Century of Scottish Governorship in the Swedish Empire, 1574–1700, in: A. MACKILLOP / S. MURDOCH (eds.), Military Governors and Imperial Frontiers c. 1600–1800, Leiden / Boston 2003, pp. 53–78.

exports (c.1628–30), the Swedish military governor of Stralsund also happened to be a Scot.[138] Perhaps these geo-political contingencies might serve to explain a particularly strong Stralsund-Scotland connection during the central years of the seventeenth century, or a generally strong link between Scottish and Swedish ports in the mid-1600s, which in relative terms appears to have been stronger for instance than the connections between Scotland and Hamburg and Bremen, ports that were located much closer to Scotland and easier to reach than Stralsund.

In the early eighteenth century, this pattern changed. As mentioned above, the annexation of Hither Pomerania by Sweden after the Thirty Years' War was accompanied by a commercial policy directed at integrating Stralsund and its hinterland into the Swedish economy and subject the city's economic activities to the needs of the Swedish state.[139] Stralsund's economic decline can be captured in fairly straightforward terms: in 1720 the exemption from the Sound Toll was waived; between 1732 and 1747 the town witnessed the subsequent bankruptcy of 20 resident merchant houses. Her trade shifted towards intra-Baltic commerce but, in an unequal and almost "colonial" exchange mechanism, focused chiefly on the supply of raw materials to Sweden proper.[140] If there were exports from *Scotland* to Stralsund in the period under consideration (1700–1770), these were mainly Scots salt and, to a lesser extent, coals, the staple exports to this destination since the later sixteenth and in the seventeenth century. These exports, however, levelled off after 1746 (see below), after which Stralsund becomes virtually absent from Scottish customs accounts as a declared destination.[141] The detailed discussion on the salt trade below will demonstrate that what had once been a considerably large market for Scots salt – mainly Danzig, but presumably Stralsund as well – in the eighteenth century was all but non-existent. Scotland in turn did not usually import anything in substantial quantities from Stralsund, either between 1770 and 1770 (or, for that matter, other Baltic German ports). *Rostock* which during the seventeenth century had also received notable quantities of Scots salt and coals at times[142], in the eighteenth century virtually disappeared as an export or import declaration from the Scottish customs accounts.[143]

In general, therefore, Scottish-German trade in the eighteenth century went through the North Sea and mainly via Hamburg and Bremen. Notwithstanding some marks of decline observable in Baltic ports after 1700, the preceding remarks on the

138 Between 1679 and 1697 the Swedish governor again was a Scot, one Peter MacLean. Generally speaking Scots appear to have been the largest group of foreign mercenaries as well as higher military officials enlisted in the Swedish Army during the Thirty Years War. GROSJEAN, Scottish Governorship, pp. 62s., and Tab. 3 (pp. 60s.) and 5 (p. 70f).

139 LANGER, Stralsund, p. 128.

140 R. KUSCH, Stralsund von 1720 bis 1815, in: H. EWE (ed.), Geschichte der Stadt Stralsund, Weimar 1984, pp. 202–233, at p. 202–204.

141 With the exception of 1749, when one ton of coals was exported thence from Bo'ness, and 1752, when 16 tons 10 cwt of lead and one ton of coals were exported from Leith and Bo'ness, respectively. No imports were recorded during 1743–55.

142 OLECHNOWITZ, Handel, p. 95.

143 Due to a 3 per cent excise on imports, Rostock lost some shares of her trade to Lübeck, where this excise was not levied. BEUTIN, Seehandel, p. 83.

Sound Toll Registers should also have clarified that the conclusion of a mere reduction of the Baltic in terms of its share in world trade vis-à-vis the Atlantic would be premature.[144] It has been explained in the introduction that, due to the better nature and larger quantity of Scottish records, time series on the Scottish-German trade volume need to be based mainly on the Scottish series of records. Any discussion on structure and fluctuations in the eighteenth-century Scottish-German trade volume thus needs to start with British (read: Scottish) records. Thus the following remarks on the general pattern of mutual trade between Scotland and Germany will bear out a decidedly British/Scottish viewpoint.

144 J. A. FABER, Structural Changes in the European Economy during the Eighteenth Century as Reflected in the Baltic Trade, in: W. G. HEERES / L. M. J. B. HESP / L. NOORDEGRAAF / R. C. W. VAN DER VOORT (eds.), From Dunkirk to Danzig. Shipping and Trade in the North Sea and the Baltic, 1350–1850, Amsterdam 1988, pp. 83–94.

3. STRUCTURAL ASPECTS, TRENDS AND FLUCTUATIONS IN SCOTTISH-GERMAN TRADE, 1700–1770

3.1 Fluctuations: Trends and Cycles

Scottish-German trading relationships are old and can with confidence be dated back to the Middle Ages. "By the later thirteenth century merchants from western Germany were visiting Scotland. Little is known about their trade, though they probably shipped wool, wool fleeces, and hides to the Low Countries."[145] To Scotland came mostly manufactured items. During the Scottish Wars of Independence (1296–1328), for instance, German merchants supplied the Scots with arms and victuals; some of this traffic was even routed via England.[146] In 1297 the political administrator of Scotland's *communitas regni* after the death of the Scottish monarch (Alexander II), William "Braveheart" Wallace, wrote a letter to the Hansa towns of Lübeck and Hamburg, urging them to continue trading with Scotland. This activity had been slightly discouraged by the attempts at establishing a complete embargo on Scotland's foreign trade by the English king's military campaigns. "Soon afterwards, direct trade with western Germany ceased, although Rhenish wine continued to be imported via the Low Countries. Contacts with northern Germany continued, but remained generally limited. Beer was probably the most important import from this region."[147] There appear, however, to have been regular shipping links between Bremen and Edinburgh throughout the fourteenth century. During the same period the Hanseatic League appears to have had resident factors in Leith, Dundee, Aberdeen and Glasgow.[148] In the fifteenth to seventeenth centuries there was a regular yet comparatively small direct trade between Scotland and Germany as well. The main exports from Scotland to German ports were coals, (woollen, later linen) cloth and salt.[149] Bremen and Hamburg merchants commenced on their direct fish imports from the Shetlands in the later fifteenth century.[150] From German ports such as Hamburg, Rostock and Stralsund came timber items.[151] In the 1690s,

145 D. DITCHBURN, Trade with Northern Europe: Scottish Ports, in: P. G. B. MCNEILL / H. L. MACQUEEN (eds.), Atlas of Scottish History to 1707, Edinburgh 1996, p. 262.

146 D. DITCHBURN, Trade with Northern Europe: Baltic Ports, in: MCNEILL / MACQUEEN (eds.), Atlas, p. 264–5, p. 264. W. STANFORD REID, Trade, Traders, and Scottish Independence, in: Speculum, XXIX, 2, 1 (1954), pp. 210–222, at p. 218; J. W. DILLEY, German Merchants in Scotland, 1297–1327, in: Scottish Historical Review, XXVII, 103 (1948), pp. 142–155.

147 DITCHBURN, Trade with Northern Europe: Baltic Ports, p. 265.

148 S. G. E. LYTHE / J. BUTT, An Economic History of Scotland, 1100–1939, Glasgow / London 1975, pp. 57s.

149 M. LYNCH / D. DITCHBURN / J. BROWN, Scottish Trade in the Seventeenth Century, in: MCNEILL / MACQUEEN (eds.), Atlas, pp. 266–283. D. DITCHBURN, Scotland and Europe: The Medieval Kingdom and its Contacts with Christendom, c.1215–1545, Vol. 1: Religion, Culture and Commerce, East Linton 2000, p. 178–180, p. 188.

150 Ibid., pp. 147s.

151 Ibid., p. 159.

> [i]mports from Hamburg and Bremen were purchased in the Forth by exports of coal; most of the loaded incoming ships were German boats sailing for Leith, which received four or five a year in the early sixteen-eighties. Trade with the area was thus very slight, though it supported a Scottish factor there in the sixteen-nineties. The animosity of the Merchant Adventurers of England to all Scottish subjects trading at their Hamburg staple may have had something to do with it, but the Germans themselves could find little to offer in exchange for Scots coal.[152]

This is perhaps not an entirely fair assessment. Preserved volumes of the Hamburg Admiralty Toll accounts from the mid-seventeenth century seem to confirm that in fact many ships sailed to Scotland in ballast, but timber products, mainly barrel staves, honey, copper and copper manufactures, as well as alum and some tobacco would reach Scottish ports from Hamburg, too. Coal and salt were literally the only articles received from Scotland in return.[153] This situation was, however, different with regard to the Shetland trades, one specialty of Hamburg merchants. In exchange for salt fish, as well as butter and fish oil, the Hamburg merchants, which normally also were ship's captains, frequently sent essentials such as salt, meal, beer and iron tools to the Shetland Islands.[154] This overall pattern was to change after 1707. With the inclusion of Scots traders into the framework of the English Navigation Acts, imports of German linens, as well as re-exports of rice, tobacco and sugar became increasingly important.

The short-lived and quite ill-fated "Scottish East and West India Company", which has become famous for the abortive colonization scheme in the Isthmus of Darien (Panama), also sought to establish exclusive commercial relations with the larger Atlantic and Baltic German sea-ports. The former were seen as potential continental markets for the company's anticipated sales of West and East India goods. The venture had been founded and set up as a joint-stock Scottish East India and Africa Company in 1696.[155] In the same year the Company commissioned the construction of four ships in Hamburg. It also presented accounts for subscription in the same place, which for obvious reasons caused English resistance. Whilst the English successfully managed to prevent a broad subscription outside Scotland, the negotiation of a free or staple trade, however, proceeded for some time. The Hamburg interest in this venture was understandable since – in case the establishment of the Scottish Company had turned out successful – it would have amounted to a short-circuiting of London with regard to supplying colonial goods to the German

152 T. C. SMOUT, Scottish Trade on the Eve of Union 1660–1707, Edinburgh / London 1963, p. 166.

153 M. REIßMANN, Die hamburgische Kaufmannschaft des 17. Jahrhunderts in sozialgeschichtlicher Sicht, Hamburg 1975, pp. 56–58.

154 Ibid., pp. 71–73.

155 Its official name was "Company of Scotland Trading to Africa and the Indies". Even though Scots Law and the fact that until 1707 Scotland remained a sovereign state both permitted the establishment of such a company, from the English point of view the establishment of a Scottish East India Company was a clear break of the charter of the London-based English East India Company. The Scottish Company was thus from the point of its foundation doomed to failure, as the English did their best at destroying it right from the beginning. C. A. WHATLEY (with D. PATRICK), The Scots and the Union, Edinburgh 2006, pp. 166–175; M. LYNCH, Scotland. A New History, Edinburgh, 8th ed. 1997, pp. 307–9. G. P. INSH, The Company of Scotland Trading to Africa and the Indies, London / New York 1932, pp. 82–105.

consumer. But English pressure proved abortive to all components of the trading proposal; the overall fate of the Darien scheme is well known.[156]

Scots even made inroads far into central German areas much earlier than that. Mostly they did so as itinerant hucksters, peddlers and petty traders. From at least the later fifteenth century onwards the term "Schotte" became so proverbial in certain areas of Germany and the continent, from the Tyrol far up to Poland-Lithuania and Prussia, that by then in all probability it covered virtually all peddlers, regardless whether they were actually Scottish, Irish or members of another ethnic community. The Articles of Meran for instance, issued by the town of the same name during the German Peasants' War (1525), lamented upon itinerant and ubiquitous Scots, as well as people from the Netherlands and Savoy. The latter groups, being peddlers alike, were by that date already subsumed under the heading "Scot", which conveys a great deal about the perception of Scots (and Irishmen, which in contemporary usage, as well as by the Latin term *Scotus*, were covered under the label "Scots", too) in central Germany. Scots hucksters, according to the Meran articles (1525), carried their circulating capital on their backs ("*meniger umb etlich hŭndert gŭlden krămerei in den kŏrben auf iren rŭcken tragen*"); their goods and economic activity remained untaxed and thus freed from the grip of state and society alike ("*unnd nit nach vermŏgen der war allenthalben abgezolt wirdet* [...] *unnd weder mit stetn oder gerichtn stwern oder raisn, heben noch legen*"), – they were beyond control and thus seen as a potential danger to the stability of an essentially static economy and society.[157] Around the same time the mining town of Annaberg in Saxony dealt with complaints against Scots who had applied for citizenship. It was done *inter alia* on the grounds that these traders accepted the ubiquitous cheap and debased sorts of currency anxiously looked upon by the common folk. In the same way as in the Meran Articles it was alleged that the "Schotten" were still were able to use and export these small denominations with a profit – an opportunity precluded to most members of society.[158]

Eighteenth century commercial fluctuations between Scotland and Germany can be reconstructed from the Scottish customs accounts and trade statistics in fairly precise quantitative terms. Between 1743 and 1770 the picture obtains as follows:

156 See works referred to in the previous note. By the Treaty of Union (1707), however, the Scots gained full legal access to England's Atlantic empire and its commodities (sugar, tobacco, rum, rice, slaves) and thus received part of what they had hoped to achieve with their misconceived attempt at colonization in Panama (Isthmus of Darien). Only participation in the (East) India trades (mainly tea and spices) remained as limited to personal membership after 1707 as it had been before (English East India Company).

157 Meran Articles, 1525, quoted in H. WOPFNER (ed.), Acta Tirolensia. Urkundliche Quellen zur Geschichte Tirols, Vol. 3. Quellen zur Geschichte des Bauernkriegs in Deutschtirol 1525, Pt. I, Innsbruck 1908, pp. 40s.

158 Acts and minutes anent itinerant Scots, Annaberg City Council, 16. Century, quoted in: FÖRDERVEREIN ZUR WIEDERERRICHTUNG DES BARBARA UTHMANN-DENKMALS AUF DEM ANNABERGER MARKT E.V. (eds.), Barbara Uthmann in Annaberg, Annaberg-Buchholz 2002. I am indebted to Ms. K. Morgenstern for bringing this document to my attention.

Figure 6: Scottish Trade with Germany, 1743–1770

1743–1755, NAS, E504. 1755–1770, TNA, Customs 14.

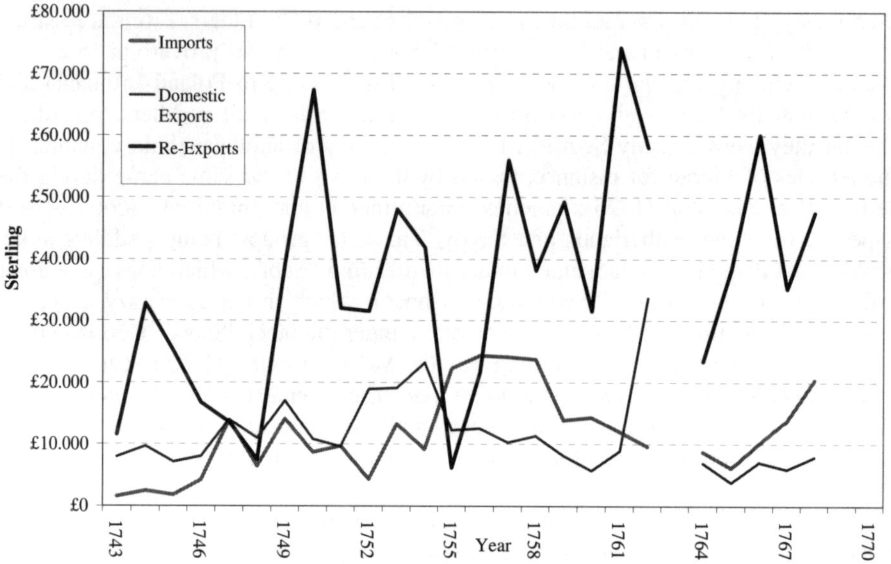

Exports and re-exports were not subject to any apparent similar cyclical movement, as is borne out by a coefficient of correlation of R = .08 for domestic exports and re-exports from Scotland to Germany, 1743–1770. Without doubt the overall pattern, however, was driven by re-exports. The statistical material, which is admittedly incomplete (1763, 1769 values are missing), points towards two seven-year cycles (exports), the first running from 1748 to 1755, and the second from 1755 to 1762–3 (each trough to trough). Both can be retraced in remote form in the general pattern of Scotland's gross total trade of which we know that slumps were experienced in 1755 and 1762. Without doubt this cycle was caused in part by the Seven Years' War, which led to temporary disruptions of (mainly English) shipping and a shortfall of supplies in particular of colonial goods to European markets. Here – at least with regard to the German market – the Scots "jumped in", increasing their re-export activity to continental markets at the expense of the English (chapter 4, section IV.2.2).

But apart from war, the second half of the 1750s was also a time of repeated harvest failures and thus saw a general increase in the price level for consumables all across Germany, which were not just due to war-induced interruptions and shortfalls of shipping. In Scotland's case, this situation even further stimulated re-exports to this destination.

Figure 7: Prices for selected Colonial Goods on the North German Market (Hamburg)

H.-J. GERHARD / K.-H. KAUFHOLD (eds.), Preise im Vor- und Frühindustriellen Deutschland. Nahrungsmittel – Getränke – Gewürze, Rohstoffe und Gewerbeprodukte, Stuttgart 2001.

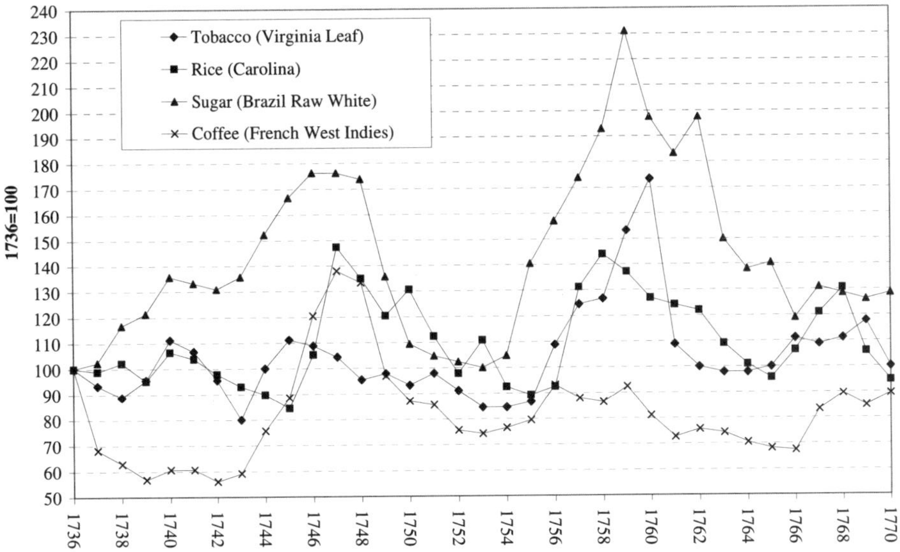

Scottish exports to Hamburg likewise expanded throughout the century.

Figure 8: Scottish Exports to Hamburg, 1733–1800[159]

SCHNEIDER et al. (eds.), Statistik. Scotland: NAS, E504 (customs accounts).

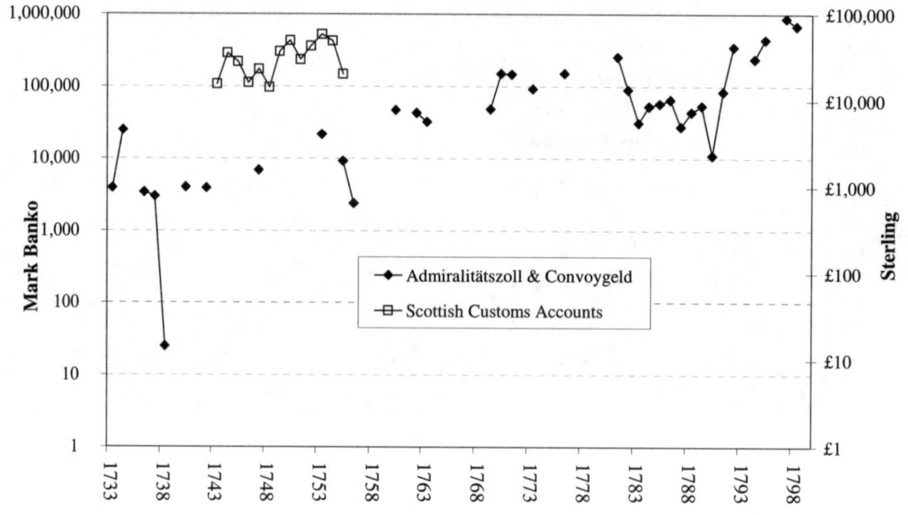

But whilst between 1755 and 1770 Scotland's total exports were on an almost continuously expanding trajectory, the pattern in total exports to Germany was highly erratic. Total imports from Germany on the other hand, followed a modestly increasing trend. It is likewise important to bear in mind that to infer too much into a pattern of Scottish trade with Germany, which on average accounted for less than five per cent of Scotland's gross total trade, means to infer trends which on a macro-level might not be too significant.

The "bottom line" of Scottish-German trade in the eighteenth century can be worked out most clearly from an examination of the series' linear trends. Without doubt a notable and most characteristic feature of the series for Scottish trade with Germany was the fact that trade was driven by re-exports.[160]

159 I should like to express my thanks to Mr Frank Schulenburg for providing the Hamburg data via email attachment.

160 Cf. RÖSSNER, In the Wake, ch. 8.

Figure 9: The Long-term Trend in Scottish Imports from, Exports and Re-exports to German Ports, 1743–1770

Source: Fig. 4.

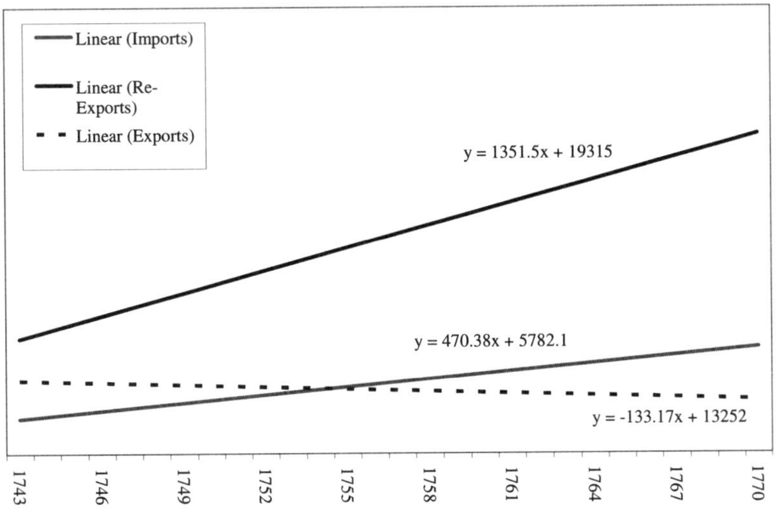

Re-exports clearly showed the strongest expansionary dynamics over the period. They drove the trades and determined the cyclical pattern of total exports. It was tobacco, sugar and rice, which not only accounted for the largest share in total exports from Scotland to Germany. These commodities also determined the pattern in a way that could perhaps be formulated in generalized terms thus: "Overseas merchant x resident in port y, mainly active in the American trades, regularly dispatched his tobacco and rice to Germany, if he had any cargoes left after he had sent ships with the same commodities to the Netherlands. In addition he filled up extra space in the ship with some domestically manufactured stockings." The initial reason for trading to Germany was not German demand for Scottish domestic products, such as woollen stockings or salt, but for overseas non-essentials, which the German consumer could not obtain directly (see sections below). Thus, the structure and composition of the Scottish-German trade volume needs some elaboration prior to a detailed analysis of the fluctuations in the commodity trades.

3.2 The Share of "Germany" in the Scottish Volume of Trade

Tables 1.1.1–2 in the Appendix provide an overview on total Scottish trade with Germany and the weight of imports and exports to Germany in Scotland's total trade, 1755–1770. From this, an average of two per cent obtains for imports, three per cent for exports, and seven per cent for re-exports. Although these figures were subject to considerable inter-annual variation and are moreover highly marred and in parts unreliable, they can probably be seen as a rough yet valid estimate. Overall, Germany appears to have been of minor importance in Scotland's gross total trade. The same certainly applies to the reverse case. Recorded and taxed imports from Scotland into Hamburg were about as significant for Hamburg's (import) trade as Hamburg was for Scotland.[161] The situation probably applied to Germany in general.

Nevertheless, there were branches of trade with Germany which regularly exceeded the average figures. In other words: there were a group of commodities for which German ports represented either the largest or by any standard a significant market in the eighteenth century. For imports, this was not at all surprising, German linens, competing with Scotch and Irish plain items in the British colonies. For exports, this was Scots salt, coal, at times vitriol oil, and most importantly fish. Amongst re-exports, it was rice that occupied a share well above average, dispatched mainly to Bremen. Tobacco did so, too, but on a much smaller scale. All of these commodities will be looked at in greater detail below (chapter 4). What can be said about the regional distribution of these trades? On the German side such a discussion is impossible as only the Hamburg records have been surveyed so far; these records however, as has been mentioned in chapter two, only covered select branches of the Hamburg commodity trades, so that a break-down of these figures into regional shares would be unlikely to heighten our overall understanding of the prevailing trade pattern much further.

3.3 Scottish Ports Involved in the German Trades

If the full set of Scottish port books (customs accounts) examined for the years 1743–1755 with regard to trade with Germany is taken as a sample, Scotland's gross total trade with Germany can be broken down as follows[162]:

161 Personal conversation and email correspondence with Mr Frank Schulenburg. See also figures in KRAWEHL et al. (eds.), Statistik.

162 The following classification has been employed: East: Alloa, Anstruther, Bo'ness, Dunbar, Dundee, Kirkcaldy, Leith, Montrose, Perth, Prestonpans. West: Ayr, Campbeltown, Dumfries, Greenock, Irvine, Kirkcudbright, Port Glasgow, Portpatrick, Stranraer, Wigtown. Highlands & Islands: Caithness, Fort William, Inverness, Orkney, Shetland.

Table 5: The Distribution of the Scottish-German Trade Volume by Scottish Regions, 1743–1755 (gross total trade, £Sterling in 1755 values)

NAS, E504, Full Set of Scottish Customs Accounts

	Sterling	
EAST	£285,687	42%
WEST	£292,942	43%
HIGHLANDS & ISLANDS	£101,393	15%
TOTAL	£680,022	100%

It appears as though trade was fairly evenly distributed between the eastern and western region of Scotland.[163] Monitoring these patterns by gross total trade, however, presents the danger of over-looking basically different patterns prevailing for total imports and exports. Moreover, defining a complete run of 13 adjacent years as a sample rather than a time series might conceal certain shifts in patterns that took place within this (admittedly) short run of years, 1743–1755. Thus, a slightly more detailed view can be presented in the following way.

Shetland appears to have been the largest outport (Customs precinct) involved in *exports of domestic produce* from Scotland to Germany in value terms. This was due to the large exports of cod and ling fish and related commodities arising as by-products from the particular feudal exchange mechanism by which landlords appropriated these fish.[164]

Table 6: Scottish Exports to Germany by Ports (4-year-averages), 1743–1755 (Shares)

1751–1755: five year average
NAS, E504, Full Set of Scottish Customs Accounts

	Glasgow	Leith	Aberdeen	Shetland	Others
1743/46	0%	5%	3%	67%	25%
1747/50	0%	16%	4%	54%	27%
1751/55	0%	9%	38%	40%	13%

In terms of domestic exports to Germany, Greenock and Port Glasgow were entirely irrelevant. As with re-exports (see below), Aberdeen gained in commercial importance in the later 1740s; in the case of domestic exports somewhat at the expense of Shetland.

With regard to *re-exports from Scotland to Germany*, an interesting development can be observed in the late 1740s and early 1750s. At that time, Aberdeen and Leith experienced a sharp yet short-lived increase in their commercial activity, due to re-exports of tobacco to Germany. This took place obviously at the expense of Glasgow (and Bo'ness, which in this instance needs to be seen as a "Glaswegian" outport). Orkney also rose to quite large dimensions at times (re-export trade in American goods), which in the case of the rice trade, and according to contemporaries, could be

163 For a comprehensive discussion see ROESSNER, Foreign Trade, ch. 5.

164 SMITH, Shetland.

explained by the fact that the northern route across the Atlantic was favoured over the southerly routes, due to the risk of capture posed by (French) privateers.

Table 7: Scottish Re-exports to Germany by ports (4-year-averages), 1743–1755 (Shares)

1751–1755: five year average
NAS, E504, Full Set of Scottish Customs Accounts

	Glasgow	Bo'ness	Ayr	Leith	Aberdeen	Orkney	Other
1743/46	84%	5%	1%	6%	0%	4%	0%
1747/50	74%	9%	0%	6%	6%	1%	3%
1751/55	45%	0%	9%	5%	31%	2%	7%

In absolute figures, both Aberdeen's exports, as well as re-exports rose quickly between 1749 and 1752/1754, only too fall back again thereafter. Most of it was tobacco (87 to 100 per cent).[165]

The pattern of *imports* was fairly straightforward. As will be shown below[166], more than two-thirds of total imports into Scottish ports from Germany were linens, mostly of the Narrow German type, which were not normally consumed within Scotland, but rather sent on to the Americas. With Bo'ness and Leith attaining the highest shares, it is clear that these linens were preferably imported through East coast ports, presumably not only due to navigational convenience, but also because the east coast's commercial relations to the German states were stronger than the West's. Bo'ness was favoured by the Glaswegian colonial trades as an eastern outlet, which explains its considerable weight in imports from Germany.

165 NAS, E504/1/1–6. According to the information contained in the Aberdeen customs accounts as to the names of exporting merchants, this quick but brief expansion, which also made Aberdeen's share of total re-exports to Germany rise quickly to levels of over ten per cent, was mainly due to the activity of: William and Alexander Copland, Gilbert More, Alexander Livingston, a company or co-partnership for which no records could be traced so far.

166 Ch. 4.

Figure 10: Scottish Imports from Germany by Ports, 1743–1755 (Shares)

NAS, E504.

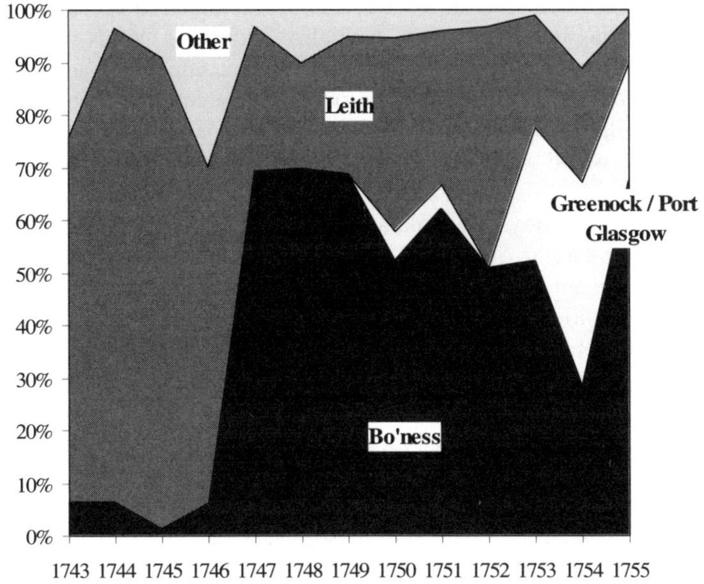

If the complete set of customs accounts examined for 1743–1755 is interpreted as a time series rather than a sample (although it is critical to infer significant commercial trends based on a set of evidence covering only 13 years), it appears as though Bo'ness shortly gained at the expense of Leith, only to lose some of its weight shortly thereafter to Glasgow. After 1753 Glasgow merchants seem to have increasingly resorted to direct imports of linen rather than relying on Bo'ness and Leith.

3.4 The Composition of the Scottish-German Trade Volume – A Sketch of Explanations

The structure of the German-Scottish trade volume can be explained in several ways. Trade theory for instance has it that countries specialize, exporting goods in which they enjoy a comparative advantage. Those goods in which the comparative advantage is greatest, i.e. in which country x (*Home*) has the smallest relative production factor input requirement (or the largest productivity differential compared to country y or *Foreign* or "the rest of the world") will be exported in first place, and then down the line of declining productivity differentials. From the point (commodity) in which *Foreign* (or rest of the world) enjoys a comparative advantage, commodities will be imported into *Home*. The largest item on *Home's* import account will be the commodity in which *Foreign* enjoys the largest comparative advantage, and so on.

There are several difficulties with this model if it is to be used as a heuristic approach to a historical phenomenon such as Scottish-German trade 1700–1770. First, it is essentially a bilateral model, even though the implicit assumption is that *Foreign* equals "rest of the world". A truly bilateral view of trade, as in the present case Scottish trade with Germany, may be an analytical isolation that does not necessarily reflect comparative advantage accurately on either side (the Scottish economy; the German economy). It could in fact distort the impression to an uninformed reader, who from the observation that Scotland's domestic exports to Germany were dominated by fish, coal, lead and salt, might conclude that Scotland enjoyed a general comparative advantage in the production of fish and minerals (which it might have, but these items were of no great significance in Scotland's total exports in the same period). We know for instance that Scots salt, which attained significantly high shares in domestic exports to Germany at times (see Appendix and chapter four), was of negligible importance in terms of its share in *total* Scottish exports at the time, as by the middle of the century, the Scottish salt industry had been finally overtaken in terms of its competitiveness on world markets by the English, facing harsh competition from better and more efficient producers across the north-western European shore, mainly Portugal, Spain, France and England. Thus one ought not to be misled just from the partial analysis of Scottish-German trade to take these commodities as representative for successful production branches of the early eighteenth-century Scottish economy as such.

Secondly, the comparative advantage model, whether based on differential factor endowment or wage and production cost differentials, simplifies reality by dealing with countries, thus potentially concealing regional differences prevailing *within* these countries or economies. Thus it could be expected that, if coal and lead were exported from Scotland, they would be so predominantly from the Firth of Forth ports adjacent to the mineral-rich deposits of the central-lowland area, but not from ports in the Orkneys or Shetlands. The Shetlands on the other hand would be the main, or at times sole, port of origin of exports of cod and ling fish to German ports, due to the adjacent fishing grounds. The same almost certainly applied to Germany as well. Therefore, statistical units of measure such as "Scotland" and "Germany" are to a certain extent an arbitrary choice, neglecting the existence of prevailing differential regional economies.

Generally speaking, early modern European economy and society were no particularly favourable environment for mutual foreign trade relationships to develop beyond very modest levels. Trade levels per capita were small; the Europeans' propensity to trade was low, compared to the post-1800 era. The Scottish-German trade volume was accordingly small and its composition "unspectacular". The only real or significant source of dynamics was re-exports. The latter, via imports of German linens and exports of sugar and tobacco from Scotland to Germany, connected the Holy Roman Empire with the British-American or Atlantic trades, which expanded considerably after 1740.

Upper ceilings on productivity and per capita incomes, which had been reached in the sixteenth century, and which were perhaps been temporarily left later in the seventeenth century, were reached in fact again in most of early eighteenth century German territories, particularly after 1740 (although the absence of more data and the difference in regional structures strictly speaking does not allow such a generalized statement). On average, as in most areas of the continent at the time, the pre-industrial consumer's budget would have been limited and subject to multiple constraints:

> In the normal run of events the plenty of the harvest home gave way in due course to the short commons of the spring. Lent was as much an economic necessity as a religious obligation. Those – perhaps the minority – for whom the rotting meat of winter had been made more palatable by a lavish addition of spices needed little compulsion to restrict their diet of fish in March while the majority eked out their dwindling supplies of grain till the new harvest. As feasts punctuated with gluttony the tedium of a more restricted dietary, so fasts gave official sanction to curbs on consumption which would nonetheless have been necessary. Good harvests ensured a prospect of reasonable food supplies through the winter: bad harvests meant stringency and malnutrition for many and starvation for some.[167]

In the same way eighteenth-century German society and economy were characterized by low per capita incomes and an extreme inequality in the distribution of wealth.[168] Social and economic historians have even labelled the eighteenth century a "Century of Hunger", an observation borne out by the results of the Abel School with regard to a general decline in real wages and living standards and thus very probably per capita national income throughout many areas of Europe, in particular after 1740.[169] During the time under consideration, for about 75 to 80 per cent of the population there would not have been left much of an additional spending margin over subsistence

167 W. MINCHINTON, Patterns and Structure of Demand, 1500–1750, in: C. M. CIPOLLA (ed.), The Fontana Economic History of Europe, Vol. 2. The Sixteenth and Seventeenth Centuries, Glasgow 1974, pp. 83–176, at p. 116.

168 NORTH, Von der Atlantischen Handelsexpansion bis zu den Agrarreformen, p. 173, p. 187. C. M. CIPOLLA, Before the Industrial Revolution. European Society and Economy 1000–1700, London / New York, 3rd ed. 1993, pp. 22–37.

169 M. MONTANARI, La fame e l'abbondanza, Rome / Bari 1993, German trans., Der Hunger und der Überfluß. Kulturgeschichte der Ernährung in Europa, Munich, 2nd ed. 1999, chs. 28–33; ABEL, Agrarkrisen, Engl. Transl. Agricultural Fluctuations in Europe from the Thirteenth to the Twentieth Centuries, London 1980; ID., Massenarmut und Hungerkrisen im vorindustriellen Deutschland, Göttingen 1971; ID., Stufen der Ernährung. Eine historische Skizze, Göttingen 1981; B. H. SLICHER VAN BATH, The Agrarian History of Western Europe, A.D. 500–1850, London 1963. W. ACHILLES, Landwirtschaft in der Frühen Neuzeit, Munich 1991, esp. pp. 63–89.

requirements.[170] Somewhat in consequence the rural areas of Germany, including the smaller or agrarian towns, were largely self-sufficient in the early modern period and remained so during the eighteenth century.[171] Under these parameters the German (and Scottish) propensity to trade would have been low on a virtually permanent basis, ruling out particularly large levels of mutual trade.

Accordingly, and very unsurprisingly, Scottish *domestic exports* – small as they were in relative terms – to Germany were dominated by primary products.

Table 8: The Changing Composition of Scotland's Domestic Exports to Germany, 1745–9 and 1755–9

Source: 1745–9: NAS, E504; 1755–9: TNA, Customs 14
Five-year-averages. Limit to total imports of £10 or over.

	1745/9			1755/9		
	£ Sterling			£ Sterling		
Animal Products	6,487		57%	6,390		63%
Vegetable Products	2,150		19%	178		2%
Minerals	2,121		19%	1,612		16%
Worsted Stockings		591	5%		938	9%
Woollendries		13	0%			
Leather Manufactures		38	0%		209	2%
Vitriol Oil					792	8%
Total Manufactures	642		6%	1,938		19%

The share of primary exports declined slightly from a total of 76 per cent (1745–9) to 63 per cent (1755–9), as did minerals (coal, salt, lead); both at the expense of "manufactures". The latter was mainly due to a spectacular, yet temporary, expansion of vitriol oil exports, which dwindled away after 1760 and only experienced a further expansion in the 1780s. Primary exports were dominated by fish, mainly cod and ling, but also herring and salmon. Exports of cereals declined towards the end of the period, as since the late 1750s Scotland became a permanent net-importer of grain.[172]

Scottish *imports* from Germany were dominated by the item *Narrow German* linen, a label which appears without further comment as to the type and origin of this product in the Scottish customs accounts.[173] As the bulk of these linens was imported through Bremen, they presumably originated chiefly in the big west-central German

170 Especially the rise of the "sub-peasant" strata in rural society in many German territories would have represented one key barrier to economic growth: W. TROSSBACH, Bauern 1648–1806, Munich 1993, pp. 31–44 and ACHILLES, Landwirtschaft, pp. 107–120. H. WUNDER, Agriculture and Agrarian Society, in OGILVIE (ed.), Germany, Vol. II, pp. 63–99. E. BENZ, Population Change and the Economy, in: ibid., pp. 39–62, esp. at pp. 45–51. For the implications of rural social stratification on employment, incomes and economic growth in the period briefly: S. C. OGILVIE, Proto-Industrialization in Germany, in: ID. / M. CERMAN (eds.), European Proto-industrialization, Cambridge 1996, pp. 118–136.

171 KELLENBENZ, Wirtschaftsgeschichte, Vol. I, p. 344; ID., Außenhandel.

172 Figures for imports and exports of cereals into / from Scotland can be obtained from A. BALD, The Farmer and Corn-Dealer's Assistant, Edinburgh 1780, pp. 437–442. For some critical remarks vide COCHRAN, Scottish Trade with Ireland, pp. 93–114, esp. p. 94, p. 96, pp. 102–105. England: M. OVERTON, Agricultural Revolution in England. The Transformation of the Agrarian Economy 1500–1850, Cambridge 1996, p. 89, Fig. 3.8.

173 See ch. 4, section 4.3.1 below.

linen-weaving belt that included areas such as Westphalia and Osnabrück (hence the term *Osnaburgh*). These areas were located within the Bremen "catchment area", for which the river Weser and thus the port of Bremen served as a distribution channel. The German linens, by their pricing, quality and a generous draw-back upon re-export, were much sought-after in the British colonies, and lent themselves to profitable re-export trading on British account. From the late 1750s and thereafter, a second group of commodities became increasingly important, gaining at the relative expense of linens: cereals, mainly oats, rye and wheat. This was due to Scotland (like England) becoming a net-importer of grain for good after c.1760.

But as mentioned above, the main source of dynamics for Scottish trade with Germany – in fact for eighteenth century trade in general – were re-exports. *Re-exports* dominated Scottish-German gross total trade in value terms. At first sight this corresponded to the commercial patterns of other nations – above all the Dutch, the English, the French, later on the Danes and Swedes. But at second sight, the caesura of 1740, when re-exports of many European countries started to gather momentum appears to be somewhat surprising. From 1740 onwards at latest – the Sound Toll Registers suggest an early starting period around 1720[174] – there was a massive expansion of re-exports of tropical non-essentials, such as tobacco, sugar, coffee from the main colonial powers – England, Scotland and France, and to an extent Denmark-Norway as well – to continental ports all across north-western Europe.[175] But in many areas on the continent the 1740s on the other hand also saw a turning point in economic fluctuations, witnessing sharp declines in real wages and probably per capita real national incomes as well. Possibly it was the general rise of population levels after 1740, which in combination with a progressive decrease in real prices for these products would have created additional demand for re-exports. Scottish-German trade therefore makes for a good case study of eighteenth-century European trade and the distribution of economic power, as one of the subjects examined – Scotland – was part of the "core" or colonial powers, whilst the other – Germany – largely remained on the receiving end; it needs to be remembered that all German attempts at establishing overseas colonies failed during the eighteenth century.

Due to the absence of large trading companies and the fact that no German state maintained overseas colonies on a permanent or cost-effective basis, tropical groceries and beverages, such as tea, sugar, cocoa, coffee and rice could neither be produced in Germany nor be obtained directly on German account; intermediaries had to be used. (Tobacco was an exception as it was widely cultivated in Germany; but the German crop never matched the high-quality brands from the Americas.)[176] Whilst in the mid-

174 STEENSGARD, Long-distance Trade, p. 105, Tab. 3.1.

175 It has been shown in section 3.1 above that England's and Scotland's overseas trade expanded considerably between c. 1740 and 1770, and that this phenomenon was linked to a boom in the re-export trades. (England tended to export more sugar, tea and coffee, alongside rice and tobacco, but Scotland's re-export trade was biased towards tobacco).

176 F.-W. HENNING, Handbuch der Wirtschafts- und Sozialgeschichte Deutschlands, Vol. 1: Deutsche Wirtschafts- und Sozialgeschichte im Mittelalter und in der Frühen Neuzeit, Paderborn 1991, pp. 861s.; NORTH, Kommunikation, p. 26. C. SHAMMAS, The Revolutionary Impact of European Demand for Tropical Goods, in: J. J. MCCUSKER / K. MORGAN (eds.), The Early Modern Atlantic Economy, Cambridge 2000, pp. 163–185.

seventeenth century, Hamburg merchants had a direct trade with the West Indies[177] (they were offered free access to the Danish Caribbean sugar islands / *Dansk Vestindien* in 1767[178]), these direct trades remained small in comparison, as the larger colonial powers, especially Britain, tried, and between 1700 and 1770 largely managed, to safeguard their trading prerogative with the New World.[179] Therefore, from the point of view of the German consumer, intermediaries were needed for the supply of these products, relying on mainly France, then Britain, the Netherlands, and it has to be added, Denmark, for their supply of tobacco, sugar, coffee, ginger and rice.[180] Scotland, which by Act and Treaty of Union since 1707 had full legal access to the English colonies overseas, or better: the commodities enumerated in the English Navigation Acts, thus in theory benefited from the role of being a supplier (or better: intermediary) of these products (consider also the implications of the "staple thesis"). In fact (see section 3.1 above) Scottish overseas trade became, in reaction to these geo-political and institutional constellations, biased towards re-exports of tobacco.

Some dynamics were also observable. During the eighteenth century British real freight rates on tobacco and rice declined progressively, in tobacco's case in the order of approximately 80 per cent between c. 1700 and 1775.[181] Successful business techniques developed by Glaswegian tobacco merchants created asymmetrical credit relationships between "motherland" (here: Glasgow) and the "colonies" (in contemporary language the term "colony" was unknown; the term plantation was used instead), enabling Glaswegian tobacco merchants to offer the product at unbeatable prices to European consumers, as they dictated both the purchasing price in America, as well as the prices for their goods produced in Britain, which they sold to the colonies in return.[182] Without doubt such changes on the supply side had its effects on the final price at which British traders were willing to offer their products to the European consumer. Whilst throughout the eighteenth century, tobacco prices in Germany increased very moderately, victual prices increased faster[183], resulting in a

177 REIßMANN, Kaufmannschaft, pp. 75s.

178 E. KLESSMANN, Geschichte der Stadt Hamburg, Hamburg 2002, p. 228.

179 Most effectively at times when their navies were not too occupied with naval warfare.

180 Not much can be said about the supply of goods provided by the other two major colonial powers, Portugal and Spain, to Germany in the period.

181 R. R. MENARD, Transport Costs and Long-Range Trade, 1300–1800: Was there a European 'Transport Revolution' in the Early Modern Era?, in: TRACY (ed.), Political Economy of Merchant Empires, pp. 228–75. With regard to productivity gains realized in the Glasgow tobacco trades, see J. M. PRICE, The Rise of Glasgow in the Chesapeake Tobacco Trade, 1707–1775, in: William and Mary Quarterly, II (1954), pp. 179–199.

182 See especially T. M. DEVINE, The Tobacco Lords. A Study of the Tobacco Merchants of Glasgow and their Trading Activities 1740–1790, Edinburgh 1975; ID., The Colonial Trades and Industrial Investments in Scotland, c.1700–1815, in: P. EMMER / F. GAASTRA (eds.), The Organization of Interoceanic Trade in European Expansion, 1450–1800, Aldershot 1996, pp. 299–312; I. W. STEVENSON, Some Aspects of the Geography of the Clyde Tobacco Trade in the Eighteenth Century, in: The Scottish Geographical Magazine, LXXXIX (1973), pp. 19–35.

183 H.-J. GERHARD / K.-H. KAUFHOLD (eds.), Preise im Vor- und Frühindustriellen Deutschland. Nahrungsmittel – Getränke – Gewürze, Rohstoffe und Gewerbeprodukte, Stuttgart 2001, Tab. pp. 124s., Tab. A1.08.07. The equation for the linear trend of this time series between 1736 and 1770 works out at $y = 0.2576x + 42.517$, which is a comparatively modest increase (vis-à-vis trends in Abel's graphs on cereal prices during the same period).

long-term decline in the relative or real price of tobacco for the German consumer, c. 1740–1770.

Tobacco and sugar created their own markets, but the purchaser had some saying as well. Especially in free ports such as Hamburg and Altona, where trading was open to all nations at favourable customs rates, the colonial powers had to compete against each other for the German consumer. They did so largely via the price mechanism. In the eighteenth century for instance France's sugar and coffee sales on the Hamburg market always outpaced British sales.[184] This was due to an aggressive, and for the German consumer attractive, pricing policy of the French. In this regard eighteenth-century British suppliers of colonial re-exports to Europe faced a competitive market.

Scottish re-exports to Germany consisted mainly of tobacco and rice, supplemented by insignificant quantities of sugar, tea and coffee. This took account of newly-emerged consumption habits, which were by no means uniform across Europe, even though more precise statements have to await fuller investigation. Tea, sugar and tobacco are believed to have become items of mass consumption in eighteenth-century England, if "mass consumption" is defined as regular, meaning daily, consumption by at least 25 per cent of the population.[185] For continental Europe on the other hand it has also been suggested for example that "sugar and tobacco, like tea, made the leap during the seventeenth century from the exclusive luxury price level down to the mass consumption level."[186] This, however, provides no further insights as to observable sociological patterns of consumption, i.e., where this happened, when exactly, which socio-economic classes in the Weberian sense would have been involved in this process. Here conclusions need to remain speculative, tentative and wide-sweeping. According to MENNINGER, using modern-day average consumption figures, regular daily consumption would have to be formularized thus: tea : coffee : chocolate / cocoa nuts = 0.25 : 1 : 2, or the physical amount necessary for a daily consumption of chocolate for instance would have amounted to about eight times the raw amount of tea necessary for stilling one's daily quench for the item.[187] Needless to say that finding a true average of amounts used is impossible; contemporary guides on how coffee and tea could be "stretched" are legion. There are indications that all classes could have consumed the items under consideration, yet with varying degrees of "purity" of these beverages, an aspect which would have kept the lower classes out of

184 M. A. DENZEL, Zur Geschäftspraxis eines Nanteser Handelshauses: Der Preiskurant von Pelloutier & Cie (1763–1793), in: J. HOOCK / W. REININGHAUS (eds.), Kaufleute in Europa. Handelshäuser und ihre Überlieferung in vor- und frühindustrieller Zeit, Dortmund 1997, pp. 61–87, at p. 78.

185 C. SHAMMAS, The Pre-industrial Consumer in England and America, Oxford 1990, pp. 76–86. England was of course an exceptional performer in early modern European economic history. Being an island, politically unified and a large colonial power, her population benefited from relatively high per capita incomes (or "stage of development"), and thus enjoyed per capita consumption levels of what were in the strictest sense non-essentials such as tea, tobacco, sugar and spices, that were higher than most of the rest of continental Europe.

186 K. GLAMANN, The Changing Patterns of Trade, in: E. E. RICH / C. H. WILSON (eds.), The Cambridge Economic History of Europe, Vol. V: The Economic Organization of Early Modern Europe, Cambridge 1977, pp. 185–289, at p. 212.

187 A. MENNINGER, Genuss im kulturellen Wandel. Tabak, Kaffee, Tee und Schokolade in Europa (16. – 19. Jahrhundert), Stuttgart 2004, pp. 315s.

the phenomenon of "mass-consumerism" in the sense of historical sociology.[188] Given these constraints, one might assume that on the level of the individual consumer, demand for colonial non-essentials in the eighteenth century could be determined by factors such as: (a) disposable personal income; (b) preference or taste (which might explain why tea did not become particularly fashionable in Germany in the eighteenth century whilst coffee would); (c) interest or curiosity; (d) the stimulating, hunger-suppressing, or even mildly hallucinogenic effects of some if consumed in large-enough quantities; (e) conspicuous consumption with the aim at (α) visualizing social stratification or (β) exclusivity within the same social stratum (clubs, societies etc.); (f) conspicuous consumption aimed at pretending or sporting an affiliation to a higher social class the imitation of which (in terms of manners and consumption patterns) appears to be particularly desirable; (g) gender; (h) locality / residence (urban dwellers can be seen as overall more likely to consume exotic non-essentials); and (i) geography in general (i.e. variance in consumption patterns according to different regions).[189] As the present work is not intended to be a study in historical sociology or pre-modern German consumption patterns – such a study is in fact still wanting – these remarks will be left as they stand. They ought to keep the reader aware of the fact that the criteria influencing the composition and size of re-exports to Germany (on Scottish, English, French and Danish accounts chiefly), especially the prevailing consumption patterns, are manifold enough in order to forbid generalized or mono-causal explanations.

As opposed to England, tea made no significant inroads into German consumption patterns before 1800 – even though, as Menninger has carefully observed, there were a growing number of complaints pointing towards the opposite, which, however, need to be viewed with a due pinch of salt.[190] German per capita consumption figures for coffee on the other hand seem to have outpaced the British figure by a factor of 2.5 in

188 IBID., pp. 313–320, pp. 337s.

189 R. SANDGRUBER, Genußmittel. Ihre reale und symbolische Bedeutung im neuzeitlichen Europa, in: Jahrbuch für Wirtschaftsgeschichte (1994/1), pp. 73–88, therein references to further literature; W. SCHIVELBUSCH, Das Paradies, der Geschmack und die Vernunft. Eine Geschichte der Genußmittel, Munich / Vienna, 2nd ed. 1981; N. BRÜBACH, 'This Precious Stinke' – Zur Wirtschaftsgeschichte des Tabaks, 1500 – ca. 1800, in: H. POHL (ed.), The European Discovery of the World and its Economic Effects on Pre-industrial Society 1500–1800, Stuttgart 1990, pp. 141–152; J. SCHNEIDER, Produktion, Handel und Konsum von Kaffee (15. bis Ende 18. Jh.), in: Ibid., pp. 122–140; P. K. O'BRIEN, European Industrialization: From the Voyages of Discovery to the Industrial Revolution, in: Ibid., pp. 154–177, esp. at pp. 164–169; S. W. MINTZ, Sweetness and Power. The Place of Sugar in Modern History, New York 1985; H. PIETSCHMANN, Produkte und Techniken aus Übersee in den Europäischen Ökonomien, 12.–18. Jahrhundert: Nahrungsmittel in Westeuropa. Ein Forschungsbericht, in: S. CAVACIOCCHI (ed.), Prodotti e Tecniche d'Oltremare nelle Economie Europee Secc. XIII–XVIII, Prato 1998, pp. 175–204, at pp. 184s. A. EIRAS ROEL, Los productos alimentarios de ultramar. La Europa mediterránea, in: Ibid., pp. 99–144; R. WENDT, Überseeische Ernährungsprodukte im frühneuzeitlichen Zentraleuropa, in: Ibid., pp. 145–174; K. MORGAN, Transatlantic Rice in the European Market in the Eighteenth Century, in: Ibid., pp. 465–475; J. SCHNEIDER, Die neuen Getränke: Schokolade, Kaffee und Tee (16.–18. Jahrhundert), in: Ibid., pp. 541–590; P. SCHMIDT, Tobacco – Its Use and Consumption in Early Modern Europe, in: Ibid., pp. 591–617; MONTANARI, Hunger; ABEL, Stufen; SHAMMAS, Revolutionary Impact.

190 MENNINGER, Genuss, pp. 337s.

the later eighteenth century.[191] Thus disposable income might not necessarily be the main determinant for per capita consumption figures for extra-European non-essentials. Tobacco was mass consumed in many German areas since the mid-seventeenth century (chapter four). Sugar and coffee made this leap later. Rice was a staple crop in southern Europe, and thus an essential; yet it was not consumed in large quantities in north-western Europe. This discussion will be taken up again in the detailed sections on the rice and tobacco trades. Notwithstanding all difficulties of formulating a robust scenario of consumption of tropical non-essentials in eighteenth century Germany (see above), it is clear that German demand for colonial (American) goods increased considerably during the eighteenth century, focusing on sugar, coffee, and tobacco.[192] Amongst 67 small retailers (*Krämer* or *Hoken*) in Hanover in 1764 for instance, 47 sold coffee and 31 colonial sugar on a regular basis. As mentioned previously, most of the colonial foodstuffs imported from America into Bremen and Hamburg on a regular basis were usually quoted regularly on the large German inland fairs of Brunswick, Leipzig and Frankfurt-on-the-Main as well, 1700–1770. A widespread and increasing number of unsuccessful prohibitions relating to the sale of colonial goods have also been taken by historians as evidence for a broad expansion of the consumption of these goods in the period under consideration.[193] Coffee possibly reached a position of a "good of mass-consumerism" by the end of the eighteenth century, but, together with sugar, would in the first half of the century clearly have to be classified as a non-essential item still, being no regular component of the average diet yet.[194] The consumption of tea and chocolate on the other hand does not appear to have become widespread in Northern Germany until very late in the eighteenth century, the first perhaps due to reasons of taste, but chocolate certainly due to the fact that it was the most expensive out of the range of non-essential colonial consumables.[195] They can thus be left out of a discussion on Scottish (or British)-German trade in the eighteenth century, as can be sugar and coffee, which Germany mostly received from France and the Netherlands in the period rather than from Britain.

In this way, Germany – and most parts of continental Europe – experienced a different and slightly lagged pattern of consumption compared to Britain (probably only England), where quite extraordinary levels of per capita consumption of sugar and its three complementary beverages, tea, coffee and chocolate, were reached early

191 Ibid., pp. 334s., Tab. 12 on p. 334.

192 KRIEDTE, Handel, pp.. 34s., SCHIVELBUSCH, Paradies, pp. 82–90.

193 KRIEDTE, Handel, pp. 33s.; SCHNEIDER, Produktion, Handel und Konsum von Kaffee, pp. 132–135; ABEL, Stufen, pp. 55s. Abel, however, stressed the fact that coffee remained a luxury item, even though its consumption spread down the strata of society during the eighteenth century (to rich peasant households – which after 1740 might have benefited from increasing cereal prices).

194 SANDGRUBER, Genußmitttel, p. 74; SCHNEIDER, Schokolade, Kaffee und Tee, pp. 559–563. Supply necessary for "mass consumption": F. BRAUDEL, Civilization and Capitalism, Vol. 1: The Structures of Everyday Life, London, 4th ed. 1986, pp. 251s. MINTZ, Sweetness and Power, ch. 3.

195 SCHNEIDER, Schokolade, Kaffee und Tee, pp. 551–3; ABEL, Stufen, p. 57; SANDGRUBER, Genußmittel, p. 77. Chocolate appears to have been more fashionable in the South (Vienna and other Austrian metropoleis).

in the eighteenth century.[196] Likewise, it needs to be stressed that demand for colonial non-essentials was regionally differentiated in England.[197] There is ample analytical reason to assume a similar situation for the German states.

Thus the general growth dynamics observable in European trade, especially within the quantitative and institutional framework of the "Atlantic Economy" after the 1720s, including British, French, Danish and Swedish "colonial trades", as well as the "triangular system" connecting Africa, the West Indies, North America and the continental "global players" such as England-Scotland, France, Holland, and to a lesser extent the Iberian Peninsula, explain the dominant role which re-exports of colonial goods played in *Scottish-German trade* in the eighteenth century. Having explained the basic composition of the Scottish-German trade volume in broad terms, some commodities of particular importance will now be discussed. These, as hinted above, will be such commodities for which Germany either represented the most significant market or, as in salt's case, commodities coming from Scotland, which were the most important foreign specimens sold in Germany.

196 MINTZ, Sweetness and Power, pp. 109–113, p. 149. SCHIVELBUSCH, Genussmittel, pp. 90–95. Coffee consumption expanded considerably in England until after c.1750, when coffee was replaced by tea.

197 England: D. RICHARDSON, The Slave Trade, Sugar, and British Economic Growth, 1748–1776, Journal of Interdisciplinary History, XVII, 4 (Spring 1987), pp. 739–769, at pp. 748, 751s. For Scotland there are no firm (or even tentative) results available.

IV. THE COMMODITY TRADES

1. DOMESTIC EXPORTS TO GERMANY

1.1 Sea Fish

In the early modern period sea fish was an important consumption item, in particular within the daily diet of urban dwellers. Its durability and a remote outer and textural similarity to meat rendered it useful for a variety of substitution processes subject to the needs of both ecclesiastical (fasting), as well as profane purposes. When budget constraints did not allow the purchase of meat, fish could be an attractive alternative.[1]

Fish usually ranged amongst the most important primary products Scotland had to offer on world markets, but Germany in particular. During the first half of the century, fish normally attained shares in the area of ~50 per cent of total Scottish exports to Germany. This share was higher than total exports of fish to total exports from Scotland (1755–59) – in this way the fish trade was a particularly "Scottish-German thing". Furthermore, it was indicative of a pre-industrial economy with a strong weight of primary products amongst total exports. The fish trades were also indicative of different regional economies, as the main fish exported to German ports was cod, virtually exclusively dispatched from the Shetlands. From 1743 on, the customs accounts, in combination with the inspector general's ledgers of imports and exports after 1755, provide the following picture:

1 A. LAMPEN, Stadt und Fisch: Konsum, Produktion und Handel im Hanseraum der Frühzeit, in: Vierteljahrschrift für Sozial- und Wirtschaftsgeschichte, LXXXVII (2000), pp. 281–307, at pp. 286–289.

Figure 1: Total Scottish Fish Exports to Germany, 1743–1770

NAS, E504; TNA, Customs 14

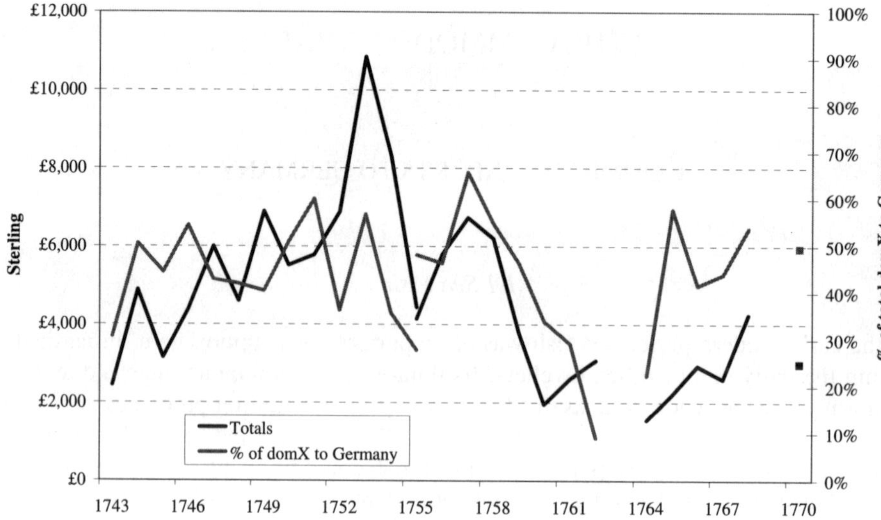

Figure 2: Scottish Exports of Cod, Ling, Salmon and Herring to Germany, 1743–1770

Sources: As Fig. 1. Salmon and Herring on secondary axis.

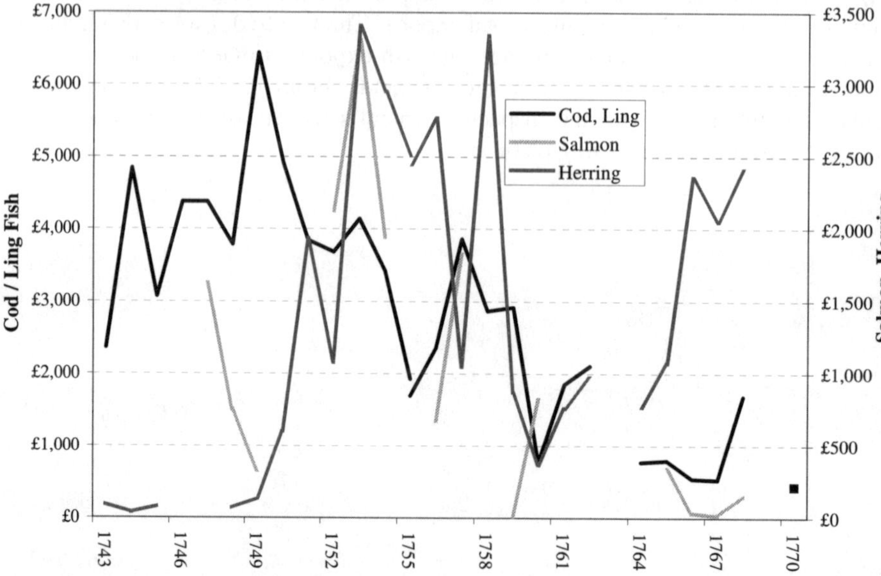

An increase in fish exports c.1743–1753, accounting for a share of fish amongst total domestic exports to Germany of normally 40 to 50 per cent, was followed by a decline, 1753–1762, accompanied by a similar decline in export shares. At present it is impossible to determine exactly the underlying causalities. (But strictly speaking the very size of the fish trades to Germany and their share in total Scottish and German overseas trade do not even permit the quest for a macro-pattern – therefore the following needs to remain to an extent descriptive). The most important type of sea fish sent from Scotland to German ports was cod.

1.1.1 Cod and Ling

Cod, one of the largest sea fish caught in northern Atlantic waters, easily weighing 10 kilos and more per fish, could be rendered useful for many purposes. Their heads were cheap food for humans and animals alike. Parts of their meat might be expensive and served on the tables of contemporary gourmets only; their liver was an ample source of oil. The catches had to be heavily salted on board the fishing boats and ships, in order to be storable for a longer time, which made them suitable for ships' provisions on long-distance voyages. Cod and ling fish were also popular meat substitutes during fasting times.[2]

Scottish exports of cod and ling fish were centred on Shetland. The history and markets of the Shetland cod fisheries, as well as their socio-economic framework are well documented.[3] The German link and major branch of these trades, however, has not been studied extensively, which occasions a few further remarks.

In monetary terms cod and ling represented the major type of fish dispatched from Scotland to Germany. In the eighteenth century, Scotland, or better: Shetland not only became the main Scottish production centre for cod and ling in general, but also, along Norway and Newfoundland, one of the main suppliers of these fish to world markets. Shetland exported her cod & ling fish chiefly to the large North Sea ports of Bremen and Hamburg, which had become her largest foreign outlet from the 1640s onwards. A similar situation obtained in the reverse: from the middle of the seventeenth century onwards, the Shetlands were, after the Netherlands, the most important fish supplier overseas to the Hamburg market, even though the beginnings of regular contacts between the Shetlands and German Hansa towns date back to the early 1400s. Existing Hamburg customs records and merchants' business papers testify to the importance of the *Hitlandfahrt* (Shetland trade) to Hamburg fish merchants at that time (1400s).[4] These trades, however, really expanded later on, chiefly in the seventeenth and eighteenth centuries. The eighteenth century witnessed a slight change in the commercial pattern. First, the commercial agents changed: whilst prior to 1707 the Shetland fish trades had been mostly in the hands of German carriers, after 1707 exports went exclusively on British account. Secondly, in the eighteenth century, Shetland's cod fish

2 J. G. KRÜNITZ (ed.), Oekonomische Encyklopaedie oder Allgemeines System der Land-, Haus- und Staatswirthschaft, 242 vols. Berlin 1773–1858, Art. "Kabeljau", in: Vol. 32 (1784).

3 H. D. SMITH, Shetland Life and Trade, 1550–1914, Edinburgh 1984; R. J. COULL, The Sea Fisheries of Scotland. A Historical Geography, Edinburgh 1996.

4 COULL, Sea Fisheries, pp. 86–92; K. FRIEDLAND, Der Hansische Shetlandhandel, in: ID., Mensch und Seefahrt zur Hansezeit, Cologne / Weimar / Vienna 1995, pp. 190–205, at p. 191, p. 201; M. REIßMANN, Die hamburgische Kaufmannschaft des 17. Jahrhunderts in sozialgeschichtlicher Sicht, Hamburg 1975, pp. 71–73.

exports mainly went to Hamburg rather than Bremen (whence they had been dispatched chiefly in the seventeenth century).

Between the 1500s and roughly until 1710, it had been mostly native German and largely Bremen merchants, often resident in Shetland, who had been carrying fish to Germany.[5] After a slight time lag, local landowners and British merchants took the marketing of Shetland fish into their own hands, stimulated by the Navigation Acts and the bounty on fish exports since 1727. The available post-1742 Scottish customs accounts suggest that the export trade was by then virtually entirely in the hand of *British* merchants resident in the Shetlands. The change roundabout 1707/10 went together with an apparent slump in fish exports to Hamburg, which contemporaries observed and lamented upon. This phenomenon may be explained by the change in the institutional framework in 1707 (Union of the Kingdoms of England and Scotland).

The application of the institutional framework of the English Navigation Acts, which became applicable in Scotland as of Mayday 1707, prohibiting the import of foreign salt in foreign ships[6] and charging non-British denizens higher customs duties on imports, clearly discouraged a continuation of a trade pattern controlled by Hamburg and Bremen merchant-captains prior to 1707.[7] Although Shetland's balance of trade with Germany was a positive one in normal times, and exports of fish were free of charge, regardless whether or not shipped in British ships or by British subjects, some imports would have been required to balance the books. Obvious candidates were staves and hoops for the fish barrels, which were in short supply in timber-scarce Shetland. These items were imported preferably from German ports and were liable to import duty.

A contemporary opinion (1709) seems to confirm that taxation, above all else, was the real reason for the temporary slump, partly caused by the withdrawal of German traders formerly resident in the Shetlands for good:

> The Hamburgers had a trade to Zetland and brought money to that place for fishes which they loaded therewith. Now these ships come not because of the customes paid for the forraign goods and they have fallen upon Norway as yet of venting their commodities So that money is scarce in Zetland.[8]

But this situation altered nothing in terms of the general pattern. Notwithstanding temporary disruptions and a complete restructuring of the distribution network, Germany, or better Hamburg, continued to be Shetland's main market until late in the eighteenth century.

The second component of the structural change in and after 1707 lay in the export destination for Shetland sea fish. In the eighteenth, as opposed to the seventeenth, century, Shetland's exports of fish, if they went to Germany (which they did predomi-

5 SMITH, Shetland Life, pp. 10–20, pp. 35–68.

6 Ibid., p. 77.

7 Foreigners were liable to the *Petty Custom* upon import, a duty levied according to and on top of the *Old Subsidy*, amounting to 1.25 per cent of the goods' value given in the Book of Rates. H. CROUCH, A Complete View of the British Customs […], 4th ed. London 1745, p. 11.

8 NAS, GD150/2543/17 (transferred to Shetland Archives; microfilm copy in NAS, RH4/137), *George Robertson to the Earl of Morton*, 21 June 1709.

nantly), were almost exclusively destined for Hamburg rather than Bremen. At present it cannot be established why exactly this was the case. But be that as it may, the overall trend appears to have been an increase in exports until about 1749 and a pronounced decline thereafter. This decline in exports of salted dry fish (cod, ling) to German markets c. 1749–1770, took place vis-à-vis total Scottish export levels of cod and ling that were stable in the long run.[9] Thus, the German market share in total exports of cod & ling somewhat declined over the period under consideration. Perhaps German demand for sea fish, which in terms of their price per calorific unit were more expensive than basic cereals (such as rye or oats)[10] declined slightly after 1740. Perhaps suppliers other than Shetland became important on the Hamburg and Bremen fish market. A scissor-like movement between cod & ling fish on the one, and herring and salmon (see next section) on the other hand seems to suggest that declining exports of Scots cod to Germany were partly compensated for by increasing herring (and to a lesser extent salmon) exports (note that in figure 2 above herring and salmon are displayed on the secondary axis).

If allegations of profit margins of up to 100 per cent on Shetland cod and ling are anywhere near economic reality, this business would have been an extremely profitable one for those controlling the supply and distribution channels – i.e. after 1707 the resident British fish merchants.[11] Although salt fish exported to places outside Britain had to be cured with foreign salt by law (apart from the fact that Scots salt was often of too poor quality to be useful for this purpose), this made the British fish trade no less profitable. Import duties paid on foreign Portuguese, Spanish (and sometimes French) salt, apart from a drawback of 83 per cent (1708–1747/55) and 88 per cent after 1747/55 on Spanish and Portuguese Salt, were virtually repaid by the bounty on top of the draw-back of customs duties, which was normally financed by drawing on the funds yielded by the *Excise on Foreign Salt Inwards*.[12]

The seasonal trading pattern, as it appears from the customs accounts, was a fairly regular one. In the first half of the year, usually during Midsummer and into Michaelmas quarter (May–June), ships arrived from Altona, laden with white Spanish, Portuguese or French salt. Ships coming from Hamburg had been loaded with hoops and staves for the barrels in which the catches would later be shipped back right to the place where the barrel hoops and staves had come from. The bulk of cod and ling fish were exported later during Michaelmas quarter.[13] This quarter also witnessed the yearly remittance of customs yields from Shetland to Edinburgh.[14]

9 SMITH, Shetland Life, p. 68, Fig. 14.

10 W. ABEL, Stufen der Ernährung. Eine historische Skizze, Göttingen 1981, pp. 49s.

11 COULL, Sea Fisheries, pp. 87s.

12 French salt could draw back only 30 per cent (1708–1747/55) and 38 per cent (thereafter) of duties paid upon importation. Bounty: NAS, RH15/93/17/24–25 (1720). *Exchequer Order and Customs Certificates Relating to Fish Debentures, Shetland.* Duties and drawbacks calculated using information contained in T. LANGHAM, The Neat Duties (All Discounts and Abatements deducted) of all Merchandize Specify'd in the Book of Rates, London 1708; 3rd ed. 1715; 7th ed. 1754; and CROUCH (1725, 1731, 1738, 1745, 1755).

13 July–September.

14 NAS, E504/32/1–2, passim.

1.1.2 Herring

Herring were the second-most important category of sea fish exported from Scotland to Germany. They made for a counter-cycle to cod and ling fish in the 1740s and 1750s (Figure 2 above), shortly after Scottish herring shipments to other destinations, for instance the Baltic, had for the first (and sole) time displaced Dutch shipments to the same destination (see below). Shortly – between c. 1720 and 1750 – Scotland became one of Europe's major suppliers of herring to continental markets, of which German destinations represented one important component.

Since the later seventeenth century the main export markets for Scots herring had been the Baltic, France, Ireland and the Caribbean[15], although western Germany did play a not unimportant role. In the eighteenth century, herring were exported to Germany chiefly from Shetland, in insignificant quantities also from the Firth of Forth, Montrose and Aberdeen.[16] Although patterns and structures prevailing on the seventeenth- and eighteenth-century world market for herring are not well understood, it is usually acknowledged that these patterns were at least co-determined by Scots traders.

The comparative advantage enjoyed by the Dutch herring fisheries during the seventeenth century had initially led to the latter monopolizing the European herring supply.[17] Since the 1680s and 1690s, however, and through to the end of the eighteenth century, there was a prolonged decline of Dutch market shares, most notably in the Baltic.[18] Other suppliers, such as Scotland, more or less competed successfully, with a price-reducing effect, quite obviously at the expense of Dutch market shares. It seems, for instance as though shortly after the decline of Dutch herring shipments eastwards through the Øresund had set in, Scottish herring exports eastwards to the Baltic expanded (c. 1700–1730), reaching levels of up to a third of total shipments at times (of herring eastwards through the Sound). (The winner in this race, however, would be Norway in the end).[19] Unfortunately no data on Scottish-German trade are available for this apparently crucial period in the history of the Scottish herring fisheries (c. 1700–1730). Therefore no affirmative assessment as to the role of the western European, especially the German, market in this process of restructuring and re-allocation of supply channels can be made. Suffice it to recall from the previous section that the expansion of herring exports went parallel to a decline in cod fish exports, but, more

---

15 COULL, Sea Fisheries, pp. 73–76.

16 This is somewhat contrary to what one might have expected, given that the main herring fishing grounds of Scotland were located near the Firths of Forth and Clyde. COULL, Sea Fisheries, pp. 61s.

17 This had been achieved by curing the fish on board the vessels right after the catch, thus shortening the time between catch and sale, and providing their vessels with a larger operational range, which allowed them to invade traditional British and Scandinavian fishing grounds and in the end to dictate European market prices. R. W. UNGER, Dutch Herring, Technology and International Trade in the Seventeenth Century, in: Journal of Economic History, XL (1980), pp. 253–279, at p. 255.

18 Ibid., p. 262; p. 273, Fig. 3.

19 A. R. MICHELL, The European Fisheries in Early Modern History, in: E. E. RICH / C. H. WILSON (eds.), The Cambridge Economic History of Europe, Vol. V: The Economic Organization of Early Modern Europe, Cambridge 1977, pp. 133–185, esp. at pp. 147s., p. 165, Fig. 5, pp. 181–184. S. HÖGBERG, Utrikeshandel och sjöfart på 1700-talet. Stapelvaror i svensk export och import 1738–1808, Lund 1969.

importantly, that it really gathered momentum after the mid-1740s. This furthermore coincided with the rise of the Irish market for Scots herring. In combination these aspects might point towards a competitive gain of the Scots (herring) fisheries, presumably at the expense of the Dutch.

Herring were treated preferentially in British-German trade agreements. On January 31st in 1711, for instance, a treaty was signed between Britain and Hamburg, granting British merchants access to the Hamburg fish market on favourable terms equal to those enjoyed by the Dutch.[20] Effectively this meant duty-free access, as Dutch imports were generally freed from the payment of the *Admiralitätszoll* (admiralty toll).[21] For Scottish fish merchants this was without doubt a powerful incentive, as not only were certain regional economies within Scotland heavily dependent on the herring fisheries, but Hamburg was also their main foreign outlet prior to the emergence of the Irish market in the mid-1750s.[22] A waiving of import duties on herring, reducing their final sales price, would have acted as a powerful commercial stimulus, shifting outwards both the supply as well as the demand curve for that product. The Hamburg consumer, by granting custom-free access to the major northern European herring producers and rivals (Scotland, Netherlands), in the early decades of the eighteenth century would thus reap the benefits of a highly competitive market and an accordingly competitive pricing of the product.

Around 1715/1716 Scottish herring shipments through the Sound reached record levels and led to Scotland temporarily becoming the largest herring supplier to the Baltic. At precisely the same time Bartholomew Bludworth, a Scots merchant resident in Hamburg, acting as a factor for his fellow countryman Alexander McIntosh (an Inverness fish merchant), commented upon the low price Scots herring fetched on an obviously glutted Hamburg fish market. By believing that this was still due in particular to the superior methods employed by the Dutch, he suggested that the Scottish herring fisheries still relied on less effective and obsolete production methods, which led to bad timing and thus deficient sales levels. He wrote:

> Our fishmongers are so very much overstocked [?] if they bidd any price at all [...] t'will be a very poor one. [...] You still give the Hollanders all the Advantage of your Herring Trade which is a very Choice one well manag'd as they do it, therefore every step they take [...] ought to be nicely observed. We begin to Fish when they have supply'd all Marketts & made all Topping Prices. Why can't we go out as soon & as farr at sea as they do, & have al help & necessarys aboard to cure 'em as they have; Why can't we have sound & well made season'd Cask of very same fashion make & bigness of theirs; Why can't we be as Curious in our Packing them (after they have lain their full Time in salt); throwing aside thinn ?Cask? & press them so fast into the barrills [?] they can't give way & want a lay or 2 when they arrive.[23]

20 Hamburg, 31 January 1711. NLS, Pamphlet Series, 1.22(96).

21 O.-E. KRAWEHL, Die Admiralitätszoll- und Convoygeldeinnahmebücher als handelsstatistische Quelle, in: J. SCHNEIDER / O.-E. KRAWEHL / M. A. DENZEL (eds.), Statistik des Hamburger seewärtigen Einfuhrhandels im 18. Jahrhundert. Nach den Admiralitätszoll- und Convoygeld-Einnahmebüchern, St. Katharinen 2001, pp. 9–18, at p. 11.

22 Which it had been for a long time preceding the Union. See SMITH, Shetland Life.

23 NAS, GD23/6/33/2, 8 (copy), identical wording but different dates (29 November 1715, 10 December 1716).

This passage presents a bit of a conundrum with regard to changes in what was certainly an important branch of seventeenth and eighteenth-century European economic activity. Perhaps Bludworth was unaware that the dominant market position enjoyed by the Dutch had been the result not only of comparative advantage, but also of duty-free access to the Hamburg market, which their main rivals, the English and the Scots, had been denied until recently (1711). This would have increased the competitive advantage of the Dutch without altering their comparative advantage. The above brief passage is also a clear warning against taking the Sound Toll Registers as more than they are[24], assuming a gain in competitiveness of the Scottish herring fisheries just on the grounds that they appear to have (temporarily) displaced the Dutch on the Baltic market. Clearly, there were markets other than the Baltic – the North Sea littoral for instance, later on Ireland – in which the Scots were by no means very competitive, not even after the abolition of import duties (Hamburg, 1711), if the contemporary assessments were correct. This might have changed in the mid-1750s, when exports of Shetland herring to Ireland and Germany – their main markets – started to increase significantly. But again the loss of the Scottish customs accounts between 1707 and 1742 is a rather unfortunate incidence. Significant changes in the European fish trade patterns, in which the Scots might have played a dominant role, obviously fell precisely into the period in which Scottish records (customs accounts, chapter 2) are silent.

Generally speaking, however, it is difficult to infer general European patterns (and shifts in them) from a partial analysis such as the present one on Scotland and Germany – both of which were only partial suppliers (and purchasers) on the world market – regardless whether the products under consideration were fish, or commodities to be discussed below, such as tobacco, rice or salt. It was only the salt trades which were based on a close and particularly Scottish-German connection in the seventeenth and eighteenth centuries. In the eighteenth century the German market proved to be crucial for the Scottish salt industry, being its last market of significance on the Continent. Scots salt also was frequently the most important foreign marine salt sold in Bremen, even surpassing Lüneburg brine salt sales at times. In fact, the success of Scots salt on the Bremen market, particularly in the seventeenth, but also in the eighteenth century, was inextricably linked to the demise of the Lüneburg salt works in the same period.

---

24 W. S. UNGER, Trade through the Sound in the Seventeenth and Eighteenth Centuries, in: Economic History Review, Second Series, XII, 2 (1959), pp. 206–221, J. A. FABER, Structural Changes in the European Economy during the Eighteenth century as Reflected in the Baltic Trade, in: W. G. HEERES / L. M. J. B. HESP / L. NOORDEGRAAF / R. C. W. VAN DER VOORT (eds.), From Dunkirk to Danzig. Shipping and Trade in the North Sea and the Baltic, 1350–1850, Amsterdam 1988, pp. 83–94.

1.2 Salt[25]

1.2.1 The Significance of Salt

Salt is one of the oldest manufactured products known to mankind. It has been an essential component of human diet across the globe from the Stone Age until the present time, quite regardless of people's age, colour, race, socio-economic and cultural background, or a whole society's stage of economic development. A constant intake of salt is crucial for maintaining one's health (in the very long term an overdose might be as critical as a deficit), further to its use as a preservative, as animal food, or its usefulness in a variety of chemical processes.

Salt can be obtained using a variety of procedures. In the pre-modern period the essential options would have been: mining (rock salt), or evaporating brine, using artificial heat, yielding the most superior and accordingly most expensive types of salt (for instance Lüneburg salt). A third – most common – option was to evaporate sea water, thus obtaining marine salt using natural heat provided by sunlight (French, Spanish and Portuguese salt) or artificial heat (coals; Scots and English salt).[26] Whilst nowadays in contemporary European cuisine marine salt ranges slightly above the mass-produced basic table salts which can be obtained in any corner store and hypermarket, in pre-modern times, sea salt was the more basic item, affordable by even the lower ranks of society on a daily basis. Evaporating sea water was in fact the easiest and cheapest way of obtaining salt suitable for preserving and seasoning food in the pre-industrial period.

Some producers, most notably in the north-east of England and in Scotland, used small or refuse coals, a decidedly cheap and dirty fuel that was unfit for all but the crudest and most basic firing purposes, such as heating gigantic iron or lead pans, in order to increase the amount of refined salt that could be produced per time unit in these comparatively sun-less countries. Arguably this resulted in a fairly high degree of impurity of the final product (sea salt) which might radically decrease a prospective consumer's willingness and ability to use this salt for nutritional purposes, a problem commonly faced by Scots salt producers in the period under consideration. By all means this would have had a considerable price-reducing effect, partly offsetting the obvious quality deficiencies of the product.

That being said, salt was one of the earliest commodities in history to be traded over long distances. It remained one of the most obvious items to be exported by salt producing nations (such as Scotland and England) and to be imported by non- or small producers. Thus to state that there was a regular and large trade in salt between Scotland and Germany in the eighteenth century might on the one hand be mistaken for a statement of the obvious. Everyone needed the item on a daily basis, after all, and if per capita yearly salt requirements calculated for Bohemian servant classes around

25 The subsequent paragraph on the Scottish-German salt trades draws heavily on P. R. ROESSNER, 'New Light on Whatley's Numbers'. The German Market for Scots Salt in the Eighteenth Century, in: Scottish Historical Review, 1 / 2008 (forthcoming), as well as Id., Scottish Trade in the Wake of Union, 1700–1760. The Rise of a Warehouse Economy, Stuttgart 2008, ch. 7, section 7.3.2.

26 J.-C. HOCQUET, Le Sel et le Pouvoir. De l'an mil à la Revolution française, Paris 1985, p. 15; R. P. MULTHAUP, Neptune's Gift. A History of Common Salt, Baltimore / London 1978, pp. 20–30.

1700 were correct (c. 11 kg per annum, see below) such a situation, if applicable to Europe in general, should have resulted in a lively intra-European salt trade. But the knowledge that both "nations" were salt producers, as well as importers themselves in the period under consideration might on the other hand puzzle the reader. Germany was a salt producing country after all – consider the famous Lüneburg salt works catering for the north German market – so why should there have been regular imports of Scots salt into German ports, 1700–1760? Scotland was a large salt producer and exporter herself – consider the hundreds of Scottish salt pans spread all across Scotland's "inland sea", the Firth of Forth – and yet she imported large quantities of Portuguese, Spanish and French salt in the eighteenth century.

The answer lies within the medium layers of the pre-industrial northern European economy and society, somewhat hidden below the surface of the obvious historical facts. Modern economics would coin the lapidary term "graded preference" for this phenomenon. Scots salt was a very basic, impure and grey specimen, unfit for all but the most basic nutrition purposes. It could not be used for curing fish for exporting – for this purpose Scots fish merchants needed to import the "whiter" marine salts from Portugal, Spain and France. Yet some of the northern producers, such as Lüneburg, whilst manufacturing an extremely pure and thus valuable product, could not sell their salt at prices affordable to the lower classes of society within their immediate vicinity (that is, adjacent territories). This is where producers of low-quality salt like the Scots came in. Lower incomes meant lower quality of the products to be consumed on a day-to-day basis. In fact, until roughly 1770 Scots salt found a ready market close-by across the North Sea, where average incomes were low and on the whole declining – Germany.

The Scottish-German salt trades attained a significance which far outpaced salt's mere weight in total exports of Scotland to German ports. In fact, exports of Scots salt to the Holy Roman Empire present a prime example of a close and peculiarly Scottish-German trading connection, in terms of a domestic Scottish export for which German ports represented the major foreign outlet, as well as an item consumed on the German side, which was mostly supplied by Scots. Whilst the early modern *Scottish* salt industry has been the subject of several exemplary and definitive studies by Whatley[27], the *Bremen* salt market was analyzed by the late K. H. Schwebel, who pointed out the significance of Scots salt in this city.[28] Neither of these studies, however, drew particular and due attention to the German market for the Scottish product as such. Much more than being a story of the German market for salt (the demand side), the following will tell an interesting tale of decline of a formerly vital Scottish export economy, a loss in international competitiveness (the demand side) of an industry which was artificially kept alive and sometimes revitalized by the German market.

---

27 C. A. WHATLEY, The Scottish Salt Industry 1570–1850. An Economic and Social History, Aberdeen 1987; ID., 'That Important and Necessary Article'. The Salt Industry and its Trade in Fife and Tayside c1570–1850, Dundee: Abertay Historical Society Publications, Vol. 22 (1984); ID., Salt, Coal and the Union of 1707: A Revision Article, in: Scottish Historical Review, LXVI, 1, Nr. 181 (April 1987), pp. 26–45; ID., Sales of Scottish Marine Salt c.1714–1823, in: Scottish Economic and Social History, VI (1986), pp. 4–17.

28 K. H. SCHWEBEL, Salz im Alten Bremen, Bremen 1988.

In fact the eighteenth century appears as a watershed period for the Scottish salt industry in terms of the competitiveness of its product on continental markets. Whatley has been able to show that a definite and protracted decline in exports of Scots salt took place during the first half of the eighteenth century, with levels approaching zero in the 1750s, from which they never again recovered.[29] This was a considerable change in the commercial pattern, and most certainly in the relative productivity record of the industry, in comparison to previous centuries, especially the early 1600s. At that time Scotland had been a large salt exporter accounting for significant shares of total salt sales on continental European, but in particular Baltic, markets.[30] 150 years later the tides had turned completely against Scotland, which then exported only fractional amounts of production levels, which overall appear to have remained constant, 1700–1760.

Having said all this, the following aspects are of significance for the following discussion: (1) In the eighteenth century, Germany in fact became not only the largest, but virtually the last foreign market for what at that time had become a virtually non-exportable item.[31] (2) North Sea ports (Bremen, Emden, Hamburg) became the main importers of Scots salt. Quite obviously they did so at the expense of Baltic ports. Stralsund for instance ceased to import Scots salt after 1746, as did most other German, quasi-German and non-German ports in the Baltic. (3) The shift towards Atlantic ports went ahead with another interesting phenomenon. During the eighteenth century Scots salt frequently remained as significant to the Bremen and north-western German consumer, as Bremen was of importance to the Scottish industry as the last major foreign outlet for its sea salt. In 1738/39 for instance, Scots salt still was the most important type of foreign marine salt sold on the Bremen market, in the same way as Bremen at that time was by far the major export destination for Scots salt producers. On the one hand this was a mere continuation of a pattern that had set in around 1600 at latest. But given the complete loss of overseas markets for the Scottish industry 1700–1760 on the other hand, holding on to this old pattern was remarkable. Given the average quality of the Scottish product and the harsh competition faced on northern European salt markets, a continuation of a strong Scotland-Bremen connection in salt trading was by no means historically inevitable. (4) It is also clear that the north-German (in particular Bremen's) preference for Scots salt can hardly be explained in terms of a special taste for Scots salt. The Scottish product was price- but not quality-competitive vis-à-vis its rival products from Cheshire, France and the Iberian Peninsula. One would suppose that within an environment of multiple budget constraints, due mainly to declining living standards and real wages in particular after c.1740[32], a cheap and

29 WHATLEY, Salt Industry, p. 46, Fig. 3.

30 S. G. E. LYTHE, The Economy of Scotland in its European Setting, 1550–1625, Edinburgh 1960, p. 160.

31 WHATLEY, Salt Industry, ch. 2.

32 The classic account remains W. ABEL., Agrarkrisen und Agrarkonjunktur in Mitteleuropa vom 13. bis zum 19. Jahrhundert, Hamburg / Berlin, 3rd ed. 1978; Engl. Translation: Agricultural Fluctuations in Europe from the Thirteenth to the Twentieth Centuries, London 1980, passim. See also ID., Stufen, ch. 2; ID., Geschichte der deutschen Landwirtschaft vom frühen Mittelalter bis zum 19. Jahrhundert, Stuttgart, 3rd ed. 1978. This view, put forward in the original (1935) edition, was adopted for good in European economic historiography; see e.g. B. H. SLICHER VAN BATH, The Agrarian History of Western Europe, A.D. 500–1850, London 1963, pp. 221–238. For a critical

competitively-priced essential such as Scots salt would by definition have represented an attractive alternative to other available and more expensive types of marine or brine salt. Lüneburg salt for instance – a salt of the latter type – would have been unaffordable to the lower ranks of society. This was due not least to various barriers to trade in the shape of external, internal and transit tolls and customs on cross-border traffic, resulting from Germany's extreme political fragmentation. These considerably increased the price charged by the Lüneburg salt works, the main producer in Northern Germany. By the same token they made Atlantic or North Sea salt extremely attractive on the north German market. Due to the short distance compared to the main competitors Portugal, Spain and France, an accordingly short period of travel and thus modest transport costs, Scotland was an obvious competitor on the German market. The large German sea ports accordingly ranged amongst the most obvious foreign outlets for Scots salt works in the period. In fact Scotland had been amongst the major suppliers to the German market since the later Middle Ages.

review of the Abel thesis by an agrarian economist, however, see W. ACHILLES, Landwirtschaft in der Frühen Neuzeit, Munich 1991. More recent accounts on German economic history in the early modern period have not been able to contribute anything substantially new to Abel's view of the eighteenth century European socio-economic framework. K.-H. KAUFHOLD, Deutschland 1650–1850, in: W. FISCHER / J. A. VAN HOUTTE / H. KELLENBENZ / I. MIECK / F. VITTINGHOFF (eds.), Handbuch der Europäischen Wirtschafts- und Sozialgeschichte, Vol. 4: Von der Mitte des 17. zur Mitte des 19. Jahrhunderts, Stuttgart 1993, pp. 530–588, in particular at p. 554, pp. 558s.; F.-W. HENNING, Handbuch der Wirtschafts- und Sozialgeschichte Deutschlands, Vol. 1: Deutsche Wirtschafts- und Sozialgeschichte im Mittelalter und in der Frühen Neuzeit, Paderborn 1991, pp. 282s., pp. 792–804; R. METZ, Säkulare Trends der Deutschen Wirtschaft, in: M. NORTH (ed.), Deutsche Wirtschaftsgeschichte. Ein Jahrtausend im Überblick, Munich, 2nd ed. 2005, pp. 427–500.

1.2.2 Sales of Scots Salt on the German Market

In order to correctly assess the role of the German market for Scots salt in the eighteenth century, it is necessary to extend the analysis backwards, in order to get an extended picture of the continental European market for Scots salt over time, and spatially, in this instance by customers (nations, export destinations) purchasing the item. The heydays of Scottish salt exports in terms of peak levels and most certainly export-to-output ratios had been reached early in the seventeenth century, with Baltic markets (Germany, Sweden, Denmark, Danzig) being the most important.[33] In the Baltic Scotland in fact surpassed England in terms of domestic salt (i.e. re-exports of French, Portuguese and Spanish salt not considered) sold during most years between c. 1660 and 1700 still, as suggested by the Sound Toll Registers (Figure 4 below).

Figure 3: Sales of Scots and English Salt on Baltic Markets, 1671–1760 (last)

N. E. BANG / K. KORST (eds.), Tabeller over Skibsfart og Varetransport gennem Øresund 1661–1783 og gennem Storebælt 1701–1748, Vol. 1.1: Copenhagen / Leipzig 1939; Vol. 1.2: Copenhagen / Leipzig 1945.

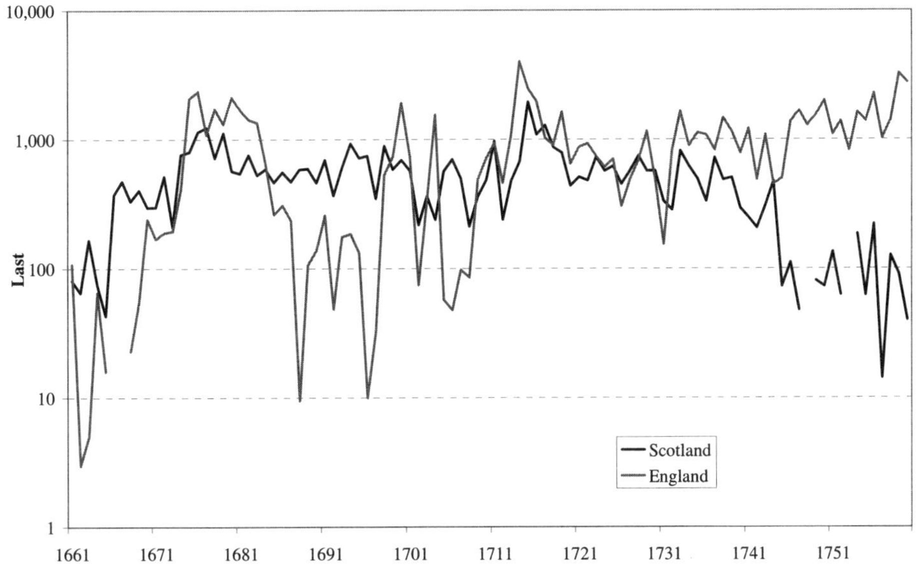

At that time salt markets had been buoyant all across north-west Europe, as salt was an essential the demand of which was fairly inelastic. During much of the sixteenth and the first two decades of the seventeenth century, the German population had expanded continuously in line with a general expansion in European population. If a roughly constant per capita consumption of salt is assumed, this would have translated into a general increase in the demand for salt, providing ample marketing opportuni-

33 D. DITCHBURN, Scotland and Europe: The Medieval Kingdom and its Contacts with Christendom, c.1215–1545, Vol. 1: Religion, Culture and Commerce, East Linton 2000, p. 160; WHATLEY, Salt Industry, pp. 33–44.

ties for the major European salt producers.[34] Even though amongst the latter Scotland ought to be seen as a marginal supplier, compared to the Portuguese, Spanish and French industries, she held up reasonably well against English competition. Scots salt played an intrinsic part of the story of the European salt market and followed, or at times perhaps even co-determined, European patterns of salt trading.

The North-West German territories, however, were all located within the market boundaries (determined by transport costs, internal and transit tolls and customs duties as a component of the final market price) of the Lüneburg salt works.[35] Not only did the Lüneburg salt works operate closer to the large North German markets than the Atlantic producers (Portugal, Spain, France, England, Scotland), and thus would, thanks to a relatively dense network of rivers and canals, have captured a potentially large market. Their product was also qualitatively better than French, Portuguese, Spanish, English or Scots salt, due to a variety of reasons, one of which was the extraordinary degree of purity (or natural saturation with salt) of the brine of 25.5 per cent.[36] Moreover, protective taxation or outright prohibition in some of the adjacent territories, such as the Duchy of Brunswick, where the sale of Scottish salt was prohibited by statutory law, should, and at times would, have stimulated Lüneburg's sales.[37] And yet Scots salt was extremely successful on the North-West German market early on.

Scots salt entered the competitive scene right at a time when output levels and market shares of the Lüneburg salt works commenced on their long-term and once-and-for-all decline in the 1580s/1600s, which suggests that it might have played – however minor – a part in the process.[38] This process might in fact have amounted to a significant structural change in the North-west German salt market. Even though Scotland was certainly not the most important supplier of salt to continental markets, the scissor-like movement of Scots exports vis-à-vis Lüneburg production and export levels in the late sixteenth and early seventeenth centuries is too obvious to be purely coincidental.[39] According to Witthöft this decline in Lüneburg's production capacities was a deliberate reduction of desired capacities rather than due to an exhaustion of physical resources. Witthöft thus attributed the decline in Lüneburg's importance for the Northern European salt markets to three factors: the dwindling of Lübeck (a Baltic port) in international trade, possibly indicative of a general gravitational shift in the commercial patterns from the Baltic towards the Atlantic; the rise of Mercantilism and related economic policies which tended to mutually reduce the size of export markets for certain products by erecting artificial barriers to trade (tariffs, prohibition etc.); and

34 HENNING, Handbuch, Vol. 1, p. 649, p. 721.

35 E. HOFFMANN, Lübeck im Hoch- und Spätmittelalter: Die große Zeit Lübecks, in: A. GRAßMANN (ed.), Lübeckische Geschichte, Lübeck, 2nd ed. 1989, pp. 79–340, at pp. 207s.

36 MULTHAUP, Neptune's Gift, p. 7. H. WITTHÖFT, Struktur und Kapazität der Lüneburger Saline seit dem 12. Jahrhundert, Wiesbaden 1976.

37 H.-J. VON WITZENDORF, Bremens Handel im 16. und 17. Jahrhundert, in: Bremisches Jahrbuch, XLIV (1955), pp. 128–174, at p. 146.

38 S. G. E. LYTHE, Scottish Trade with the Baltic 1550–1650, in: J. K. EASTHAM (ed.), Economic Essays in Commemoration of the Dundee School of Economics 1931–1955, Coupar Angus 1955, pp. 63–84, at p. 76, p. 81 (Table).

39 WITTHÖFT, Struktur, p. 111 / graph XII; p. 112 / graph XIII.

the price-competitiveness of Atlantic sea salt (English, Scots, French, Spanish, Portuguese).[40] Of these reasons it would be the last-mentioned which needs to be seen as the most important factor in the present analysis – the story of Scots salt imports into German ports, 1700–1770.

Tracing sales of Scots salt on the northern German market after 1738/1742 – when the Bremen *Schlachteangabebücher* and *Scottish customs accounts* (chapter 2) commence – is a fairly straightforward task. For this purpose the Scottish port books (Customs collectors' quarterly accounts, see chapter 2)[41], which are preserved in virtually complete series for all Scottish ports after Christmas quarter 1742, have been examined with regard to (salt) exports to Germany. As the incentives to smuggle were small at this point – salt was exported duty free; smuggling incentives would have been larger at the point of *production*, where excise duty was charged – the customs series can be seen as fairly indicative of factual exports of salt to German ports. For *total* exports of Scots salt in the period, Whatley's figures have been used.[42] After 1755, on the other hand, the inspector general's ledgers of imports and exports have been used in establishing the share of "Germany" in total exports of Scots salt.[43] This evidence has been supplemented by Bremen customs records (*Schlachteangabebücher*, available from 1738 onwards)[44], as well as the Sound Toll Registers[45], which have been examined with regard to traffic of Scots salt to Baltic ports located within the German Empire.[46] Thus, whilst post-1742 the German market share can be captured linking the customs evidence with Whatley's export figures, the picture is much less reliable for any time prior to 1742. Nevertheless the picture is reasonably clear. First, after 1700 German ports became the largest and at times sole market for Scots salt sold abroad, until exports finally reached and stayed at levels near zero since the late 1750s.[47] Second, it would now be the North Sea ports of Germany – Bremen and Emden in particular – rather than Baltic German ports, which received most of the quantities. Lübeck and Stralsund (Swedish Pomerania), which had been large and

40 Ibid., p. 7, p. 104, p. 107.

41 NAS, E504/2/1–3 (Alloa), E504/6/1–4 (Bo'ness), E504/20/1–3 (Kirkcaldy), E504/30/1–2 (Prestonpans), the only ports from which salt was exported to Germany in the period.

42 WHATLEY, Salt Industry, p. 46, Fig. 3. As Whatley has expressed total exports of salt from Scotland in a five-year moving average, the share of salt exported to Germany in total Scots salt exports is an approximation (see table 1 below).

43 TNA, Customs 14. These are to be seen as not entirely reliable, though, as they generally record lower amounts of salt exports than the customs accounts. Differences could be explained by deviations in recording practice of the customs collectors and ex post corrections of original customs declarations that were made known to the inspector general of imports and exports (but are neither preserved nor traceable by the modern-day researcher).

44 *Staatsarchiv, Bremen*, 2–Ss.2.a.4.f.1seq., *Schlachteangabebücher* (Schlachte Toll Accounts), 1738–9, 1754 seq.

45 BANG / KORST (eds.), Tabeller.

46 These destinations were: Lübeck, Rostock, Stralsund, Wismar, "Øvrige Pommern". Apart from Lübeck, these ports were all under Swedish rule since 1648. As Swedish Pomerania was part of the German Empire, and the Swedish kings were Imperial Princes for these dominions, these ports have been included in the discussion.

47 Then Scots salt was replaced by English (Cheshire, Liverpool) salt on the Bremen market. See below.

regular outlets for Scots salt in the seventeenth and isolated years of the eighteenth century, declined in terms of their importance between the 1720s and 1740s.

For the early decades of the eighteenth century, no quantitative materials other than the Sound Toll Registers exist. Alternatively one might draw on the impressionistic account written by Henry Kalmeter. He was a Swedish denizen travelling in Scotland undercover in 1720–1, involved in some form of economic espionage. Kalmeter reckoned that around 1720, Scots salt was, apart from Bremen, still dispatched in small quantities to Sweden, but "the greater part of the Scottish salt is disposed of at Danzig".[48] "Sweden" in this account might well have represented or at least included Stralsund, a quasi-German port, as this part of Pomerania had become Swedish territory by the Treaty of Westphalia in 1648. But in this regard, Kalmeter was unspecific. The Sound Toll Registers, however, seem to suggest that Stralsund was not a particularly significant export destination for Scots salt in the first four decades of the eighteenth century any more (Figure 5 below).

Figure 4: Destinations of Scots Salt in the Baltic (German Empire), 1700–1760 (weys)

1 wey = 40 bushels á 56lbs = 2,240lbs = 1 standard metric ton.
BANG / KORST (eds.), Tabeller.
Pomerania excl. Stralsund: Rostock, Wismar, "Øvrige Pommern" (=other Pomeranian ports).

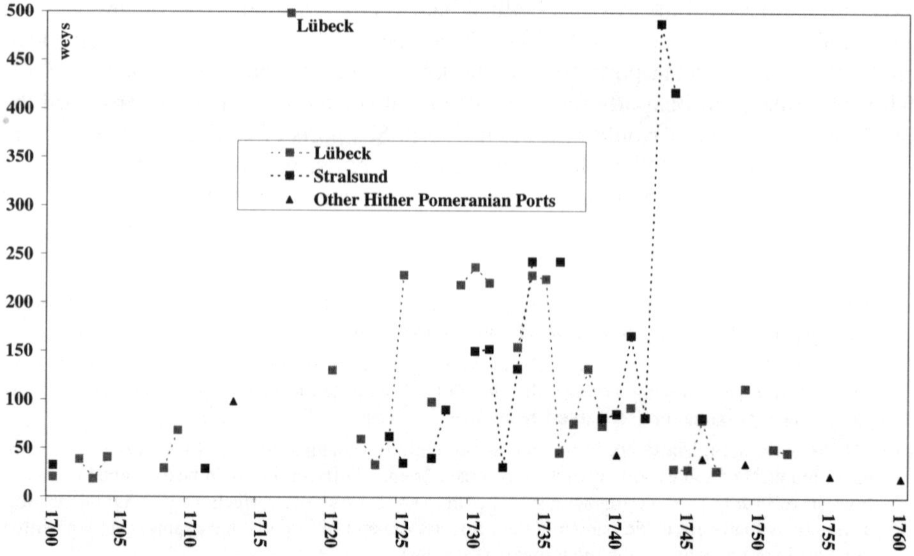

There only appears to have been a brief revival of the Baltic ports of the Empire as an export destination for Scots salt between c. 1725 and 1745, with Lübeck, a proper German port, being the most important destination in most years.

48 T. C. SMOUT (ed.), Journal of Henry Kalmeter's Travels in Scotland 1719–1720, in: SCOTTISH HISTORY SOCIETY (ed.), Scottish Industrial History. A Miscellany, Edinburgh 1978, pp. 1–52, at p. 49.

If Kalmeter's basic observation was accurate that Scandinavian or Baltic markets in general – i.e. not just the German and quasi-German Baltic ports – were the main destinations for Scots salt sent abroad in the 1710s and 1720s still (this observation cannot be tested statistically), the 1710s and 1720s would have seen a prolongation of the seventeenth-century commercial patterns. Without doubt this changed some time after Kalmeter's report, as the post-1742 Scottish customs accounts suggest a fundamentally different story. After 1742 German ports proper, located chiefly in the North Sea, were favoured by Scots salt traders (see Table 1 below). On the Baltic market, Scottish producers lost out against English producers after 1715, as Figure 4 above demonstrates. The north-west German market on the other hand would not be taken over by English salt until the 1770s. It is interesting to note, however, that both series experienced a decline between 1715 and 1745 before their trends depart. In a sense, therefore, the success story of English salt on Baltic markets did not begin strictly speaking prior to 1744.

Whereas exports of Scots salt to Baltic German ports continued after 1720 and even experienced an "Indian summer" c. 1725–1745 (Figure 5 above), they were always dwarfed by exports to the North Sea ports of Emden, Bremen and Hamburg.[49] Within the framework of overall declining Scottish salt exports, German North Sea ports in the late 1740s and early 1750s thus increased their share at the expense of the Baltic, becoming the most important destination for Scots salt on the continent, with shares frequently above 50 per cent of total exports of Scots salt.[50]

49 Whilst the average number of salt *weys* dispatched to the latter obtains at 568 in the period 1743–1755, the same figure for salt dispatched to Baltic ports located within the Empire works out at 112 *weys*, or less than one-fifth of the former. Calculated from NAS, E504/2/1–3 (Alloa), E504/6/1–4 (Bo'ness), E504/20/1–3 (Kirkcaldy), E504/30/1–2 (Prestonpans).

50 Cf. Appendix. 1738–9 figures referred to in subsequent sections are approximate values, obtained by converting the Bremen salt *last* into British *bushels*. The Bremen last has been assumed to equal 4,410 lbs, which is a conservative estimate. SCHWEBEL, *Salz*, p. 73.

Table 1: Exports of Scots Salt, 1743–59 (bushels)[51]

1743–1755: NAS, E504; 1755–1770: TNA, Customs 14; Totals 1745, 1750–55: WHATLEY, Salt Industry, p. 46, Fig. 3.

	(1) Germany (E504)	(2) Germany (Cust14)	(3) Total Salt X (Cust 14)	(4) 5-yr-mov-av (1)	(5) 5-yr.-mov.-av.totals (Whatley)	(6) Share of Germany in total sales abroad
1743	17,776					
1744	30,040					
1745	41,632			32,453	75,000	43%
1746	37,720					
1747	35,100					
1748	17,780					
1749	27,200					
1750	19,780			20,917	28,000	75%
1751	22,426			19,281	25-28,000	73%
1752	17,400			14,961	25-28,000	56%
1753	9,600			13,710	25-28,000	52%
1754	5,600				25-28,000	
1755	13,525	13,525	16,725		25-28,000	81%
1756		17,750	24,943			71%
1757		4,600	9,100			51%
1758		16,010	35,248			45%
1759		2,516	9,732			26%
1760						
1761			1,022			0%
1762			1,014			0%
1763						
1764			1,050			0%
1765		4,000	10,000			40%
1766			18,824			0%
1767		7,888	34,118			23%
1768		10,040	24,440			41%
1769						
1770		5,500	12,942			42%

51 Market shares in (6), 1745, 1750–1753 have been approximated by computing a five-year-moving average matching WHATLEY's series. The customs accounts indicate 16,725 bushels as total exports of Scots salt in 1755, rather than 15,960 bushels as given in TNA, Customs 14 (but the latter generally appears to have under-recorded trade).

Bremen remained the largest German destination for Scots salt in "Germany" for the rest of the period under consideration. For those years after 1755 for which salt exports were recorded (1756–9, 1765, 1767–8, 1770) it retained a market share of normally between 72 and 100 per cent.

1.2.3 The Bremen Salt Market

Scots salt, especially its widespread trade and use, due to its extremely competitive pricing, had in fact been lamented upon by the Lüneburg salt masters, one of the main providers of salt to the north-west German market, since the later Middle Ages. If these complaints are to be taken literally, the Lüneburg masters would have lost the Bremen salt market to Scots producers as early as the second half of the sixteenth century.[52] True, price differentials between Scots salt and comparable other products on the Baltic market had been notorious as early as 1485; it is more than likely that this situation applied to the areas surrounding the North Sea littoral as well.[53] But it was the seventeenth century, which saw a rocketing increase in the number of complaints, relating *inter alia* to the fraudulent declaration of Scots as Lüneburg salt in Lübeck and Bremen, resulting from the apparently popular practice of re-filling Scots salt into Lüneburg bottoms and thus counterfeiting the latter.[54] In these years Scots salt frequently surpassed even Lüneburg salt in terms of yearly quantities sold in Bremen, as is suggested by surviving shipping records from 1617, 1626 and 1628.[55] It is striking that the Lüneburg salt works were so much closer to the Bremen and north-west German markets than any of the western European producers' (England, Scotland, Portugal, Spain, France) and yet failed to displace Scots salt from the northern markets. The commercial problems which the Lüneburg salt masters were facing underline the unintended effectiveness of artificial barriers to trade in terms of radically reducing the size of markets. A large number of tolls and customs, a result of territorial fragmentation and more or less random Mercantilist tax base enlargement, considerably reduced market sizes and the growth potential of the fragmented German economy in the early modern period.[56] But the success of Scots salt on these markets also seems to underline the importance of demand for cheap products in times of heavy budget constraints for the average consumer. In this market segment, Scots salt was subject to fierce competition from Spanish, Portuguese and French products. The latter, whilst at that time allegedly only marginally different from the Lüneburg product in terms of quality, still sold in Bremen for half the price of Lüneburg salt most of the time and thus directly competed with the Scottish product, moving within about the same price

---

52 SCHWEBEL, Salz, p. 21. But such complaints should always be taken – the trivial expression might be allowed here! – with a "pinch of salt".

53 DITCHBURN, Scotland and Europe, p. 186, quoting P. DOLLINGER, Die Hanse, Stuttgart, 3rd ed. 1981, p. 512.

54 Lübeck: MEYER-STOLL, Kaufmannschaft, p. 103, n. 4. Bremen: SCHWEBEL, Salz.

55 SCHWEBEL, Salz, pp. 36s.

56 H.-J. GERHARD, Merkantilpolitische Handelshemmnisse (im territorialen Vergleich) am Beispiel eines territorial relativ einheitlichen Gebietes, in: H. POHL (ed.), Die Auswirkungen von Zöllen und anderen Handelshemmnissen auf Wirtschaft und Gesellschaft vom Mittelalter bis zur Gegenwart, Stuttgart 1987, pp. 59–83.

bracket, and thus the same market segment (i.e. the rather quality-indifferent customer).[57] Nevertheless, even though it would not have matched Portuguese, Spanish or French salt in terms of quality, Scots salt remained amongst the most popular types sold in Bremen throughout the seventeenth and eighteenth century.

Figure 5: Exports of Scots Salt to "Germany" (totals) and Bremen, 1738–1770

NAS, E504; *StA Bremen*, 2.Ss.2.a.4.f.1., Vol. 1. Bremen figures for 1767–8 and 1770 are critical.

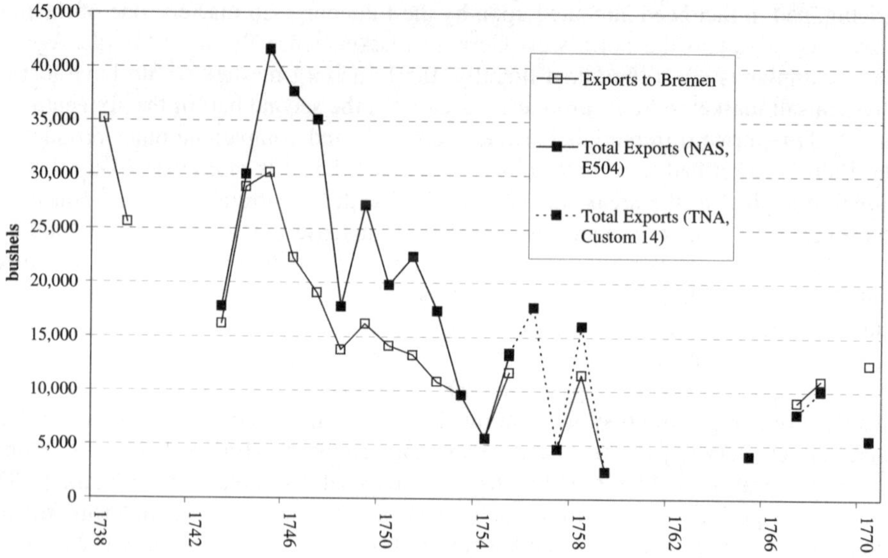

Overall or in absolute terms, however, the available evidence from the Bremen *Schlachte* Toll Accounts (1738–9), in combination with the Scottish customs accounts (1743–1755) and the ledgers of the Scottish inspector general of imports and exports, indicates a protracted decline in total sales of Scots salt on the Bremen market, 1738–1770. This was in line with and in a similar order as the general decline of exports of domestic salt from Scotland. Although the Bremen market share remained roughly constant and large throughout most of the time, levels of Scots salt exports to Bremen had, even on the most conservative estimates, been significantly higher in the late 1730s and prior to that date than they would be in the 1740s and 1750s.

But not only was Bremen the most important, and in many years the only, purchaser of Scots salt abroad until late in the eighteenth century. Scots salt also continued to be the most important type of sea-borne salt imported into Bremen. This appears to have been a remarkable continuation of a pattern first observable in the early seventeenth century (see above). According to the Bremen *Schlachte* toll accounts for instance, Scots salt still accounted for 85 per cent of total recorded sea-borne imports of salt into Bremen in 1738 and for 93 per cent in 1739.[58] This predominant role seems only to have been temporarily eroded between the later 1660s and c.1700. In

57 SCHWEBEL, Salz, p. 14.

58 *StA Bremen, Schlachteangabebücher, 2–Ss.2.a.4.f.1.*

part this was due to edicts prohibiting the consumption of Scots salt in Prussian and Hanoverian territory (1685 to 1716), which ruled out the river Weser as a convenient route for water-borne re-exports from Bremen to central-German territories.[59] A flickering increase of Lüneburg's sales on the Bremen market, reminiscent of pre-1580 "heyday" times, was certainly one of the direct results of these legislations. But apparently the Lüneburg salt masters later scored an own goal and undermined their position by implementing a staple or factory system for the marketing of Lüneburg salt in North Western German states (an attempt at a monopolistic pricing policy). By keeping the price for their product at too high a level to be particularly attractive to the purchaser, this, circa 1700, once again led to an increase in the price differential of Lüneburg vis-à-vis Scots salt and thus an increase in the competitive position of the latter on the Bremen salt market. Whilst Lüneburg salt was quoted at 40–42 Rix Dollars per last in Bremen in 1700/1702, Scots salt sold at slightly more than 1/2 this price, at 23–24 Rix Dollars per last.[60] Similar prices were maintained for the rest of the century. In 1733 for instance, the Bremen salt merchant Diederich (Dietrich) Ratien, consignee of the Edinburgh-based smaller merchant John Carmichael, disposed of the latter's Scots salt at 26 Rix Dollars per last. In 1740 he was even able to fetch a sales price of 29 and 30 Rix Dollars respectively per last for another consignment sent to him by Carmichael.[61]

Scots salt thus yielded regular sales in Bremen, always fetching prices well below those quoted for Lüneburg salt. Its significance on the Bremen and Northern German market is furthermore attested to by a plethora of acts and regulations that dealt expressively with Scots salt, issued for instance by Bremen, or Emden City Council in 1723 (see following figure).

59 SCHWEBEL, Salz, pp. 68s.

60 Ibid., pp. 71–75.

61 But prices were certainly volatile. Earlier the same year (1740) the last of Scots salt had been quoted at about 24–26 Rix Dollars in Bremen, and Ratien had accordingly anticipated a lower sales price. NAS, AC9/1525, *Invoice and Letter Diederich Ratien (Bremen) to John Carmichael (Edinburgh)*, 14 September 1740 (prospects of sales prices); 3 December 1740 (invoice of sale). 1733 sale: NAS, AC9/1525, *Invoice and Letter relating to salt sales in Bremen on Carmichael's account*, 1733. See P. R. RÖSSNER, Scottish Trade in the Wake of Union (1700–1760). The Rise of a Warehouse Economy, Stuttgart 2008, ch. 8.

Edict anent the Declaration of Scots as Lunenburg Salt, Emden 1723

Stadtarchiv Emden, I, 863b

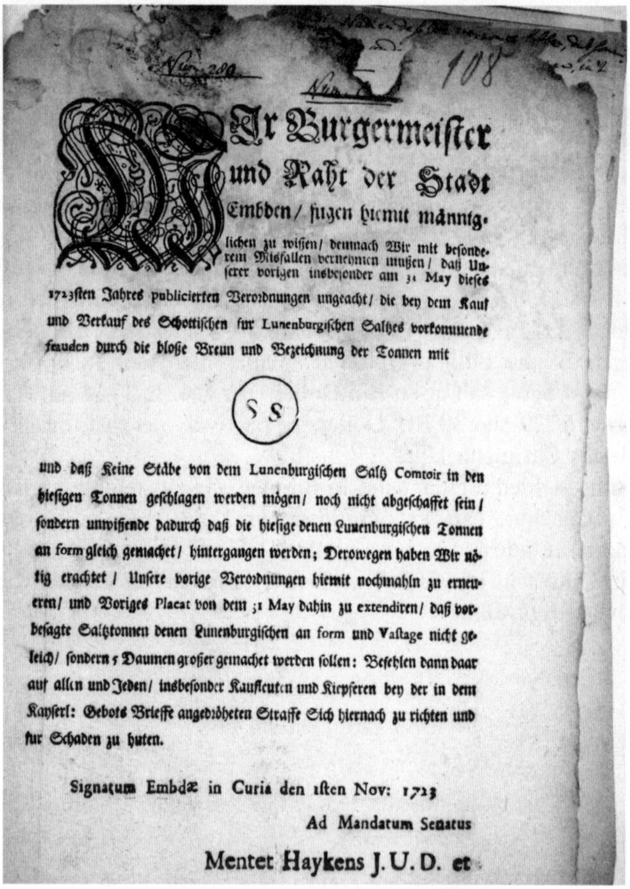
Wir Burgermeister und Raht der Stadt Embden / fugen hiemit männiglichen zu wissen / demnach Wir mit besonderem Mißfallen vernehmen mußen / daß Unserer vorigen insbesonder am 31 May dieses 1723sten Jahres publicierten Verordnungen ungeacht / die bey dem Kauf und Verkauf des Schottischen fur Lunenburgischen Saltzes vorkommende frauden durch die bloße Breun und Bezeichnung der Tonnen mit

(S S)

und daß Keine Stäbe von dem Lunenburgischen Saltz Comtoir in den hiesigen Tonnen geschlagen werden mögen / noch nicht abgeschaffet sein / sondern unwißende dadurch daß die hiesige denen Luenburgischen Tonnen an form gleich gemachet / hintergangen werden; Derowegen haben Wir nötig erachtet / Unsere vorige Verordnungen hiemit nochmahln zu erneueren / und Voriges Placat von dem 31 May dahin zu extendiren / daß vorbesagte Saltztonnen denen Lunenburgischen an form und Vastage nicht gleich / sondern 5 Daumen großer gemachet werden sollen: Befehlen dann daar auf allen und Jeden / insbesonder Kaufleuten und Kiepferen bey der in dem Kayserl: Gebots Brieffe angedrohéten Straffe Sich hiernach zu richten und fur Schaden zu huten.

Signatum Embdæ in Curia den 1sten Nov: 1723

Ad Mandatum Senatus

Mentet Haykens J. U. D. et

Numerous and frequent complaints of the Lüneburg salt masters in the sixteenth and seventeenth centuries, anent frauds, such as selling Scots salt in Lüneburg measures etc., continued into the eighteenth century, expressing a similar discomfort with this particular type of competition.[62] Thus, Scots salt maintained a roughly constant, and by no means insignificant, position on the north-west German market, in a framework of a continuing decline in exports c. 1700–1760, with stable and in fact sometimes even increasing sales prices. It was not before the 1760s/70s that Scots salt would be replaced for good by English (Cheshire) salt on the Bremen market (see below).[63]

62 SCHWEBEL, Salz, p. 33, p. 41.

63 Ibid., p. 75, pp. 82–91.

What happened to Scots salt once it had been landed in Bremen? As a fairly non-perishable good, salt could be stored for considerable periods; therefore, salt sales and salt consumption might not match or coincide for every year examined. Only a fraction of Scots salt dispatched to Bremen would have been consumed there on the spot. Large quantities would be either re-shipped seawards east (westwards would not have made sense, as the Netherlands, Europe's largest carrier of bulk goods such as Iberian sea salt lay close-by), or more likely, shipped up the River Weser into adjacent Prussian, Hanoverian and Danish territory. Perhaps it was – due to its generally low quality – mainly used for feeding animals. The area around Bremen, especially the Frisian plains, was at that time, as it still is today, marked by a high weight of pastoral farming and stock rearing in overall agricultural activity.[64] This might explain the large imports of low-grade salt via Bremen (and not via Hamburg, an otherwise much more obvious port of calling at the German end of the trades), as well as the collapse in and after 1770/2, years which saw a hunger crisis in Germany, coupled with a wide-spread reduction in the animal stock.[65] If sold on the spot in Bremen, salt was allegedly purchased by wholesalers down to small retailers (Höker, peddlers) alike. Another option was to produce refined salt before re-sale (*Solt van Solte* – "salt upon salt").[66] It is therefore fair to say that during the seventeenth and eighteenth centuries, Scots salt would have penetrated deep into German territories and, by virtue of amounts sold and its pricing, have captured large market shares in northern Germany.

And where exactly did the salt come from? During the period for which the customs accounts have been examined comprehensively, Kirkcaldy (head port, including its creeks, smaller salt ports) appears as the main port of dispatch for Scots salt sent to Germany. The Scottish customs accounts indicate that in the 1740s exports were still dispatched from Bo'ness in fairly large numbers, but that from the early 1750s onwards, Kirkcaldy gained at the expense of Bo'ness. This seems to confirm Whatley's observation that the salt works situated on the southern littoral of the Firth of Forth after 1750 further reduced their export activity and focused on the buoyant urban market of Edinburgh and the Lothians instead.[67]

64 J. BÖLTS, Die Rindviehhaltung im oldenburgisch-ostfriesischen Raum vom Ausgang des 16. Jahrhunderts bis zum Beginn des 19. Jahrhunderts, in: H. WIESE / J. BÖLTS, Rinderhandel und Rinderhaltung im nordwesteuropäischen Küstengebiet vom 15. bis zum 19. Jahrhundert, Stuttgart 1966, pp. 133–271, esp. at pp. 137–140, 170, 180–183, 186, Tab. 13; H. WIESE, Der Rinderhandel im nordwesteuropäischen Küstengebiet vom 15. Jahrhundert bis zum Beginn des 19. Jahrhunderts, in: ibid., pp. 1–132, especially pp. 9–13. K. H. KAUFHOLD, Die Wirtschaft in der frühen Neuzeit: Gewerbe, Handel und Verkehr, in: C. VAN DEN HEUVEL / M. VON BOETTICHER (eds.), Geschichte Niedersachsens, Vol. 3 / Pt. 1: Politik, Wirtschaft und Gesellschaft von der Reformation bis zum Beginn des 19. Jahrhunderts, Hanover 1996, pp. 351–574, at pp. 551s.; pp. 681s. D. SAALFELD, Ländliche Gesellschaft in der frühen Neuzeit I: Ländliche Wirtschafts- und Sozialgeschichte vom Beginn des 16. bis zur Mitte des 17. Jahrhunderts, in: ibid., pp. 637–732, at pp. 681s.

65 Suggested by Prof. Dr. Markus A. Denzel (Leipzig), personal communication.

66 SCHWEBEL, Salz, p. 17f, p. 22, p. 26, p. 36f, p. 39, p. 41, p. 44, p. 48.

67 WHATLEY, Salt Industry, pp. 52–4.

Table 2: Share of Ports in total Exports of Salt to Germany

Average figures for 1743–1755 (13 yrs)
NAS, E504

	Alloa	Bo'ness	Kirkcaldy	Prestonpans
Germany	4%	27%	64%	5%
Bremen	2%	36%	59%	3%

1.2.4 Explanations

It is certain therefore that Scots salt played a considerable role on the Northern German market between 1600 and 1770; a role that was perhaps more considerable than in the case of any other product traded from Scotland to Germany during the same period. Having established the share of the German market for the Scottish salt industry as basically the last remaining foreign outlet of significance c. 1700–1760, but in particular after 1740, some comment would be in order, as to the reasons for this. What was it that made Scots salt so attractive on the Bremen and northern German market? Needless to say that unless a statistically robust amount of micro-evidence was unearthed yielding some reliable evidence as to the composition of the average "German consumption expenditure" in the period under consideration, the following remarks will have to remain highly conjectural.

It is suggested here that quality and price are the essential two components of the explanation. Both were on the lower margin. Otherwise certain phenomena, such as the continuous and somewhat rapid decline of export markets 1700–1770, the simultaneous and resulting rise of the domestic market in Scotland, and the pronounced anxiety of Scottish salt makers to protect their market from English competition by retaining a mutual tariff barrier on Scottish-English salt trade after 1707, could hardly be explained.[68] Whilst it has been suggested that "too much emphasis has been placed on the [Scottish salt] industry's export performance"[69], it is nonetheless clear that, first, the export share of a particular product is quite indicative of this industry's productivity record, as secondly would be this product's share in total domestic exports.[70] By these standards, the Scottish salt industry, with salt accounting for 0.12 per cent of domestic and 0.06 per cent of total exports from Scotland (average 1755–59) respectively, was hopelessly uncompetitive on international markets around the middle of the eighteenth century. And as has been shown in the preceding sections, total exports of Scots salt declined from still quite reasonable levels in the 1710s and 1720s down to zero by about 1760/70. Likewise, the export share of the industry, i.e. the share of total exports to total marketed output of Scots salt, experienced a dramatic decline, 1700–1770. Whilst it had attained quite reasonable levels of up to 60 per cent of total marketed output at varying periods during the seventeenth century, it still stood at

68 C. A. WHATLEY, Salt, Coal and the Union of 1707: A Revision Article, in: Scottish Historical Review, LXVI, 1, Nr. 181 (April 1987), pp. 26–45.

69 WHATLEY, Salt Industry, p. 44.

70 P. TEMIN, Two Views of the British Industrial Revolution, in: Journal of Economic History, LVII (1997), pp. 63–82.

about 30 per cent in the first decade of the eighteenth century.[71] After 1730, however, this share rapidly declined to levels below five per cent (1730–1760). It did so in line with the decline in total exports of Scots salt from Scotland. Thus there was a dramatic loss of competitiveness of the industry on international markets after the Union 1707, i.e. a decrease in the industry's productivity, at least compared to other producers. Clearly, English producers have to be looked for as the major factor contributing to the loss of export markets of the Scottish industry on the continent. The discovery of rock salt in Cheshire in 1670 and subsequent improvements in the transport network until 1757 for instance led to a rocketing increase of Cheshire's production. This caused the Scottish industry the final and definite loss of its last remaining continental market (Bremen) since 1770.[72] One would have occasion to speculate that in order for the Scots product to be displaced from the German market, English salt must have been available at a comparable price and better quality. But then one needs to raise the question: what had been the main reason for the initial success of Scots salt in Bremen (again: North-West Germany) before the final demise?

As mentioned in the introductory paragraph[73], Scots salt was sea salt obtained using artificial heat.[74] The fact that the thermal energy applied to the evaporation process was obtained by burning large amounts of "small" or refuse coal from adjacent coalmines, a type of coal that was virtually unsuitable for any purpose other than firing huge salt-pans, could have accounted for two scenarios directly influencing Scots salt's competitive position, yet in different directions, making for an ambiguous net outcome. Firstly, the availability of an abundant and cheap fuel supply would have resulted in a higher output per unit of time.[75] This would have increased the competitive position of the Scottish product. But secondly, the particular type of coal used might have accounted for a large degree of carbonate residuals and impurities in the final product. There is ample contemporary evidence that Scots salt was rather unsuitable for all but very basic nutritional requirements and chemical applications:

> Salt made from sea-water, unlike brine or rock salt, contains significant quantities of calcium and magnesium compounds which give the product a bitter taste and make it an inefficient preservative. Newcastle salt was grudgingly accepted as kitchen salt but neither as fine table salt nor for curing provisions that were to be kept for any length of time. [...] Both the strength and texture of salt depend on the size of the grains, and boiling sea-water rapidly produced fine-grained salt which soaked up moisture readily and was considered inferior to the larger, coarser-grained salt made by slower evaporation. These shortcomings reduced its appeal to those customers who could afford to pay for quality and restricted it to a smaller market and lower price range.[76]

---

71 WHATLEY, 'Important and Necessary Article', p. 29.

72 ID, Salt Industry, p. 49; SCHWEBEL, Salz, pp. 82–91; MULTHAUP, Neptune's Gift, pp. 58s.

73 Present chapter, section 1.2.1.

74 WHATLEY, Salt Industry.

75 The Scottish coal and salt industries were in fact complementary to one another, a situation which frequently resulted in vertically integrated large business units along the Firth of Forth littorals. WHATLEY, Salt Industry; B. F. DUCKHAM, A History of the Scottish Coal Industry, Vol. 1: 1700–1815. A Social and Industrial History, Newton Abbot 1970, pp. 14–16.

76 J. ELLIS, The Decline and Fall of the Tyneside Salt Industry 1660–1790: A Re-examination, in: Economic History Review, Second Series, XXXIII, 1 (1980), pp. 45–58, at p. 46.

Furthermore, like the northern English sea salt yielded around Newcastle, Scots salt

> was also the product of a process requiring substantial inputs. Enormous quantities of fuel are needed to extract the 3 per cent of salt dissolved in sea-water. Contemporary accounts show it took no less than 6 or 8 tons of coal to make 1 ton of salt at Shields and fuel was the largest element in the total production costs. […] At Shields, in contrast to most other salt-works, the "pancoal" used was not bought from mines sunk specifically or even mainly to supply this demand; it was the by-product of an industry geared to the production of high-quality "shipcoal" for sale in the coastal and export markets. The majority of consumers were householders who wanted large, regular lumps of coal which did not burn as quickly or as fiercely as small coal. However it was impossible, even in the best collieries, to work good shipcoal without encountering a certain amount of this "crusty, drossy, mouldering coal" for which there was very little demand. Its sale to the pans, although at much reduced prices, was therefore welcome as it was thought to help maintain the coalowners' profit margins.[77]

In fact most of the Scottish salt was of an inferior dark or "grey" type, obtained using those types of refuse coal mentioned in the above paragraph, which would have accounted for a comparatively low quality of the final product (Whatley). British Customs legislation prohibited its use for curing exported salt fish. On the German market and in terms of quality, Scots salt could neither match the Lüneburg product made from brine, nor for that matter, its rival sea salts from the Bay of Biscay.[78]

Therefore, in order to fetch sales on foreign markets, Scots salt needed to be cheap and competitively priced. This was certainly the case: as shown above, at the beginning of the eighteenth century, Scots salt sold at slightly more than one-half the price of Lüneburg salt per last on the Bremen market. This was most likely due to considerable differentials in quality, production and transport costs – presumably a combination of the three.[79] Although due to the absence of suitable price evidence a direct comparison between Scots and Atlantic sea salt on the other hand cannot be made, the fact that Scots salt seems to have outperformed its Spanish, Portuguese and French rival products on the Bremen market for most of the seventeenth and eighteenth centuries, is a strong indication that it was priced accordingly, i.e. below Iberian or Bay salt. There is even some indication that Scots salt was frequently sold below cost-price.[80] This would have made sense for instance if a merchant planned a trading voyage with multiple links, the first one being a German port, where he anticipated purchasing cargoes for re-shipping to a further destination in continental Europe and thus needed to make a sale first, in order to raise liquid funds. Lest the ship sailed completely empty, he might as well fill it up with Scots salt as ballast which he could afford to sell at slightly less than he had paid for it to the Scots salt master, thus reducing the overall costs of the ship's voyage.

Thus from c. 1715 through to 1770, German markets accounted for 50 to 100 per cent of total sales of Scots salt abroad. Germany, particularly Bremen, became the last "lifeline" of an industry which faced rapidly declining export shares. In Bremen, Scots

77 Ibid., p. 46–47.

78 Schwebel, Salz, pp. 12–14, p. 21, p. 27, p. 33s., p. 36s., pp. 39–75.

79 Ibid., pp. 71–75.

80 Whatley, 'Important and Necessary Article', p. 32.

salt continued to be sold in notable quantities throughout the eighteenth century, being frequently the most important item imported from overseas. There existed an old, well-established, even intimate, connection between the salt masters located at the Firth of Forth littoral and the Free Imperial City of Bremen, which, if some documents are to be taken literally, would have dated back to the later Middle Ages. What had once been a major customer amongst others (Bremen) during the Scots salt industry's finest hours, in the end proved to be a most loyal companion, accompanying the Scots export industry on its death bed on its final voyage into oblivion. This was the point in time when Scots salt was finally displaced from its continental markets by its English rival in the 1760s and 1770s. After 1770, the Scottish domestic market would absorb 100 per cent of Scots salt for good.

1.3 Other Domestic Exports from Scotland to German Ports

Other than salt and fish, domestic exports from Scotland to Germany were of rather mediocre importance, both in terms of their macro-economic significance (for Scotland), as well as their weight in total exports from Scotland. *Woollen stockings* were an exception, inasmuch as these were exported in quite considerable quantities to German ports in the period under consideration. This might appear slightly strange, as Henning for instance maintains (without a differentiation according to the types of woollen goods) that production costs for woollen goods would have been about equal in Germany and Britain in the period.[81] Exports of woollen goods to Germany concentrated in two particular areas: Aberdeenshire and the Shetlands. The production of stockings had developed around *Aberdeen* along proto-industrial lines early on. In the first half of the eighteenth century, Aberdeen merchants provided circulating capital to "as many as thirty thousand mainly part-time weavers and knitters"[82] in Aberdeenshire and Kincardineshire on a putting-out basis and disposed of large quantities of higher-grade woollen manufactures weekly.[83] Accordingly, Aberdeen was, prior to the rise of the Scottish woollen industry in the Scottish Borders in the 1790s, the largest port of dispatch for woollen manufactures from Scotland. In *Shetland*, woollen stockings were sometimes appropriated via a feudal exchange mechanism and made up additional cargo for the ships that were mainly laden with cod and destined for either Hamburg or Bremen.[84]

Coal, lead and *vitriol oil* will not be considered at present. Figures are provided in the appendix. Neither did these industries' output attain large shares in Scottish national income, nor did it reach significantly high levels amongst total domestic exports

81 HENNING, Handbuch, Vol. 1, p. 839. For the Scottish industry, see: I. BARNES, The Aberdeen Stocking Trade, in: Textile History, VIII (1977), pp. 77–98, Fig. 1; C. GULVIN, The Union and the Scottish Woollen Industry, 1707–1760, in: Scottish Historical Review, L (1971), pp. 121–137, at p. 122. NAS, RH2/5/11, *Memorandum concerning the manufacture of woollens in Aberdeenshire.*

82 C. A. WHATLEY, Scottish Society. Beyond Jacobitism, Towards Industrialization, Manchester / New York 2000, p. 129.

83 H. HAMILTON, An Economic History of Scotland in the Eighteenth Century, Oxford 1963, p. 157s.

84 SMITH, Shetland Life.

from Scotland to German ports. Re-exports on the other hand are much more interesting, and, when it comes to the assessment of multilateralism or the Atlantic economy, they prove to be a much more significant component of the overall framework put forward in the present book.

2. TRADED COMMODITIES (II): RE-EXPORTS

As shown above[85], re-exports occupied a significant role and attained increasing shares in total exports of most of those nations in eighteenth century Europe that possessed overseas colonies or trading companies. Scotland, which had full legal access to the English colonial empire *qua* Treaty of Union (1707), was no exception, and the German market for re-exports channelled via Scotland seems to have corresponded fairly closely to the general continental European market patterns for colonial non-essentials, such as tobacco, sugar, tea, coffee, cocoa, spices and the like.

Amongst total re-exports from Scotland, not only to Germany, but in fact the entire north-west of Europe, tobacco and rice were the most significant commodities. The German market was, as developed en detail in chapter eight of my *In the Wake*[86], normally part of a circular commercial system operated by British traders, comprising various locations on either side of the Atlantic for both commodity, as well as bill of exchange transactions.

2.1 Tobacco

Tobacco is a "sedative stimulant" with both stimulating and calming effects, depending upon the forms of use, intake and consumption habits. An occasional smoker for instance will be immediately stimulated by the first few draws from a smoke she is having after several weeks without cigarettes, but a regular smoker will be nervous and restless, unless he is granted a regular supply with nicotine spread evenly over the day.[87] Tobacco can be very addictive, and therefore had, if sold cheaply and in large amounts, using economies of scale in the supply and distribution chain, one of the highest average profit mark-ups in eighteenth-century world trade. Partly this was also due to the fact that the good branches were chiefly produced in those global areas that lay within the most powerful empires of their time – British and French America – and that the tobacco trades were thus monopolized.

Tobacco consumption had spread across north-western Europe since the early 1600s and had reached dimensions of mass consumerism after the mid-seventeenth century. In England and the Netherlands for instance, per capita consumption levels of

85 Ch. 3.

86 RÖSSNER, In the Wake, ch. 8.

87 Based upon the author's own experience, as well as countless nights out with habitual and dogmatic smoker Prof. Ian Blanchard at Maxi's and the Centraal (Edinburgh).

1.5 lbs or more had been reached since the 1670s, which would, according to historians, allow the use of the term "mass-consumption".[88] Per capita consumption figures, usually derived from retained imports, however, do not reveal anything on this product's consumption *patterns*, which might vary with or be determined by socio-economic macro-classification schemes, such as class, status, and stratum. Likewise, within a country defined by political boundaries, the role of a particular good may vary considerably between regions. This prevents one from making all but very general statements.

In Germany, tobacco was reported to have been smoked on a mass basis by soldiers in the Thirty Years' War. In this way, wide regions – essentially those affected by the war – might have reached per capita consumption levels similar to England and the Netherlands even slightly earlier than the latter countries.[89] The famous satirist Grimmelshausen for instance wrote of day labourers and other common folks towards the end of the Thirty Years' War that they

> [t]heils sauffen Taback, andere fressen ihn, von namentlichen wird er geschnupft, also daß mich wundert, warum sich noch keener vorgefunden, der ihn auch in die Ohren steckt. Und weiß ein jedweder zu sagen, wofür er ihn gebrauche und wozu er ihm wohl bekomme.[90]

By the 1750s at latest mass consumerism of tobacco would have been an unquestionable phenomenon in Germany.[91] In the eighteenth century it was not a question of consumption as such any more, but rather *how* tobacco was consumed, which retained a distinctive and distinguishing element of social stratification. It was smoked by the lower social classes and snuffed by the more affluent groups of society. Snuffing tobacco went along with an extremely tedious framework of rules of courteousness, as well as the requirement of artistically sophisticated and thus very expensive snuff

---

88 N. BRÜBACH, 'This Precious Stinke' – Zur Wirtschaftsgeschichte des Tabaks, 1500 – ca. 1800, in: H. POHL (ed.), The European Discovery of the World and its Economic Effects on Pre-industrial Society 1500–1800, Stuttgart 1990, pp. 141–152; P. SCHMIDT, Tobacco – Its Use and Consumption in Early Modern Europe, in: S. CAVACIOCCHI (ed.), Prodotti e Tecniche d'Oltremare nelle Economie Europee Secc. XIII–XVIII, Prato 1998, pp. 591–617, esp. at p. 610–12. J. GOODMAN, Tobacco in History. The Cultures of Dependence, London / New York 1993, p. 60, Tab. 4.1 and discussion, pp. 72s., Tab. 4.3 (based on Nash). C. SHAMMAS, The Pre-industrial Consumer in England and America, Oxford 1990, pp. 78–81, p. 79 / Tab. 4.2. Cf. also M. BERG, Consumption in eighteenth- and early nineteenth–century Britain, in: R. FLOUD / P. JOHNSON (eds.), The Cambridge Economic History of Modern Britain, Vol. I: Industrialisation, 1700–1860, Cambridge 2004, pp. 357–387, at p. 367, Tab. 13.3; R. SANDGRUBER, Genußmittel. Ihre reale und symbolische Bedeutung im neuzeitlichen Europa, in: Jahrbuch für Wirtschaftsgeschichte (1994/1), pp. 73–88, at p. 75, p. 79. For late seventeenth-century mass consumption in Jamaica: N. ZAHEDIEH, London and the Colonial Consumer in the Late Seventeenth Century, in: Economic History Review, Second Series, XLVII, 2 (1994), pp. 239–261, at p. 252.

89 BRÜBACH, Wirtschaftsgeschichte des Tabaks, pp. 149–152. GOODMAN, Tobacco, ch. 4, esp. pp. 56–61; ch. 6, esp. p. 142, p. 144.

90 "Some of them drink tobacco, others eat it, and others again take it as snuff, so that I am actually quite surprised that I have not come across a single person who has stuck it into their ears yet. And everyone you ask will have a ready answer as to which use he will put it to and what good it does to his health". Quoted in BRÜBACH, Wirtschaftsgeschichte des Tabaks, p. 150.

91 A. MENNINGER, Genuss im kulturellen Wandel. Tabak, Kaffee, Tee und Schokolade in Europa (16. – 19. Jahrhundert), Stuttgart 2004, pp. 284–286.

boxes. This allowed the urban middle and upper classes to develop new means of creating and preserving social exclusivity in the consumption of a product, which as such had become affordable to large groups below their social stratum.[92]

But by no means did this aspect translate into a generally veritable demand for overseas (French, Dutch, British-American, Spanish-American) tobacco just by definition. Tobacco was cultivated to considerable extent all over Germany and across other parts of north-western Europe since the later seventeenth century. During 1700 to 1750 for instance, the volume of tobacco imported from British America into *Dutch* ports ranged between 50 and 100 per cent of the amount grown in the Netherlands *in situ*. It is likely that the situation was similar in Germany; generally American tobacco represented only an addition to total supply on the German market.[93] But a certain predominance of British (Virginia) supply on continental European markets was acknowledged by contemporaries, as the American tobaccos would have tasted better than the continental specimens.[94] As late as 1780, the Prussian king Frederick the Great was so concerned about the drainage of funds due to ever-increasing imports of Virginia leaf tobacco that he encouraged import substitution processes, by establishing a prize fund towards developing chemical substances that would improve Prussian-grown tobaccos.[95]

Again, if Britain was an additional or marginal supplier, within the British supply Scotland can be seen as a marginal supplier, as well. It was not until the early 1770s that Scottish ports began to overtake English ports in terms of re-exports of tobacco to the continent. This again prevents the formulation of firm and causative statements in terms of the importance of the German market for Scottish merchants.

---

92 W. SCHIVELBUSCH, Das Paradies, der Geschmack und die Vernunft. Eine Geschichte der Genußmittel, Munich / Vienna, 2nd ed. 1981, pp. 143–158.

93 P. KRIEDTE, Spätfeudalismus und Handelskapital. Grundlinien der europäischen Wirtschaftsgeschichte vom 16. bis zum Ausgang des 18. Jahrhunderts, Göttingen 1980; Engl. translation: Peasants, Landlords and Merchant Capitalists. Europe and the World Economy, 1500–1800, Leamington Spa 1983, p. 67, Tab. 19.

94 SCHMIDT, Tobacco, pp. 605s.

95 T. KUSTER, 500 Jahre kolonialer Rohrzucker – 250 Jahre europäischer Rübenzucker, in: Vierteljahrschrift für Sozial- und Wirtschaftsgeschichte, LXXXV (1998), pp. 477–512, at pp. 493s.

Figure 6: Total Re-Exports of Raw ("unmanufactured") Tobacco from Scotland to "Germany"; Wholesaler's Price for "Virginia Leaf" Tobacco in Hamburg, 1736–1770

Source: Re-exports; 1743–1755: NAS, E504; 1755–1770: TNA, Customs 14. Hamburg Prices: H.-J. GERHARD / K. H. KAUFHOLD (eds.), Preise im Vor- und Frühindustriellen Deutschland. Nahrungsmittel – Getränke – Gewürze, Rohstoffe und Gewerbeprodukte, Stuttgart 2001, pp. 124s., Tab. A1.08.07. Price quotes in Shillings Banko

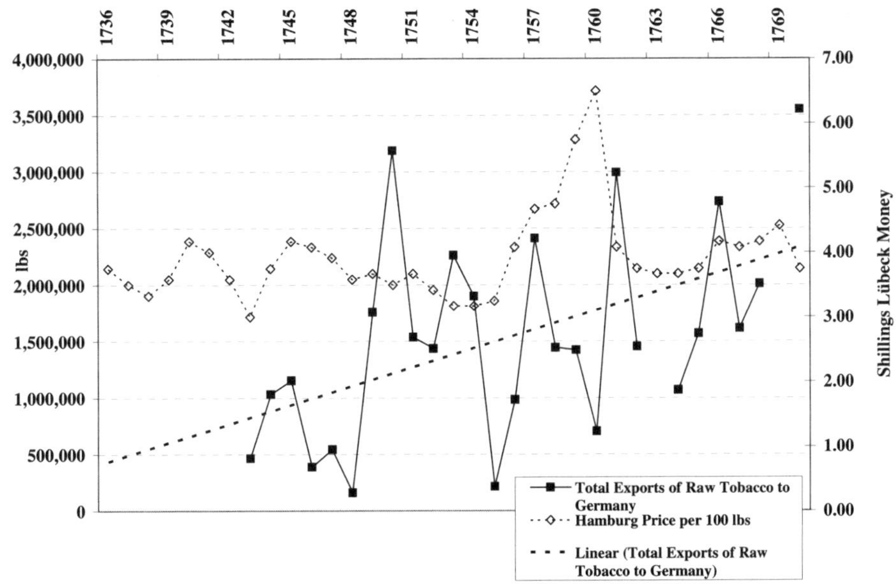

In eighteenth-century Germany the price movement for tobacco was partly contingent upon political developments. The increase in the price level between 1754 and 1760 for instance can almost certainly be attributed to the Seven Years' War, as well as a generally inflationary trend in the price level due to deficient European harvests at the beginning of the 1750s.[96] In this way the story of tobacco is similar to the story of rice (see below). The fall after 1760 on the other hand might – other than the end of the war – be attributed to a switch from France to Britain as Hamburg's main supplier of colonial goods. As France in 1760 cancelled a 1716 commercial treaty with Hamburg, French colonial goods now became dearer, due to an increase in French duties. The successful change to British suppliers resulted in a rocketing of British exports of colonial goods to Hamburg after 1760, and an according reduction in the prices quoted on sugar, tobacco and rice was achieved as early as 1763.[97]

But no apparent correlation can be detected for the Hamburg price of tobacco, assuming that it was representative of the entire North of Germany on the one, and total exports of raw tobacco from Scottish ports to Germany on the other hand. This might be due to several factors. First, there were other suppliers to Germany, chiefly Eng-

96 M. A. DENZEL / H.-J. GERHARD, Inflationäre Prozesse in Nordwestdeutschland im 18. Jahrhundert, in: Vierteljahrschrift für Sozial- und Wirtschaftsgeschichte, XC (2003), pp. 1–25, at pp. 8–10.

97 Ibid.

land and the Netherlands, which were more important than Scotland.[98] Merchants also frequently sent over cargoes at random, i.e. were prepared to take losses when the market conditions in Germany for their tobacco proved to be unfavourable for protracted periods, i.e. for more than a year or so after consigning the cargo to a German port. Sales could be delayed for several years, if cargoes were sent on consignment, in order to fetch an optimal market price.[99] In general, the best explanation would be that Germany was not the main market for American tobacco supplied via Scotland, and that Scotland was not the main source of supply for tobacco to Germany. Nevertheless, German ports were an intrinsic component of markets for tobacco traded through Scotland; they were part of the European "other end of the chain".[100]

Rice again makes for a close Scottish-German trading connection in the eighteenth century. Its significance, however, was limited to certain periods, most notably the Seven Years' War, and thus due almost entirely to changing political, rather than economic, contingencies.

98 In Bremen Dutch, and later on Brazilian, tobacco was favoured since the 1730s over tobacco obtained from British America. L. Beutin, Drei Jahrhunderte Tabakhandel in Bremen, in: H. Kellenbenz (ed.), Ludwig Beutin, Gesammelte Schriften zur Wirtschafts- und Sozialgeschichte, Cologne / Graz 1963, pp. 98–131, at pp. 104s.

99 Rössner, In the Wake, ch. 8, esp. section 8.2 (Buchanan & Simson).

100 See also P. R. Roessner, Scottish Foreign Trade towards the End of the Pre-industrial Period, 1700–1760, Unpubl. University of Edinburgh PhD Thesis, Edinburgh 2007, passim, esp. chs. 7, 8; Id., Warehouse Economy.

2.2 Rice

2.2.1 General Remarks

Scotland imported and re-exported considerable quantities of rice since the time in which the available source material commences (1742). Accounting for up to 46 per cent of total re-exports (£Sterling) from Scotland to Germany, the percentages fluctuated quite erratically.[101] But at some point Germany emerged as the main market for this commodity, if traded through Scottish ports. Given the socio-economic framework of consumption and distribution sketched out in chapter three, rice represents a different and interesting case of slightly opposed and equally unconvincing theories as to its use in consumption, i.e. its north-western European market.[102] But prior to proceeding with a detailed examination of German market conditions faced by Scots merchants trading American rice, some general remarks on the eighteenth century rice trades are in order.

During the period under consideration, in particular the boom in the Scottish rice trades in the late 1750s and early 1760s, Scotland's re-export to import quota for rice obtained at 96% per cent. In other words, rice was not normally or only in tiny quantities consumed in Scotland at all (unless Scotland received its rice from English ports, which is unlikely).

Table 3: Total Imports and Re-exports of Rice, Scotland, 1755–1762

TNA, Customs 14; T36/13

	Imports	Re-exports	Re-X/M
	cwt	cwt	
1755	8,704	8,556	98%
1756	17,213	19,612	114%
1757	17,486	16,523	94%
1758	38,912	33,634	86%
1759	52,035	53,494	103%
1760	33,003	32,840	100%
1761	32,526	28,399	87%
1762	25,938	22,625	87%
AVE			96%

This phenomenon can partly be explained by the fact that rice was taxed at prohibitive levels, amounting to 85 per cent of its prime cost in 1755, if retained for domestic consumption.[103] It could on the other hand draw back up to 90 per cent of customs

101 See figures 7, 8 below and appendix, Table 1.3.2.

102 Its role on the southern European market on the other hand is fairly clear and unambiguous. R. C. NASH, South Carolina and the Atlantic Economy in the Late Seventeenth and Eighteenth Centuries, in: Economic History Review, Second Series, XLV, 4 (1992), pp. 677–702; slightly different view: M. NORTH, The European Rice Trade in the Eighteenth and early Nineteenth Centuries, in: K. FRIEDLAND (ed.), Maritime Food Transport, Cologne / Vienna 1994, pp. 313–323.

103 In 1755, the total duty on imported rice was 6s 4d 2 farthings per cwt, whereupon its f.o.b. valuation (import) amounted to 7s 6d per cwt. CROUCH, View (1755), TNA, Customs 14.

duties paid upon import at any time during the eighteenth century, if it was re-exported within three years after the import declaration had been made (see chapter 3 above, section 3.1). This and the alleged fact that around the middle of the century, net profits to be made in the rice trade were in the order of 50 per cent of its *f.o.b.* price in Carolina[104], suggest that rice was somewhat predestined for profitable entrepôt trading on British/Scottish account within the framework of an otherwise prohibitive taxation regime (British Customs System). Not much is known about the composition of prices, but if a mid-century (1757) source from South Carolina is to be believed, transport costs amounted to £4 10s to £5 per metric ton, which, given an average f.o.b. value of £7 10s per ton of rice, would have amounted to about 42 per cent of the c.i.f. price (profit margin not considered). Between "prime cost" (f.o.b. or ex works) in Carolina and Scotland, the price of one ton of rice would at least double, as the following speculative exercise suggests.

Table 4: Pricing of Imported Rice per Metric Ton[105]

	£Sterling
1 ton of rice @ "prime cost" (f.o.b.)	£7.50
Freight	£4.75
Insurance @ 15 per cent (of prime cost+freight)	£1.13
Non-refundable customs duties	£0.63
End price f.o.b. (Scotland), excl. profit margin	£14.01
Possible profit margin (.49*f.o.b.)	£3.68
End price f.o.b. (Scotland), incl. profit margin	£17.69

Source: f.o.b. price: TNA, Customs 14. Freight & insurance charges: LITTLEFIELD, Rice and Slaves, p. 69, quoting NAS, GD219/290 (1757); customs duties: CROUCH, View (1755).

The wholesale price in Germany would be considerably higher, accounting for the costs of shipping, as well as a profit margin for the re-exporting Scots merchant.

There were, then, two possibilities of shipping American rice to its European consumers. The most obvious option from the modern point of view was direct traffic between South Carolina and its main European markets (Iberian Peninsula, Netherlands, Germany). This however was notionally prohibited *qua* Navigation Laws, unless a special licence was obtained, a bond given and an exemption fee was paid.[106] As far as can be determined on the basis of an evaluation of the complete set of Scottish customs accounts for the years 1743–1755, direct rice shipments *on Scottish ac-*

104 "[T]he Rice would not produce less than £3 Sterling per Barrel at home which is you know 720£ amount. (…)[T]he neat proceeds will not be more than about £350 (…)." Quotation taken from D. C. LITTLEFIELD, Rice and Slaves. Ethnicity and the Slave Trade in Colonial South Carolina, Urbana / Illinois, pbk, 1991, p. 69.

105 1 ton = 2,240 lbs. Freight: £4 15s Sterling. Another source quotes a freight rate of only £4 10s per ton of rice from Charleston in 1757. NAS, AC9/2152/48, *David Loch vs. Donald Edie & Co* (1768), Bill of Loading for 180 bbl of rice shipped from Charleston to "Leith & Hamburg or Bremen", in the ship Helen, master Donald Edie, on account of David Loch (Edinburgh), 5 April 1757. See also present chapter, section 2.2.5 below.

106 Act of Parliament: 5 Geo II cap. 9 sec. 1. An entry was to be made in the Scottish customs accounts on these shipments if Scots merchants were involved. See also J. M. PRICE, The Imperial Economy, 1700–1776, in: P. J. MARSHALL (ed.), The Oxford History of the British Empire, Vol. II: The Eighteenth Century, Oxford / New York 1998, pp. 78–104, at p. 85s.

count took place, but exclusively to Portugal (Lisbon).[107] The other option was the one which English Mercantilism sought to achieve in general: shipment via a British port under payment of customs duties; the rice cargoes then had to be declared regularly as an import, and subsequently as a re-export and were recorded accordingly in identical quantities in the Scottish customs accounts.[108] With regard to supplying the north-western European market (Germany, Netherlands) this was in fact quite a sensible option, as Scotland, especially the Orkney Islands, for instance, lay *en route* between Carolina and Germany. Especially in times of war, the route around the North of Scotland proved to be the safer bet, compared to the alternative southern route to London via the English Channel. This explains to an extent, why Scottish re-exports of rice to German ports took off in the late 1740s and early 1750s, only to level off again in the 1760s. This period, partly coinciding with the Seven Years' War, also happened to be a period of increased activity of French privateers in the southern waters of the North Atlantic. At that time there was also an increasing, yet humble level of illegal direct trade between Carolina and Bremen: in 1755 for instance seven ships laden with rice made a direct voyage between South Carolina and Bremen; eight in 1756. In other years, apart from 1769, such shipments never amounted to more than one or two each year.[109] Thus, the take-off of the Scottish rice trades and the German market for American rice was to a large extent a product of political contingencies.[110]

2.2.2 Scottish Re-exports of Rice to Germany, c. 1740–1770: A Story of Successful Interloping?

Again, the trading pattern to be discussed below has a significance reaching far beyond either Germany's or Scotland's eighteenth-century economic history. Germany for a relatively brief period (1755–63) emerged as the main market for rice traded through Scottish ports, surpassing exports from Scotland to Holland, as well as English re-exports of rice to German ports. This period, roughly coinciding with the Seven Years' War, was also of considerable significance for Scotland's trading activity in general. During these years Scottish re-exports of colonial goods increased faster than English re-exports (Fig. 7).

---

107 Hugh Clerk, brother of Sir John Clerk of Penicuik, for instance was involved in it. NAS GD18/5321/66, 21 March 1751.

108 Or more commonly: providing bonded security in lieu of payment, if a re-export was anticipated.

109 VON WITZENDORF, Beiträge, p. 365.

110 For the subsequent discussion the simplified assumption will therefore be that all exports of rice to Germany *on Scottish account* can be captured from the Scottish customs records (i.e. there was no direct traffic between Charleston and Bremen or Hamburg on Scottish account). Whilst the Scottish customs accounts indicate some direct traffic between Charleston and Lisbon on Scottish account, no indications as to direct shipments to either Hamburg or Bremen could be traced by the present author. There are, however, entries relating to direct rice imports from the Carolinas into Bremen in the *Schlachte* toll accounts. Due to the absence of respective entries in the Scottish customs accounts, it needs to be assumed that these direct rice imports into Bremen took place on English account, or were shipped illegally. *StA Bremen*, 2–Ss.2.a.4.f.1, Vol. 2, entry Nr. 201; Nr. 305.

Figure 7: Scottish and English Re-exports, 1755–1770 (official valuations), £'000s Sterling

Source: TNA, Customs 3, Customs 14

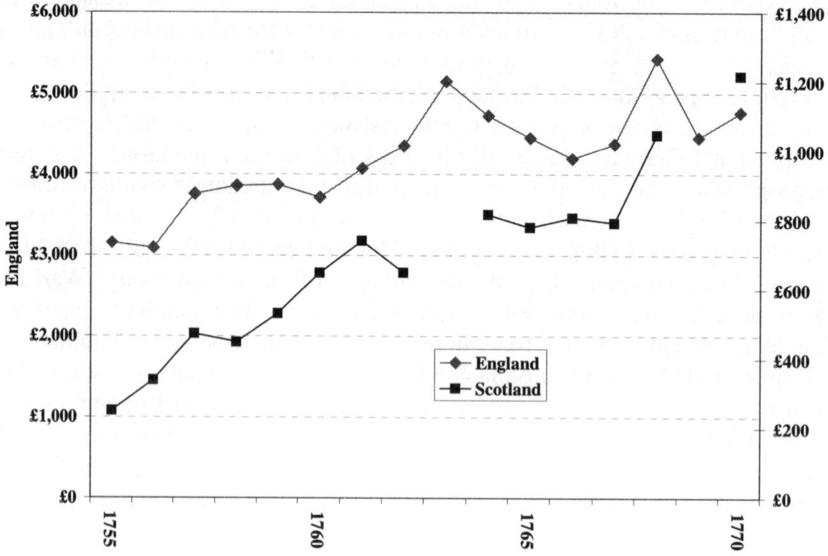

This could mean that Scots traders reaped some windfall gains at the expense of the English whose Navy was occupied with battling the French in the southern waters of the North Atlantic. Obviously wars between the big players in the game (England, France) stimulated the commercial opportunities offered in world trade accruing to smaller nations, such as Scotland (or Sweden, Denmark–Norway).

In the period for which figures are available, the pattern of Scottish re-exports of American rice to German ports appears as follows:

Figure 8: Re-exports of Rice to German Ports on Scottish account, 1743–1770

Source: NAS, E504; TNA, Customs 14

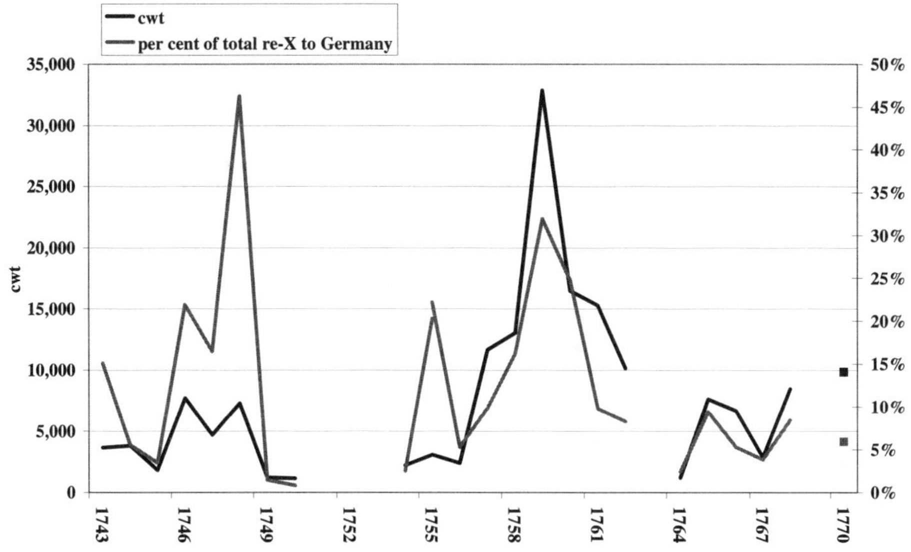

In most years, England re-exported larger quantities of rice to Germany than Scotland (direct shipments not considered).

Figure 9: Scotland's and England's Re-exports of Rice to German Ports Compared

England: NASH, South Carolina, Tab. 5 (four-year-averages). Scotland: NAS, E504 (1743–1755), TNA, Customs 14 (1755–1770)

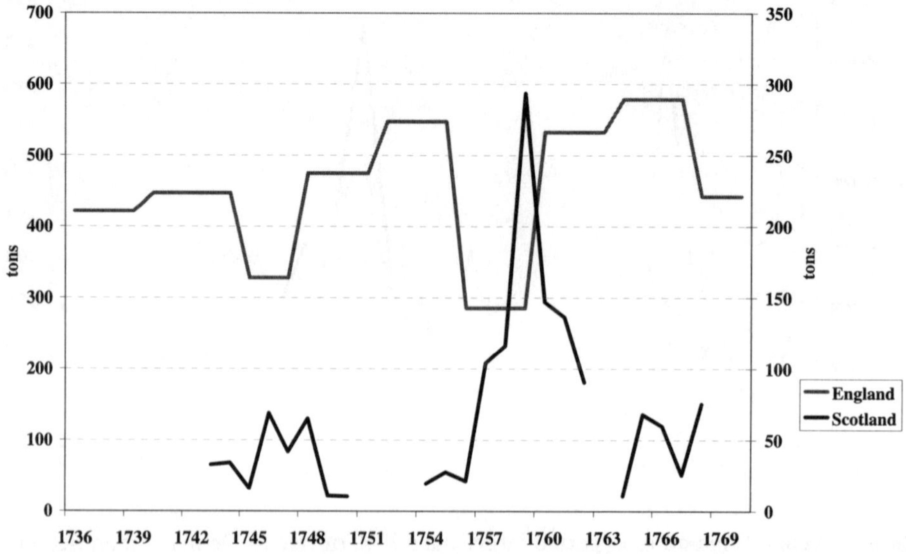

This was just a result of the generally larger propensity to trade of the English[111], and not due to a particularly English propensity to rice trading. Germany, however, was not England's main market for rice (the Netherlands were). Scotland's case was not much different: between 1755 and 1762, for instance, the Dutch share of rice traded via Scotland obtained at an average of 67 per cent, the German market at 33 per cent. Other destinations were largely irrelevant.[112] There were, however, years, when the German market surpassed the Dutch in terms of sales from Scotland (1757, 1759, and 1761).

111 As shown in ch. 3, the English per capita trade volume was usually about four times as large as the Scottish one (in official figures).

112 TNA, Customs 14; T36/13. Cf. also NASH, South Carolina, Tab. 5.

Figure 10: Scottish Re-exports of Rice to "Germany"; Retail Price Quoted for "Carolina Rice" per 100 *Pfund* Weight in Hamburg, 1736–1770

Shipments: 1743–1755: NAS, E504; 1755–1759: TNA, Customs 14. Price quotes taken from GERHARD / KAUFHOLD (eds.), Preise, pp. 48s., Tab. A1.01.01. Price quotes in *Mark Lübeck Current Money* á 16s.

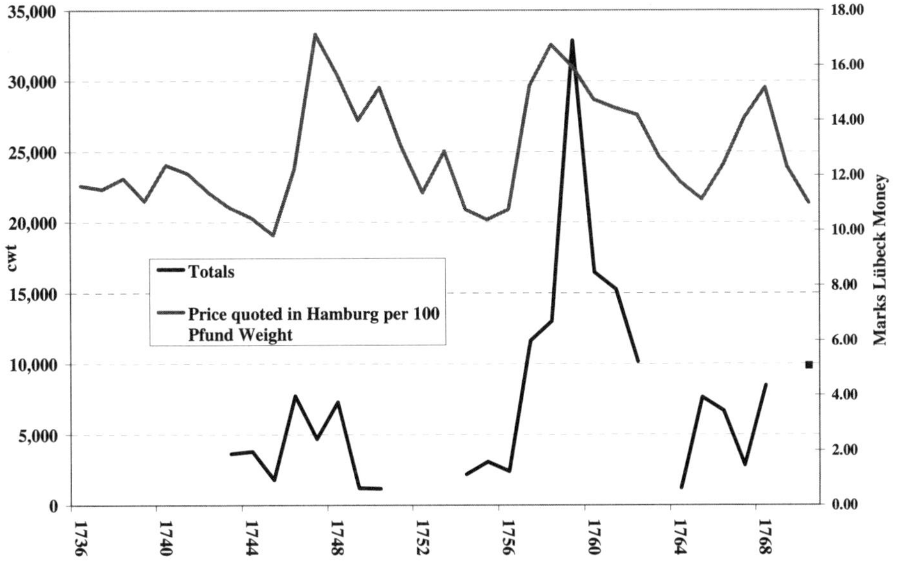

Whilst generally, re-exports of Carolina rice from Scotland to German ports fluctuated quite erratically, two periods appear as particularly significant: the later 1740s, as well as the later 1750s and early 1760s.

Table 5: Average Re-exports of Rice from Scottish Ports to Germany

NAS, E504, TNA, Customs 14. 1 ton = 20 cwt = 2,240 lbs.

Period	Metric tons	STDV
1743-50	196	2,559.48
1755-62	656	9,508.05
1764-68	268	3,166.33

Clearly, with the highest yearly average amounts shipped and standard deviation, the period 1755–1762 stands out from the rest, in terms of a considerable increase in traffic in general, but also an increase in the oscillations. It is debatable whether this phenomenon was supply- or demand-driven, as indications for both can be observed (see below). On the one hand this growth of rice re-exports from Scotland to German ports during the second half of the 1750s coincided with a general increase in grain prices in Germany. This would have stimulated sales of cereals and cereal substitutes in general.[113] But the available circumstantial evidence, apart from being sparse, suggests that this pattern was less determined by changes in German demand for rice, which might well have been contingent upon fluctuations in the German harvest cycle, but rather the political situation English merchants – the larger suppliers – were facing. The rapid increase of rice re-exports to Germany from Scottish ports 1756–1759 in the order of 1,270 per cent coincided with a 60 per cent decrease of rice exports from England to the Netherlands and a 50 per cent decrease of rice re-exports from England to German ports.[114] It further led to a temporary rise of the German share of total re-exports of rice from Scotland to levels between 50 and 70 per cent during 1756–1761.[115]

113 HENNING, Handbuch, Vol. 1, p. 791, Fig. 128. M. A. DENZEL / H. J. GERHARD, Global and Local Aspects of Pre-Industrial Inflations: New Research on Inflationary Processes in XVIIIth-Century Central Europe, in: Journal of European Economic History, XXXIV, 1 (2005), pp. 149–185, at pp. 157s.

114 NASH, South Carolina, p. 688, Tab. 5.

115 TNA, Customs 14.

Table 6: Scottish Re-exports of Rice to Germany (in per cent of total English and British re-exports of rice to "Germany"; values approximated).

Scotland: 1743–1754: customs accounts, E504; 1755–1762: TNA, Customs 14; T36/13. England: Figures from NASH, South Carolina, Tab. 5. Figures for the Scottish share are approximations, as Nash's figures are four-year averages for periods which do not overlap with data from the Scottish customs accounts.

	per cent of English re-exports	per cent of British Re-Exports
1743	7%	7%
1744	8%	7%
1745	5%	5%
1746	21%	17%
1747	13%	11%
1748	14%	12%
1749	2%	2%
1750	2%	2%
1751		
1752		
1753		
1754	4%	3%
1755	5%	5%
1756	8%	7%
1757	36%	27%
1758	41%	29%
1759	103%	51%
1760	28%	22%
1761	26%	20%
1762	17%	15%
1763	0%	0%
1764	2%	2%
1765	12%	11%
1766	10%	9%
1767	4%	4%
1768	17%	15%
1769	0%	0%
1770	20%	17%

A further surprising trend regarding the movements of rice prices over time can be observed. The supply price quoted in Charleston and the wholesale price quoted in Hamburg appear to have been inversely correlated throughout most of the time under consideration. Only sometimes did the two move in unison.[116]

116 A Charleston resident for instance reported a 220 per cent rise in its price, from 12s 6d to 40s per bbl, in 1747. The 1746–7 Hamburg price quotes mirror this increase. NAS, GD237/1/154/4, Letters from James Meikle (South Carolina), mentioning the ship *Magdalene* and her captain James McKenzie (which had sailed for Bremen in 1746 with a total of 1974.23 cwt of rice at Leith in Michaelmas 1746). Cf. also GD237/1/154/3, 29 March 1747. GD18/5321/66, *Hugh Clerk to Sir John Clerk of Penicuik*, 21 March 1751; GD219/290, *John Murray of Murraywhat* (South Carolina), 31 January 1756.

Figure 11: Charleston Rice Prices and Hamburg Wholesale Prices for Imported "Carolina" Rice, 1736–1771

Charleston: NASH, South Carolina, p. 680, Tab. 1. Hamburg: GERHARD / KAUFHOLD (eds.), Preise, p. 48f, Tab. A1.01.01. Four year averages based on periods used by Nash.

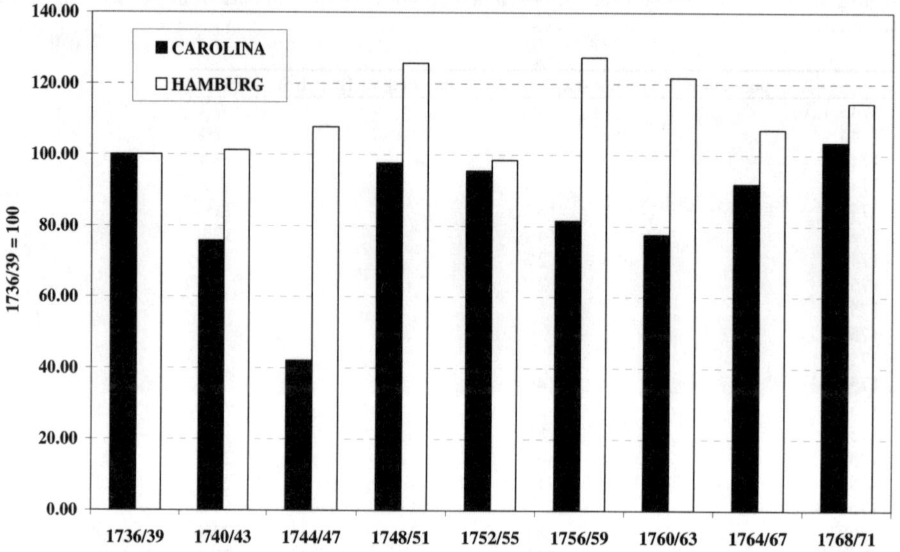

Thus, on the one hand 1740–1760 was a period of depression of rice exports from Carolina to England, and from England to continental European markets.[117] Without doubt this had a price-reducing effect on the purchasing price of rice quoted in America. On the other hand precisely the same period saw Scottish shipments from Carolina to Scotland and on to German and Dutch ports soar to previously and subsequently inexperienced levels. Scotland even temporarily surpassed England in terms of total rice traded to German destinations, when absolute imports of rice into Scotland, as well as Scotland's share in total British rice imports soared to record levels (Table 7).[118] Clearly Scots traders took away some of the traditionally English market shares on the continent at that time, thus realising economic gains from the depression in Carolina and English shipping activity. How is this to be explained?

The answer is "interloping". In a nutshell, the solution lay in a bundle of four criteria. (a) During the Seven Years' War, roughly coinciding with the rise of Scottish rice re-exports at the expense of the English, French privateers roamed the southern waters of the North Atlantic. This made the route from South Carolina to England (London) via the English Channel extremely dangerous. (b) The shipping route across the northern North Atlantic, touching Britain at the north tip of Scotland (Orkney Islands, head port Kirkwall), was, although by no means safe from French privateers either, nevertheless the more sensible bet for the rational merchant from the mid-1750s through to the mid-1760s. This can be attested using contemporary merchants' correspondence (see below). Both links (Carolina⇨Scotland; Scotland⇨Germany)

117 NASH, South Carolina, p. 679f; pp. 687s.; p. 688, Tab. 5.

118 Ibid., p. 691, Tab. 7, cols. 3, 4.

somewhat predestined Scotland as a centre for rice exports to Northern Europe during war times which involved French and English warships.[119] (c) This instable political situation caused a depression in overall exports from South Carolina, and thus led to a decline in the market of rice, which kept the price quotes in South Carolina down. Freight and insurance rates would go up, partly offsetting the more attractive purchase price of rice. These aspects [a–c] point towards a *supply-driven* mechanism determining the pattern of rice re-exports to German ports. It is only the last criterion [d] which lends itself to a *demand-driven* explanation. (d) A decline in continental European living standards after 1740 would have led "the German urban dweller" or some other statistical average or similarly fictitious figure to increasingly resort to grain substitutes. If rice was one of those, which is debated amongst scholars[120], demand for it would have risen, too. This might explain a trend increase in the price of imported rice on the German market, which would have acted as a commercial stimulus to British traders.

Inflationary trends were indeed observable in Germany between c. 1755 and 1765.[121] Quite obviously this coincided with the Seven Years' War, which increased the prices for colonial goods. On the other hand the 1750s saw a series of bad harvests across Germany as well. As a result, the upsurge of the market for colonial rice presumably was a combination of supply-determined and demand-driven components. Both economic (aggregate supply in Germany), as well as political (Seven Years' War, interruption in supply of shipping services and colonial goods) contingencies proved favourable for a small interloping nation – Scotland – to enter what was only temporarily a profitable option. In combination these aspects seem to explain the considerable yet temporarily limited upsurge of rice re-exports to Germany on Scottish account in the 1740s and again in the later 1750s and early 1760s. As soon as the Seven Years' War was over, English traders would again take the "big" business into their own hands.

Some remarks ought to be included on the socio-economic framework of rice consumption in Germany. This requires a short examination of the German market as part of the eighteenth-century world market for rice, as well as a few comments on the applicable socio-economic framework of rice consumption. Unfortunately previous research on early modern consumption patterns, whilst contributing a rich body of evidence as to the consumption of new "tropical and sub-tropical non-essentials" such as tobacco, sugar, tea, coffee and cocoa, has established nothing substantial with regard to rice. It cannot be determined for certain why exactly rice, apart from direct shipments from Carolina to Portugal, was traded almost exclusively to Germany and the Netherlands, without being consumed for instance within Britain. Research has also as yet failed to explain the growth of rice imports into German ports as such, i.e. the inroads it made into German consumption patterns since the 1700s. Did rice become an essential consumption item in eighteenth-century Germany, or did its consumption remain a phenomenon pertaining to the *haute cuisine*, food eaten on Sundays and feast days on the tables of the well-to-do as a curiosity?

---

119 NAS, GD219/290, *John Murray of Murraywhat Letter Book*, 13 April 1756.

120 See section 2.2.4 below.

121 DENZEL / GERHARD, Inflationäre Prozesse, pp. 8–10.

2.2.3 The German Market as Part of the World Market for Rice

Unfortunately this question cannot be answered for certain. Rice had been imported in small quantities, yet regularly into the port of Hamburg since the early 1620s. Towards the end of the eighteenth century the famous encyclopaedist Krünitz believed that, alongside Amsterdam, Hamburg was Europe's second-largest rice importer. Initially, France and Italy had been the main suppliers, but towards the turn of the century, the market was taken over increasingly by the newly-emerged supplier on world markets: South Carolina.[122] Whilst it seems unlikely that rice became a staple import into German ports prior to the mid-eighteenth century, it was quoted regularly in the price currents of the Brunswick fairs towards the end of the eighteenth century.[123] This would point towards a regular supply of this commodity, as well as an increased permeation into central-German markets after 1750 at latest, perhaps arguing against the view that it was mostly consumed within the cities where the rice had been landed. But it is also clear that a merely regular quote of the item on the price currents of the larger inland fairs does not necessarily point towards *mass-consumption* of the item in central Germany, or a high degree of permeation into the lower middle and underclasses of contemporary German society.

Rice was shipped chiefly to Hamburg, less so to Bremen; Baltic ports were irrelevant as a destination (notwithstanding possible shipments via Hamburg). These rice imports from Scotland, or for that matter, total imports of foreign rice into German Atlantic ports in general, represented only a marginal addition to total supply of foodstuffs on the German market. But since rice was not native in northern Europe, these rice imports however, would not have been additional supplies of *rice;* the only way of obtaining and consuming rice in north-west Germany was to import the item from overseas.

---

122 NORTH, European Rice Trade, pp. 317s., Tab. 2, 3.

123 M. A. DENZEL, Die Braunschweiger Messen als regionaler und überregionaler Markt im norddeutschen Raum in der zweiten Hälfte des 18. und im beginnenden 19. Jahrhundert, in: Vierteljahrschrift für Sozial- und Wirtschaftsgeschichte, LXXXV (1998), pp. 40–93, at p. 47.

2.2.4 The Significance of Rice

Rice cultivation had been introduced in South Carolina in the 1690s. It was largely dependent on slave labour, and, it has been suggested, specialist indigenous knowledge, which might have been brought to the Carolinas from Africa by the African slaves that were acquainted with native rice cultivation.[124] Within Europe, on the other hand, rice was predominantly produced and consumed in the South (Iberian Peninsula, France, Italy). In the area of *San Lucar de Barrameda* for instance, Spanish farmers in the eighteenth century developed a cultivation system yielding up to four harvests per year from an almost entirely infertile patch of land which was made fertile through a sophisticated irrigation system, drawing on the water supplies of the river Guadalquivir.[125] There were several types of rice available in Europe, both imported and produced *in situ*. In contemporary appreciation Carolina rice, the corns being fairly white, without husks and thus held to be very palatable, ranged in the same area as Italian (Milan, Verona), and Turkish or Levant rice, whilst several other types, such as Spanish or African rice were held to be inferior.[126]

Direct shipments from Carolina to Lisbon, or re-exports from Scottish and English ports to Southern Europe therefore only contributed a marginal addition to total available supply of what would have been a native crop there.[127] Northern Europe, however, clearly represents a different case, since rice was neither native there, nor was it an established component of the prevailing diet until late. Here, South Carolina was the major supplier of what would still have been a comparatively alien product to the consumer. Yet some scholars maintain that rice in the eighteenth century already occupied a role of an essential foodstuff, fundamentally different in its socio-cultural meaning and economic significance from other colonial re-exports such as sugar and tobacco.

These differing interpretations of rice's role in eighteenth-century German consumption patterns may be crystallized into two streams of thought. The first approach is to ascribe rice the economic role of an "emergency grain" or cereal substitute. Scholars favouring this explanation have referred to phenomena on the supply side, or more specifically, shortfalls in European aggregate supply of cereals over demand. Then – given that rice would indeed have been a cereal substitute and inferior good – north-west European demand for rice would have been determined mainly by fluctuations in the harvest cycle. A second option would be to explain an increase in total re-exports of rice to Northern Europe with changes in preference and taste, phenomena occurring on the demand side. This demand would have been much less contingent upon fluctuations in German aggregate or total agrarian supply (harvest cycle).[128] Neither explanation has its particular virtues. The main problem is the absence of suitable

---

124 LITTLEFIELD, Rice and Slaves, ch. 4.

125 J. G. KRÜNITZ (ed.), Oekonomische Encyklopaedie oder Allgemeines System der Land-, Haus- und Staatswirthschaft, 242 Vols. Berlin 1773–1858, Vol. 123 (1813), entry "Reiß".

126 Ibid.

127 A. EIRAS ROEL, Los productos alimentarios de ultramar. La Europa mediterránea, in: CAVACIOCCHI (ed.), Prodotti, pp. 99–144, at pp. 101s.

128 In its early times, for example, American rice was classified as a "drug" in English customs (Book of Rates) nomenclature.

micro-data, such as statistically significant sets of household account books etc., which makes either of the explanations mentioned above tautological in a sense.

The supply-determined view has been formulated as follows:

> Europeans ate [rice] as a relatively minor, substitute commodity for other cereals and as a complementary cheap grain with other foodstuffs – the reverse of the situation in Asia where of course it has long been a primary staple product and an essential part of the people's diets. […] By the mid-eighteenth century, food shortages among the European population could be severe, owing to demographic pressures and a run of indifferent harvests; about three-quarters of western Europe required basic foodstuffs from overseas, and rice was one of several commodities, including wheat and corn, that met the demand. […] Only good quality rice was generally dispatched to Europe.[129]

Whilst the assumption of a contingency of north-west European rice imports upon the north-west European harvest cycle on the one, and a preference of the north-west European customer for "good quality rice" on the other hand appears to be a slight contradiction in terms (would a customer experiencing budget constraints not have happily resorted to cheaper rice, if rice was a grain substitute inferior to the staple bread cereals?), Montanari has made a similar remark.[130] The main weakness of this explanation is that it has failed to present sound numerical evidence on how the north-west European, mainly the Dutch and German, harvest cycle fits into the picture and which consumption patterns prevailed, both of which would be essential for their argument.[131] Indeed Abel long ago showed that after 1740, all across Europe grain prices began to increase faster than wages, thus presumably leading to a decline in real wages. If the Abel framework was correct, one of its implications would be the uniformity of movement between "real wages" and per capita incomes, which on the whole would have tended to decline after 1740 (if the Abel framework was correct). Furthermore, severe harvest failures can be asserted all across Germany and Europe for instance in 1738–41[132] and 1772–3.[133] No scholar, however, has so far been able to prove a strong positive correlation between harvest shortfalls and per capita income declines on the one, and an increasing propensity to rice imports on the other hand – which should have been an observable pattern if the supply-determined explanation was correct. Whilst without doubt there were periodic harvest shortfalls in Germany after the mid-1730s, which might well have amounted to aggregate supply shocks in each instance, there is no *a priori* evidence that rice automatically became an increas-

129 K. MORGAN, Transatlantic Rice in the European Market in the Eighteenth Century, in: CAVACIOCCHI (ed.), Prodotti, pp. 465–475, at pp. 468s., without direct proof of evidence as to rice being consumed mainly by the urban poor.

130 M. MONTANARI, La fame e l'abbondanza, Rome / Bari 1993, German transl., Der Hunger und der Überfluß. Kulturgeschichte der Ernährung in Europa, Munich, 2nd ed. 1999, p. 156.

131 Such as price series and related evidence. NASH, South Carolina, pp. 681–692.

132 A. E. IMHOF, Aspekte der Bevölkerungsentwicklung in den nordischen Ländern 1720–1750, 2 Vols. Bern 1976; J. D. POST, Climatic Variability and the European Mortality Wave of the early 1740s, in: Journal of Interdisciplinary History, XV, 1 (1984), pp. 1–30; ID., Food Shortage, Climatic Variability, and Epidemic Disease in Preindustrial Europe. The Mortality Peak in the early 1740s, Ithaca / London 1985.

133 W. ABEL, Massenarmut und Hungerkrisen im vorindustriellen Deutschland, Göttingen 1971.

ingly resorted-to emergency product, in the same way as the better-documented cases of peas, beans, buck-wheat and the potato.

But it cannot be doubted on the other hand that rice has got some fortuitous physiological qualities which quite set it apart from proper grains or cereals, as "no puede eludirse la importancia económica y social de este producto, considerando su riqueza en proteínas de alto valor biológico, su alta capacidad de asimilación por el organismo humano, y sobre todo, su elevada productividad, muy superior incluso a la del maiz."[134] In terms of nutritional value (calories yielded per unit), and by virtue of its being potentially apt to yield up to three harvests per year, rice was somewhat superior to cereals such as wheat, rye and oats. The fact of its admittedly quiet taste if unsalted and unseasoned is a characteristic rice shares with all major cereals. Moreover, the fact that rice is normally prepared and eaten hot in the shape of gruel or porridge, and thus physically resembles the standard day-to-day dish of the "average eighteenth century German consumer" (oats or rye porridge mostly) would have made it a very obvious cereal substitute.[135] But, in order to be classified as a cereal substitute, rice ought to have been a cheap product. So long as its nutritional value relative to prevailing main bread grains (rye, oats, to a lesser extent, wheat) exceeded its relative price (relative to rye, oats, and wheat) rice ought to have been preferred for consumption.

But relative to bread grains, rice was in fact no cheap product in the eighteenth century *per se*. Eiras Roel for instance has been able to demonstrate that in eighteenth century Spain – where rice was in a sense native – the price quotes for rice per calorific unit (not unit of measure) regularly exceeded the price of all other available food crops.[136] There is little ground that in northern Europe the situation would have been radically different. As rice was no cheap commodity *per se*, particularly if it were true that only the better types were shipped from Carolina to the German ports, it is hard to classify it as a grain substitute and inferior commodity – unless, of course the consumer was subject to constant "calorific illusion".[137]

Nor has the second line of thought been formulated in terms that would be particularly valid for the macro-economy. This approach views rice not as an inferior good (supply-determined), but stipulates instead that in the eighteenth century demand for rice was determined by preference and taste (demand-determined). North for instance has suggested that

---

134 EIRAS ROEL, Productos alimentarios, p. 102.

135 P. MÜNCH, Lebensformen in der Frühen Neuzeit. 1500 bis 1800, Frankfurt-am-Main 1992, pp. 276s.; R. WENDT, Überseeische Ernährungsprodukte im frühneuzeitlichen Zentraleuropa, in: CAVACIOCCHI (ed.), Prodotti, pp.145–174, at p. 173.

136 EIRAS ROEL, Productos alimentarios, p. 103, p. 141, Tab. V.

137 This consumer might not have been able to precisely establish rice's calorific value and thus – perhaps because rice increases in size when boiled – constantly misinterpreted rice as being cheaper than wheat, rye and oats per currency unit expended.

> [i]n Northern Germany the upper urban class ate rice in the form of rice cakes and chiefly of sweet boiled rice, the so-called "Reisbrei"[...]. This "Reisbrei" was spread as a part of conspicuous consumption into the country in the late 18th century, when the burghers began to eat rice together with their meat on Sundays. Rich peasants of the marshes along the German North Sea coast offered boiled rice together with sugar and raisins – also expensive import commodities – as one course during the wedding banquets and to Sunday guests.[138]

Whilst this explanation is diametrically opposed to the supply-driven scenario summarized previously, it is as impossible to prove on grounds other than speculative reasoning and surviving stray household accounts and perhaps the odd recipe book of a wealthy farmer's wife. The contemporary encyclopaedist Krünitz for instance believed that of all types of rice available in eighteenth-century Europe, the item produced in South Carolina ranged amongst the most beautiful and palatable types, being long, fairly white and without husks, thus matching those high-quality sorts produced in the area of Milan (Italy), Java and China. He added that it was predominantly used as a basic foodstuff during fasting times, particularly so in Catholic areas; he also listed more than forty recipes for rice dishes common in Germany at the time.[139] This might or might not support a demand-determined scenario, but a firm answer needs to be left to future research on rice's role in eighteenth-century consumption patterns.[140]

The present section on rice may be concluded by ways of a case study, illustrating the risks and general mechanisms of the business in the second half of the 1750s.

---

138 NORTH, Rice Trade, pp. 320s.

139 KRÜNITZ, Vol. 123, entry "Reiß".

140 An assessment of rice on the German market in the eighteenth century therefore needs to remain inconclusive, pending further research on consumption patterns leading to more plausible explanations. There can be no doubt that an impoverishment of diet took place from the late 1500s onwards, a tendency that might have been partly reversed during the so-called "agrarian depression" c. 1640–1740, but which became particularly pronounced with a significant further fall in real wages and incomes since the 1740s. For the economic aspects see KAUFHOLD, Deutschland 1650–1850, p. 554, pp. 558s.; HENNING, Handbuch, Vol. 1, pp. 792–804; ABEL, Stufen, ch. 2; Id., Agrarkrisen, pp. 196–203; ID., Landwirtschaft, pp. 282s.; SLICHER VAN BATH, Agrarian History, pp. 221–238. MONTANARI, Hunger. For a discussion of the pitfalls of constructing real wage series for pre-industrial European economies, see: P. K. O'BRIEN / C. KEYDER, Economic Growth in Britain and France 1780–1914. Two Paths to the Twentieth Century, London 1978, pp. 68–76.

2.2.5 The Voyage of the Helen, 1757— A Case Study

A good example of the procedures and risks of the rice trade[141] with particular regard to a Scottish merchant providing the German market with rice is provided by a voyage of the ship *Helen* in 1757. The *Helen* had been trafficking between Scotland, Carolina and Germany prior to that date on a regular basis. The voyage under consideration was commissioned by David Loch, a resident merchant in Leith, the port of Edinburgh, in 1757. From the customs accounts, David Loch appears as the typical early modern "all-rounder", an overseas merchant operating on a large financial scale, with his hands in all branches of the Atlantic trades. The case under consideration relates to his rice business, which linked South Carolina with Scotland and Germany.

The *Helen* had returned to Leith from Hamburg and Altona in May 1756, presumably a rice voyage, as well[142], and was subsequently loaded with Scots linen, iron manufactures, claret and coals, bound for Charleston in Carolina.[143] On 27 September 1756, David Loch insured the cargo with four fellow Edinburgh merchants at the usual conditions prevailing in the London insurance market (which was taken as a benchmark for premiums negotiated in the northern British markets), the insured sum being £200 Sterling, the premium eight per cent. At eight per cent, the policy covered loss due to adverse weather conditions, capture at sea by men of war, fire, piracy, or other "thieves", *provided the ship sailed in convoy*, i.e. within a group of merchant ships accompanied by at least one British war-ship.[144] A voyage without convoy would have cost 12 to 15 per cent of the insured value of the cargo; the insurance contract stated expressively that Loch would forfeit the insured sum if the ship was captured by privateers or pirates whilst sailing without convoy.[145]

The ship arrived safe and according to schedule, in Charleston "about the end of November 1756", where it discharged its cargo and was re-loaded with rice, totalling more than 300,000 lbs (ca. 134 metric tons), as well as 128 bbl pitch, 40 bbl tar, 4 ½ tons Brazil wood, 4 tons logwood, 200 ft mahogany, 1,590 (13.25 ct or long hundred) hogshead staves, 1,260 lbs coffee, 3,469 lbs indigo and 550 gallons Jamaica rum.[146] These goods were insured at a total of £1,540 Sterling for the voyage back from Charleston to Leith.[147] The ship was fully loaded, "very deep so be sure to make Insurance"[148], and cleared Charleston in convoy in May 1757. The convoy was accompanied by one man-of-war and one sloop-of-war, all bound for Halifax in Nova Sco-

141 Which technically was no business of its own, but frequently connected to the Caribbean indigo, coffee, rum and sugar trades.

142 NAS, AC9/2152/71, provisions invoice, Hamburg, 20 May 1756; AC9/2152/74: carpenter's account Altona, 20 June 1756, AC9/2152/75: butcher's account for provisions (beef), 28 May 1756; see also AC9/2152/77, 79, 82.

143 NAS, AC9/2152/43, account/invoice of sales, Charleston, 27 April 1757.

144 NAS, AC9/2152/12–13.

145 NAS, AC9/2152/35, copy of a letter David Loch to Hog & Kinloch, 30 April 1757.

146 NAS, AC9/2152/19, Deposition of David Ross (shipmate); AC9/2152/10, 51, 22 April 1757, bills of lading, Charleston; NAS, AC9/2503–4/9.

147 NAS, AC9/2152/22, Account (bill of loading) for the Helen, Charleston, 12 April, 28 April, 31 May, 25 June 1757.

148 NAS, AC9/2152/37, Donald Edie to David Loch, Charleston 26 April 1757.

tia.[149] Loch, however, had planned for a different route. It was intended to call at the Orkney Islands (Scotland), Leith and then to sail on to Hamburg or Bremen. This meant that for the best part of the voyage across the Atlantic the ship would sail without convoy, against which ship and cargo were not insured.[150] At that time (1757) this was not exactly prudent choice, as French privateers roamed these waters, in particular the latitudes stretching between the Caribbean and South-west England. Having sailed from Charleston towards Halifax for 30 leagues, the *Helen* parted the convoy eastwards, and set sail for the Orkney Islands. Shortly thereafter the ship was indeed taken by French privateers.[151] The French took out some of the indigo, rum, coffee and sugar, but discarded the rest. They then burnt and sunk the ship, took the crew captive and to Louisburg and then to Brest (France), from which they were returned eventually to Portsmouth.[152] Loch accordingly forfeited the insurance, on the grounds of the ship and cargo having been insured as sailing under convoy, at a premium lower by about 50 per cent than the current rate for ships sailing without convoy. By Loch not accepting the forfeiture, one more court case was filed before the Scottish High Court of Admiralty.[153]

Thus the depression in rice exports from South Carolina and accordingly lower prices quoted at the point of production were the result of a reduced trading activity at recurring intervals between 1740 and 1760. This, however, did not translate into lower wholesale prices in Europe (German market), because first, the generally increased risk of shipping the cargo in the same period would have led to an increase in insurance premiums and overall freight costs. Secondly, the general macro-economic constellations in Germany would have tended to keep prices for foodstuffs at a high, and in its long-term linear trend increasing, level.

Moreover, Scotland as a stop en route was somewhat favoured vis-à-vis England by the political geography of the later 1750s. The route across the northern Atlantic to Scotland rather than London or other ports in the south-west of England was safer. A point which supports this notion is the temporary upsurge of Kirkwall (Orkney Islands head port) as a trading centre for rice around the mid-1750s, as is borne out by the

149 NAS, AC9/2152/17, Statement by Andrew Cowan and Archibald Inglis, 1764; AC9/2152/19, Deposition of David Ross, Shipmate.

150 NAS, AC9/2152/37, Letter by Donald Edie to David Loch, Charleston 26 April 1757; AC9/2152/38, Letter by David Deas, Charleston to David Loch, 3 March 1757.

151 NAS, AC9/2152/19, Deposition of David Ross, shipmate.

152 NAS, AC9/2152/28, statement sworn upon oath by Donald Edie and James Robertson, London, 21 January 1758.

153 The jurisdiction of the Scottish High Court of Admiralty – which by §19 of the Treaty of Union (1707) continued to exist as a separate Scottish institution afterwards – covered all sorts of maritime matters such as contracts, crimes, piracy etc. that had occurred at sea or in relation to a seafaring voyage and which had given rise to dispute. In the eighteenth century the court appears to have been favoured by merchants especially for settling commercial matters (such as unpaid bills, wages, expenses), rather than strictly criminal offences. Cases could be brought before the court by anyone, i.e. regardless of status, class or nationality. Thus the Admiralty Court, by providing impartial justice at the expense of the convicted, was essential for providing a stable environment (institutional framework) for overseas trade, lowering transaction costs and thus facilitating commercial expansion and economic growth in the long-run.

Scottish customs accounts.[154] Clearly this was a very direct effect of the naval interruptions caused by the Seven Years' War.

Therefore, this particular market constellation appears to have been fortuitous for Scottish merchants in the 1750s and might have stimulated Scottish purchases in South Carolina and shipments to Germany in the period. Between 1756 and 1759, exports of rice from Scotland to German ports surged by more than ten times, perhaps initially stimulated by a 61 per cent increase in the wholesaler's price of Carolina rice quoted in Hamburg (from 10 Mark 6 s to 16 Mark 12 s *Lübeck* current money).[155] These factors seem, at least for Scots merchants, to have partly offset the rise in shipping costs and insurance premiums resulting from the increased activity of French privateers. The more so, as the insurance premiums apparently – if negotiated prudently – covered the risks of Scots active in the rice trades quite sufficiently, as a contemporary exile Scot-temporarily-turned-Carolina-resident pointed out in 1756:

> however contradictory the maxim may appear our Merchts find their Interest as much in the Capture of their Rice as if it had gone to a Ready market in the time of war; they must pay a certain price to the Planter here, they must pay an Extravagant freight home, and it would be the highest Imprudence not to Insure though the Premium be high. With all these charges the Rice market is often Uncertain in foreign countreys, and when the Merchts have got it there it sometimes happens that they are brought in Debt by it. Can we wonder then that they should be concerned at the Capture when in place of an uncertain Market they have a Sure & a fixed Value from the underwriters?[156]

The above evidence seems to suggest that the spectacular, yet short-lived, increase in rice shipments via Scotland c. 1755–1762/3 was simply due to a business advantage gained at the expense of English traders, which would disappear as soon as English shipping routes were safer again. The chronological coincidence of this pattern with the Seven Years' War (1756–1763) thus may well have been a pattern of causation rather than correlation. If the English merchant marine was heavily engaged in naval warfare with the French, Scots traders may have taken this as an incentive to realise some short-lived windfall gains, because they had the safer shipping routes – via the North Atlantic and the Orkney Islands – and thus could ship their rice to continental European destinations more cheaply than the English during 1755–1763. Much more research on Scottish interloping activities during wartime involving the British (but mainly English) Navy thus needs to be done, but the above-quoted case of the *Helen* and David Loch's insurance claim, as well as the present quote from 1756 relating to insurance claims due to French piracy, seem to suggest that French privateers were at times fairly successful in capturing British ships and their cargoes. The Scots did not hesitate to use this aspect to their own advantage.

154 NAS, E504/26/3.

155 16s *Lübisch* current money = 1 *Mark Lübisch* current money.

156 NAS, GD219/290, *John Murray of Murraywhat Letter Book*, 13 April 1756.

2.3 Other Re-exports: Sugar, Coffee, Ginger

Other re-exports from Scotland to Germany may be dealt with very briefly, due to their insignificant overall relevance. Mintz's study has dealt at length with the phenomenon *sugar* and all its possible socio-economic ramifications[157]; coffee, tea and chocolate – which were all re-exported from Scotland to Germany at times, yet in marginal and very insignificant quantities – have been usefully synopsized very recently by MENNINGER.[158] Firm conclusions on early eighteenth century Scotland or Germany are impossible, on the grounds discussed at length in chapter three of the present work. Again, Scotland was not the main supplier to the German market. Nor was Germany Scotland's main customer of sugar. In fact it appears as though on the Hamburg market for instance, British suppliers were constantly undersold by the *French* in the eighteenth century. At times of political instability, neutral states such as Hamburg might be able to choose who they bought their goods from entirely on the grounds of the price offered, without subjecting their purchasing decisions to political deliberations. On these markets British merchants were price takers. With regard to sugar and coffee, it was very often France which could – and mostly did – offer better terms to the Hamburg merchants than Britain.[159] If Scots merchants occasionally did send over sugar and coffee on consignment to a German port, it was usually part of a larger cargo comprising mainly rice and tobacco. Sugar was, it appears, shipped rather in order to fill the ship, as long as market prospects promised a profit, however small, on the overall voyage. The same applies to coffee, tea, chocolate and ginger, which were dispatched from Scottish ports to Germany at times. To devote a separate paragraph to them would mean to over-stretch their significance in Scottish-German trade; figures might be found in the appendix (Tab. 1.3.2–3). It is now time to discuss the main Scottish imports from Germany, prior to drawing a tentative conclusion on the Scottish-German commodity trades in the eighteenth century.

---

157 S. W. MINTZ, Sweetness and Power. The Place of Sugar in Modern History, New York 1985.

158 MENNINGER, Genuss, esp. chs. III.2, 4, and V.2.

159 Hamburg for instance appears to have received the lion's share of its coffee from France throughout the eighteenth century. J. SCHNEIDER, Die neuen Getränke: Schokolade, Kaffee und Tee (16.–18. Jahrhundert), in: CAVACIOCCHI (ed.), Prodotti, pp. 541–590, at pp. 572–5.

3. TRADED COMMODITIES (III): IMPORTS FROM GERMANY

3.1 Linens

In the period under consideration, Narrow German linens (including items from Prussia and Russia), accounting for up to 94 per cent of total imports from Germany into Scottish ports, represented by far the largest single item in yearly Scottish imports from the Holy Roman Empire. In this way, trade with Germany around the middle of the century was an intrinsic component of Scotland's more recently developed Atlantic trading pattern.

Linen was one of the most popular and basic manufactures in the early modern period and traded over large distances. Contemporaries were well aware of linen's role for early modern society:

> Der allgemeine Gebrauch desselben bey Reichen und Armen, giebt dessen Nothwendigkeit, und daher auch Wichtigkeit im Handel genugsam zu erkennen. Bey den meisten Menschen ist die erste Bekleidung, wenn sie ans Tages Licht erscheinen, die Leinwand, und wenn sie von der Welt abscheiden, die letzte Mitgabe. Sie macht das nothwendigste Stück der Kleidung aus, und ist im Hause so wohl zur Reinlichkeit als Zierde, am Tische, in der Küche, und im Bette unentbehrlich. Da nun aber fast keiner der Leinwand entbehren kann, so ists auch natürlich, daß so viele Menschen sich mit Verfertigung derselben beschäftigen, so wie auch der verschiedene Gebrauch derselben, viele verschiedene Sorten davon verlangen muß. Daher entstehen die mancherley Gattungen der Leinwand, und sie ist, grob oder fein, roh oder gebleicht, Haus= oder Kaufleinwand. Die grobe und feine ist leicht zu unterscheiden, wie auch die rohe und gebleichte. Jene ist entweder grob, und wird zu Säcken, zum Packen und Umschlagen der Waaren, und dergleichen gebraucht; oder fein, und dient zu leichter Sommerkleidung und Unterfutter. Von der ersten wird aus Deutschland viel nach Holland und England, von der letztern viel aus Holland nach Italien verführet.[160]

German linens ranked high in contemporary appreciation, as their fabric was light, yet so robust as to be fairly tight and nearly impervious to wind and water.[161] Although in theory the domestic sale of German linens within Britain was allowed, a high nominal duty on retained imports of German linens made the latter uncompetitive on the British market (in particular as one of the major producers, Ireland, lay close-by and Irish linens could be imported into Britain duty free). In the American colonies, however,

---

160 Roughly translates as: "The most obvious proof of linen's inevitability and ubiquity is its widespread use by rich and poor alike. Man is clothed in linen from the cradle to the grave. Our most important garments are made of it, as well as napkins, diapers and bed covers. Since linen is such an inevitable component of our daily lives, it is neither surprising to find so many engaged in its production, nor to observe a multitude of specimens being manufactured according to manifold purposes. There are fine and coarse, raw or bleached linens, linen cloth for domestic consumption and linen clothes for sale. Coarse linens are used chiefly for sacking and packing, the finer types you will find worn by people during the hot days or as an under garment. Most of the linens sent to England and Holland are coarse German linens, but the finer items are sold by the Dutch to the Italians." KRÜNITZ (ed.), Encyklopaedie, Vol. 107 (1799), entry: "Leinwand".

161 ID. (ed.), Encyklopaedie, Vol. 107 (1799), entry: "Leinwandhandel".

demand for the German products proved to be considerable. It would have been particularly stimulated by a rather generous drawback (customs duties refund upon re-export), which ranged from 82 to 89 per cent of customs duties paid or secured on bond upon import between 1708 and 1770.[162] If re-exported to the colonies, the effective level of taxation on Narrow German linens therefore normally worked out at circa two per cent, as the following table demonstrates (1755 price structure, application of the 1660 legislation or rates).

Table 7: Taxation schedule for "Narrow German" linens (1755), ct ells

CROUCH, View (1755), p. 190. Level of duties computed for British denizens.

	£ Sterling	% of 1755 Valuation
1755 Import Valuation (TNA, Customs 14)	5.5	
Total of Customs Duties	0.869	16%
Drawback	0.774	14%
Level of Taxation if retained for domestic consumption		16%
Drawback if re-exported regularly (% of 1755 valuation)		14%
Effective Tax Rate if re-exported (% of 1755 valuation)		2%

Although the Mercantilist framework did not want these manufactures within Britain, with an effective tax rate of two per cent it did not necessarily put those sending them on to a further destination outside the British Isles at the same disadvantage as those importing (and re-exporting) *French* linens. Again this was a consequence of the 1660 English Customs System, with customs duties and regulations designed in a way so as to make Britain a "warehouse of the world" (chapter three, section 3.1 above).

For the present discussion two aspects ought to be borne in mind: first, imports of Narrow German linens from Germany did not normally equal *total* imports of Narrow German linen into Scotland, as minor quantities were shipped down the Rhine via Amsterdam or Rotterdam. Secondly, a considerable amount of German linens destined for sale in the Americas by Glaswegian merchants were in fact purchased and consigned in London.[163] Therefore, total re-exports of German linens from Scottish ports did not necessarily equal total imports of German linens into Scotland from Germany within a given year.

The expansion of imports and re-exports of German linens in the late 1730s coincided with the general rise of the Atlantic trades since c. 1736 (chapter three). There appear to have been two linen import (and thus re-export) cycles, 1747–1757, and 1757/8–1771 (Figure 12).

162 T. LANGHAM, The Neat Duties […] of all merchandize Specify'd in the Book of Rates […], London 1708; 3rd ed. 1715; CROUCH, View (London, 1725; 2nd ed. 1731; 3rd ed. 1738; 4th ed. 1745; 5th ed. 1755); H. SAXBY, The British Customs, London 1757. S. BALDWIN, A Survey of the British Customs […], London 1770.

163 J. M. PRICE, Buchanan & Simson, 1759–1763: A Different Kind of Glasgow Firm trading to the Chesapeake, in: William and Mary Quarterly, XL (1983), pp. 3–41, at p. 35.

Figure 12: Imports and Re-exports of "Narrow German" Linens, 1738–1776

1738–1748: NAS, Mitchell Papers, RH 2/5/11/18, *Account of the quantities of the several sorts of foreign linens imported into Scotland, Christmas 1738 to Christmas 1748*; 1748–1755: imports from Germany only, customs accounts NAS, E504. 1755–1776: TNA, Customs 14.
Note that imports of Narrow German linen from Germany did not always or necessarily equal total imports of Narrow German linen; therefore the figures for 1748–1755 might be too low in some years.

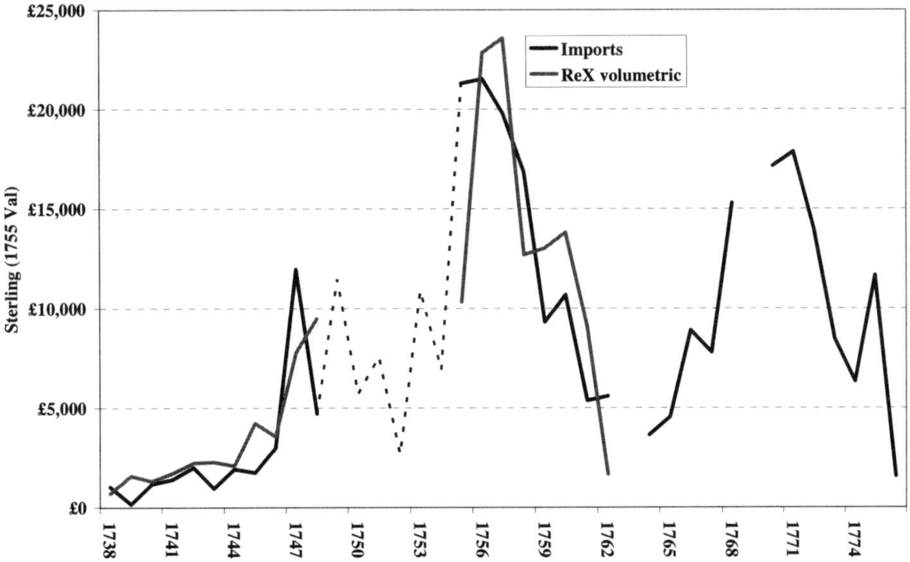

Scholars have attributed the stagnation in re-exports of German linens to the Americas in the 1750s to the introduction of the linen bounty in 1743[164], which certainly further encouraged and stimulated the Scottish and Irish linen industries and their total exports.[165] Contemporary thinkers were likewise convinced that the bounty was responsible not only for an upsurge in the domestic production, but also for a growing export share of Scottish linens in total linens exported, an increase somewhat at the expense of German items, 1742–1752. A contemporary British politician for instance wrote in 1752, that

> The Bounty has enabled us at a very small Expence to the Government to send considerable Quantities of our own Linens to the Plantations, which were formerly supplied with foreign, & must be so again if the Bounty is not continued. (…) The Exportation of our Coarse Linens has been the Cause of opening new Branches of Trade between Scotland and the Plantations, whereby the Revenue has been increased & Smuggling discouraged.[166]

But as during the first six years of the bounty's existence (1742–7), imports of German linens continued to expand and only slightly declined thereafter, it is not evident

164 An export subsidy granted on Scotch and Irish linens.

165 PRICE, Imperial Economy, p. 88.

166 Lord Deskford. NAS, Seafield MSS, GD 248/954/5/38, *Reasons for Continuing the Bounty on Low Priced British Linens.*

that this duty replaced the German linens and priced them out of the market immediately or by necessity. Quite to the contrary, as the second cyclical increase between c. 1753 and 1758 demonstrates.[167] This was most certainly due to the abolishment of the bounty after the parliamentary session in 1753–4, after which a subsidy was granted to the Scottish linen industry instead, which contemporaries thought to be inadequate in order to price the German linens out of the colonial markets. Whilst during its times of existence the bounty on exports of Scottish (and Irish) linens had lowered the price of the item at which Scots traders were willing to offer it to the colonial consumer, thus partly pricing the German re-exports out of the colonial market, the second upsurge of imports and re-exports of "narrow German" linens from Scottish ports, 1753–58, was indicative of a still highly uncompetitive Scottish industry which captured large export markets only within a framework of protection and subsidization. Whenever this framework was lessened or broke apart, i.e. tariffs on foreign linens were lowered, or bounties (export subsidies) abandoned, some market shares would be lost to foreign competition.[168]

If imported from Germany to Scotland, Narrow German linens were exclusively shipped from either Bremen or Hamburg, but none through Emden or the Baltic ports.[169] Tiny quantities would also be imported through Dutch (Amsterdam, Rotterdam), Danish (Altona), Polish (Danzig) and Russian ports (St Petersburg).[170] Although there were considerable fluctuations in the share of the two ports, Bremen emerges as the most important point of dispatch, 1743–1755.

Table 8: German Ports of Dispatch, "Narrow German" linens (£Sterling).

Yearly averages for periods given, excl. Altona.
NAS, E504 (1743–1755); TNA, T36/13 (1760–1765), ct ells (120) have been valued at 1755 rate
Full Table in Appendix

	Hamburg		Bremen	
1743-1755	2,017	35%	5,476	70%
1760-65	1,161	31%	4,876	89%

The picture was symmetrical: towards the end of the eighteenth century, most of total German linen exports overseas were channelled through Bremen, followed by Hamburg, Altona and other Atlantic ports.[171] Unfortunately, the Scottish customs accounts

167 See Figure 13 above.

168 A. J. DURIE, The Markets for Scottish Linen, 1730–1775, in: Scottish Historical Review, LII, 1 (1973), pp. 30–49, at pp. 42–4.

169 NAS, E504.

170 NA, T36/13, Account of linens imported into Scotland, 1760–1762. Linen imported from St Petersburg were normally labelled "Narrow Russia or Muscovy". E. SCHMITZ, Leinengewerbe und Leinenhandel in Nordwestdeutschland, Cologne 1967, p. 87, n. 494. Silesian linen exported via Altona: J. HANWAY, An Historical Account of the British Trade over the Caspian Sea. With the Author's Journal of Travels from England through Russia into Persia; and back through Russia, Germany and Holland, Vol. II, London, 2nd ed. 1754, p. 17.

171 K.-H. KAUFHOLD, Gewerbelandschaften in der frühen Neuzeit (1650–1800), in: H. POHL (ed.), Gewerbe und Industrielandschaften vom Spätmittelalter bis ins 20. Jahrhundert, Stuttgart 1986, pp. 112–202, at p. 170, p. 180.

are indifferent as to the specific material identity of Narrow German linens. As there were several types available, this rules out a precise answer, as to where the German linens imported had been produced, or what types of linen exactly were imported. As of 4 & 5 W. & M. cap. 5 (Act of Parliament)

> [a]ll Linen of *Germany* or *High Dutchland*, and *Silesia*, not above three Quarters and an Half broad, shall be accounted narrow Linen; and all above that Breadth shall be accounted as broad, and pay accordingly.[172]

The customs accounts therefore did not differentiate according to the several places of origin (such as *Polonia, Hanovers, Westphalia, Hartford (Herford), plain Napkining, Hinderlands from Prussia and Polonia*[173] etc.) and generally applied the same valuation and taxation rate to what could be a bewildering array of different linen specimens imported from Germany. But due to the significance of Bremen in Scottish imports of the specimen under consideration, however, it can be assumed that the majority of Narrow German linens imported into Scotland had been produced in central-west Germany. Production had developed mainly in regions such as Westphalia (Tecklenburg, Lingen, Minden, Ravensberg), or those smaller territories bordering the River Weser, such as the Duchy of Brunswick and the Bishopric of Hildesheim. These regions were characterized by a strong weight of the linen textile manufacturing sector in total employment. Production was largely organized within a proto-industrial economic framework (often under the putting-out system, *Verlag*, but independent producers were also important), thus mainly carried out in the countryside, by people whose main source of income was not agriculture and who were producing for inter-regional and overseas markets.[174] The industry was boosted and probably experienced productivity gains since the later seventeenth century, not only by state control (the so-called *Leggen*, central places where the final product received an official quality check, similar to the stamp masters established by the Board of Trustees in Scotland 1727), but also by various funds put up by various governments in order to encourage textile production.[175] The distribution chain was in the hands of Bremen overseas merchants and freight carriers. It has been alleged for instance that Bremen haulers not only controlled the transportation and logistics of the trades, but also supplied the central German producers with colonial goods imported via Bremen in turn. These goods were paid for by the linens received; but usually there remained a positive balance accruing to the Bremen merchants and haulers, which led to asymmetrical credit relationships in the long run, possibly very similar to those described with regard to the Glaswegian colonial trades.[176] Generally speaking, the central-west German linens,

---

172 LANGHAM, Duties (1708), p. 92; CROUCH, Guide (1755), p. 190.

173 The latter would be labelled "Narrow East Country", but it is unclear whether some of the Narrow German linens in the customs accounts might have included East Country linens as well.

174 W. REININGHAUS, Gewerbe in der Frühen Neuzeit, Munich 1990, pp. 26–29; KAUFHOLD, Gewerbelandschaften, pp. 124s., p. 136, p. 162, pp. 164s., pp. 168–170, pp. 182s., pp. 186–202.

175 HENNING, Handbuch, Vol. I., p. 822, pp. 846s.

176 KRÜNITZ (ed.), Encyklopaedie, Vol. 107 (1799), entry: "Leinwandhandel". Glasgow tobacco trades: T. M. DEVINE, The Tobacco Lords. A Study of the Tobacco Merchants of Glasgow and their Trading Activities 1740–1790, Edinburgh 1975.

which were mainly traded via Bremen, were held to be the best of their kind available for sale.[177]

Hamburg on the other hand, as shown above (chapter three), was a channel for the production of Lower Saxony and areas further east, reaching deep into the Silesian (Prussian) territories. Emden had lost its role as the major exporting port for the north-west German production areas after the sixteenth century and was of no importance in the eighteenth century any more in terms of exports to Scotland or Britain in general.[178]

During the period for which the customs accounts have been completely examined, German linens were mainly imported via Bo'ness.[179]

Table 9: Imports of Narrow German Linens from Germany by Scottish Ports (ct ells)

NAS, E504. 1 *ct* (*centum*, long hundred) = 120

	Bo'ness		Greenock		Leith		Other	
1743					174	100%		
1744					357	100%		
1745					270	100%		
1746					403	88%	55	12%
1747	1,590	73%			550	25%	50	2%
1748	747	87%			111	13%		
1749	1,662	80%			425	20%		
1750	762	73%			275	27%		
1751	1,076	78%			299	22%		
1752	279	57%			209	43%		
1753	1,196	60%	571	29%	344	17%		
1754	418	33%	594	47%	133	11%	114	9%
1755	2,693	71%	887	23%	236	6%		
AVE		47%		8%		44%		2%

Bo'ness, located in the Firth of Forth just a few miles to the north-west of Edinburgh, was an extended "eastern arm" or east coast port of Glasgow, even prior to the construction of the Forth-Clyde canal linking the two directly in the 1790s. It can with regard to the linen trades be labelled a Glasgow port, as it was chiefly via Bo'ness that the Atlantic merchants of Glasgow obtained their supplies of German linen, increasingly so after the mid-1740s.

So much for the linen trades, which were the most important imports Scotland received from Germany during the eighteenth century. Only cereals deserve some further, yet short, comment.

177 KRÜNITZ (ed.), Encyklopaedie, Vol. 107 (1799), entry: "Leinwandhandel".

178 SCHMITZ, Leinengewerbe, p. 87, n. 491–3.

179 The full name of the town used to be Borrowstounness, but the abbreviation "Bo'ness" has become official nomenclature.

3.2 Cereals

England became a net-importer of grain from c. 1760 onwards.[180] For Scotland – based on a source which prior to the lifting of the Corn Laws probably under-stated imports[181] – an identical scenario obtains:

Figure 3: Scottish Net-exports of all Cereals (excl. Rice), 1708–1776.

Source: BALD, Assistant.

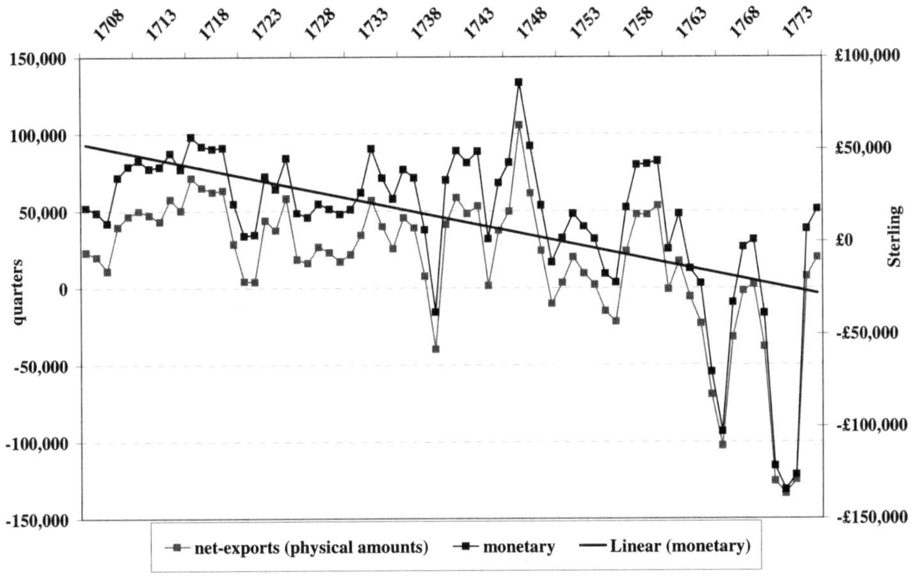

Basically, the Scottish pattern of net-exports of grain was similar to the one detected for England. From the mid-1760s, net-exports appear to have fallen below zero and remained there for most years. From 1765 on, cereals began to be imported into Scotland on a more regular basis. Some quantities came from Germany, too, attaining shares of up to 34 per cent in total imports. The socio-economic implications of this (was this a "Malthusian" or "Rostovian" scenario?) need not be discussed here. Likewise, too much should not be read into the mutual Scottish-German cereal trades, as the Netherlands and Poland (Danzig) were certainly a much more important grain supplier to Scotland and England than the German ports proper.

Other imports do not appear to have loomed large on the Scottish import bill incurred in Germany. Timber items received from Germany, such as clapboards and

180 M. OVERTON, Agricultural Revolution in England. The Transformation of the Agrarian Economy 1500–1850, Cambridge 1996.

181 A. BALD, The Farmer and Corn-Dealer's Assistant, Edinburgh 1780, provides some import-export data allegedly derived from (now lost) "customhouse books". L. E. COCHRAN, Scottish Trade with Ireland in the Eighteenth Century, Edinburgh 1985, pp. 93–114, esp. p. 94, p. 96, pp. 102–105.

pipe or barrel staves were part of a larger general supply for Scots coopers producing the barrels and casks needed by their fisheries and wine merchants.[182]

Having discussed exports, re-exports and imports in turn, it would be in order to move on to the micro-level of individual Scots merchants involved in the trades to Germany. Similar to Newman's observation on English trade with Hamburg in the late seventeenth and early eighteenth centuries[183], much of Scottish-German trade was but a part of a wider, multilateral network and system of trade balances and payments. This is where the truly European or even global contingencies enter the picture. As a detailed examination of these mechanisms has already been presented elsewhere[184], this thematic approach will not be pursued or followed up here.

182 Appendix, Table 1.4.2–3.

183 K. NEWMAN, Hamburg in the European Economy, 1660–1750, in: Journal of European Economic History, XIV, 1 (1985), pp. 57–93, esp. at pp. 88–90.

184 RÖSSNER, In the Wake, ch. 8.

V. CONCLUSION

This study of Scottish-German Trade, 1700–1770[1] has shown how closely integrated trade between Scottish and German ports was into (1) the British Atlantic economy – defined by the nascent British Empire, its commercial and institutional foundations (Navigation Acts), (2) the general north-western European system of commodity exchange and (3) financial transactions, the corollary of the former in accounting terms. Each of the three incorporated locations beyond either Scotland or Germany. With regard to (1), trade between Scotland and Germany was dominated by *re-exports* of those staple commodities obtained in the British Colonies that accounted for the major observable commercial dynamics in the period – chiefly tobacco, sugar, rice and coffee. With regard to *imports* from Germany, this particular trade flow linked back into the "Atlantic economy" by the imports of German linens, which were re-exported to the British Colonies. As commercial dynamics resting upon an exponentially increasing amount of re-exports of tropical goods since c.1740 were in fact observable for most of the European economies that had colonies in those tropical latitudes or access to their products (France, the Netherlands, England, Scotland, Denmark) the Scottish pattern of trade and one of its particular markets, Germany, again closely fit into a pan-European contingency table of economic development prior to the Industrial Revolution.

But this was by no means limited to the re-export trade in colonial non-essentials. As has been demonstrated with regard to Scottish *domestic exports* of herring, cod fish and salt to German ports, these trades were often part of a larger goods' circuit that spanned, apart from Germany and Scotland, the Netherlands and the Iberian Peninsula as well. Outstanding balances were, so to speak, settled multilaterally. Domestic exports from Scotland were dominated by commodities such as fish, salt, lead, coal and stockings, the traditional bulk staples Scotland had been exporting to continental European destinations since the early 1500s. Scots salt in the 1740s still attained shares of up to 12 per cent in total exports to Germany. The German market, particularly Bremen, thus proved to be the lifeline of what was an industry facing stiff competition on continental markets.

Accordingly, trade between Scotland and Germany went mainly through the large North Sea ports of Hamburg and Bremen, the main German points of arrival for colonial or sub-tropical goods in the period under consideration. Especially Hamburg was a "free" port since the 1720s, offering attractive trading conditions to anyone, regardless of the political conditions of the day, by the application of only modest customs duties. Bremen and Hamburg, therefore, not only by the token of their close proximity to Scotland's east coast ports, but also by attractive conditions offered to British traders, were amongst the most obvious destinations for sea-borne trade, particularly for

1 The results formulated at present need to be seen in combination with the findings in P. R. RÖSSNER, Scottish Trade in the Wake of Union 1700–1760. The Rise of a Warehouse Economy, Stuttgart 2008, chapter 8.

low-value and bulk commodities such as salt and fish, trade in which became increasingly unprofitable with an increase in distance from their point of dispatch. Hamburg and Bremen however were chiefly transit or re-exporting ports in either direction. By the lack of direct access to colonial non-essentials these large German entrepôts were predestined for a profitable trade in these commodities via the nations possessing colonies or direct access to the much sought-after goods such as tobacco, sugar, coffee. They supplied the entire North, as well as central areas of Germany with colonial goods; their linen supply areas likewise reached deep into central-western German production areas, in Hamburg's case deep into Prussian and Silesian production areas. Bremen's markets, in particular for tobacco and Scots salt, comprised *inter alia* the states of Hanover, Brunswick and Oldenburg, the Weser area, Hesse and Westphalia.

These ports, by operating a commercial policy towards "free trade", however not only channelled British imports. In fact the same commodities which normally came in via Britain were also obtained from "rival" nations such as France and the Netherlands. Accordingly, British, or in the present case, Scots traders frequently faced stiff competition on the German market, conditions of which were more often than not determined by Dutch, French and Spanish sales on German and "quasi-German" markets. This applied to tobacco and sugar, the former a Scottish, the latter an English staple, but also to rice. Even though towards the end of the period under consideration (1770) Scottish ports at times handled more than 50 per cent of British tobacco imports and re-exports, the powerful Glaswegian monopoly in British colonial tobacco did not translate into a monopoly on the German market. Apart from the fact that some tobacco was being cultivated in Germany itself, German demand seems to have favoured Dutch and Spanish colonial tobacco. Thus on the German market Scottish tobacco traders were price takers, and profit opportunities presumably contingent upon the much larger supply of other colonial powers. The French also determined to an extent the level of sales and profits made on American tobacco sold in Germany on Scottish account. If for instance, the French tobacco buyers purchased too much or made a bulk purchase of tobacco in Glasgow or Edinburgh earlier than expected, there would be no cargo available in Glasgow to be shipped to the German market. And since France was a direct supplier of sugar and coffee to the German market, profit and sales' levels on this market were entirely dependent upon direct supplies via France. If a larger amount of sugar and coffee from the French West Indies had been dispatched to Hamburg recently, there would be no point in sending over some sugar and coffee from the British West Indies, as the French constantly undercut the British on the Hamburg coffee and sugar market. These aspects have been used to clarify to how little extent Scottish-German trade in the period was actually determined by mutual German demand and Scottish supply for products, or vice versa; it all took place within a larger pan-European contingency matrix.

The detailed examination of the rice trades has likewise demonstrated the geographical-political contingencies that reached far beyond the narrow perspective of Scotland⇔Germany, which market conditions for a particular product could be subjected to. These constellations for instance led to a considerable yet temporary upsurge in Scotland's share of American rice traded to German (and Dutch) destinations during times when English shipping routes were endangered by French privateers. At one point in time (1759), Scotland even handled the lion's share of American rice traded to Germany on British account, perhaps even to continental European destinations in general. Once English shipping routes were safer again, however, this business advantage vanished as quickly as it had been gained.

Has the choice of the topic therefore been too much of an analytical reduction to bear much historical relevance and significance? – To the contrary. Apart from the fact that the choice of topic in fact reflects a simple ceteris paribus condition, in order to gain a comprehensive and statistically manageable analytical insight into an infinitely complex working mechanism ("the eighteenth-century Atlantic economy"), German markets did in fact represent the major markets for certain Scottish products at times during the eighteenth century. Salt has been a case in point, even presenting the opportunity of a bilateral analysis that made historical sense. For the Scottish salt industry, which since the early 1700s faced an increasingly unfavourable position on continental markets vis-à-vis English (Cheshire) producers, German ports effectively acted as a lifeline after the 1740s. Whilst total exports of Scots salt, and accordingly the export share of the industry, experienced a continuous decline, c. 1740–1770, the German market retained a nearly constant market share. It was in particular Bremen and its commercial hinterland, where Scots salt continued to be consumed in extraordinary quantities. It appears to have been the most common and popular type of foreign salt sold on the Bremen salt market at times. The best explanation for this is the close proximity to the main Scottish salt producers in the Firth of Forth, accordingly modest transport costs, as well as the alleged fact that at that time Scots salt was often sold below cost-price. An examination of select merchant's papers has suggested that frequently these sales were less profit-orientated than driven by the desire to raise cash in a foreign currency with which further purchases would be made on the German market.

As shown elsewhere[2], the contingencies of Scottish-German trade fluctuations were such that not only was this trade flow dependent upon general European commodity market conditions. It was by the nature of trade balances and trading practice also firmly embedded into the corollary of the commodity markets: the system of north-western European finance and cashless transactions. This situation can only be fully appreciated if the discussion is taken from the macro- or statistical viewpoint, down to the level of individual merchants or firms active in the trades with Germany. A discussion of select merchant's papers and accounts has shown that trade between Scottish and German ports normally involved at least three, and more often many more links, resembling a web of financial and commodity transactions spun all across north-western Europe, even comprising parts of America and Africa. The mechanism operating in this sphere closely corresponded to the mechanism of the north-western European financial system examined and analyzed in-depth by M A Denzel. Strictly speaking, therefore, bi-lateral trade, or in the present instance, "Scottish-German trade" probably did not exist as such, or at least was not representative of average conditions. Transactions were almost never completely balanced, but required either further financial streams or commodity transfers, covering locations and time frameworks different from those obtaining in the initial commodity trades. Money for cargoes received from Scotland for instance was probably not normally remitted directly back to Glasgow or Edinburgh from Hamburg or Bremen.

2 Ibid.

Thus, trade between Scottish and German ports – regardless the type of commodities and merchants or business size involved – was normally multilateral and firmly integrated into what scholars have variously called the "Atlantic economy", or the "European-centred world trading system". In fact it was a phenomenon of truly global dimensions.

Sources are the same as in Table 1.1 for all subsequent tables, unless otherwise indicated.

Table 1.1: Total Scottish Imports from / Exports to Ports within the Holy Roman Empire, 1743–1770

Table 1.1.1: At 1755 valuations (£Sterling)

	Imports				Exports				Re-exports			
	German Ports		Altona	Stralsund	German Ports		Altona	Stralsund	German Ports		Altona	Stralsund
	E504	CUST14	E504	E504	E504	CUST14	E504	E504	E504	CUST14	E504	E504
1742	1,562		17	152	1,070				1,333			
1743	1,523		161		7,957			407	11,535			
1744	2,434		142		9,657			374	32,757			
1745	1,783		570		7,082				25,102			
1746	4,218		131		8,028			69	16,738		11,531	
1747	13,911		111		13,976				13,544			
1748	6,475		583		10,972				7,484			
1749	14,088		607		17,034			15	39,428		3,840	
1750	8,667		362		10,809				67,341			
1751	9,679		225		9,614				31,990			
1752	4,330		251		18,942			1,298	31,537			
1753	13,248		247		19,109		8		48,019			
1754	9,188		237		23,216				41,872			
1755	22,272	22,270	119		15,955	8,588			7,221	5,141		
1756		24,344				12,490				21,629		
1757		24,125				10,249				55,979		
1758		23,718				11,314				38,182		
1759		13,902				8,178				49,248		
1760		14,360				5,766				31,558		
1761		12,008				8,931				74,212		
1762		9,635				33,650				58,056		
1763												
1764		8,728				6,913				23,410		
1765		6,124				3,813				38,469		
1766		10,081				7,066				60,112		
1767		13,842				5,913				35,173		
1768		20,394				7,892				47,491		
1769												
1770		25,655				6,033				78,994		

1743–1755: Customs Accounts, Scotland (NAS, E504). Full list given in bibliography.
1755–1770: Scottish Inspector General's Ledgers of Imports and Exports (TNA, Customs 14).

Table 1.1.2: Official Sterling Valuations (1755–1770)

	Totals (Scotland)				Trade with German Ports							
	Imports	Exports	Re-exports	TotalX	Imports	%	Exports	%	Re-exports	%	TotalX	%
1755	465,412	284,691	250,876	535,567	22,270	5%	8,588	3%	5,141	2%	13,729	3%
1756	480,425	285,892	339,088	624,980	24,344	5%	12,490	4%	21,629	6%	34,119	5%
1757	619,836	348,686	472,778	821,464	24,125	4%	10,249	3%	55,979	12%	66,228	8%
1758	659,165	399,661	449,013	848,673	23,718	4%	11,314	3%	38,182	9%	49,496	6%
1759	605,888	416,896	529,090	945,986	13,902	2%	8,178	2%	49,248	9%	57,426	6%
1760	850,793	437,384	648,968	1,086,352	14,318	2%	5,772	1%	31,558	5%	37,330	3%
1761	748,640	424,479	741,335	1,165,814	12,002	2%	8,599	2%	74,212	10%	82,811	7%
1762	708,925	347,890	650,347	998,237	9,621	1%	32,073	9%	58,056	9%	90,129	9%
1763	903,891	n/a	n/a	1,091,436	4,842	1%	n/a	n/a	n/a	n/a	20,650	2%
1764	886,353	426,758	817,170	1,243,927	8,804	1%	6,621	2%	23,410	3%	30,032	2%
1765	922,401	400,928	779,940	1,180,868	6,025	1%	3,794	1%	38,469	5%	42,263	4%
1766	980,990	355,627	808,077	1,163,704	10,049	1%	6,893	2%	60,112	7%	67,005	6%
1767	1,023,197	452,298	793,192	1,245,490	12,697	1%	5,793	1%	35,167	4%	40,959	3%
1768	1,236,648	454,757	1,047,392	1,502,150	19,742	2%	7,862	2%	47,491	5%	55,353	4%
1769	1,225,530	n/a	n/a	1,563,053	18,434	2%	n/a	n/a	n/a	n/a	50,131	3%
1770	1,213,360	510,576	1,217,341	1,727,918	24,825	2%	6,029	1%	79,015	6%	85,044	5%

TNA, Customs 14
Missing totals for 1763, 1769: NLS, Ms 60.

Table 1.2: Scottish Domestic Exports to Germany (1743–1770)

1.2.1: Primary Products

1.2.1.1: Primary Products (I): Animal Products

	Cod, Ling						Herring					
	cwt		Sterling		% of total domX		bbl		Sterling		% of total domX	
	E504	Cust14	E504	Cust14	E504	Cust14	E504	Cust14	E504	Cust14	E504	Cust14
1743	4,707		£2,354		30%		115		£92		1%	
1744	9,690		£4,845		50%		46		£37		0%	
1745	6,140		£3,070		43%		100		£80		1%	
1746	8,750		£4,375		54%						0%	
1747	8,750		£4,375		31%						0%	
1748	7,566		£3,783		34%		84		£67		1%	
1749	12,870		£6,435		38%		169		£135		1%	
1750	9,840		£4,920		46%		750		£600		6%	
1751	7,690		£3,845		40%		2,421		£1,936		20%	
1752	7,365		£3,683		19%		1,345		£1,076		6%	
1753	8,280		£4,140		22%		4,260		£3,408		18%	
1754	6,845		£3,423		15%		3,688		£2,950		13%	
1755	3,851	3,385	£1,925	£1,692	12%	20%	3,142	3,061	£2,514	£2,449	16%	29%
1756		4,710		£2,355		19%		3,459		£2,767		22%
1757		7,728		£3,864		38%		1,308		£1,046		10%
1758		5,728		£2,864		25%		4,173		£3,338		30%
1759		5,832		£2,916		36%		1,089		£871		11%
1760		1,531		£765		13%		460		£368		6%
1761		3,701		£1,851		21%		950		£760		9%
1762		4,206		£2,103		6%		1,216		£973		3%
1763												
1764		1,549		£774		11%		964		£771		11%
1765		1,593		£796		21%		1,338		£1,070		28%
1766		1,086		£543		8%		2,945		£2,356		33%
1767		1,059		£529		9%		2,565		£2,052		35%
1768		3,361		£1,681		21%		3,012		£2,410		31%
1769												
1770		866		£433		7%		3,192		£2,554		42%

Table 1.2.1.1: Contd.: Primary Products (I): Animal Products

	Salmon						Total Fish			
	bbl		Sterling		% of total domX		Sterling		% of total domX	
	E504	Cust14	E504	Cust14	E504	Cust14	E504	Cust14	E504	Cust14
1743					0%		£2,446		31%	
1744					0%		£4,882		51%	
1745					0%		£3,150		44%	
1746					0%		£4,375		54%	
1747	650		£1,625		12%		£6,000		43%	
1748	300		£750		7%		£4,600		42%	
1749	130		£325		2%		£6,895		40%	
1750					0%		£5,520		51%	
1751					0%		£5,781		60%	
1752	850		£2,125		11%		£6,883		36%	
1753	1,324		£3,310		17%		£10,858		57%	
1754	778		£1,944		8%		£8,317		36%	
1755					0%	0%	£4,439	£4,141	28%	48%
1756		269		£673		5%		£5,795		46%
1757		731		£1,828		18%		£6,738		66%
1758						0%		£6,202		55%
1759		3		£6		0%		£3,793		46%
1760		330		£824		14%		£1,957		34%
1761						0%		£2,611		29%
1762						0%		£3,076		9%
1763										
1764						0%		£1,546		22%
1765		136		£340		9%		£2,207		58%
1766		15		£36		1%		£2,935		42%
1767		7		£16		0%		£2,598		44%
1768		63		£156		2%		£4,246		54%
1769										
1770						0%		£2,987		50%

	Butter						Fish / Train Oil					
	bbl		Sterling		% of total domX		Tons		Sterling		% of total domX	
	E504	Cust14	E504	Cust14	E504	Cust14	E504	Cust14	E504	Cust14	E504	Cust14
1743	169		£674		8%		0.38		£7		0%	
1744	410		£1,640		17%		0.38		£7		0%	
1745	406		£1,624		23%				£0		0%	
1746	108		£432		5%				£0		0%	
1747	248		£992		7%				£0		0%	
1748	278		£1,112		10%		13		£230		2%	
1749	637		£2,547		15%		18		£329		2%	
1750	129		£516		5%		11		£192		2%	
1751	112		£448		5%				£0		0%	
1752	333		£1,332		7%		24		£442		2%	
1753	6		£24		0%		220		£4,011		21%	
1754	50		£200		1%		66		£1,211		5%	
1755	32	34	£128	£136	1%	2%	38	40	£687	£724	4%	8%
1756				£0		0%		72		£1,319		11%
1757		142		£568		6%		16		£298		3%
1758		143		£572		5%		34		£629		6%
1759		62		£248		3%		19		£347		4%
1760		57		£228		4%		54		£976		17%
1761		104		£416		5%		34		£611		7%
1762		48		£192		1%		26		£475		1%
1763				£0						£0		
1764		172		£688		10%		106		£1,933		28%
1765				£0		0%		7		£128		3%
1766		100		£400		6%		30		£548		8%
1767		30		£120		2%		57		£1,034		17%
1768		18		£73		1%		11		£198		3%
1769				£0						£0		
1770		11		£44		1%		2		£27		0%

1.2.1.2: Primary Products (II): Cereals

	Totals Barley				**Oats, Oatmeal**					
	Sterling		% of total domX		quarters		Sterling		% of total domX	
	E504	Cust14	E504	Cust14	E504	Cust14	E504	Cust14	E504	Cust14
1743	£0		0%				£0		0%	
1744	£287		3%				£0		0%	
1745	£0		0%				£0		0%	
1746	£0		0%				£0		0%	
1747	£551		4%				£0		0%	
1748	£1,288		12%		59		£50		0%	
1749	£2,966		17%		100		£85		0%	
1750	£414		4%				£0		0%	
1751	£152		2%				£0		0%	
1752	£461		2%				£0		0%	
1753	£0		0%				£0		0%	
1754	£263		1%				£0		0%	
1755	£273	£44	2%	1%			£0	£0	0%	0%
1756		£0		0%				£0		0%
1757		£0		0%				£0		0%
1758		£0		0%				£0		0%
1759		£0		0%				£0		0%
1760		£0		0%				£0		0%
1761		£919		10%		1000		£850		10%
1762		£16,316		48%		8224		£6,990		21%

	Rye						**Wheat**					
	quarters		Sterling		% of total domX		quarters		Sterling		% of total domX	
	E504	Cust14	E504	Cust14	E504	Cust14	E504	Cust14	E504	Cust14	E504	Cust14
1743	13		£10		0%		1,350		£1,789		22%	
1744							12		£15		0%	
1745												
1746												
1747							1,460		£1,935		14%	
1748							351		£464		4%	
1749							154		£204		1%	
1750	150		£120		1%		15		£20		0%	
1751							46		£61		1%	
1752							80		£106		1%	
1753												
1754												
1755												
1756												
1757												
1758												
1759												
1760								250		£331		6%
1761								482		£638		7%
1762		212		£169		1%		423		£560		2%

No grain exports recorded after 1762.

Table 1.2.1.2 Contd.: Primary Products (II): Cereals

	Malt						Total Cereals			
	quarters		Sterling		% of total domX		Sterling		% of total domX	
	E504	Cust14	E504	Cust14	E504	Cust14	E504	Cust14	E504	Cust14
1743	653		£653		8%		£2,452		31%	
1744	675		£675		7%		£977		10%	
1745	245		£245		3%		£245		3%	
1746	335		£335		4%		£335		4%	
1747	41		£41		0%		£2,526		18%	
1748	1,724		£1,724		16%		£3,526		32%	
1749	863		£863		5%		£4,118		24%	
1750	2,595		£2,595		24%		£3,149		29%	
1751	100		£100		1%		£313		3%	
1752							£567		3%	
1753									0%	
1754							£263		1%	
1755	466	466	£466	£466	3%	5%	£739	£510	5%	6%
1756						0%		£0		0%
1757						0%		£0		0%
1758						0%		£0		0%
1759		426		£426		5%		£426		5%
1760						0%		£331		6%
1761		971		£971		11%		£3,379		38%
1762		3,952		£3,952		12%		£27,987		83%
1763										
1764		469		£469				£469		7%
1765				£0				£0		0%
1766				£0				£0		0%
1767				£0				£0		0%
1768				£0				£0		0%
1769										
1770		302		£302				£302		5%

Table 1.2.2: Industrial Products

Table 1.2.2.1: Products of the Extractive Industries (I): Salt, Lead

	Salt						Lead					
	weys		Sterling		% of total domX		Tons		Sterling		% of total domX	
	E504	Cust14	E504	Cust14	E504	Cust14	E504	Cust14	E504	Cust14	E504	Cust14
1743	444		£370		5%		10		£165		2%	
1744	751		£626		6%		13		£206		2%	
1745	1,041		£867		12%		12		£198		3%	
1746	943		£786		10%		85		£1,403		17%	
1747	878		£731		5%		170		£2,806		20%	
1748	445		£370		3%		15		£248		2%	
1749	680		£567		3%		101		£1,658		10%	
1750	495		£412		4%				£0		0%	
1751	561		£467		5%		24		£396		4%	
1752	435		£363		2%		55		£908		5%	
1753	240		£200		1%		2		£33		0%	
1754	140		£117		1%		12		£198		1%	
1755	338	319	£282	£266	2%	3%	110		£1,808	£0	11%	0%
1756		444		£370		3%		6		£103		1%
1757		115		£96		1%		100		£1,650		16%
1758		400		£334		3%		14		£231		2%
1759		63		£52		1%		112		£1,848		23%
1760								30		£495		9%
1761										£0		0%
1762								17		£285		1%
1763												
1764										£0		0%
1765		100		£83		2%				£0		0%
1766										£0		0%
1767		197		£164		3%				£0		0%
1768		251		£209		3%		13		£206		3%
1769						n/a						
1770		138		£115		2%						

Table 1.2.2.1.1: German Markets for Scots Salt

	(a) Including Stralsund							(b) Excluding Stralsund					
	Bremen	Hamburg	Lübeck	Emden	Stralsund	Other	Totals	Bremen	Hamburg	Lübeck	Emden	Other	Totals
	weys / tons							weys / tons					
1743	404	40			488		933	404	40				444
1744	722		30		418		1169	722		30			751
1745	755		29	257			1041	755		29	257		1041
1746	558		80	306	83		1026	558		80	306		943
1747	477		28	374			878	477		28	374		878
1748	345			100			445	345			100		445
1749	405		113	163			680	405		113	163		680
1750	355			140			495	355			140		495
1751	333		50	178			561	333		50	178		561
1752	271		46	118			435	271		46	118		435
1753	240						240	240					240
1754	140						140	140					140
1755	293					45	338	293				45	338
	Bremen	Hamburg	Lübeck	Emden	Stralsund	Other	Totals	Bremen	Hamburg	Lübeck	Emden	Other	Totals
1743	43%	4%	0%		52%		100%	91%	9%				100%
1744	62%		3%		36%		100%	96%		4%			100%
1745	73%		3%	25%			100%	73%		3%	25%		100%
1746	54%		8%	30%	8%		100%	59%		8%	32%		100%
1747	54%		3%	43%			100%	54%		3%	43%		100%
1748	78%			22%			100%	78%			22%		100%
1749	60%		17%	24%			100%	60%		17%	24%		100%
1750	72%			28%			100%	72%			28%		100%
1751	59%		9%	32%			100%	59%		9%	32%		100%
1752	62%		11%	27%			100%	62%		11%	27%		100%
1753	100%						100%	100%					100%
1754	100%						100%	100%					100%
1755	87%					13%	100%	87%				13%	100%

Table 1.2.2.1.2: Scottish Ports from whence Salt was Shipped to German Ports

	Alloa	Bo'ness	Kirkcaldy	Prestonpans	Totals	Alloa	Bo'ness	Kirkcaldy	Prestonpans	Totals
1743	178		180	86	444	40%		41%	19%	100%
1744		347	302	103	751		46%	40%	14%	100%
1745		425	479	137	1,041		41%	46%	13%	100%
1746	63	545	306	30	943	7%	58%	32%	3%	100%
1747	69	340	403	66	878	8%	39%	46%	8%	100%
1748		128	317		445		29%	71%		100%
1749		263	418		680		39%	61%		100%
1750			495		495			100%		100%
1751			491	70	561			88%	12%	100%
1752			435		435			100%		100%
1753			240		240			100%		100%
1754		90	50		140		64%	36%		100%
1755		113	226		338		33%	67%		100%

Table 1.2.2.2: Products of the Extractive Industries (II): Coal

1 Chalder *Newcastle (NCL) measure* = 72 bushels

	Coal								Totals Coal			
	chalders (NCL)		Sterling		Tons		Sterling		Sterling		% of total domX	
	E504	Cust14	E504	Cust14	E504	Cust14	E504	Cust14	E504	Cust14	E504	Cust14
1743					170		£43		£43		1%	
1744					130		£33		£33			
1745	55		£55		483		£121		£176		2%	
1746	183		£183		100		£25		£208		3%	
1747	301		£301		178		£45		£345		2%	
1748	92		£92		180		£45		£137		1%	
1749	101		£101		10		£3		£104		1%	
1750	126		£126		118		£30		£156		1%	
1751	120		£120		140		£35		£155		2%	
1752	166		£166		622		£155		£321		2%	
1753	245		£245		1,289		£322		£567		3%	
1754	109		£109		1,626		£407		£516		2%	
1755	133	133	£133	£133	2,285	2,190	£571	£548	£704	£681	4%	8%
1756		314		£314		2,846		£712		£1,026		8%
1757		115		£115		1,549		£387		£502		5%
1758		230		£230		1,274		£319		£549		5%
1759		95		£95		1,036		£259		£354		4%
1760		25		£25		846		£212		£236		4%
1761		14		£14		896		£224		£238		3%
1762		181		£181		715		£179		£360		1%
1763												
1764		106		£106		1,846		£462		£568		8%
1765		410		£410		1,653		£413		£823		22%
1766		227		£227		2,677		£669		£896		13%
1767		168		£168		2,283		£571		£739		12%
1768		44		£44		1,994		£499		£543		7%
1769												
1770		118		£118		2,954		£739		£857		14%

Table 1.2.2.3: Manufactures

	Vitriol Oil						Worsted Stockings					
	lbs		Sterling		% of total domX		dz pairs		Sterling		% of total domX	
	E504	Cust14	E504	Cust14	E504	Cust14	E504	Cust14	E504	Cust14	E504	Cust14
1743							733		£697		9%	
1744							850		£808		8%	
1745							858		£815		12%	
1746							500		£475		6%	
1747							417		£396		3%	
1748							625		£594		5%	
1749							710		£674		4%	
1750							725		£689		6%	
1751	2,961		£74		1%		2,083		£1,979		21%	
1752	2,081		£52		0%		8,225		£7,814		41%	
1753	6,136		£153		1%		2,933		£2,787		15%	
1754	32,609		£815		4%		11,538		£10,961		47%	
1755	39,391	39,391	£985	£985	6%	11%	6,383	1,100	£6,064	£1,045	38%	12%
1756		86,320		£2,158		17%		1,377		£1,308		10%
1757								417		£396		4%
1758		32,640		£816		7%		875		£831		7%
1759								1,167		£1,108		14%
1760								742		£705		12%
1761								1,000		£950		11%
1762								1,217		£1,156		3%
1763												
1764								833		£792		11%
1765								575		£546		14%
1766		79,530		£1,988		28%		225		£214		3%
1767								1,308		£1,243		21%
1768		50,699		£1,267		16%		500		£475		6%
1769												
1770		30,161		754		12%		500		£475		8%

Table 1.2.2.3.1: Points of Dispatch of Worsted Stockings, 1743–1755 (dz pairs)

	Aberdeen		Shetland		Totals	
1743			733	100%	733	100%
1744			850	100%	850	100%
1745			858	100%	858	100%
1746			500	100%	500	100%
1747			417	100%	417	100%
1748			625	100%	625	100%
1749			710	100%	710	100%
1750	200	28%	525	72%	725	100%
1751	1,500	72%	583	28%	2,083	100%
1752	7,300	89%	925	11%	8,225	100%
1753	2,600	89%	333	11%	2,933	100%
1754	10,980	95%	558	5%	11,538	100%
1755	6,150	96%	233	4%	6,383	100%

Table 1.3: Scottish Re-Exports to Germany (1743–1770) / Table 1.3.1: Tobacco

	"Unmanufactured" Tobacco						Roll Tobacco		
	lbs		Sterling		% of total Re-X		lbs	Sterling	% of total Re-X
	E504	Cust14	E504	Cust14	E504	Cust14	E504	E504	E504
1743	463,565		£9,658		84%				
1744	1,033,462		£21,530		66%		9,006	£375	1%
1745	1,153,805		£24,038		96%				
1746	386,848		£8,059		48%				
1747	541,395		£11,279		83%				
1748	161,139		£3,357		45%		1,827	£76	1%
1749	1,756,305		£36,590		93%				
1750	3,187,318		£66,402		99%		4,559	£190	0%
1751	1,535,523		£31,990		100%				
1752	1,436,016		£29,917		95%		27,356	£1,140	4%
1753	2,259,817		£47,080		98%		3,606	£150	
1754	1,899,039		£39,563		94%		8,684	£362	1%
1755	212,677	214,333	£4,431	£4,465	61%	68%			
1756		983,508		£20,490		95%			
1757		2,410,913		£50,227		90%			
1758		1,442,391		£30,050		79%			
1759		1,422,190		£29,629		60%			
1760		705,522		£14,698		47%			
1761		2,992,420		£62,342		84%			
1762		1,452,239		£30,255		52%			
1763									
1764		1,067,768		£22,245		95%			
1765		1,567,677		£32,660		85%			
1766		2,732,988		£56,937		95%			
1767		1,612,740		£33,599		96%			
1768		2,008,603		£41,846		88%			
1769									
1770		3,550,414		£73,967		94%			

	Cut Tobacco			Snuff						Totals Tobacco	
	lbs	Sterling	% of total Re-X	lbs		Sterling		% of total Re-X	lbs	% of total Re-X	
	E504	E504	E504	E504	Cust14	E504	Cust14	E504	Cust14	E504	Cust14
1743										84%	
1744										67%	
1745										96%	
1746	34,080	£2,130	13%							61%	
1747										83%	
1748	4,796	£300	4%							50%	
1749	34,565	£2,160	5%							98%	
1750										99%	
1751										100%	
1752	1,904	£119	0%							99%	
1753				202		£12		0%		98%	
1754	10,136	£634	2%	100		£6		0%		97%	
1755	1,657	£104	1%							63%	68%
1756											95%
1757											90%
1758					10,369		£1,167		3%		82%
1759											60%
1760											47%
1761											84%
1762											52%
1763											
1764											95%
1765											85%
1766											95%
1767					132		£8		0%		96%
1768											88%
1769											
1770											94%

Table 1.3.2: Re-exports: Sugar, Rice

	Muscovado Sugar						Rice					
	cwt E504	Cust14	Sterling E504	Cust14	% of total Re-X E504	Cust14	cwt E504	Cust14	Sterling E504	Cust14	% of total Re-X E504	Cust14
1743							3,666		£1,741		15%	
1744	1,380		£2,070		6%		3,816		£1,813		6%	
1745							1,817		£863		3%	
1746	1,777		£2,665		16%		7,719		£3,666		22%	
1747							4,693		£2,229		16%	
1748							7,291		£3,463		46%	
1749	47		£70		0%		1,211		£575		1%	
1750							1,159		£550		1%	
1751												
1752												
1753												
1754							2,202		£1,046		2%	
1755							3,084	3,084	£1,465	£1,465	20%	22%
1756								2,399		£1,139		5%
1757								11,654		£5,536		10%
1758								13,022		£6,185		16%
1759		2,371		£3,557		7%		32,876		£15,736		32%
1760		3,195		£5,793		18%		16,468		£7,822		25%
1761		3,014		£4,521		6%		15,269		£7,253		10%
1762		13,783		£20,674		36%		10,138		£4,816		8%
1763												
1764								1,191		£566		2%
1765		1,366		£2,049		5%		7,624		£3,621		9%
1766								6,684		£3,175		5%
1767								2,847		£1,352		4%
1768		9		£14		0%		8,446		£4,012		8%
1769												
1770								9,845		£4,676		6%

Table 1.3.3: Other

	Cocoa						Tea					
	cwt E504	Cust14	Sterling E504	Cust14	% of total Re-X E504	Cust14	lbs E504	Cust14	Sterling E504	Cust14	% of total Re-X E504	Cust14
1744	1,394		£6,969		21%							
1745							94		£38		0%	
1755							1,123		£449		6%	
1762		5		£23		0%						

Table 1.3.4: Re-exports of Rice from Scotland and England to German Ports, 1736–1770 (cwt)

	a	b	c	d	e	f	g
	Scotland				**England**	**Scottish X as %**	**Scottish X as %**
	Hamburg E504	Bremen E504	Totals E504	CUST14	4-year-AVE	**of English Totals**	**of British Totals**
1736					47,232		
1737					47,232		
1738					47,232		
1739					47,232		
1740					50,089		
1741					50,089		
1742					50,089		
1743		3,666	3,666		50,089	7%	7%
1744	3,816		3,816		50,089	8%	7%
1745	1,817		1,817		36,696	5%	5%
1746	5,745	1,974	7,719		36,696	21%	17%
1747	3,224	1,469	4,693		36,696	13%	11%
1748	5,315	1,976	7,291		53,214	14%	12%
1749		1,211	1,211		53,214	2%	2%
1750		1,159	1,159		53,214	2%	2%
1751					53,214		
1752					61,339		
1753					61,339		
1754	2,202		2,202		61,339	4%	3%
1755		3,084	3,084	3,084	61,339	5%	5%
1756				2,399	31,964	8%	7%
1757				11,654	31,964	36%	27%
1758				13,022	31,964	41%	29%
1759				32,876	31,964	103%	51%
1760				16,468	59,643	28%	22%
1761				15,269	59,643	26%	20%
1762				10,138	59,643	17%	15%
1763					59,643		
1764				1,191	64,821	2%	2%
1765				7,624	64,821	12%	11%
1766				6,684	64,821	10%	9%
1767				2,847	64,821	4%	4%
1768				8,446	49,554	17%	15%
1769					49,554		
1770				9,845	49,554	20%	17%

English figures R. C. NASH, South Carolina and the Atlantic Economy in the Late Seventeenth and Eighteenth Centuries, Economic History Review, Second Series, XLV, 4 (1992), pp. 677–702.

Table 1.4: Scottish Imports from Germany (1743–1770):

1.4.1. Linen

	Narrow German						Other				Totals Linen			
	ct ells E504	Cust14	Sterling E504	Cust14	% of total M E504	Cust14	Sterling E504	Cust14	% of total M E504	Cust14	Sterling E504	Cust14	% of total M E504	Cust14
1743	174		£955		63%						£955		63%	
1744	357		£1,964		81%						£1,964		81%	
1745	270		£1,486		83%						£1,486		83%	
1746	458		£2,521		60%		£138		3%		£2,660		63%	
1747	2,191		£12,050		87%		£178		1%		£12,228		88%	
1748	857		£4,714		73%		£69		1%		£4,783		74%	
1749	2,087		£11,478		81%		£561		4%		£12,039		85%	
1750	1,037		£5,704		66%		£5		0%		£5,709		66%	
1751	1,375		£7,562		78%		£229		2%		£7,790		80%	
1752	488		£2,684		62%		£95		2%		£2,779		64%	
1753	1,980		£10,893		82%		£168		1%		£11,061		83%	
1754	1,259		£6,925		75%		£479		5%		£7,404		81%	
1755	3,815	3,815	£20,982	£20,981	94%	94%	£395	£361	2%	2%	£21,377	£21,342	96%	96%
1756		3,608		£19,844		82%		£1,843		8%		£21,687		89%
1757		3,502		£19,263		80%		£2,090		9%		£21,353		89%
1758		3,049		£16,771		71%		£2,438		10%		£19,209		81%
1759		1,461		£8,037		58%		£906		7%		£8,943		64%
1760		1,813		£9,973		69%		£1,875		13%		£11,848		83%
1761		958		£5,268		44%		£64		1%		£5,332		44%
1762		836		£4,596		48%		£29		0%		£4,625		48%
1763														
1764		519		£2,856		33%		£1,506		17%		£4,362		50%
1765		808		£4,443		73%		£163		3%		£4,606		75%
1766		1,598		£8,788		87%		£51		1%		£8,839		88%
1767		1,406		£7,736		56%		£59		0%		£7,794		56%
1768		2,760		£15,181		74%		£99		0%		£15,281		75%
1769														
1770		3,080		£16,939		66%		£2,061		8%		£19,000		74%

Table 1.4.1.1: German Ports of Dispatch for *Narrow German* Linens

	Hamburg		Bremen		Total
1743	369	39%	587	61%	955
1744		0%	1,965	100%	1,964
1745	1,486	100%			1,486
1746	1,825	72%	696	28%	2,521
1747	6,284	52%	5,765	48%	12,050
1748	605	13%	4,109	87%	4,714
1749	1,131	10%	10,346	90%	11,478
1750	632	11%	5,072	89%	5,704
1751	1,646	22%	5,915	78%	7,562
1752	725	27%	1,959	73%	2,684
1753	4,794	44%	6,098	56%	10,893
1754	4,340	63%	2,584	37%	6,925
1755	365	2%	20,618	98%	20,982
1760	899	9%	9,073	91%	9,973
1761		0%	5,169	100%	5,169
1762	1,306	28%	3,290	72%	4,596
1763	1,965	100%			1,965
1764	475	16%	2,406	84%	2,881
1765			4,443	100%	4,443

Sources: 1743–1755: Customs Accounts, NAS, E504; 1760–1765: TNA, T36/13

Table 1.4.1.2: Scottish Ports Importing *Narrow German* Linens (ct ells)

	Bo'ness		Greenock		Leith		Other		Totals
1743					174	100%			174
1744					357	100%			357
1745					270	100%			270
1746					403	88%	55	12%	458
1747	1,590	73%			550	25%	50	2%	2191
1748	747	87%			111	13%			857
1749	1,662	80%			425	20%			2087
1750	762	73%			275	27%			1037
1751	1,076	78%			299	22%			1375
1752	279	57%			209	43%			488
1753	1,196	60%	571	29%	344	17%			1980
1754	418	33%	594	47%	133	11%	114	9%	1259
1755	2,693	71%	887	23%	236	6%			3815

Table 1.4.2: Timber

	Clapboards						Staves			
	ct		Sterling		% of total M		ct/Sterling		% of total M	
	E504	Cust14	E504	Cust14	E504	Cust14	E504	Cust14	E504	Cust14
1743	33		£211		14%					
1744	52		£339		14%		8		0%	
1745	34		£219		12%		35		2%	
1746	28		£184		4%		25		1%	
1747	23		£150		1%		144		1%	
1748	34		£220		3%		151		2%	
1749	75		£489		3%		184		1%	
1750	13		£83		1%		271		3%	
1751	45		£293		3%		278		3%	
1752	42		£274		6%		284		7%	
1753	49		£319		2%		161		1%	
1754	6		£39		0%		59		1%	
1755	14	13	£88	£85	0%	0%	72	72	0%	0%
1756		54		£348		1%		124		1%
1757								57		0%
1758		50		£322		1%		94		0%
1759		4		£26		0%		33		0%
1760		1		£3		0%		17		0%
1761								135		1%
1762		1		£7		0%		240		2%
1763										
1764		5		£33		0%		17		0%
1765										
1766		47		£306		3%		25		0%
1767		20		£127		1%		4		0%
1768		17		£107		1%				
1769										
1770		38		£249		1%		5		0%

1.4.2 Contd.: Timber

	Other Timber				Totals Timber	
	Sterling E504	Cust14	% of total M E504	Cust14	% of total M E504	Cust14
1743	£38		3%		16%	
1744					14%	
1745					14%	
1746	£43		1%		6%	
1747	£71		1%		3%	
1748	£91		1%		7%	
1749	£703		5%		10%	
1750	£850		10%		14%	
1751	£707		7%		13%	
1752	£128		3%		16%	
1753	£708		5%		9%	
1754	£370		4%		5%	
1755	£268	£265	1%	1%	2%	2%
1756		£258		1%		1%
1757		£249		1%		1%
1758		£957		4%		4%
1759		£81		1%		1%
1760		£75		1%		1%
1761		£193		2%		2%
1762		£367		4%		4%
1763						
1764		£98		1%		2%
1765		£539		9%		9%
1766		£204		2%		5%
1767		£29		0%		1%
1768		£1		0%		1%
1769						
1770						1%

Table 1.4.3: Cereals

(Imports of rye not considered.[1])

	Barley			Oats, Oatmeal			Wheat			Total Cereals	
	quarters	Sterling	% of total M	quarters	Sterling	% of total M	quarters	Sterling	% of total M	Sterling	% of total M
1757							150	£199	1%	£199	1%
1765				395	£336	5%				£336	5%
1766				60	£51	1%				£51	1%
1767	840	£672	5%	3,941	£3,350	24%	488	£646	5%	£4,668	34%
1768	425	£340	2%	1,929	£1,639	8%	460	£610	3%	£2,677	13%
1769											
1770				3,307	£2,811	11%				£2,811	11%

Sources: as in Table 1.1.1

1 The only recorded import of rye from Germany into Scotland was 110 quarters in 1768.

Table 1.5: Scottish Trade with Germany by Scottish Ports

Table 1.5.1: Exports (£Sterling)

	Aberdeen	Alloa	Anstruther	Ayr	Boness	Caithness	Dumfries	Dunbar	Dundee	Greenock
1743	£1,069				£148			£1,472		
1744		£5			£330				£302	£6
1745		£10			£417					
1746		£52			£642					
1747		£558	£91		£833			£408	£563	
1748	£750				£512	£419				
1749	£325		£578		£336			£225	£298	£79
1750	£787	£7			£126			£746	£57	
1751	£1,425				£106			£214		
1752	£9,274	£26			£151			£265		
1753	£4,112	£134	£8		£221			£511		
1754	£12,173	£79			£346					
1755	£6,327	£97			£175				£70	

	Inverness	Kirkcaldy	Leith	Montrose	Orkney	Perth	Port Glasgow	Prestonpans	Shetland	Totals
1743		£193	£165	£653			£31	£403	£3,823	£7,957
1744		£445		£675	£613			£85	£7,197	£9,657
1745		£664	£43	£245				£114	£5,589	£7,082
1746		£275	£1,403	£335			£15	£25	£5,282	£8,028
1747	£1,625	£375	£3,683		£23			£55	£5,763	£13,976
1748	£244	£738	£1,238	£995		£139			£5,937	£10,972
1749	£287	£348	£3,606	£863					£10,089	£17,034
1750		£1,031		£1,328					£6,726	£10,809
1751		£444	£484	£170				£108	£6,663	£9,614
1752		£462	£559	£60				£796	£7,351	£18,942
1753	£1,492	£656	£3,289	£72				£171	£8,442	£19,109
1754	£475	£380	£825	£263				£846	£7,830	£23,216
1755		£708	£2,417	£466				£1,002	£4,695	£15,955

Table 1.5.1: Contd.: Exports (%)

	Aberdeen	Alloa	Anstruther	Ayr	Boness	Caithness	Dumfries	Dunbar	Dundee	Greenock
1743	13%				2%			18%		0%
1744		0%			3%				3%	0%
1745		0%			6%					0%
1746		1%			8%					0%
1747		4%	1%		6%			3%	4%	0%
1748	7%	0%			5%	4%				0%
1749	2%	0%	3%		2%			1%	2%	0%
1750	7%	0%			1%			7%	1%	0%
1751	15%				1%			2%		0%
1752	49%	0%			1%			1%		0%
1753	22%	1%	0%		1%			3%		0%
1754	52%	0%			1%					0%
1755	40%	1%			1%				0%	0%

	Inverness	Kirkcaldy	Leith	Montrose	Orkney	Perth	Port Glasgow	Prestonpans	Shetland	Totals
1743		2%	2%	8%			0%	5%	48%	100%
1744		5%		7%	6%			1%	75%	100%
1745		9%	1%	3%				2%	79%	100%
1746		3%	17%	4%				0%	66%	100%
1747	12%	3%	26%		0%		0%	0%	41%	100%
1748	2%	7%	11%	9%		1%			54%	100%
1749	2%	2%	21%	5%					59%	100%
1750		10%	0%	12%					62%	100%
1751		5%	5%	2%				1%	69%	100%
1752		2%	3%	0%				4%	39%	100%
1753	8%	3%	17%	0%				1%	44%	100%
1754	2%	2%	4%	1%				4%	34%	100%
1755		4%	15%	3%				6%	29%	100%

Table 1.5.2: Re-exports (£Sterling)

	Aberdeen	Alloa	Anstruther	Ayr	Boness	Caithness	Dumfries	Dunbar	Dundee	Greenock
1743				£1,036						£3,357
1744										£4,058
1745			£177							£907
1746					£3,910					£5,886
1747					£4,293					£6,327
1748					£5,289					
1749	£567				£1,898					£17,857
1750	£6,912									£16,648
1751	£4,129						£2,294			£13,639
1752	£19,574							£1,442		£383
1753	£10,715			£3,126			£5,037			£5,567
1754	£13,659			£8,267						£7,225
1755	£1,905			£2,630					£40	

	Inverness	Kirkcaldy	Leith	Montrose	Orkney	Perth	Port Glasgow	Prestonpans	Shetland	Totals
1743					£1,741		£5,402			£11,535
1744			£900		£913		£26,886			£32,757
1745					£863		£23,155			£25,102
1746			£4,116	£80			£2,746			£16,738
1747			£1,202	£183	£1,539					£13,544
1748			£2,195							£7,484
1749			£3,578	£1,543			£13,985			£39,428
1750		£2,706	£550	£1,057			£39,467			£67,341
1751			£1,201	£1,498			£9,230			£31,990
1752			£1,391	£2,150			£6,597			£31,537
1753			£4,952				£18,622			£48,019
1754			£50		£1,047		£11,623			£41,872
1755			£1,127		£1,519					£7,221

Table 1.5.2 Contd.: Re-Exports (%)

	Aberdeen	Alloa	Anstruther	Ayr	Boness	Caithness	Dumfries	Dunbar	Dundee	Greenock
1743				9%						29%
1744										12%
1745			1%							4%
1746					23%					35%
1747					32%					47%
1748					71%					
1749	1%				5%					45%
1750	10%									25%
1751	13%						7%			43%
1752	62%							5%		1%
1753	22%			7%			10%			12%
1754	33%			20%						17%
1755	26%			36%					1%	

	Inverness	Kirkcaldy	Leith	Montrose	Orkney	Perth	Port Glasgow	Prestonpans	Shetland	Totals
1743					15%		47%			100%
1744			3%		3%		82%			100%
1745					3%		92%			100%
1746			25%	0%			16%			100%
1747			9%	1%	11%					100%
1748			29%							100%
1749			9%	4%			35%			100%
1750		4%	1%	2%			59%			100%
1751			4%	5%			29%			100%
1752			4%	7%			21%			100%
1753			10%				39%			100%
1754			0%		3%		28%			100%
1755			16%		21%					100%

Table 1.5.3: Imports (£Sterling)

	Aberdeen	Alloa	Anstruther	Ayr	Boness	Dunbar	Dundee	Greenock
1743			£84		£99			
1744	£7		£79		£155			
1745					£25			
1746			£250		£254	£44		
1747			£9		£9,633	£70		
1748					£4,530	£75		
1749			£279		£9,711	£14	£43	
1750	£24		£227		£4,539			£477
1751			£35		£6,019	£47		£426
1752					£2,200	£130		
1753					£6,937			£3,354
1754	£45		£5		£2,598			£3,568
1755	£6		£49		£15,033			£4,956

	Inverness	Kirkcaldy	Leith	Montrose	Orkney	Perth	Prestonpans	Shetland	Totals
1743		£68	£1,054	£31		£188			£1,523
1744			£2,193						£2,434
1745		£139	£1,596				£22		£1,783
1746		£141	£2,707	£51	£770				£4,218
1747	£32		£3,825					£342	£13,911
1748	£35	£284	£1,285	£46			£220		£6,475
1749		£278	£3,678	£85					£14,088
1750		£26	£3,183	£191					£8,667
1751		£291	£2,836	£18				£6	£9,679
1752			£1,990	£10					£4,330
1753		£76	£2,821	£36	£24				£13,248
1754		£494	£1,991	£14	£475				£9,188
1755		£189	£2,014	£26					£22,272

Table 1.5.3 Contd.: Imports (%)

	Aberdeen	Alloa	Anstruther	Ayr	Boness	Dunbar	Dundee	Greenock
1743			6%		6%			
1744	0%		3%		6%			
1745					1%			
1746			6%		6%	1%		
1747			0%		69%	1%		
1748					70%	1%		
1749			2%		69%	0%	0%	
1750	0%		3%		52%			6%
1751			0%		62%	0%		4%
1752					51%	3%		
1753					52%			25%
1754	0%		0%		28%			39%
1755	0%		0%		67%			22%

	Inverness	Kirkcaldy	Leith	Montrose	Orkney	Perth	Prestonpans	Shetland	Totals
1743		4%	69%	2%		12%			100%
1744			90%						100%
1745		8%	90%				1%		100%
1746		3%	64%	1%	18%				100%
1747	0%		27%					2%	100%
1748	1%	4%	20%	1%			3%		100%
1749		2%	26%	1%					100%
1750		0%	37%	2%					100%
1751		3%	29%	0%				0%	100%
1752			46%	0%					100%
1753		1%	21%	0%	0%				100%
1754		5%	22%	0%	5%				100%
1755		1%	9%	0%					100%

Table 1.6: Scottish Trade with Germany by German Ports

Table 1.6.1: Imports

	Hamburg	Bremen	Lübeck	Altona	Other	TOTALS
1743	£588	£936		£161		£1,685
1744	£86	£2,337		£142		£2,565
1745	£1,486	£297		£570		£2,353
1746	£3,223	£995		£131		£4,349
1747	£7,863	£6,048		£111		£14,022
1748	£1,910	£4,566		£583		£7,059
1749	£2,504	£11,584		£607		£14,695
1750	£3,235	£5,359	£73	£362		£9,029
1751	£3,017	£6,483	£179	£225		£9,904
1752	£1,818	£2,462		£251	£50	£4,581
1753	£6,711	£6,537		£247		£13,495
1754	£6,295	£2,818		£237	£76	£9,426
1755	£846	£21,241		£119	£185	£22,391
1743	35%	56%		10%		100%
1744	3%	91%		6%		100%
1745	63%	13%		24%		100%
1746	74%	23%		3%		100%
1747	56%	43%		1%		100%
1748	27%	65%		8%		100%
1749	17%	79%		4%		100%
1750	36%	59%	1%	4%		100%
1751	30%	65%	2%	2%		100%
1752	40%	54%		5%	1%	100%
1753	50%	48%		2%		100%
1754	67%	30%		3%	1%	100%
1755	4%	95%		1%	1%	100%

Table 1.6 Contd.

Table 1.6.2: Exports of Domestic Products

	Hamburg	Bremen	Emden	Lübeck	Altona	Stralsund	Other	TOTALS
1743	£5,818	£2,139				£407		£8,364
1744	£8,820	£812		£25		£374		£10,031
1745	£5,992	£817	£249	£24				£7,082
1746	£7,089	£465	£408	£67		£69		£8,098
1747	£12,615	£805	£533	£23				£13,976
1748	£10,509	£298	£165					£10,972
1749	£15,396	£1,382	£163	£94		£15		£17,050
1750	£10,119	£543	£147					£10,809
1751	£8,370	£1,026	£168	£51				£9,615
1752	£18,162	£644	£98	£39		£1,298		£20,241
1753	£16,979	£2,130			£8			£19,117
1754	£21,345	£1,871						£23,216
1755	£14,711	£1,175					£70	£15,956
1743	70%	26%				5%		100%
1744	88%	8%		0%		4%		100%
1745	85%	12%	4%	0%				100%
1746	88%	6%	5%	1%		1%		100%
1747	90%	6%	4%	0%				100%
1748	96%	3%	2%					100%
1749	90%	8%	1%	1%		0%		100%
1750	94%	5%	1%					100%
1751	87%	11%	2%	1%				100%
1752	90%	3%	0%	0%		6%		100%
1753	89%	11%			0%			100%
1754	92%	8%						100%
1755	92%	7%					0%	100%

Table 1.6 Contd.

Table 1.6.3: Re-exports

	Hamburg	Bremen	Emden	Lübeck	Altona	TOTALS
1743	£9,794	£1,741				£11,535
1744	£26,700	£6,057				£32,757
1745	£22,337	£2,765				£25,102
1746	£9,137	£6,848		£754	£11,531	£28,270
1747	£10,629	£1,891	£1,024			£13,544
1748	£3,801	£1,069	£2,614			£7,484
1749	£21,789	£15,740	£1,898		£3,840	£43,267
1750	£39,581	£27,760				£67,341
1751	£21,546	£10,235	£209			£31,990
1752	£24,940	£6,597				£31,537
1753	£41,719	£6,300				£48,019
1754	£27,719	£14,153				£41,872
1755	£5,701	£1,519				£7,220
1743	85%	15%				100%
1744	82%	18%				100%
1745	89%	11%				100%
1746	32%	24%		3%	41%	100%
1747	78%	14%	8%			100%
1748	51%	14%	35%			100%
1749	50%	36%	4%		9%	100%
1750	59%	41%				100%
1751	67%	32%	1%			100%
1752	79%	21%				100%
1753	87%	13%				100%
1754	66%	34%				100%
1755	79%	21%				100%

Table 2: A Comparison of Scottish and German Customs Records, 1747, 1754, 1755

Table 2.1: Imports from Leith into Hamburg according to Scottish and Hamburg Records (1747, 1755)

	1747				1755			
Commodities	**Mark Banko**	**%**	**Sterling**	**%**	**Mark Banko**	**%**	**Sterling**	**%**
Tobacco			476.10	11%				
Tea							449	13%
Ale / Beer / Porter								
French Cambrics							657	19%
Woolendries			61.00	1%				
Stockings								
Bed Sheets (?)								
Wheat			963.98	23%				
Lead	1,300	90%	2,557.50	61%			1,808	51%
Salt							21	1%
Coal			3.50	0%				
Vitriol Oil					600	100%		
Herring							94	3%
Butter								
Leather Goods	150	10%	96.81	2%				
Train Oil							475	13%
Furniture							40	1%
TOTAL	1,450		4,158.89	100%	600		3,543.78	100%

Scotland: Customs Accounts, NAS, E504

Hamburg: J. Schneider, O.-E. Krawehl and M. A. Denzel (eds.), *Statistik des Hamburger seewärtigen Einfuhrhandels im 18. Jahrhundert. Nach den Admiralitätszoll- und Convoygeld-Einnahmebüchern* (St Katharinen, 2001), Tables, pp. 91s., pp. 121–123

Table 2.2: Traffic declared in Leith for *Hamburg*, according to Scottish Customs Accounts

(a) 1747

Quarter	Traffic	Commodity	Amount Shipped	Ship	Master	Merchant	Date of Entry
I	export	Wheat (quarter)	99	Providence	David Loch	William Reid	23 February
I	export	Wheat (quarter)	20	Providence	David Loch	James Fullerton	23 February
II	export	Coloured Woollen Cloth (yd)	800	Providence	James Reid	Robert Brown	
II	export	Musselburgh Stuffs (yd)	200	Providence	James Reid	William Sauter	
II	export	Wheat meal (quarter)	25	Providence	James Reid	George Chalmers	
II	export	Leather Tanned (lb)	630	Providence	James Reid	William Sauter	
II	export	Leather tanned / manufactured (lb)	140	Providence	James Reid	William Sauter	
II	re-export	Tobacco: un-manufactured (lb)	15,130	Providence	James Reid	William Reid	
II	re-export	Tobacco: un-manufactured (lb)	3,723	Providence	James Reid	William Reid	
III	export	Wheat (quarter)	246	Ann & Isobell	Alexander Chaplain	John Coutts / Archibald Trotter	
III	export	Wheat meal (quarter)	338	Providence	David Loch	George Chalmers	
III	export	Lead: Bar Lead (ton)	100	Young Elizabeth	Jan Johannes	Alexander Sherriff	
III	export	Lead: Bar Lead (ton)	30	Providence	David Loch	Alexander Sherriff	
III	export	Leather Tanned (lb)	731	Providence	James Reid	William ?Scouler?	
IV	export	Coloured Woollen Cloth (yd)	420	Hopefull	Hugh Walker	William Reid	04. Nov
IV	re-export	Tobacco: un-manufactured (lb)	4,000	Hopefull	Hugh Walker	William Reid	04. Nov
IV	export	Lead: Bar Lead (ton)	25	Hopefull	Hugh Walker	Alexander Pentland	28 October
IV	export	Coal: small coals (chalder)	4	Hopefull	Hugh Walker	William Reid	28 October

Source: Customs Accounts, NAS, E504

Table 2.2 Contd.: Traffic declared in Leith for *Hamburg*, according to Scottish Customs Accounts

(b) 1755

Quarter	Traffic	Commodity	Amount Shipped	Ship	Master	Merchant	Date of Entry
I	export	Whale Oil (ton)	10	Margaret & Mary	James Chrystie	David Loch	01. Apr
I	export	Cabinet ware (lb)	40	Margaret & Mary	James Chrystie	David Loch	01. Apr
I	re-export	Cambrics French (1/2piece)	284	Margaret & Mary	James Chrystie	William Crowden	02. Apr
II	export	Herring (barrel)	118	Betty	Donald Edie	Gilbert Meason	
II	export	Whale Oil (ton)	16	Betty	Donald Edie	David Loch	
III	export	Lead: Bar Lead (ton)	60	Unity	William Cuthbertson	William Moffat	
III	re-export	Salt (wey)	15	James & Jean	David Brody (Brodie)	David Loch	
III	re-export	Salt (wey)	1	James & Jean	David Brody (Brodie)	David Loch	
IV	export	Lead: Bar Lead (ton)	50	Margaret	Richard Scowgall	William Moffat	14 October
IV	re-export	Tea (lb)	1,084	Miller of Mansfield	William Smith	James Chalmers	16 October
IV	re-export	Tea (lb)	39	Miller of Mansfield	William Smith	James Chalmers	16 October

Source: Customs Accounts, NAS, E504

Table 2.3: Goods declared in Scottish ports for *Bremen* in the second half of 1754 (Michaelmas and Christmas Quarter)

Port / Customs Precinct	Year	Q	X/Re-X	Commodity, measure	Amount	Ship	Captain
LEITH	1754	III	X	Whale Oil (ton)	25.5	Tesdo	Alexander Learmonth
SHETLAND	1754	III	X	Herring (barrel)	450	?Alice?	James O'Conner
SHETLAND	1754	III	X	Herring (barrel)	430	Rouce	John Mey
SHETLAND	1754	III	X	Herring (barrel)	350	Argyll	Thomas Wilson
PRESTONPANS	1754	IV	X	Coal: great coals (ton)	30	Phoenix of Morrisonshaven	Richard Henderson
PRESTONPANS	1754	IV	X	Coal: great coals (ton)	3	Phoenix of Morrisonshaven	Richard Henderson
PRESTONPANS	1754	IV	X	Vitriol Oil (lb)	11,869	Phoenix of Morrisonshaven	Richard Henderson

Source: Customs Accounts, NAS, E504

Table 2.4: Scottish Port Books and Bremen Schlachte Toll Accounts compared: Traffic declared in Scottish Ports with the destination "Bremen" and Incoming Traffic in the Bremen Schlachte Toll Accounts, declared origin: "Scotland" or Scottish Port, 1755

(a) Scotland, Customs Accounts										(b) Bremen, Schlachteangabebücher						
Port / Customs Precinct	Year	Q	X/Re-X	Destination	Commodity, measure	Amount	Ship	Captain	Date of Declaration (out)	Date of Schlachte Entry (in)	Origin	Captain	Salt (Bremen lasts)	Weys, last @4500lbs	Herring (*Fässer*)	Purchaser
KIRKCALDY	1755	I	X	Bremen	466Salt (wey)	90	De Hoopen De Anna	Bone KeBroders	25 March	25 Apr	Scotland	?Bolck Grainger? / BoneKe Broders	30	60.27		Math. ?Tielen? & Sons
KIRKCALDY	1755	II	X	Bremen	466Salt (wey)	90.63	Lady Margareta of Bremen	Henrick Muller	23 May	18 June	Scotland	Henrick Wessels	40	80.36		Math. ?Tielen? & Sons
SHETLAND	1755	III	X	Bremen	572Herring (bbl)	300	Ann of Lerwick	Patrick Torrie	13 Aug	30 Aug	Lerwick	Patrick Torrie			301	(?Elter?) Düsing / Duising
SHETLAND	1755	III	X	Bremen	572Herring (bbl)	434	Anson Jaggar of London	John Kelway	17 Aug	30 Aug	Lerwick	John Kelway			434	(?Elter?) Düsing / Duising
SHETLAND	1755	III	X	Bremen	572Herring (bbl)	429	?Rouce? Jaggar of London	John May	18 Aug	10 Sep	Lerwick	John May			428	(?Elter?) Düsing / Duising
SHETLAND	1755	III	X	*Hamburg*	572Herring (bbl)	387.5	Ally of London	James O'Connor	29 July	29 Sep	South Wold	James O'Conner			360	(?Elter?) Düsing / Duising
										5 Oct	South Wold	John Kelway			344	(?Elter?) Düsing / Duising
BONESS	1755	IV	X	Bremen	466Salt (wey)	62.5	Gabetha & Elizabeth of Bremen	Henrick Muller	27 October	24 Nov	Scotland	Henrick Muller	30	60.27		Math. ?Tielen? & Sons
BONESS	1755	IV	X	Bremen	466Salt (wey)	50	Gabetha and Elizabeth of Bremen	Henrick Muller	27 October							
ORKNEY	1755	II	Re-X	Bremen	089Cotton Wool (lbs)	591	Industry of Leith	Andrew Cowan								
ORKNEY	1755	II	Re-X	Bremen	338Canes or Reeds (1000)	0.5	Industry of Leith	Andrew Cowan								
ORKNEY	1755	II	Re-X	Bremen	357Rice (cwt)	3084.16	Industry of Leith	Andrew Cowan	28 May							
ORKNEY	1755	II	Re-X	Bremen	549Turpentine (cwt)	33.31	Industry of Leith	Andrew Cowan								
ORKNEY	1755	II	Re-X	Bremen	648Wax Myrtle (lb)	100	Industry of Leith	Andrew Cowan								

Table 3.1 Consignments to German Ports on Account of Buchanan & Simson according to the Firm's Records

	Date	Ship	Master	Destination	Consignee	Commodity	Measure	Amount
1	16 March 1759	Jonge Lucas	Gerrit Kotter	Hamburg	Stephen Wolfenden	Tobacco	lbs	55,872
	16 March 1759	Jonge Lucas	Gerrit Kotter	Hamburg	Stephen Wolfenden	Tobacco	hhds	16
	16 March 1759	Jonge Lucas	Gerrit Kotter	Hamburg	Stephen Wolfenden	Sugar	casks	137
2	23 March 1759	Jonge Hendrick	Roloff	Hamburg	Richard Thornton	Tobacco	hhds	35
	23 March 1759	Jonge Hendrick	Roloff	Hamburg	Richard Thornton	Tobacco	hhds	3
	23 March 1759	Jonge Hendrick	Roloff	Hamburg	Richard Thornton	Tobacco	hhds	2
	23 March 1759	Jonge Hendrick	Roloff	Hamburg	Richard Thornton	Tobacco	hhds	20
3	11 June 1759	Neptune	Peter Meyer	Hamburg	Richard Thornton	Tobacco	hhds	3
	?11 June 1759?	?Neptune?	?Peter Meyer?	?Hamburg?	?Richard Thornton?	Tobacco	hhds	71?
4	22 June 1759	Corneli(u)s	Bendix Jahn	Hamburg	Stephen Wolfenden	Tobacco	hhds	16
	22 June 1759	Corneli(u)s	Bendix Jahn	Hamburg	Stephen Wolfenden	Sugar	hhds	146
5	19 September 1759	Jonge Lucas / Krone?	Gerrit Kotter / Peter Claassen?	Hamburg	Stephen Wolfenden	Tobacco	hhds	5
	19 September 1759	Jonge Lucas / Krone?	Gerrit Kotter / Peter Claassen?	Hamburg	Stephen Wolfenden	Tobacco	hhds	18
6	2 November 1759	Good Hope	Christian Janson	Hamburg	William Burrows & Son	Tobacco	hhds	10
7	2 May 1760	Anna Rosina	Johann Henry Wendt	Bremen	Frederik Schröder	Tobacco	hhds	75
	2 May 1760	Anna Rosina	Johann Henry Wendt	Bremen	Frederik Schröder	Ginger	lbs	4,113
	2 May 1760	Anna Rosina	Johann Henry Wendt	Bremen	Frederik Schröder	Coffee	cwt	146
8	?1760?	Jan of Bremen	Johann Friedrich Daniken	Bremen	Frederik Schröder	Tobacco	hhds	47
9	?1760?	Maria Theresia	Conrad Lange	Bremen	Frederik Schröder	Tobacco	hhds	87
10	June 1761	Krone (Crown)	Peter Claasen	Hamburg	Richard Thornton	Tobacco	hhds	98
	June 1761	Krone (Crown)	Peter Claasen	Hamburg	Richard Thornton	Sugar	hhds	16
11	24 July 1761	Katharina Elizabeth	Ede Dircks	Hamburg	Richard Thornton	Tobacco	hhds	65
	24 July 1761	Katharina Elizabeth	Ede Dircks	Hamburg	Richard Thornton	Sugar (refined)	hhds	12
12	4 August 1761	Jonge Christian	German	Hamburg	Stephen Wolfenden	Tobacco	hhds	79
13	29 August 1761	?Gisbert? Maria	?	Hamburg	Richard Thornton	Tobacco	hhds	190
14	23 October 1761	Elizabeth	?	Hamburg	Stephen Wolfenden	Tobacco	hhds	29
15	November / Decembe	Eleonora	Joh(a)n Brachman(n)	Hamburg	Georg Einbeck	Tobacco	hhds	52
	November / Decembe	Eleonora	Joh(a)n Brachman(n)	Hamburg	Georg Einbeck	Sugar	casks	137
16	?	Concordia	?	Hamburg	Georg Einbeck	Sugar	casks	55
17	May 1762	Maria Theresia	Conrad Lange?	Hamburg	Frederik Schröder	Tobacco	hhds	58
18	May 1762	Krone (Crown)	Peter Claasen	Hamburg	Richard Thornton	Tobacco	hhds	35
	May 1762	Krone (Crown)	Peter Claasen	Hamburg	Richard Thornton	Tobacco	hhds	4
	May 1762	Krone (Crown)	Peter Claasen	Hamburg	Richard Thornton	Tobacco	hhds	12
19	September 1762?	Concordia Sohia	Andreas ?Jordts?	Hamburg	Richard Thornton	Tobacco	hhds	56
	September 1762?	Concordia Sohia	Andreas ?Jordts?	Hamburg	Richard Thornton	Sugar	hhds	55
	September 1762?	Concordia Sohia	Andreas ?Jordts?	Hamburg	Stephen Wolfenden	Sugar	hhds	54

Table 3.2 Cargoes to German ports on account of Buchanan & Simson according to the Customs Accounts (Greenock, Port Glasgow)

Port	Year	Qu	Destination	Commodity	Amount	Ship	Master	Merchant(s)
GREENOCK	1759	I	Hamburg	Muscovado (cwt)	1,056.27	Young Lucas	Gerrit Kooter	Alexander Houston / William Hyndman
PORT GLASGOW	1759	I	Hamburg	Tobacco (lbs)	29,608.00	Young Henrick	Henrick Roelofs	George Buchanan / Robert Bailie / William Dunlop
PORT GLASGOW	1759	I	Hamburg	Tobacco (lbs)	1,919.00	Young Henrick	Henrick Roelofs	William Miller Sr.&Jr. / William Gordon & Co
PORT GLASGOW	1759	I	Hamburg	Tobacco (lbs)	2,862.00	Young Henrick	Henrick Roelofs	Andrew Ramsay / William Gordon & Co
PORT GLASGOW	1759	I	Hamburg	Tobacco (lbs)	18,022.00	Young Henrick	Henrick Roelofs	Alexander Walker / William Gordon
GREENOCK	1759	II	Hamburg	Tobacco (lbs)	70,806.00	Neptunus	Peter Meyer	George Buchanan / William & James Watson
PORT GLASGOW	1759	II	Hamburg	Tobacco (lbs)	14,662.00	Cornelius	Benedix (Benedict) Zahn	Robert & William Dunlop / William Wallace
PORT GLASGOW	1760	III	Bremen	Ginger (cwt)	4,335.52	Anna Rosina of Bremen	Johan Hendrick Wendt	William Gordon / Hugh Millikin & Co
GREENOCK	1760	III	Bremen	Coffee (lbs)	146.50	Anna Rosina	Johan Hinrich Wendt	George Buchanan / James Simson / James Watson
PORT GLASGOW	1760	II	Bremen	Tobacco (lbs)	43,999.00	Jan of Bremen	Johan Frederik Daanisken (Daanken)	George Buchanan / Gordon / Millikin & Co
PORT GLASGOW	1761	II	Hamburg	Tobacco (lbs)	16,514.00	Krone (Crown) of Altona	Peter Claasen	George Buchanan / James Simson / Robert Douglas / Robert Gregory & Co
GREENOCK	1761	III	Hamburg	Tobacco (lbs)	49,085.00	Krone (Crown) of Altona	Peter Claasen	James Simson / William & James Watson
GREENOCK	1761	II	Hamburg	Muscovado (cwt)	172.73	Krone (Crown) of Altona	Peter Claasen	Colin Dunlop / Alexander Houston / William McCunn
GREENOCK	1761	III	Hamburg	Muscovado (cwt)	503.46	Krone (Crown) of Altona	Peter Claasen	George Buchanan / William Watson & Co
GREENOCK	1761	II	Hamburg	Tobacco (lbs)	5,710.00	Catharina & Elizabeth	Ede Dircks	George Buchanan / William & James Watson
PORT GLASGOW	1761	II	Hamburg	Tobacco (lbs)	21,730.00	Catharina Elizabeth of Hamburg	Edo Direcks (?Diercks?)	Buchanan & Simson / Robert Douglas / Robert Gregory
PORT GLASGOW	1761	II	Hamburg	Refined Sugar (cwt)	74.50	Catharina Elizabeth of Hamburg	Edo Direcks (?Diercks?)	Colin Dunlop / George Buchanan / Robert Douglas / Robert Gregory
GREENOCK	1761	III	Bremen	Tobacco (lbs)	53,613.00	Young Christian	Peter Michael German	George Buchanan / William & James Watson
PORT GLASGOW	1761	III	Hamburg	Refined Sugar (cwt)	779.08	Young Christian Peter	Michael German	George Buchanan / Colin Dunlop / Robert Douglas / Robert Gregory
PORT GLASGOW	1762	II	Hamburg	Tobacco (lbs)	4,134.00	Concordia Sophia of Hamburg	Peter Jansen	James Simson / Robert Douglas / Robert Gregory
PORT GLASGOW	1762	III	Hamburg	Tobacco (lbs)	9,414.00	St Geran	Jacob Heidman	James Simson / Robert Douglas / Robert Gregory

NOTE ON WEIGHTS AND MEASURES

Abbreviations used:

bbl	= barrel
ct	= hundred
cwt	= hundredweight
ft	= feet
gl(s)	= gallon(s)
yd(s)	= yard(s)

1) The *hundredweight* (cwt) used by the British Customs administration equalled 1 cwt = 112 lbs. Deviant quotations, which are at variance with the evidence of the various Customs records might be found in R. E. ZUPKO, A Dictionary of Weights and Measures for the British Isles: The Middle Ages to the Twentieth Century (Philadelphia, 1985), entry "hundred".
2) The standard ton generally corresponded to 20 standard cwt, thus: 1 ton = 20 cwt = 2,240 lbs.
3) The salt *wey* used by the British Customs amounted to 40 standard bushels and thus corresponded to the standard metric ton, thus: 1 wey = 40 bushels @ 56 lbs each, or 1 wey = 2,240 lbs. Deviant quotes for the salt wey, which are at variance with the evidence of the various Customs records, may be found in ZUPKO, Dictionary, entry "wey".
4) The *hundred* used by the British Customs administration for timber items generally conformed to the standard of the *long hundred* of 1 ct = 120. Deviant quotations, which are at variance with the evidence of the various Customs records, might likewise be found in ZUPKO, Dictionary, entry "hundred". In some exceptions, when the *short hundred* was employed by the Customs, it was indicated as such in the respective port records.
5) Where the load-feet measure was employed instead (fir timber; timber in great balks), one *load* equalled 50 feet.
6) The *barrel* (bbl) used by the British Customs administration for ashes (pearl, pot, wood and weed) generally amounted to 200 lbs, as opposed to the suggestion by ZUPKO, Dictionary, entry "barrel", which reckons the ashes bbl at 2 standard cwt @ 112 lbs each.

British and German Currencies

1) Immediately prior to the Union of 1707, the Scots currency exchanged at 1/12 £Sterling (this rate had fluctuated until 1603 when it was fixed). Thus 1 £Scots = 1 s 8 d Sterling. This exchange rate was retained after 1707 for accounting and banking purposes and in local transactions (grain stipends, rent payments etc.)
2) The old Scots currency also included the *Merk* (Mark) Scots. 1 *Merk* Scots = 13s 4d Scots (~2/3 £Scots or ~1s 1d 1 *farthing* Sterling).
3) ***Hamburg*** had two currencies, one of which was a money of account (*Mark Banko*).
   i. The nominal relations for both were: 1 Mark = 16 s (Shillings) = 32 *Groats* (Groschen) *Lubisch* (Lübeck Money), but

ii. Mark Banko was fixed in terms of its imputed precious metal content whilst Mark Hamburg current (Lübeck) Money fluctuated in value. Mark Banko was thus available at an *agio*, as 100 Marks Banko always equalled more than 100 Marks current money.

iii. 1 *Mark* = 1/3 *Rix Dollars* (*Reichstaler*).

4) ***Bremen*** normally reckoned in Rix Dollars (*Reichstaler*) @ 64 Groats (*Groschen*) or 384 Pennies (*Pfennige*).

The following works have been used for reference:

Currency

DENZEL, M. A., 'La Practica della Cambiatura'. Europäischer Zahlungsverkehr vom 14. bis zum 17. Jahrhundert, Stuttgart 1994

ID. / SCHWARZER, O., Kurant, in: M. NORTH (ed.), Von Aktie bis Zoll. Ein Historisches Lexikon des Geldes, Munich 1995, pp. 210–12

GEMMILL, E. / MAYHEW, N., Changing Values in Medieval Scotland. A Study of Prices, Money, and Weights and Measures, Cambridge 1995

GIBSON, A. J. S. / SMOUT, T. C., Prices, Food and Wages in Scotland 1550–1780, Cambridge 1995

MCCUSKER, J. J., Money and Exchange in Europe and America, 1600–1775, Chapel Hill 1978, pp. 61–79

PETERS, L. F. , Hamburger Bank", in: NORTH (ed.), Von Aktie bis Zoll, pp. 154–5

SCHNEIDER, K., Mark II, in: ibid., pp. 235–6

SPRENGER, B., Das Geld der Deutschen. Geldgeschichte Deutschlands von den Anfängen bis zur Gegenwart, Paderborn / Munich / Vienna / Zurich 1991

Exchange Rates

As MCCUSKER, Money, does not have the eighteenth century bill rate Hamburg on London, the following works can be used instead:

REISS, W., Historical Exchange Rates, in: W. FISCHER / R. MARVIN MCINNIS / J. SCHNEIDER (eds.), The Emergence of a World Economy 1500–1914, Pt. I: 1500–1850, Wiesbaden 1986, pp. 171–190

J. SCHNEIDER / O. SCHWARZER, International Rates of Exchange: Structures and Trends of Payments Mechanism in Europe, 17th to 19th Century, in: Ibid., pp. 143–170

J. SCHNEIDER / O. SCHWARZER / F. ZELLFELDER / M. A. DENZEL (eds.), Währungen der Welt VI: Geld und Währungen in Europa im 18. Jahrhundert, Stuttgart 1992

BIBLIOGRAPHY

PRIMARY SOURCES

Abbreviations used in the text:

ECA	Edinburgh City Archives
GCA	Glasgow City Archives
NAS	National Archives of Scotland
NLS	National Library of Scotland
TNA	The National Archives (formerly Public Record Office, England & Wales)

National Archives of Scotland, Edinburgh

High Court of Admiralty, Edinburgh, Decrees

AC 7/37–8	*Dalling vs. Carmichael*, 4 August 1732

High Court of Admiralty, Edinburgh, Processes in Absence (AC8), Processes in Foro (AC9)

AC8/409	John Carmichael, Petition (1730)
AC8/836	David Gemlo vs Thomas Douglas & Co (1754)
AC8/854	William Auchterlony vs Thomas Douglas & Co (1754)
AC9/1206	Robert Dalling vs John Carmichael (1732)
AC9/1525	Diederich Ratien vs John Carmichael (1742)
AC9/1581	Robert Auchterlony vs Thomas Douglas & Co (1754)
AC9/1584	Richard Hartley vs Thomas Douglas & Co (1754)
AC9/1891	William Alexander vs Thomas Douglas & Co (1754)
AC9/1960	John Carmichael vs George Seaman (1755)
AC9/2115	Robert Auchterlony vs Thomas Douglas & Co (1754)
AC9/2152	David Loch vs Donald Edie (1762)

Board of Customs & Excise, Scotland (CE)

CE1/8	Minute Book Board of Customs (11 December 1749 to 23 January 1755)
CE1/9	Minute Book (27 January 1755 to 19 April 1759)
CE 7/5	Inspector General's (of Imports and Exports) Report Book (1784–1786).
CE7/11	Instructions 1707 (1707)
CE14/1	Abstract of General Orders of the Honourable Board of Customs in Scotland (1707–c.1806)
CE51/2/1	Port of Dumfries, Board to Collector, Letter & Order Book (1727–1748)
CE56/5/1	"Prestonpans Custom Book" (Files of Masters' Reports Inwards, Port of Prestonpans, 1708–1718)
CE57/2/172a	Port of Leith, Board to Collector, Board's General Orders (1707–1803)
CE87/1/1	Port of Aberdeen, Collector to Board et al., Letter Book (1728–1732)

Court of Session (CS)

Buchanan & Simson (Glasgow, c.1759–1763)

CS96/502–503	Invoice Books
CS96/504–5	Journals
CS96/506/1–2	Ledgers
CS96/507	Letter Book

Semple, Jamieson & Lawson (Glasgow)

CS96/1176–81
CS96/1183–4
CS96/1186
CS96/1191–2
CS96/1195
CS96/1197
CS96/3870–1

Exchequer Records (E)

Writs of Extent against Thomas Douglas & Co.

E371/41–48	(1753–54)
E371/56	
E371/58	(1758)

E501/1–72	*Customs General Accounts* (Customs Yields, Scotland, 1707–1770)

E504	*Customs Collectors' Quarterly Accounts ("customs accounts", "port books"), full set Christmas 1742–Christmas 1755*
E504/1/1–6	Aberdeen
E504/2/1–3	Alloa
E504/3/1–3	Anstruther
E504/4/1–2	Ayr
E504/6/1–4	Bo'ness
E504/7/1–2	Caithness / Thurso
E504/8/1–2	Campbeltown
E504/9/1–2	Dumfries
E504/10/1–3	Dunbar
E504/11/1–3	Dundee
E504/12/1–2	Fort William
E504/15/1–7	Greenock
E504/17/1–2	Inverness
E504/18/1–3	Irvine
E504/20/1–3	Kirkcaldy
E504/21/1–2	Kirkcudbright
E504/22/1–7	Leith
E504/23/1	Lochbroom / Ullapool (Jun 1743 – Jun 1747)
E504/24/1–3	Montrose
E504/26/1–3	Orkney (Kirkwall)
E504/27/1–3	Perth
E504/28/1–7	Port Glasgow
E504/29/1–3	Portpatrick
E504/30/1–2	Prestonpans
E504/32/1–2	Shetland (Lerwick)
E504/34/1–2	Stranraer
E504/37/1–2	Wigtown

General Deposit Series (GD)

Clerk of Penicuik Muniments

GD18/5321/66
GD18/5321/69

GD22/6/33	(1715–1718) Merchants' letters relating to herring fishery and herring trade to Hamburg. Correspondence between Bartholomew Bludworth (Hamburg) and Alexander Mackintosh (Edinburgh)
GD45/24/37	D'AVENANT, Charles, A Report to the Honourable The Commissioners For putting in Execution the Act, intitled An Act, for the Taking, Examining, and Stating the Publick Accounts of the

Kingdom (London 1712)

GD219/290	*John Murray of Murraywhat Letter Book*

Trinity House (Leith) Records

GD 226/7/1	*Crown Money Book*
GD 226/18/250	*Table of Shore-Dues*
GD 229/13/36	*Tables of Shore Dues,* Leith (1761–1780, 1788–1827)

GD237/1/154/3
GD237/1/154/4

Photostat Copies of Treasury and Customs Materials (London)
Ledgers of Imports and Exports – TNA (ex P.R.O.), Customs 14

RH 2/4/10	1755–1758
RH 2/4/11	1759–1762
RH20/1	1762
RH 2/4/17	1764
RH 2/4/14	1765
RH 2/4/20	1766
RH 2/4/16	1767
RH 2/4/15	1768
RH 2/4/18	1770
RH2/4/460	Treasury Out-Letters, 1755

Mitchell Papers

RH 2/5/11/18	Account of the Quantities of the several sorts of Foreign Linens imported into Scotland from Xmas 1737 to Xmas 1748
RH 2/5/11/19	Account of Foreign Linens re-exported out of Scotland to the Plantations in America from Xmas 1737 to Xmas 1748
RH 2/5/11/20	Account of the Quantity of Linen Cloth exported out of Scotland from Lady Day 1743 to Xmas 1748 upon which Bounties have been paid, distinguishing British and Irish
RH 2/5/11/23–24	Memorandum on the Common Practice used in importing Foreign Linen etc.

Miscellaneous (RH)

RH4/137	Microfilm copy of NAS, GD150/2543/17 (transferred to Shetland Archives), *George Robertson to Earl of Morton*, 21 June 1709
RH 4/170	Misc. microform copies of TNA, E122/219 records (Exchequer series)
RH4/203/1	Papers of Lawrence Dundas
RH15/14/99	Papers of Alexander Campbell, merchant in Edinburgh (c.1700–1707); Misc. papers relating to Port of Leith (1706–7)

RH15/38/91	John Mathie (Bremen) to John Carmichael, merchant in Edinburgh (1740–1), concerning state of repair of the ship.
RH15/38/92	John Carmichael to Diederich Ratien (Bremen), his consignee in Bremen (1740–1)
RH15/92/32	Papers of Robert Menzies of Coulterallars (second Inspector General of Exports and Imports of Scotland, 1764)

National Library of Scotland

Manuscript Sources

Ms 60	*The Value of all Goods, Wares and Merchandize Imported into & exported from Scotland Compared with the Excess of Each Country Commencing Anno 1755.*
Pamphlet Series	*1.22(96) Copy of Treaty between Britain and Hamburg, granting British merchants access to the Hamburg fish market on favourable terms equal to those enjoyed by the Dutch, Hamburg, 31 January 1711*

University of Edinburgh, Main Library, Special Collections

Laing MSS

La.II.491/11/4, Customs Accounts Port of Kirkcaldy, Midsummer 1737

Edinburgh City Archives, Edinburgh

Convention of Royal Burghs, Scotland

SL30/4/6, Box 1, Bdl. 2, *Rules and Directions for the Better Regulating the Coast Trade, and preventing Frauds by Ships and Vessels trading Coastways* (1773)

Dundee City Archives

Montrose Outport Records (transferred from NAS)

CE53/1/3	Collector (Port of Montrose) to Board of Customs, 1738–1744
CE53/2/6	Board of Customs to Collector (Port of Montrose), 1752–1770

Glasgow City Archives, Mitchell Library

Outport Records Port Glasgow & Greenock

CE 60/1/1	Collector to Board of Customs, Letter Book (1749–1752)
CE 60/1/2	Letter Book Collector to Board of Customs (1755–1758)
CE 60/2/359	Board of Customs to Collector, Order and Letter Book, Surveyor's Copy (?)
CE 60/2/387	Index to Board's Orders (1742–1789)
CE 60/4/10	Instruction Manual (1708–1856)

The National Archives (formerly Public Record Office), London

Board of Customs & Excise

Customs 14	Scottish Inspector General's Ledgers of Imports and Exports, 1755–1770 (Photostat copies in NAS).

Treasury

T1/447/242–243	*Memorial of the Commissioners for Managing His Majesty's Customs in Scotland*
T36/13	Misc. Accounts Relating to Scotland

Staatsarchiv, Bremen

2–Ss.2.a.4.f.1seq.	*Schlachteangabebücher* (1738–9, 1754 seq.).

Stadtarchiv, Emden

Stadtarchiv Emden, I, 863b	Edict anent the Declaration of Scots as Lunenburg Salt, Emden 1723

PRIMARY SOURCES, PRINTED BOOKS AND VOLUMES PRIOR TO 1800

BALD, A., The Farmer and Corn-Dealer's Assistant, 1st ed. Edinburgh 1780

BALDWIN, S., A Survey of the British Customs [...], London 1770

BANG, N. E. / KORST, K. (eds.), Tabeller over Skibsfart og Varetransport gennem Øresund 1661–1783 og gennem Storebælt 1701–1748: Vol. 1.1, Copenhagen / Leipzig 1939; Vol. 1.2, Copenhagen / Leipzig 1945

CROUCH, H., A Complete View of the British Customs [...], Part I, London 1725

———, A Complete View of the British Customs [...], Part II, London 1728

———, A Complete View of the British Customs [...], 2nd ed., London 1731

———, A Complete View of the British Customs [...], 3rd ed., London 1738

———, A Complete View of the British Customs [...], 4th ed., London 1745

———, A Complete View of the British Customs [...], 5th ed., London 1755

HANWAY, J., An Historical Account of the British Trade over the Caspian Sea. With the Author's Journal of Travels from England through Russia into Persia; and back through Russia, Germany and Holland, Vol. II, 2nd ed. London 1754

KRÜNITZ, J. G. (ed.), Oekonomische Encyklopaedie oder Allgemeines System der Land-, Haus- und Staatswirthschaft, 242 vols. Berlin 1773–1858

LANGHAM, T., The Neat Duties (All Discounts and Abatements deducted) of all Merchandize Specify'd in the Book of Rates, London 1708

———, The Neat Duties (All Discounts and Abatements deducted) of all Merchandize, Specified in the Book of Rates, 3rd ed., London 1715

———, The Nett Duties and Drawbacks payable upon Importation and Exportation Of all Sorts of Merchandize, Digested into an Easy Method [...], 7th ed., London 1754

H. SAXBY, The British Customs, London 1757

PUBLISHED AND UNPUBLISHED THESES AND DISSERTATIONS

BOKELOH, K. H., Emder Wirtschaftsgeschichte 1744–1806. Preußischer Absolutismus der zweiten Hälfte des 18. Jahrhunderts in einer Randprovinz, University of Tübingen PhD Thesis, Tübingen 1984

COCHRAN, L. E., Scottish Trade with Ireland in the Eighteenth Century, Unpubl. University of Stirling PhD Thesis, 2 vols. Stirling 1980

DENHOLM, P. C. / ROSS, K. G., The Cash Accounts of the Ship Leith Galley. A Study in Eighteenth Century Ship-Operation, Unpubl. Manuscript, NAS, Edinburgh 1972

KOUFOPOULOS, A. J., The Cattle Trades of Scotland, 1603–1745, Unpubl. University of Edinburgh PhD Thesis, Edinburgh 2005

RORKE, M., Scottish Overseas Trade 1275/86–1597, Unpubl. Univ. of Edinburgh PhD Thesis, 2 vols. Edinburgh 2001

ROESSNER, P. R., 'New Avenues of Trade.' Der Außenhandel Schottlands im 18. Jahrhundert zwischen Tradition und Revolution (1707–1783), Unpubl. University of Göttingen MA thesis, Göttingen 2002

———, Scottish Foreign Trade towards the End of the Pre-industrial Period, 1700–1760, Unpubl. University of Edinburgh PhD Thesis, Edinburgh 2007

SCOTT, R., The Politics and Administration of Scotland 1725–1748, Unpubl. University of Edinburgh PhD Thesis, Edinburgh 1981

SMOUT, T. C., The Overseas Trade of Scotland With Particular Reference to the Baltic and Scandinavian Trades 1660–1707, Unpubl. University of Cambridge PhD Thesis, Cambridge 1959

SECONDARY WORKS

ABEL, W., Agrarkrisen und Agrarkonjunktur in Mitteleuropa vom 13. bis zum 19. Jahrhundert, Berlin 1935; Hamburg / Berlin, 3rd ed. 1978

———, Massenarmut und Hungerkrisen im vorindustriellen Deutschland, Göttingen 1971

———, Geschichte der deutschen Landwirtschaft vom frühen Mittelalter bis zum 19. Jahrhundert, Stuttgart, 3rd ed. 1978

———, Agricultural Fluctuations in Europe from the Thirteenth to the Twentieth Centuries, London 1980

———, Stufen der Ernährung. Eine historische Skizze, Göttingen 1981

ACEMOGLU, D. / JOHNSON, S. / ROBINSON, J. A., The Rise of Europe: Atlantic Trade, Institutional Change and Economic Growth, Centre for Economic Policy Research Discussion Paper Nr. 3712 (January 2003)

ADAMS, D. G., Trade in the Eighteenth and Nineteenth Centuries, in: G. JACKSON / S. G. E. LYTHE (eds.), The Port of Montrose: A History of its Harbour, Trade and Shipping, Tayport 1993, pp. 125–149

ALLEN, R., Agriculture During the Industrial Revolution, in: R. FLOUD / D. N. MCCLOSKEY (eds.), The Economic History of Britain since 1700, Vol 1: 1700–1860, Cambridge, 2nd ed. 1994, pp. 96–122

ASHTON, T. S., An Economic History of England: The Eighteenth Century, London 1955

———, Introduction, in: E. B. SCHUMPETER, English Overseas Trade Statistics, 1697–1808, Oxford 1960, pp. 1–14

ÅSTRÖM, S. E., From Cloth to Iron. The Anglo-Baltic Trade in the Late Seventeenth Century, Pt. I: The Growth, Structure and Organization of the Trade, Helsingfors 1963

———, From Cloth to Iron. The Anglo-Baltic Trade in the Late Seventeenth Century, Pt. II: The Customs Accounts as Sources for the Study of the Trade, Helsingfors 1965

———, The Swedish Economy and Sweden's Role as a Great Power, 1632–1697, in: M. ROBERTS (ed.), Sweden's Age of Greatness 1632–1718, London / Basingstoke 1973, pp. 58–101

———, North European Timber Exports to Great Britain, 1760–1810, in: P. L. COTTRELL / D. H. ALDCROFT (eds.), Shipping, Trade and Commerce. Essays in Memory of Ralph Davis, Leicester 1981, pp. 81–98

AUBIN, H. / ZORN, W. (eds.), Handbuch der Deutschen Wirtschafts- und Sozialgeschichte, Vol. 1:Von der Frühzeit bis zum Ende des 18. Jahrhunderts, Stuttgart 1971

BAASCH, E., Zur Statistik des Ein- und Ausfuhrhandels Hamburgs Anfang des 18. Jahrhunderts, in: Hansische Geschichtsblätter, LIV (1929)

BANG, N. E. / KORST, K. (eds.), Tabeller over Skibsfart og Varetransport gennem Øresund 1661–1783 og gennem Storebælt 1701–1748, Vol. 1.1, Copenhagen / Leipzig 1939

———, Tabeller over Skibsfart og Varetransport gennem Øresund 1661–1783 og gennem Storebælt 1701–1748, Vol. 1.2, Copenhagen / Leipzig 1945

BARNES, I., The Aberdeen Stocking Trade, in: Textile History, VIII (1977), pp. 77–98

BECHTEL, H., Wirtschaftsgeschichte Deutschlands. Vom Beginn des 16. zum Ende des 18. Jahrhunderts, Munich 1952

BENZ, E., Population Change and the Economy, in: S. OGILVIE (ed.), Germany. A New Social and Economic History, Vol. II: 1630–1800, London / New York 1996, pp. 39–62

BERG, M., Consumption in Eighteenth- and early Nineteenth-century Britain, in: R. FLOUD / P. JOHNSON (eds.), The Cambridge Economic History of Modern Britain, Vol. I: Industrialisation, 1700–1860, Cambridge 2004, pp. 357–387

BESTMANN, U. / IRSIGLER, F. / SCHNEIDER, J. (eds.), Hochfinanz, Wirtschaftsräume, Innovationen. Festschrift für Wolfgang von Stromer, 3 Vols., Trier 1987

BEUTIN, L., Der Deutsche Seehandel im Mittelmeergebiet bis zu den Napoleonischen Kriegen, Neumünster 1933

———, Drei Jahrhunderte Tabakhandel in Bremen, in: H. Kellenbenz (ed.), Ludwig Beutin, Gesammelte Schriften zur Wirtschafts- und Sozialgeschichte, Cologne / Graz 1963, pp. 98–131

BLANCHARD, I., 'Russia's Age of Silver'. Precious Metal Production and Economic Growth in the Eighteenth Century, London 1989

———, GOODMAN / NEWMAN, J. (eds.), Industry and Finance in Early Modern History, Stuttgart 1992

———, Northern Wools and Netherlands Markets at the Close of the Middle Ages, in: G. G. SIMPSON (ed.), Scotland and the Low Countries 1124–1994, East Linton 1996, pp. 76–88

BOG, I. (ed.), Der Außenhandel Ostmitteleuropas 1450–1650, Cologne / Vienna 1971

BOGUCKA, M., Handelsbeziehungen im Ostseeraum: Der Handel zwischen Danzig/Gdansk und Stockholm in der 1. Hälfte des 17. Jahrhunderts, in: K. FRIEDLAND / F. IRSIGLER (eds.), Seehandel und Wirtschaftswege Nordeuropas im 17. und 18. Jahrhundert, Ostfildern 1981, pp. 38–47

BOJE, P., Denmark's Role in the World Economy, 1750–1950, in: M. NORTH (ed.), Nordwesteuropa in der Weltwirtschaft 1750–1950 / Northwestern Europe in the World Economy 1750–1950, Stuttgart 1993, pp. 21–38

BÖLTS, J. Die Rindviehhaltung im oldenburgisch-ostfriesischen Raum vom Ausgang des 16. Jahrhunderts bis zum Beginn des 19. Jahrhunderts, in: H. WIESE / J. BÖLTS, Rinderhandel und Rinderhaltung im nordwesteuropäischen Küstengebiet vom 15. bis zum 19. Jahrhundert, Stuttgart 1966, pp. 133–271

H. BRANIG, Geschichte Pommerns (ed. W. Buchholz), Pt. II: Von 1648 bis zum Ende des 18. Jahrhunderts, Cologne / Weimar / Vienna 2000

BRAUDEL, F., Civilization and Capitalism 15th – 18th Century, Vol 1: The Structures of Everyday Life, London 2002, pbk

———, Civilization and Capitalism 15th – 18th Century, Vol. 2: The Wheels of Commerce, London 2002, pbk

BRÜBACH, N., 'This Precious Stinke' – Zur Wirtschaftsgeschichte des Tabaks, 1500 – ca. 1800, in: H. POHL (ed.), The European Discovery of the World and its Economic Effects on Pre-industrial Society 1500–1800, Stuttgart 1990, pp. 141–152

———, Die Reichsmessen von Frankfurt am Main, Leipzig und Braunschweig (14.–18. Jahrhundert), Stuttgart 1994

BRÜCK, T., Korporationen der Schiffer und Bootsleute. Untersuchungen zu ihrer Entwicklung in Seestädten an der Nord- und Ostseeküste vom Ende des 15. bis zum Ende des 17. Jahrhunderts, Weimar 1994

BUCHHOLZ, W., Öffentliche Finanzen und Finanzverwaltung im entwickelten frühmodernen Staat. Landesherr und Landstände in Schwedisch-Pommern 1720–1806, Cologne / Weimar / Vienna 1992

———, (ed.), Deutsche Geschichte im Osten Europas, Vol. 9. Pommern, Berlin 1999

———, Das schwedische Pommern vom Westfälischen Frieden bis zum Wiener Kongress, in: ID. (ed.), Deutsche Geschichte im Osten Europas, Vol. 9. Pommern, Berlin 1999, pp. 237–305

BURMESTER, R., Lübecks Wirtschaft in den letzten 175 Jahren (1751–1926), in: A. REY (ed.), Lübeck seit Mitte des 18. Jahrhunderts (1751). Ein Jubiläumsbeitrag zur 700-Jahrfeier der Reichsfreiheit Lübecks, Lübeck 1926, pp. 39–52

BURTON, F. N., Contemporary Trade, Oxford 1984

BUTT, J. / WARD, J. T. (eds.), Scottish Themes. Essays in Honour of S. G. E. Lythe, Edinburgh 1976

CAMPBELL, R. H., An Economic History of Scotland in the Eighteenth Century, in: Scottish Journal of Political Economy, XI (1946)

———, The Anglo-Scottish Union of 1707.II. The Economic Consequences, in: Economic History Review, Second Series, XVI, 3 (1964), pp. 472–474

———, The Industrial Revolution: A revision article, in: Scottish Historical Review, XLVI (1967), pp. 36–55

———, Scotland since 1707. The Rise of an Industrial Society, Edinburgh, 2nd revised ed. 1985

CANNY, N. (ed.), The Oxford History of the British Empire, Vol. I: The Origins of Empire. British Overseas Enterprise to the Close of the Seventeenth Century, Oxford 1998

CARRIERE, C., Négociants marsellais au xviiie siècle, in: Institut historique de Provence, 1973, Vol, 1, pp. 375–388, pp. 462–464, reprinted in: M. MARGAIRAZ (ed.), Histoire Économique XVIIIe–XXe Siècle, Paris 1992, pp. 526–538

CARUS-WILSON, E. M. / COLEMAN, O., England's Export Trade 1275–1547, Oxford 1963

CAVACIOCCHI, S. (ed.), Prodotti e Tecniche d'Oltremare nelle Economie Europee Secc. XIII–XVIII, Prato 1998

CIPOLLA, C. M. (ed.), The Fontana Economic History of Europe, Vol. 2: The Sixteenth and Seventeenth Centuries, Glasgow 1974

———, Before the Industrial Revolution. European Society and Economy 1000–1700, London / New York, 3rd ed. 1993

CLARK, G. N., Guide to English Commercial Statistics 1696–1782, London 1938

COCHRAN, L. E., Scottish-Irish Trade in the Eighteenth Century, in: T. M. DEVINE / D. DICKSON (eds.), Ireland and Scotland 1600–1850. Parallels and Contrasts in Economic and Social Development, Edinburgh 1983, pp. 151–162

———, Scottish Trade with Ireland in the Eighteenth Century, Edinburgh 1985

COLE, W. A., Trends in Eighteenth Century Smuggling, in: Economic History Review, Second Series, X (1957/58), pp. 359–410

CONNOR, A. D. / SIMPSON, A. D. C., Weights and Measures in Scotland: A European Perspective, East Linton 2004

COTTRELL, P. L. / ALDCROFT, D. H. (eds.), Shipping, Trade and Commerce. Essays in memory of Ralph Davis, Leicester 1981

COULL, R. J., The Sea Fisheries of Scotland. A Historical Geography, Edinburgh 1996

CRAFTS, N. F. R., English Economic Growth in the Eighteenth Century: A Re-examination of Deane and Cole's Estimates, in: Economic History Review, Second Series, XXIX (1976), pp. 226–235

———, British Economic Growth during the Industrial Revolution, Oxford 1985

CRAIG, L. A. / FISHER, D., The European Macroeconomy. Growth, Integration and Cycles 1500–1913, Cheltenham / Northampton 2000

CULLEN, L. M., Anglo-Irish Trade, 1660–1800, Manchester 1968

DAVIS, R, English Foreign Trade, 1660–1700, in: Economic History Review, Second Series, VI (1954), pp. 150–166

———, English Foreign Trade, 1700–1774, in: Economic History Review, Second Series, XV (1962), pp. 285–303

———, A Commercial Revolution. English Overseas Trade in the Seventeenth and Eighteenth Centuries, London 1967

———, The Industrial Revolution and British Overseas Trade, Leicester 1979

DEANE, P. / COLE, W. A., British Economic Growth 1688–1959. Trends and Structure, Cambridge, 2nd ed. 1967

DEANE, P., The First Industrial Revolution, Cambridge / London / New York / Melbourne 1967

DENNISON, E. P. / DITCHBURN, D. / LYNCH, M. (eds.), Aberdeen Before 1800. A New History, East Linton 2002

DENZEL, M. A., 'La Practica della Cambiatura'. Europäischer Zahlungsverkehr vom 14. bis zum 17. Jahrhundert, Stuttgart 1994

——— / SCHWARZER, O., Kurant in: M. NORTH (ed.), Von Aktie bis Zoll. Ein Historisches Lexikon des Geldes, Munich 1995, pp. 210–12

———, Die Braunschweiger Messen als regionaler und überregionaler Markt im norddeutschen Raum in der zweiten Hälfte des 18. und im beginnenden 19. Jahrhundert, in: Vierteljahrschrift für Sozial- und Wirtschaftsgeschichte, LXXXV (1998), pp. 40–93

———, Die Integration Deutschlands in das internationale Zahlungsverkehrssystem im 17. und 18. Jahrhundert, in: E. SCHREMMER (ed.), Wirtschaftliche und soziale Integration in historischer Sicht, Stuttgart 1996, pp. 58–109

———, Zur Geschäftspraxis eines Nanteser Handelshauses: Der Preiskurant von Pelloutier & Cie (1763–1793), in: J. HOOCK / W. REININGHAUS (eds.), Kaufleute in Europa. Handelshäuser und ihre Überlieferung in vor- und frühindustrieller Zeit, Dortmund 1997, pp. 61–87

——— (ed.), Währungen der Welt XI: Dänische und nordwestdeutsche Wechselkurse 1696–1914, Stuttgart 1999

——— / GERHARD, Inflationäre Prozesse in Nordwestdeutschland im 18. Jahrhundert, in: Vierteljahrschrift für Sozial- und Wirtschaftsgeschichte, XC (2003), pp. 1–25

——— / ———, Global and Local Aspects of Pre-Industrial Inflations: New Research on Inflationary Processes in XVIIIth–Century Central Europe, in: Journal of European Economic History, XXXIV, 1 (2005), pp. 149–185

DEVINE, T. M., The Tobacco Lords. A Study of the Tobacco Merchants of Glasgow and their Trading Activities 1740–1790, Edinburgh 1975

DEVINE, T. M. / DICKSON, D. (eds.), Ireland and Scotland 1600–1850. Parallels and Contrast in Economic and Social Development, Edinburgh 1983

——— / R. MITCHISON (eds.), People and Society in Scotland, Vol. I: 1760–1830, Edinburgh 1988

———, Urbanisation, in: ID. / R. MITCHISON (eds.), People and Society in Scotland, Vol. I: 1760–1830, Edinburgh 1988, pp. 27–52

——— / JACKSON, G. (eds.), Glasgow. Volume I: Beginnings to 1830, Manchester / New York 1995

———, The Golden Age of Tobacco, in: ID. / G. JACKSON (eds.), Glasgow, Vol. I: Beginnings to 1830, Manchester / New York 1995, pp. 139–183

———, The Colonial Trades and Industrial Investments in Scotland, c.1700–1815, in: P. EMMER / F. GAASTRA (eds.), The Organization of Interoceanic Trade in European Expansion, 1450–1800, Aldershot 1996, pp. 299–312

———, The Scottish Nation. A History 1700–2000, New York 1999

———, Scotland's Empire 1600–1815, London 2003

———, Scotland in: R. FLOUD / P. JOHNSON (eds.), The Cambridge Economic History of Modern Britain, Vol. I: Industrialisation, 1700–1860, Cambridge 2004, pp. 388–416

——— / LEE, C. L. / PEDEN, G. C. (eds.), The Transformation of Scotland. The Economy Since 1700, Edinburgh 2005

———, The Modern Economy: Scotland and the Act of Union, in: ID. / C. L. LEE / G. C. PEDEN (eds.), The Transformation of Scotland. The Economy Since 1700, Edinburgh 2005, pp. 13–33

DE VRIES, J., European Urbanization 1500–1800, London 1985

DE VRIES, J. / VAN DER WOUDE, A., The First Modern Economy. Success, Failure, and Perseverance of the Dutch Economy, 1500–1815, Cambridge 1997

DILLEY, J. W., German Merchants in Scotland, 1297–1327, in: Scottish Historical Review, XXVII, 103 (1948), pp. 142–155

DITCHBURN, D., Trade with Northern Europe, 1297–1540, in: M. LYNCH / R. M. SPEARMAN / G. STELL (eds.), The Scottish Medieval Town, Edinburgh 1988, pp. 161–179

———, Trade with Northern Europe: Scottish Ports, in: P. G. B. MCNEILL / H. L. MACQUEEN (eds.), Atlas of Scottish History to 1707, Edinburgh 1996, p. 262

———, Trade with Northern Europe: Baltic Ports, in: P. G. B. MCNEILL / H. L. MACQUEEN (eds.), Atlas of Scottish History to 1707, Edinburgh 1996, pp. 264–5

———, Scotland and Europe: The Medieval Kingdom and its Contacts with Christendom, c.1215–1545, Vol. 1. Religion, Culture and Commerce, East Linton 2000

DOLLINGER, P., Die Hanse, Stuttgart, 3rd ed. 1981

DOROSENKO, V. V., Quellen zur Geschichte des Rigaer Handels im 17. und 18. Jahrhundert und Probleme ihrer Erforschung, in: K. FRIEDLAND / F. IRSIGLER (eds.), Seehandel und Wirtschaftswege Nordeuropas im 17. und 18. Jahrhundert, Ostfildern 1981, pp. 3–25

DOTZAUER, W., Die Deutschen Reichskreise in der Verfassung des Alten Reiches und ihr Eigenleben (1500–1806), Darmstadt 1989

DUCKHAM, B. F., A History of the Scottish Coal Industry, Vol. 1: 1700–1815. A Social and Industrial History, Newton Abbot 1970

DUFFILL, M., The Africa Trade from the Ports of Scotland, 1706–66, in: Slavery and Abolition, XXV, 3 (2004), pp. 102–122

DURIE, A. J., The Markets for Scottish Linen, 1730–1775, in: Scottish Historical Review, LII, 1 (1973), pp. 30–49

———, The Scottish Linen Industry in the Eighteenth Century, Edinburgh 1979

DYBDAHL, V., Dänemark 1650–1850, in: W. FISCHER / J. A. VAN HOUTTE / H. KELLENBENZ / I. MIECK / F. VITTINGHOFF (eds.), Handbuch der Europäischen Wirtschafts- und Sozialgeschichte, Vol. 4: Von der Mitte des 17. zur Mitte des 19. Jahrhunderts, Stuttgart 1993, pp. 281–297

DYRVIK, S. / FOSSEN, A. B. / GRØNLIE, T./ HOVLAND, E. / NORDVIK, H. / TVEITE, S. (eds.), Norsk Økonomisk Historie 1500–1970, Vol. 1. 1500–1850, Bergen / Oslo / Tromsø 1979

EASTHAM, J. K., (ed.), Economic Essays in Commemoration of the Dundee School of Economics 1931–1955, Coupar Angus 1955

EIRAS ROEL, A., Los productos alimentarios de ultramar. La Europa mediterránea, in: S. CAVACIOCCHI (ed.), Prodotti e Tecniche d'Oltremare nelle Economie Europee Secc. XIII–XVIII, Prato 1998, pp. 99–144

ELLIS, J., The Decline and Fall of the Tyneside Salt Industry 1660–1790: A Re-examination, in: Economic History Review, Second Series, XXXIII, 1 (1980), pp. 45–58

EMMER, P. / GAASTRA, F. (eds.), The Organization of Interoceanic Trade in European Expansion, 1450–1800, Aldershot 1996

ENGERMAN, S. L., Mercantilism and Overseas Trade, 1700–1860, in: FLOUD, R. / MCCLOSKEY, D. (eds.), The Economic History of Britain since 1700, Vol. I: 1700–1860, Cambridge, 2nd ed. 1994, pp. 182–204

EWE, H. (ed.), Geschichte der Stadt Stralsund, Weimar 1984

FABER, J. A., Structural Changes in the European Economy during the Eighteenth century as Reflected in the Baltic Trade, in: HEERES, W. G. / HESP, L. M. J. B. / NOORDEGRAAF, L. / VAN DER VOORT, R. C. W. (eds.), From Dunkirk to Danzig. Shipping and Trade in the North Sea and the Baltic, 1350–1850, Amsterdam 1988, pp. 83–94

FELDBÆK, O., Den lange fred 1700–1800 (=O. OLSEN (ed.), Gyldendal og Politikens Denmarkshistorie, Vol. 9), Copenhagen 1990

FISCHER, T., The Scots in Germany, Edinburgh 1902

———, The Scots in Eastern and Western Prussia, Edinburgh 1903

———, The Scots in Sweden, Edinburgh 1907

FISCHER, W. / MARVIN MCINNIS, R. / SCHNEIDER, J. (eds.), The Emergence of a World Economy 1500–1914, Pt. I: 1500–1850, Wiesbaden 1986

FISCHER, W. / KUNZ, A. (eds.), Grundlagen der Historischen Statistik von Deutschland. Quellen, Methoden, Forschungsziele, Opladen 1991

FISCHER, W. / VAN HOUTTE, J. A. / KELLENBENZ, H. / MIECK, I. / VITTINGHOFF, F. (eds.), Handbuch der Europäischen Wirtschafts- und Sozialgeschichte, Vol. 4: Von der Mitte des 17. zur Mitte des 19. Jahrhunderts, Stuttgart 1993

FLADBY, R., Norwegen 1650–1850, in: W. FISCHER / J. A. VAN HOUTTE / H. KELLENBENZ / I. MIECK / F. VITTINGHOFF (eds.), Handbuch der Europäischen Wirtschafts- und Sozialgeschichte, Vol. 4: Von der Mitte des 17. zur Mitte des 19. Jahrhunderts, Stuttgart 1993, pp. 298–310

FLOUD, R. / MCCLOSKEY, D. (eds.), The Economic History of Britain since 1700, Vol. I: 1700–1860, Cambridge, 2nd ed. 1994

——— / JOHNSON, P. (eds.), The Cambridge Economic History of Modern Britain, Vol. I: Industrialisation, 1700–1860, Cambridge 2004

FRIEDLAND, K. / IRSIGLER, F. (eds.), Seehandel und Wirtschaftswege Nordeuropas im 17. und 18. Jahrhundert, Ostfildern 1981

FRIEDLAND, K. (ed.), Maritime Food Transport, Cologne / Vienna 1994

———, Mensch und Seefahrt zur Hansezeit, Cologne / Weimar / Vienna 1995

———, Der Hansische Shetlandhandel, in: ID., Mensch und Seefahrt zur Hansezeit, Cologne / Weimar / Vienna 1995, pp. 190–205

FUHSE, G., Die Freie Hansestadt Bremen in Wirtschaftsgeschichtlicher Entwicklung, Bremen 1927

GEMMILL, E. / MAYHEW, N., Changing Values in Medieval Scotland. A Study of Prices, Money, and Weights and Measures, Cambridge 1995

GERHARD, H.-J., Merkantilpolitische Handelshemmnisse (im territorialen Vergleich) am Beispiel eines territorial relativ einheitlichen Gebietes, in: H. POHL (ed.), Die Auswirkungen von Zöllen und anderen Handelshemmnissen auf Wirtschaft und Gesellschaft vom Mittelalter bis zur Gegenwart, Stuttgart 1987, pp. 59–83

——— / KAUFHOLD, K. H. (eds.), Preise im Vor- und Frühindustriellen Deutschland. Nahrungsmittel – Getränke – Gewürze, Rohstoffe und Gewerbeprodukte, Stuttgart 2001

GIBSON, A. J. S. / SMOUT, T. C., Prices, Food and Wages in Scotland 1550–1780, Cambridge 1995

GLAMANN, K., The Danish Asiatic Company, 1732–1772, in: Scandinavian Economic History Review, VIII, 1 (1960), pp. 109–149

———, European Trade, 1500–1750, in: C. M. CIPOLLA (ed.), The Fontana Economic History of Europe, Vol. 2: The Sixteenth and Seventeenth Centuries, Glasgow 1974, pp. 427–526

———, The Changing Patterns of Trade, in: E. E. RICH / C. H. WILSON (eds.), The Cambridge Economic History of Europe, Vol. V: The Economic Organization of Early Modern Europe, Cambridge 1977, pp. 185–289

GÖMMEL, R., Die Entwicklung der Wirtschaft im Zeitalter des Merkantilismus 1620–1800, Munich 1998

GOODMAN, J. / HONEYMAN, K., Gainful Pursuits. The Making of Industrial Europe 1600–1914, London / New York / Melbourne / Auckland 1988

GOODMAN, J., Tobacco in History. The Cultures of Dependence, London / New York 1993

GRAFE, R., The Globalisation of Codfish and Wool: Spanish-English-North American Triangular Trade in the Early Modern Period, London School of Economics Working Papers, Nr. 71/03 (2003)

GRANOVETTER, M., Economic Action and Social Structure: The Problem of Embeddedness, in: American Journal of Sociology, XCI, 3 (1985), pp. 481–510

GRAßMANN, A. (ed.), Lübeckische Geschichte, Lübeck, 2nd ed. 1989

GROSJEAN, A., A Century of Scottish Governorship in the Swedish Empire, 1574–1700, in: A. MACKILLOP / S. MURDOCH (eds.), Military Governors and Imperial Frontiers c. 1600–1800, Leiden / Boston 2003, pp. 53–78

——— / MURDOCH, S. (eds.), Scottish Communities Abroad in the Early Modern Period, Leiden / Boston 2005

GULVIN, C., The Union and the Scottish Woollen Industry, 1707–1760, in: Scottish Historical Review, L (1971), pp. 121–137

HAMILTON, H., An Economic History of Scotland in the Eighteenth Century, Oxford 1963

HAMMEL-KIESOW, R., Hansischer Seehandel und wirtschaftliche Wechsellagen. Der Umsatz im Lübecker Hafen in der zweiten Hälfte des 14. Jahrhunderts, 1492–6 und 1680–2, in: S. JENKS / M. NORTH (eds.), Der Hansische Sonderweg? Beiträge zur Sozial- und Wirtschaftsgeschichte der Hanse, Cologne / Weimar / Vienna 1993, pp. 77–93

HARDER (-GERSDORFF), E., Seehandel zwischen Lübeck und Rußland im 17./18. Jahrhundert nach Zollbüchern der Novgorodfahrer, Pt. I, in: Zeitschrift des Vereins für Lübeckische Geschichte und Altertumskunde, LXI (1961), pp. 43–114

HARDER-GERSDORFF, E., Handelskonjunkturen und Warenbilanzen im lübeckisch-russischen Seeverkehr des 18. Jahrhunderts, in: Vierteljahrschrift zur Sozial- und Wirtschaftsgeschichte, LVII (1970), pp. 15–45

———, Mitteleuropäische Gewerbezonen und ostbaltischer Handel im 18. Jahrhundert, in: K. FRIEDLAND / F. IRSIGLER (eds.), Seehandel und Wirtschaftswege Nordeuropas im 17. und 18. Jahrhundert, Ostfildern 1981, pp. 26–37

HARLEY, C. K., Trade: Discovery, Mercantilism and Technology, in: R. FLOUD / P. JOHNSON (eds.), The Cambridge Economic History of Modern Britain, Vol. I: Industrialisation, 1700–1860, Cambridge 2004, pp. 175–203

HARRIS, R., Scotland's Herring Fisheries and the Prosperity of the Nation, c.1660–1760, Scottish Historical Review, LXXIX, 1, Nr. 207 (2000), pp. 39–60

HARRIS, R., Government and the Economy, in: R. FLOUD / P. JOHNSON (eds.), The Cambridge Economic History of Modern Britain, Vol. I: Industrialisation, 1700–1860, Cambridge 2004, pp. 204–237

HAUSER, A., Tabakstadt Bremen, in: H. RODER (ed.), Bremen: Handelsstadt am Fluß, Bremen 1995

HEERES, W. G. / HESP, L. M. J. B. / NOORDEGRAAF, L. / VAN DER VOORT, R. C. W. (eds.), From Dunkirk to Danzig. Shipping and Trade in the North Sea and the Baltic, 1350–1850, Amsterdam 1988

HECKSCHER, E. F., Sveriges Ekonomiska Historia. Från Gustav Vasa, Vol. II, Pt. II, Stockholm 1949

———, Multilateralism, Baltic Trade and the Mercantilists, in: Economic History Review, III (1950), pp. 219–228

HENDERSON, J. M., Scottish Reckoning of Time, Money, Weights and Measures (no date / place of publication), deposited in NAS, General Register House, Historical Reading Room

HENNING, F.-W., Handbuch der Wirtschafts- und Sozialgeschichte Deutschlands, Vol. 1: Deutsche Wirtschafts- und Sozialgeschichte im Mittelalter und in der Frühen Neuzeit, Paderborn 1991

———, Das Vorindustrielle Deutschland 800-1800, Paderborn / Munich / Vienna / Zurich, 5th ed. 1994

HILTON PRICE, F. G., A Handbook of London Bankers, enlarged ed. London 1890–1

HOCQUET, J.-C., Le Sel et le Pouvoir. De l'an mil à la Revolution française, Paris 1985

HODNE, F., Norway's Role in the World Economy, 1750–1950, in: M. NORTH (ed.), Nordwesteuropa in der Weltwirtschaft 1750–1950 / Northwestern Europe in the World Economy 1750–1950, Stuttgart 1993, pp. 39–58

HOFFMANN, E., Lübeck im Hoch- und Spätmittelalter: Die große Zeit Lübecks, in: A. GRAßMANN (ed.), Lübeckische Geschichte, Lübeck, 2nd ed. 1989, pp. 79–340

HÖGBERG, S., Utrikeshandel och sjöfart på 1700-talet. Stapelvaror i svensk export och import 1738–1808, Lund 1969

HONT, I. / IGNATIEFF, M. (eds.), Wealth and Virtue. The Shaping of Political Economy in the Scottish Enlightenment, Cambridge 1983

HOOCK, J. / REININGHAUS, W. (eds.), Kaufleute in Europa. Handelshäuser und ihre Überlieferung in vor- und frühindustrieller Zeit, Dortmund 1997

HOON, E. E., The Organisation of the English Customs System 1696–1789, Newton Abbot, 2nd ed. 1968

IMHOF, A. E., Aspekte der Bevölkerungsentwicklung in den nordischen Ländern 1720–1750, 2 vols., Bern 1976

INSH, G. P., The Company of Scotland Trading to Africa and the Indies, London / New York 1932

JACKSON, G., Government Bounties and the Establishment of the Scottish Whaling Trade, 1750–1800, in: J. BUTT / J. T. WARD (eds.), Scottish Themes. Essays in Honour of S. G. E. LYTHE, Edinburgh 1976, pp. 46–66

——— / LYTHE, S. G. E. (eds.), The Port of Montrose: A History of its Harbour, Trade and Shipping, Tayport 1993

———, Glasgow in Transition, c.1660 to c. 1740, in: T. M. DEVINE / G. JACKSON (eds.), Glasgow. Vol. I: Beginnings to 1830, Manchester / New York 1995, pp. 63–105

———, The Economy: Aberdeen and the Sea, in: E. P. DENNISON / D. DITCHBURN / M. LYNCH (eds.), Aberdeen Before 1800. A New History, East Linton 2002, pp. 159–180

JACKSON, R. V., Growth and Deceleration in English Agriculture, 1660–1790, in: Economic History Review, Second Series, XXXVI (1985), pp. 333–351

JENKS, S. / NORTH, M. (eds.), Der Hansische Sonderweg? Beiträge zur Sozial- und Wirtschaftsgeschichte der Hanse, Cologne / Weimar / Vienna 1993

JOCHMANN, W. / LOOSE, H.-D. (eds.), Hamburg: Geschichte der Stadt und ihrer Bewohner, Hamburg 1982

JOOST-KRÜGER, J., Der Weserkahn, in: H. RODER (ed.), Bremen: Handelsstadt am Fluß, Bremen 1995, pp. 304–5

JÖRN, N. / NORTH, M. (eds.), Die Integration des südlichen Ostseeraumes in das Alte Reich, Cologne / Weimar / Vienna 2000

KAUFHOLD, K. H., Gewerbelandschaften in der frühen Neuzeit (1650–1800), in: H. POHL (ed.), Gewerbe und Industrielandschaften vom Spätmittelalter bis ins 20. Jahrhundert, Stuttgart 1986, pp. 112–202

———, Hauptrichtungen und wichtige Wege des binnenländischen Fernverkehrs in Niedersachsen in der frühen Neuzeit, in: U. BESTMANN / F. IRSIGLER / J. SCHNEIDER (eds.), Hochfinanz, Wirtschaftsräume, Innovationen. Festschrift für Wolfgang von Stromer, 3 Vols., Trier 1987, Vol. II, pp. 719–740

———, Deutschland 1650–1850, in: W. FISCHER / J. A. VAN HOUTTE / H. KELLENBENZ / I. MIECK / F. VITTINGHOFF (eds.), Handbuch der Europäischen Wirtschafts- und Sozialgeschichte, Vol. 4: Von der Mitte des 17. zur Mitte des 19. Jahrhunderts, Stuttgart 1993, pp. 530–588

———, Die Wirtschaft in der frühen Neuzeit: Gewerbe, Handel und Verkehr, in: C. VAN DEN HEUVEL / M. VON BOETTICHER (eds.), Geschichte Niedersachsens, Vol. 3 / Pt. 1: Politik, Wirtschaft und Gesellschaft von der Reformation bis zum Beginn des 19. Jahrhunderts, Hanover 1996, pp. 351–574

KAUKIAINEN, Y., Finland and the World Economy, in: M. NORTH (ed.), Nordwesteuropa in der Weltwirtschaft 1750–1950 / Northwestern Europe in the World Economy 1750–1950, Stuttgart 1993, pp. 59–78

KELLENBENZ, H. (ed.), Ludwig Beutin, Gesammelte Schriften zur Wirtschafts- und Sozialgeschichte, Cologne / Graz 1963

———, Der deutsche Außenhandel gegen Ausgang des 18. Jahrhunderts, in: F. LÜTGE (ed.), Die wirtschaftliche Situation in Deutschland und Österreich um die Wende vom 18. zum 19. Jahrhundert, Stuttgart 1964, pp. 4–60

———, The Rise of the European Economy. An Economic History of Continental Europe from the Fifteenth to the Eighteenth Century, London 1976

———, Deutsche Wirtschaftsgeschichte, Vol. I: Von den Anfängen bis zum Ende des 18. Jahrhunderts, Munich 1977

———, Landverkehr, Fluss- und Seeschiffahrt im Europäischen Handel (Spätmittelalter bis Anfang des 19. Jahrhunderts), in: ID., Europa. Raum Wirtschaftlicher Begegnung (=ID., Kleine Schriften, Vol. I), Stuttgart 1991, pp. 327–441

KENDALL, M. G. / BRADFORD HILL, A. (eds.), The Sources and Nature of the Statistics of the United Kingdom, Vol. 1, London / Edinburgh 1952

KJELLBERG, S. T., Svenska Ostindiska Compagnierna 1731–1813. Kryddor-Te-Porslin-Siden, Malmö 1974

KLESSMANN, E., Geschichte der Stadt Hamburg, Hamburg 2002

KOPITZSCH, F., Zwischen Hauptrezeß und Franzosenzeit 1712–1806, in: W. JOCHMANN / H.-D. LOOSE (eds.), Hamburg: Geschichte der Stadt und ihrer Bewohner, Hamburg 1982, pp. 351–490

———, Aufklärung in Hamburg. Grundzüge einer Sozialgeschichte der Aufklärung in Hamburg und Altona, Hamburg, 2nd ed. 1990

KRAWEHL, O.-E., Quellen zur Hamburger Handelsstatistik im 18. Jahrhundert, in: W. FISCHER / A. KUNZ (eds.), Grundlagen der Historischen Statistik von Deutschland. Quellen, Methoden, Forschungsziele, Opladen 1991, pp. 47–69

———, Die Admiralitätszoll- und Convoygeldeinnahmebücher als handelsstatistische Quelle, in: J. SCHNEIDER / O.-E. KRAWEHL / M. A. DENZEL (eds.), Statistik des Hamburger seewärtigen Einfuhrhandels im 18. Jahrhundert. Nach den Admiralitätszoll- und Convoygeld-Einnahmebüchern, St. Katharinen 2001, pp. 9–18

KRIEDTE, P., Spätfeudalismus und Handelskapital. Grundlinien der europäischen Wirtschaftsgeschichte vom 16. bis zum Ausgang des 18. Jahrhunderts, Göttingen 1980

———, Peasants, Landlords and Merchant Capitalists. Europe and the World Economy, 1500–1800, Leamington Spa 1983

———, Vom Großhändler zum Detaillisten. Der Handel mit Kolonialwaren im 17. und 18. Jahrhundert, in: Jahrbuch für Wirtschaftsgeschichte (1994/1), pp. 11–37

———, Trade, in: S. OGILVIE (ed.), Germany. A New Social and Economic History, Vol. II: 1630–1800, London / New York 1996, pp. 100–133

KUSCH, R., Stralsund von 1720 bis 1815, in: H. EWE (ed.), Geschichte der Stadt Stralsund, Weimar 1984, pp. 202–233

KUSTER, T., 500 Jahre kolonialer Rohrzucker – 250 Jahre europäischer Rübenzucker, in: Vierteljahrschrift für Sozial- und Wirtschaftsgeschichte, LXXXV (1998), pp. 477–512

LABROUSSE, E. / LEON, P. / GOUBERT, P. / BOUVIER, J. / CARRIERE, C. / HARSIN, P. (eds.), Histoire Économique et Sociale de la France, Vol. 2 : Des derniers temps de l'âge seigneurial aux préludes de l'âge industriel (1660–1789), Paris 1970, pp. 499–528

LAMPEN, A., Stadt und Fisch: Konsum, Produktion und Handel im Hanseraum der Frühzeit, in: Vierteljahrschrift für Sozial- und Wirtschaftsgeschichte, LXXXVII (2000), pp. 281–307

LANGER, H., Stralsund 1600–1630. Eine Hansestadt in der Krise und im Europäischen Konflikt, Weimar 1970

LEE, C. H., The British Economy Since 1700. A Macroeconomic Perspective, Cambridge 1986

———, Economic Progress: Wealth and Poverty, in: T. M. DEVINE / C. H. LEE / G. C. PEDEN (eds.), The Transformation of Scotland. The Economy since 1700, Edinburgh 2005, pp. 128–156

VON LEHE, E. / RAMM, H. / KAUSCHE, D. (eds.), Heimatchronik der Freien und Hansestadt Hamburg, Cologne, 2nd ed. 1967

LENMAN, B., An Economic and Social History of Modern Scotland 1660–1976, London 1975

P. LEON, L'élan industriel et commercial, in : E. LABROUSSE / P. LEON / P. GOUBERT / J. BOUVIER / C. CARRIERE / P. HARSIN (eds.), Histoire Économique et Sociale de la France, Vol. 2 : Des derniers temps de l'âge seigneurial aux préludes de l'âge industriel (1660–1789), Paris 1970, pp. 499–528

LEVITT, I. / SMOUT, (T.) C., Some Weights and Measures in Scotland, 1843, in: Scottish Historical Review, LVI, 2, Nr. 162 (1977), pp. 146–152

LIEBEL, H., Laissez-faire vs. Mercantilism: The Rise of Hamburg & the Hamburg Bourgeoisie vs. Frederick the Great in the Crisis of 1763, in: Vierteljahrschrift für Sozial- und Wirtschaftsgeschichte, LII (1965), pp. 207–238

LILLEHAMMER, A., The Scottish-Norwegian Timber Trade in the Stavanger Area in the Sixteenth and Seventeenth Centuries, in: T. C. SMOUT (ed.), Scotland and Europe, 1200–1850, Edinburgh 1986, pp. 97–111

———, Boards, Beams and Barrel-hoops: Contacts between Scotland and the Stavanger Area in the Seventeenth Century, in: G. G. SIMPSON (ed.), Scotland and Scandinavia 800–1800, Edinburgh 1990, pp. 100–106

LINDERT, P. H., Unequal living standards, in: R. FLOUD / D. MCCLOSKEY (eds.), The Economic History of Britain since 1700, Vol. I: 1700–1860, Cambridge, 2nd ed. 1994, pp. 357–386

LINK, T., Flensburgs Überseehandel von 1755 bis 1807. Seine wirtschaftliche und politische Bedeutung im Rahmen des Dänisch-Norwegischen Seehandels, Neumünster 1959

LITTLEFIELD, D. C., Rice and Slaves. Ethnicity and the Slave Trade in Colonial South Carolina, Urbana / Illinois, pbk 1991

LOOSE, H.-D., Das Zeitalter der Bürgerunruhen und der großen europäischen Kriege, in: W. JOCHMANN / H.-D. LOOSE (eds.), Hamburg: Geschichte der Stadt und ihrer Bewohner, Hamburg 1982, pp. 259–350

LUCHT, D., Pommern: Geschichte, Kultur und Wirtschaft, Bielefeld 1996

LÜTGE, F. (ed.), Die wirtschaftliche Situation in Deutschland und Österreich um die Wende vom 18. zum 19. Jahrhundert, Stuttgart 1964

LYNCH, M. / SPEARMAN, R. M. / STELL, G. (eds.), The Scottish Medieval Town, Edinburgh 1988

LYNCH, M., Scotland. A New History, Edinburgh, 8th ed. 1997

LYTHE, S. G. E., Scottish Trade with the Baltic 1550–1650, in: J. K. EASTHAM (ed.), Economic Essays in Commemoration of the Dundee School of Economics 1931–1955, Coupar Angus 1955, pp. 63–84

———, The Economy of Scotland in its European Setting, 1550–1625, Edinburgh 1960

——— / BUTT, J., An Economic History of Scotland, 1100–1939, Glasgow / London 1975

MCALOON, T., A Minor Scottish Merchant in General Trade: the Case of Edward Burd 1728–39, in: J. BUTT / J. T. WARD (eds.), Scottish Themes. Essays in Honour of S. G. E. Lythe, Edinburgh 1976, pp. 17–27

MCCUSKER, J. J., The Current Value of English Exports, 1697 to 1800, in: William and Mary Quarterly, XVII, 3 (1971), pp. 607–28

———, Money and Exchange in Europe and America, 1600–1775, Chapel Hill 1978

——— / MENARD, R. R., The Economy of British America, 1607–1789, Chapel Hill 1985

——— / MORGAN, K. (eds.), The Early Modern Atlantic Economy, Cambridge 2000

MACKILLOP, A. / MURDOCH, S. (eds.), Military Governors and Imperial Frontiers c. 1600–1800, Leiden / Boston 2003

McNeill, P. G. B. / MacQueen, H. L. (eds.), Atlas of Scottish History to 1707, Edinburgh 1996

Mączak, A. / Smout, (T.) C. (eds.), Gründung und Bedeutung kleinerer Städte im nördlichen Europa der frühen Neuzeit, Wiesbaden 1991

Mackay, W. (ed.), The Letter-Book of Bailie John Steuart of Inverness 1715–1752, Edinburgh 1915

Magnusson, L., An Economic History of Sweden, London / New York 2000

Maizels, A., Oversea Trade, in: M. G. Kendall / A. Bradford Hill (eds.), The Sources and Nature of the Statistics of the United Kingdom, Vol. 1, London / Edinburgh 1952, pp. 17–31

Makkai, L., Der Ungarische Viehhandel 1550–1650, in: I. Bog (ed.), Der Außenhandel Ostmitteleuropas 1450–1650, Cologne / Vienna 1971, pp. 483–206

Mann, A. J., The Scottish Book Trade, 1500–1720, East Linton 2000

Margairaz, M. (ed.), Histoire Économique XVIIIe–XXe Siècle, Paris 1992

Marshall, P. J. (ed.), The Oxford History of the British Empire, Vol. II: The Eighteenth Century, Oxford / New York 1998

Masefield, G. B., Crops and Livestock, in: E. E. Rich / C. H. Wilson (eds.), The Cambridge Economic History of Europe, Vol. IV: The Economy of Expanding Europe in the Sixteenth and Seventeenth Centuries, Cambridge 1967, pp. 275–301

Mathias, P. / Davis, J. A. (eds.), The First Industrial Revolutions, Oxford 1989

Mathias, P., The Industrial Revolution: Concept and Reality, in: Id. / J. A. Davis (eds.), The First Industrial Revolutions, Oxford 1989, pp. 1–24

Mathias, P. / Davis, J. (eds.), International Trade and British Economic Growth from the Eighteenth Century to the Present Day, Oxford / Cambridge, Mass. 1996

Mauro, F., Towards an 'Intercontinental Model': European Overseas Expansion between 1500 and 1800, in: Economic History Review, Second Series, XIV, 1 (1961), pp. 1–17

Menard, R. R., Transport Costs and Long-Range Trade, 1300–1800: Was there a European 'Transport Revolution' in the Early Modern Era?, in: J. D. Tracy (ed.), The Political Economy of Merchant Empires, New York 1991, pp. 228–75

Menninger, A., Genuss im kulturellen Wandel. Tabak, Kaffee, Tee und Schokolade in Europa (16. – 19. Jahrhundert), Stuttgart 2004

Menzies, G. (ed.), In Search of Scotland, Edinburgh 2001

Metz, R., Säkulare Trends der Deutschen Wirtschaft, in: M. North (ed.), Deutsche Wirtschaftsgeschichte. Ein Jahrtausend im Überblick, Munich, 2nd ed. 2005, pp. 427–500

Meyer-Stoll, C., Die lübeckische Kaufmannschaft des 17. Jahrhunderts unter wirtschafts- und sozialgeschichtlichen Aspekten, Frankfurt-on-the-Main / Bern / New York / Paris 1989

Michell, A. R., The European Fisheries in Early Modern History, in: E. E. Rich / C. H. Wilson (eds.), The Cambridge Economic History of Europe, Vol. V: The Economic Organization of Early Modern Europe, Cambridge 1977, pp. 133–185

Milgrom, P. / North, D. C. / Weingast, B. R., The Role of Institutions in the Revival of Trade: The Law Merchant, Private Judges, and the Champagne Fairs, in: Economics and Politics, II, 1 (1990), pp. 1–23

Minchinton, W., Patterns and Structure of Demand, 1500–1750, in: C. M. Cipolla (ed.), The Fontana Economic History of Europe, Vol. 2: The Sixteenth and Seventeenth Centuries, Glasgow 1974, pp. 83–176

Mintz, S. W., Sweetness and Power. The Place of Sugar in Modern History, New York 1985

Mitchell, B. R., British Historical Statistics, Cambridge 1988

———, International Historical Statistics: Europe 1750–2000, Basingstoke / New York, 5th ed. 2003

Mitchinton, W. E., (ed.), The Growth of English Overseas Trade in the Seventeenth and Eighteenth Centuries, London 1969

———, Introduction, in: Id. (ed.), The Growth of English Overseas Trade in the Seventeenth and Eighteenth Centuries, London 1969, pp. 1–63

MONTANARI, M., La fame e l'abbondanza, Rome / Bari 1993

———, Der Hunger und der Überfluß. Kulturgeschichte der Ernährung in Europa, Munich, 2nd ed. 1999

MORGAN, K., "Atlantic Trade and British Economic Growth in the Eighteenth Century, in: P. MATHIAS / J. DAVIS (eds.), International Trade and British Economic Growth from the Eighteenth Century to the Present Day, Oxford / Cambridge, Mass. 1996, pp. 14–33

———, Transatlantic Rice in the European Market in the Eighteenth Century, in: S. CAVACIOCCHI (ed.), Prodotti e Tecniche d'Oltremare nelle Economie Europee Secc. XIII–XVIII, Prato 1998, pp. 465–475

———, Slavery, Atlantic Trade and the British Economy, 1660–1800, Cambridge 2000

MÖRKE, O., Holstein und Schwedisch-Pommern im Alten Reich: Integrationsmuster und Politische Identitäten in Grenzregionen, in: N. JÖRN / M. NORTH (eds.), Die Integration des südlichen Ostseeraumes in das Alte Reich, Cologne / Weimar / Vienna 2000, pp. 425–472

MOWAT, S., The Port of Leith. Its History and its People, Edinburgh 1982

MÜLLER, A., Emdens Seeschifffahrt und Seehandel von der Besitzergreifung Ostfrieslands durch Preußen bis zur Eröffnung des Dortmund-Ems-Kanals 1744–1899, in: Hansische Geschichtsblätter, LV (1930)

MÜLLER, L., The Merchant Houses of Stockholm, c. 1640–1800. A Comparative Study of Early-Modern Entrepreneurial Behaviour, Uppsala 1998

———, The Swedish East India Trade and International Markets: Re-exports of Teas 1731–1813, in: Scandinavian Economic History Review, LI, 3 (2003), pp. 28–44

———, Scottish and Irish Entrepreneurs in Eighteenth-Century Sweden. East India Trade and Iron, Unpubl. Paper, Uppsala 2003

———, Kolonialprodukter i Sveriges handel och konsumtionskultur, 1700–1800, in: Historisk Tidskrift, 2/2004, pp. 225–248

MULTHAUP, R. P., Neptune's Gift. A History of Common Salt, Baltimore / London 1978

MÜNCH, P., Lebensformen in der Frühen Neuzeit. 1500 bis 1800, Frankfurt-on-the-Main 1992

NASH, R. C., The English and Scottish Tobacco Trades in the Seventeenth and Eighteenth Centuries: Legal and Illegal Trade, in: Economic History Review, Second Series, XXXV (1982), pp. 354–372

———, South Carolina and the Atlantic Economy in the Late Seventeenth and Eighteenth Centuries, Economic History Review, Second Series, XLV, 4 (1992), pp. 677–702

NEWMAN, J., 'A very delicate Experiment'. British Mercantile Strategies for Financing Trade in Russia, 1680–1780, in: I. BLANCHARD / A. GOODMAN / J. NEWMAN (eds.), Industry and Finance in Early Modern History, Stuttgart 1992, pp. 116–142

NEWMAN, K., Hamburg in the European Economy, 1660–1750, in: Journal of European Economic History, XIV, 1 (1985), pp. 57–93

NIELSEN, A., Dänische Wirtschaftsgeschichte (=Handbuch der Wirtschaftsgeschichte, Vol. 6), Jena 1933

NORTH, D. C. / THOMAS, R. P., An Economic Theory of the Growth of the Western World, in: Economic History Review, Second Series, XXIII, 1 (1970), pp. 1–17

———, The Rise of the Western World. A New Economic History, Cambridge 1973

NORTH, M. (ed.), Nordwesteuropa in der Weltwirtschaft 1750–1950 / Northwestern Europe in the World Economy 1750–1950, Stuttgart 1993

———, The European Rice Trade in the Eighteenth and Early Nineteenth Centuries, in: K. FRIEDLAND (ed.), Maritime Food Transport, Cologne / Vienna 1994, pp. 313–323.

——— (ed.), Von Aktie bis Zoll. Ein Historisches Lexikon des Geldes, Munich 1995

———, From the North Sea to the Baltic: Essays in Commercial, Monetary and Agrarian History 1500–1800, Aldershot 1996

———, Hamburg: the 'Continent's Most English City', in: ID., From the North Sea to the Baltic: Essays in Commercial, Monetary and Agrarian History 1500–1800, Aldershot 1996, paper VI, pp. 1–23

———, Kommunikation, Handel, Geld und Banken in der frühen Neuzeit, Munich 2000

———, "Integration im Ostseeraum und im Heiligen Römischen Reich, in: N. JÖRN / M. NORTH (eds.), Die Integration des südlichen Ostseeraumes in das Alte Reich, Cologne / Weimar / Vienna 2000, pp. 1–11

——— (ed.), Deutsche Wirtschaftsgeschichte. Ein Jahrtausend im Überblick, Munich, 2nd ed. 2005

———, Von der Atlantischen Handelsexpansion bis zu den Agrarreformen (1450–1815), in: ID. (ed.), Deutsche Wirtschaftsgeschichte. Ein Jahrtausend im Überblick, Munich, 2nd ed. 2005, pp. 112–196

O'BRIEN, P. K. / KEYDER, C., Economic Growth in Britain and France 1780–1914. Two Paths to the Twentieth Century, London 1978

O'BRIEN, P. K., The political economy of British taxation, 1660–1815, in: Economic History Review, Second Series, XLI (1988), pp. 1–32

———, European Industrialization: From the Voyages of Discovery to the Industrial Revolution, in: H. POHL (ed.), The European Discovery of the World and its Economic Effects on Pre-industrial Society 1500–1800, Stuttgart 1990, pp. 154–177

OGILVIE, S. (ed.), Germany. A New Social and Economic History, Vol. II: 1630–1800, London / New York 1996

OGILVIE, S. C. / CERMAN, M. (eds.), European Proto-industrialization, Cambridge 1996

OGILVIE, S. C., Proto-Industrialization in Germany, in: ID. / M. CERMAN (eds.), European Proto-industrialization, Cambridge 1996, pp. 118–136

OLECHNOWITZ, K.-F., Handel und Seeschiffahrt der späten Hanse, Weimar 1965

ORMROD, D., English Grain Exports and the Structure of Agrarian Capitalism 1700–1760, Hull 1985

OSTERHAMMEL, J., Kolonialismus. Geschichte – Formen – Folgen, Munich, 3rd ed. 2001

———, Colonialism. A Theoretical Overview, Princeton 1997

OVERTON, M., Agricultural Revolution in England. The Transformation of the Agrarian Economy 1500–1850, Cambridge 1996

PATERSON, L., The Autonomy of Modern Scotland, Edinburgh 1994

PETERS, L. F., Hamburger Bank, in: M. NORTH (ed.), Von Aktie bis Zoll. Ein Historisches Lexikon des Geldes, Munich 1995, pp. 154–5

PETRÁNOVÁ, L., Development and Possibilities of Historical Studies of Meals and Nourishment in Bohemia, in: H.-J. TEUTEBERG (ed.), European Food History. A Research Review, Leicester / London / New York 1992, pp. 236–255

PHELPS BROWN, E. H. / HOPKINS, S., Seven Centuries of the Prices of Consumables, Compared with Builder's Wage Rates, in: Economica, XXIII (1956)

PIETSCHMANN, H., Produkte und Techniken aus Übersee in den Europäischen Ökonomien, 12.–18. Jahrhundert: Nahrungsmittel in Westeuropa. Ein Forschungsbericht, in: S. CAVACIOCCHI (ed.), Prodotti e Tecniche d'Oltremare nelle Economie Europee Secc. XIII–XVIII, Prato 1998, pp. 175–204

POHL, H., Die Beziehungen Hamburgs zu Spanien und dem Spanischen Amerika in der Zeit von 1740 bis 1806, Wiesbaden 1963

——— (ed.), Gewerbe und Industrielandschaften vom Spätmittelalter bis ins 20. Jahrhundert, Stuttgart 1986

——— (ed.), Die Auswirkungen von Zöllen und anderen Handelshemmnissen auf Wirtschaft und Gesellschaft vom Mittelalter bis zur Gegenwart, Stuttgart 1987

——— (ed.), The European Discovery of the World and its Economic Effects on Pre-industrial Society 1500–1800, Stuttgart 1990

POLLARD, S. / CROSSLEY, D. W., The Wealth of Britain, 1085–1966, London 1968

POST, J. D., Climatic Variability and the European Mortality Wave of the Early 1740s, in: Journal of Interdisciplinary History, XV, 1 (1984), pp. 1–30

———, Food Shortage, Climatic Variability, and Epidemic Disease in Preindustrial Europe. The Mortality Peak in the Early 1740s, Ithaca / London 1985

PRAK, M. (ed.), Early Modern Capitalism. Economic and Social Change in Europe, 1400–1800, London / New York 2001

PRICE, J. M., The Rise of Glasgow in the Chesapeake Tobacco Trade, 1707–1775, in: William and Mary Quarterly, II (1954), pp. 179–199

———, Multilateralism and/or Bilateralism: The Settlement of British Trade Balances with 'The North', c. 1700, Economic History Review, Second Series, XIV, 2 (1961), pp. 254–274

———, France and the Chesapeake. A History of the French Tobacco Monopoly 1674–1791, and of its Relationship to the British and American Tobacco Trades, 2 Vols. Ann Arbour 1973

———, New Time Series for Scotland's and Britain's Trade with the Thirteen Colonies and States, 1740 to 1791, William and Mary Quarterly, XXXII (1975), pp. 307–325

———, Buchanan & Simson, 1759–1763: a Different Kind of Glasgow Firm Trading to the Chesapeake, in: William and Mary Quarterly, XL (1983), pp. 3–41

———, Glasgow, the Tobacco Trade, and the Scottish Customs, 1707–1730, in: Scottish Historical Review, LXIII (1984), pp. 1–36

——— / CLEMENS, P. G. E., A Revolution of Scale in Overseas Trade, in: Journal of Economic History, XLVII (1987), pp. 1–43

———, What Did Merchants Do? Reflections on British Overseas Trade, 1660–1790, in: Journal of Economic History, IL, 2 (1989), pp. 267–284

———, Tobacco in Atlantic Trade. The Chesapeake, London and Glasgow 1675–1775, Aldershot 1995

———, The Atlantic Frontier of the Thirteen American Colonies and States. Essays in Eighteenth Century Commercial and Social History, Aldershot 1996

———, Overseas Trade and Traders. Essays on Some Commercial, Financial and Political Challenges Facing British Atlantic Merchants, 1660–1775, Aldershot 1996

———, The Excise Affair Revisited. The Administrative and Colonial Dimensions of a Parliamentary Crisis, in ID., Overseas Trade and Traders. Essays on Some Commercial, Financial and Political Challenges Facing British Atlantic Merchants, 1660–1775, Aldershot 1996, pp. 257–321

———, The Imperial Economy, 1700–1776, in: P. J. MARSHALL (ed.), The Oxford History of the British Empire, Vol. II: The Eighteenth Century, Oxford / New York 1998, pp. 78–104

PRICE, R., British Society, 1680–1880. Dynamism, Containment and Change, Cambridge et al. 1999

RAMM, H., Altona, Wandsbek und die Südholsteinischen Randgebiete, in: E. VON LEHE / H. RAMM / D. KAUSCHE (eds.), Heimatchronik der Freien und Hansestadt Hamburg, Cologne, 2nd ed. 1967, pp. 263–354

REININGHAUS, W., Gewerbe in der Frühen Neuzeit, Munich 1990

REISS, W., Historical Exchange Rates, in: W. FISCHER / R. MARVIN MCINNIS / J. SCHNEIDER (eds.), The Emergence of a World Economy 1500–1914, Pt. I: 1500–1850, Wiesbaden 1986, pp. 171–190

REIßMANN, M., Die hamburgische Kaufmannschaft des 17. Jahrhunderts in sozialgeschichtlicher Sicht, Hamburg 1975

REY, A. (ed.), Lübeck seit Mitte des 18. Jahrhunderts (1751). Ein Jubiläumsbeitrag zur 700–Jahrfeier der Reichsfreiheit Lübecks, Lübeck 1926

RICE, J. Patterns of Swedish Foreign Trade in the Late Eighteenth Century, in: Geografiska Annaler, Series B, Human Geography, XLVII, 1 (1965), pp. 86–99

RICH, E. E. / WILSON, C. H. (eds.), The Cambridge Economic History of Europe, Vol. V: The Economic Organization of Early Modern Europe, Cambridge 1977

RICHARDSON, D., The Slave Trade, Sugar, and British Economic Growth, 1748–1776, in: Journal of Interdisciplinary History, XVII, 4 (Spring 1987), pp. 739–769

ROBERTS, M. (ed.), Sweden's Age of Greatness 1632–1718, London / Basingstoke 1973

RODER, H. (ed.), Bremen: Handelsstadt am Fluß, Bremen 1995

RÖSSNER, P. R., Close Encounters with the Dutch?, or: How did Scotland react on Dutch Economic Prominence During the "Long Seventeenth Century", 1600–1750?, unpubl. paper given at the *International Institute of Social History* (Leiden) Conference on "Close Encounters with the Dutch. The North Sea as Near-Core Region for a Nascent Modern World (1550–1750)", Roskilde (Denmark), 5–6 October 2007

———, Scottish Foreign Trade in the Wake of Union, 1700–1760. The Rise of a Warehouse Economy, Stuttgart 2008

———, 'New Light on Whatley's Numbers'. The German Market for Scots Salt in the Eighteenth Century, in: Scottish Historical Review, 1, 2008

ROSTOW, W. W., The Process of Economic Growth, New York, 2nd ed. 1962

——— (ed.), The Economics of Take-off into Sustained Growth, London / Basingstoke 1963

———, Stages of Economic Growth, Cambridge, 2nd ed. 1971

SAALFELD, D., Ländliche Gesellschaft in der frühen Neuzeit I: Ländliche Wirtschafts- und Sozialgeschichte vom Beginn des 16. bis zur Mitte des 17. Jahrhunderts, in: C. VAN DEN HEUVEL / M. VON BOETTICHER (eds.), Geschichte Niedersachsens, Vol. 3 / Pt. 1: Politik, Wirtschaft und Gesellschaft von der Reformation bis zum Beginn des 19. Jahrhunderts, Hanover 1996, pp. 637–732

SANDGRUBER, R., Genußmittel. Ihre reale und symbolische Bedeutung im neuzeitlichen Europa, in: Jahrbuch für Wirtschaftsgeschichte (1994/1), pp. 73–88

SAVILE, R., Bank of Scotland. A History 1695–1995, Edinburgh 1996

SCHILDHAUER, J., Hansestädtischer Alltag. Untersuchungen auf der Grundlage der Stralsunder Bürgertestamente vom Anfang des 14. bis zum Ausgang des 16. Jahrhunderts, Weimar 1992

SCHIVELBUSCH, W., Das Paradies, der Geschmack und die Vernunft. Eine Geschichte der Genussmittel, Munich / Vienna, 2nd ed. 1981

SCHLOTE, W., Entwicklung und Strukturwandlungen des englischen Aussenhandels von 1700 bis zur Gegenwart, Jena 1938

———, British Overseas Trade. From 1700 to the 1930s, Oxford 1952

SCHMIDT, P., Tobacco – Its Use and Consumption in Early Modern Europe, in: S. CAVACIOCCHI (ed.), Prodotti e Tecniche d'Oltremare nelle Economie Europee Secc. XIII–XVIII, Prato 1998, pp. 591–617

SCHMITZ, E., Leinengewerbe und Leinenhandel in Nordwestdeutschland, Cologne 1967

SCHNEIDER, J. / SCHWARZER, O., International Rates of Exchange: Structures and Trends of Payments Mechanism in Europe, 17th to 19th Century, in: W. FISCHER / R. MARVIN MCINNIS / J. SCHNEIDER (eds.), The Emergence of a World Economy 1500–1914, Pt. I: 1500–1850, Wiesbaden 1986, pp. 143–170

———, Produktion, Handel und Konsum von Kaffee (15. bis Ende 18. Jh.), in: H. POHL (ed.), The European Discovery of the World and its Economic Effects on Pre-industrial Society 1500–1800, Stuttgart 1990, pp. 122–140

———, SCHWARZER / O., ZELLFELDER, F. / DENZEL, M. A. (eds.), Währungen der Welt VI: Geld und Währungen in Europa im 18. Jahrhundert, Stuttgart 1992

———, Mark II, in: M. NORTH (ed.), Von Aktie bis Zoll. Ein Historisches Lexikon des Geldes, Munich 1995, pp. 235–6.

———, Die neuen Getränke: Schokolade, Kaffee und Tee (16.–18. Jahrhundert), in: S. CAVACIOCCHI (ed.), Prodotti e Tecniche d'Oltremare nelle Economie Europee Secc. XIII–XVIII, Prato 1998, pp. 541–590

———, KRAWEHL, O.-E. / DENZEL, M. A. (eds.), Statistik des Hamburger seewärtigen Einfuhrhandels im 18. Jahrhundert. Nach den Admiralitätszoll- und Convoygeld-Einnahmebüchern, St Katharinen 2001

SCHREMMER, E. (ed.), Wirtschaftliche und soziale Integration in historischer Sicht, Stuttgart 1996

H. SCHULTZ, Handwerker, Kaufleute und Bankiers. Wirtschaftsgeschichte Europas 1500–1800, Frankfurt-on-the-Main 1997

SCHUMPETER, E. B., English Overseas Trade Statistics, 1697–1808, Oxford 1960

SCHWARZ, K., Die Lage der Handwerksgesellen in Bremen während des 18. Jahrhunderts, Bremen 1975

SCHWARZWÄLDER, H., Geschichte der Freien Hansestadt Bremen, Vol. I: Von den Anfängen bis zur Franzosenzeit (1810), Bremen 1975

SCHWEBEL, K. H., Salz im Alten Bremen, Bremen 1988

SCOTTISH HISTORY SOCIETY (ed.), Scottish Industrial History. A Miscellany, Edinburgh 1978

SEMPLE, E. C., The Development of the Hanse Towns in Relation to Their Geographical Environment, in: Journal of the American Geographical Society of New York, XXXI, 3 (1899), pp. 236–255

SHAMMAS, C., The Pre-industrial Consumer in England and America, Oxford 1990

———, The Revolutionary Impact of European Demand for Tropical Goods, in: J. J. MCCUSKER / K. MORGAN (eds.), The Early Modern Atlantic Economy, Cambridge 2000, pp. 163–185

SHAW, J. S., The Management of Scottish Society 1707–1764. Power, Nobles, Lawyers, Edinburgh Agents and English Influences, Edinburgh 1983

SIMPSON, G. G. (ed.), Scotland and Scandinavia 800–1800, Edinburgh 1990

——— (ed.), Scotland and the Low Countries 1124–1994, East Linton 1996

SLAVEN, A., The Development of the West of Scotland 1750–1960, London 1976

SLICHER VAN BATH, B. H., The Agrarian History of Western Europe, A.D. 500–1850, London 1963

SMITH, H. D., Shetland Life and Trade, 1550–1914, Edinburgh 1984

SMITH, S. D., Prices and the Value of English Exports in the Eighteenth Century: Evidence from the North American Colonial Trade, in: Economic History Review, Second Series, XLVIII, 3 (1995), pp. 575–590

SMOUT, T. C., Scottish Trade on the Eve of Union 1660–1707, Edinburgh / London 1963

——— (ed.), Journal of Henry Kalmeter's Travels in Scotland 1719–1720, in: SCOTTISH HISTORY SOCIETY (ed.), Scottish Industrial History. A Miscellany, Edinburgh 1978, pp. 1–52

———, Where had the Scottish Economy got to by the Third Quarter of the Eighteenth Century?, in: I. HONT / M. IGNATIEFF (eds.), Wealth and Virtue. The Shaping of Political Economy in the Scottish Enlightenment, Cambridge 1983, pp. 45–72

———, (ed.), Scotland and Europe, 1200–1850, Edinburgh 1986

———, The European Lifeline, in: G. MENZIES (ed.), In Search of Scotland, Edinburgh 2001, pp. 112–135

SPERLING, J., The International Payments Mechanism in the Seventeenth and Eighteenth Centuries, in: Economic History Review, Second Series, XIV (1961–2), pp. 446–68

SPRENGER, B., Das Geld der Deutschen. Geldgeschichte Deutschlands von den Anfängen bis zur Gegenwart, Paderborn / Munich / Vienna / Zurich 1991

STANFORD REID, W., Trade, Traders, and Scottish Independence, in: Speculum, XXIX, 2, Pt. 1 (1954), pp. 210–222

STEENSGARD, N., Commodities, Bullion and Services in Intercontinental Transactions before 1750, in: H. POHL (ed.), The European Discovery of the World and its Economic Effects on Pre-industrial Society 1500–1800, Stuttgart 1990, pp. 9–23

———, The Growth and Composition of the Long-distance Trade of England and the Dutch Republic Before 1750, in: J. D. TRACY (ed.), The Political Economy of Merchant Empires, New York 1991, pp. 102–52

STEVENSON, A., Trade with the South, 1070–1513, in: M. LYNCH / R. M. SPEARMAN / G. STELL (eds.), The Scottish Medieval Town, Edinburgh 1988, pp. 180–206

STEVENSON, I. W., Some Aspects of the Geography of the Clyde Tobacco Trade in the Eighteenth Century, in: The Scottish Geographical Magazine, LXXXIX (1973), pp. 19–35

STIER, B. / VON HIPPEL, W., War, Economy and Society, in: S. OGILVIE, (ed.), Germany. A New Social and Economic History, Vol. II: 1630–1800, London / New York 1996, pp. 233–262

TEMIN, P., Two Views of the British Industrial Revolution, Journal of Economic History, LVII (1997), pp. 63–82

TEUTEBERG, H.-J. (ed.), European Food History. A Research Review, Leicester / London / New York 1992

THIRLWALL, A. P., Growth and Development. With Special Reference to Developing Economies, Basingstoke / New York, 7th ed. 2003

THOMSEN, B. N. / THOMAS, B., Dansk-Engelsk Samhandel. Et Historisk Rids 1661–1963, Arhus 1966

TRACY, J. D. (ed.), The Political Economy of Merchant Empires, New York 1991

TROSSBACH, W., Bauern 1648–1806, Munich 1993

UNGER, R. W., Dutch Herring, Technology and International Trade in the Seventeenth Century, in: Journal of Economic History, XL (1980), pp. 253–279

UNGER, W. S., Trade through the Sound in the Seventeenth and Eighteenth Centuries, in: Economic History Review, Second Series, XII, 2 (1959), pp. 206–221

VAN DEN HEUVEL, C. / VON BOETTICHER, M. (eds.), Geschichte Niedersachsens, Vol. 3 / Pt. 1: Politik, Wirtschaft und Gesellschaft von der Reformation bis zum Beginn des 19. Jahrhunderts, Hanover 1996

VAN HOUTTE, J. A., Die Niederlande 1650–1850, in: W. FISCHER / J. A. VAN HOUTTE / H. KELLENBENZ / I. MIECK / F. VITTINGHOFF (eds.), Handbuch der Europäischen Wirtschafts- und Sozialgeschichte, Vol. 4: Von der Mitte des 17. zur Mitte des 19. Jahrhunderts, Stuttgart 1993, pp. 311–363

VAN ZANDEN, J. L., Early Modern Economic Growth: a Survey of the European Economy, 1500–1800, in: M. PRAK (ed.), Early Modern Capitalism. Economic and Social Change in Europe, 1400–1800, London / New York 2001, pp. 69–87

VOGEL, W., Handelskonjunkturen und Wirtschaftskrisen in ihrer Auswirkung auf den Seehandel der Hansestädte 1560–1806, in: Hansische Geschichtsblätter, LXXIV (1956), pp. 50–64

VOTH, H. J., Living Standards and the Urban Environment, in: R. FLOUD / P. JOHNSON (eds.), The Cambridge Economic History of Modern Britain, Vol. I: Industrialisation, 1700–1860, Cambridge 2004, pp. 268–294

WALTER, R., Geschichte der Weltwirtschaft. Eine Einführung, Cologne / Weimar / Vienna 2006

WENDT, R., Überseeische Ernährungsprodukte im frühneuzeitlichen Zentraleuropa, in: S. CAVACIOCCHI (ed.), Prodotti e Tecniche d'Oltremare nelle Economie Europee Secc. XIII–XVIII, Prato 1998, pp. 145–174

WHATLEY, C. A., 'That Important and Necessary Article'. The Salt Industry and its Trade in Fife and Tayside c1570–1850, Dundee 1984

———, Sales of Scottish Marine Salt c.1714–1823, in: Scottish Economic and Social History, VI (1986), pp. 4–17

———, The Scottish Salt Industry 1570–1850. An Economic and Social History, Aberdeen 1987

———, Salt, Coal and the Union of 1707: A Revision Article, in: Scottish Historical Review, LXVI, 1, Nr. 181 (1987), pp. 26–45

———, SWINFEN, D. / SMITH, A. M., The Life and Times of Dundee, Edinburgh 1993

———, Bought and Sold for English Gold? Explaining the Union 1707, East Linton, 2nd ed. 2001

——— (with D. PATRICK), The Scots and the Union, Edinburgh 2006

WHYTE, I. D., The Function and Social Structure of Scottish Burghs of Barony in the Seventeenth and Eighteenth Centuries, in: A. MĄCZAK / (T.) C. SMOUT (eds.), Gründung und Bedeutung kleinerer Städte im nördlichen Europa der frühen Neuzeit, Wiesbaden 1991, pp. 11–30

———, 'All Kynds of Graine': The Trade in Victual c. 1680–1825, in: G. JACKSON / S. G. E. LYTHE (eds.), The Port of Montrose: A History of its Harbour, Trade and Shipping, Tayport 1993, pp. 115–124

———, Scotland before the Industrial Revolution. An Economic and Social History c1050 – c1750, London / New York 1995

———, Scotland's Society and Economy in Transition, c.1500–c.1760, Basingstoke / London / New York 1997

WIESE, H. / BÖLTS, J., Rinderhandel und Rinderhaltung im nordwesteuropäischen Küstengebiet vom 15. bis zum 19. Jahrhundert, Stuttgart 1966

WIESE, H., Der Rinderhandel im nordwesteuropäischen Küstengebiet vom 15. Jahrhundert bis zum Beginn des 19. Jahrhunderts, in: ID. / J. BÖLTS, Rinderhandel und Rinderhaltung im nordwesteuropäischen Küstengebiet vom 15. bis zum 19. Jahrhundert, Stuttgart 1966, pp. 1–132

WILSON, C., Trade and Trade Balances: The Mercantilist Problem, in: Economic History Review, Second Series, II (1949), pp. 152–161

———, Treasure and Trade Balances: Further Evidence, in: Economic History Review, Second Series, IV (1951), pp. 231–242

———, England's Apprenticeship 1603–1763, London 1965

WISKEMANN, E., Hamburg und die Welthandelspolitik von den Anfängen bis zur Gegenwart, Hamburg 1929

WITTHÖFT, H., Struktur und Kapazität der Lüneburger Saline seit dem 12. Jahrhundert, Wiesbaden 1976

VON WITZENDORF, H.-J., Beiträge zur Bremischen Handelsgeschichte in der zweiten Hälfte des 18. Jahrhunderts, in: Bremisches Jahrbuch, XLIII (1951), pp. 342–394

———, Bremens Handel im 16. und 17. Jahrhundert, in: Bremisches Jahrbuch, XLIV (1955), pp. 128–174

WOPFNER, H. (ed.), Acta Tirolensia. Urkundliche Quellen zur Geschichte Tirols, Vol. 3. Quellen zur Geschichte des Bauernkriegs in Deutschtirol 1525, Pt. I, Innsbruck 1908

WUNDER, H., Agriculture and Agrarian Society, in: S. OGILVIE (ed.), Germany. A New Social and Economic History, Vol. II: 1630–1800, London / New York 1996, pp. 63–99

ZAHEDIEH, N., London and the Colonial Consumer in the Late Seventeenth Century, in: Economic History Review, Second Series, XLVII, 2 (1994), pp. 239–261

———, Overseas Expansion and Trade in the Seventeenth Century, in: N. CANNY (ed.), The Oxford History of the British Empire, Vol. I: The Origins of Empire. British Overseas Enterprise to the Close of the Seventeenth Century, Oxford 1998, pp. 398–421

ZICKERMANN, K., 'Briteannia ist mein patria'. Scotsmen and the 'British' Community in Hamburg, in: A. GROSJEAN / S. MURDOCH (eds.), Scottish Communities Abroad in the Early Modern Period, Leiden / Boston 2005, pp. 249–273

ZOELLNER, K.-P., Vom Strelasund zum Oslofjord. Untersuchungen zur Geschichte der Hanse und der Stadt Stralsund in der zweiten Hälfte des 16. Jahrhunderts, Weimar 1974

ZORN, W., Gewerbe und Handel, 1648–1800, in: H. AUBIN / W. ZORN (eds.), Handbuch der Deutschen Wirtschafts- und Sozialgeschichte, Vol. 1: Von der Frühzeit bis zum Ende des 18. Jahrhunderts, Stuttgart 1971, pp. 531–573

ZUPKO, R. E., The Weights and Measures of Scotland before the Union, in: Scottish Historical Review, LVI, 2, Nr. 162 (1977), pp. 119–145

———, A Dictionary of Weights and Measures for the British Isles: The Middle Ages to the Twentieth Century, Philadelphia 1985

GÖTTINGER BEITRÄGE ZUR WIRTSCHAFTS- UND SOZIALGESCHICHTE

Begründet von **Wilhelm Abel** und **Karl Heinrich Kaufhold**
Herausgegeben von **Karl Heinrich Kaufhold**

1. **Wilhelm Abel,** Hrsg.: Handwerksgeschichte in neuer Sicht. 1978. VIII, 284 S., kt. *7274-8*
2. **Karl Heinrich Kaufhold:** Das Gewerbe in Preußen um 1800. 1978. XIII, 557 S. m. 19 Abb. u. 37 Tab., kt. *7275-6*
3. **Jörg Jeschke:** Gewerberecht und Handwerkswirtschaft des Königreichs Hannover im Übergang 1815–1866. Eine Quellenstudie. 1977. VIII, 530 S., kt. *7276-4*
4. **Thomas Fischer:** Städtische Armut und Armenfürsorge im 15. und 16. Jahrhundert. Sozialgeschichtliche Untersuchungen am Beispiel der Städte Basel, Freiburg i. Br. und Straßburg. 1979. 349 S., kt. *7277-2*
5. **Karl Heinrich Kaufhold:** Das Handwerk der Stadt Hildesheim im 18. Jahrhundert. Eine wirtschaftsgeschichtliche Studie. 2., überarbeitete Auflage 1980. XIII, 313 S. m. 11 Abb. u. 40 Tab., kt. *7278-0*
6. **Wieland Sachse:** Bibliographie zur preußischen Gewerbestatistik 1750–1850. 1981. VII, 392 S., kt. *7279-9*
7. **Hans-Jürgen Gerhard,** Hrsg.: Löhne im vor- und frühindustriellen Deutschland. Materialien zur Entwicklung von Lohnsätzen von der Mitte des 18. bis zur Mitte des 19. Jahrhunderts. 1984. VIII, 631 S., kt. *7280-2*
8. **John Breuilly / Wieland Sachse:** Joachim Friedrich Martens (1806–1877) und die Deutsche Ar-beiterbewegung. 1984. XV, 489 S. m. 12 Tabellen und 13 Abb. auf Kunstdrucktaf., kt. *7281-0*
9. **Rainer S. Elkar,** Hrsg.: Deutsches Handwerk in Spätmittelalter und Früher Neuzeit. Sozialgeschichte – Volkskunde – Literaturgeschichte. 1983. VIII, 328 S., kt. *7282-9*
10. **Bernd Habicht:** Stadt- und Landhandwerk im südlichen Niedersachsen im 18. Jahrhundert. Ein Wirtschaftsgeschichtlicher Beitrag unter Berücksichtigung von Bedingungen des Zugangs zum Markt. 1983. XIV, 312 S. m. 15 Abb. u. 50 Tab., kt. *7283-7*
11. **Karl Heinrich Kaufhold / Friedrich Riemann,** Hrsg.: Theorie und Empirie in Wirtschaftspolitik und Wirtschaftsgeschichte. Festschrift für **Wilhelm Abel** zum 80. Geburtstag (vergriffen)
12. **Arno Herzig / Rainer Sachs:** Der Breslauer Gesellenaufstand von 1793. Die Aufzeichnungen des Schneidermeisters Johann Gottlieb Klose. Darstellung und Dokumentation. 1987. X, 214 S. u. 8 Abb. auf Kunstdrucktaf., kt. *7284-7*
13. **Uwe Puschner:** Handwerk zwischen Tradition und Wandel. Das Münchener Handwerk an der Wende vom 18. zum 19. Jahrhundert. 1988. X, 417 S., kt. *7285-4*
14. **Reinhold Reith:** Arbeits- und Lebensweise im städtischen Handwerk. Zur Sozialgeschichte Augsburger Handwerksgesellen im 18. Jahrhundert. 1988. XII, 305 S., kt. *7286-1*
15. **Hans-Jürgen Gerhard / Karl Heinrich Kaufhold,** Hrsg.: Preise im vor- und frühindustriellen Deutschland. [1.] Grundnahrungsmittel. 1990. X, 417 S., kt. *7287-8*
16. **Margrit Schulte Beerbühl:** Vom Gesellenverein zur Gewerkschaft. Entwicklung, Struktur und Politik der Londoner Gesellenorganisation 1550–1825. 1991. VIII, 529 S., kt. *7288-5*
17. **Reinhold Reith / Andreas Grießinger / Petra Eggers:** Streikbewegungen deutscher Handwerksgesellen im 18. Jahrhundert. Materialien zur Sozial- und Wirtschaftsgeschichte des städtischen Handwerks 1700–1806. 1992. IX, 464 S. m. 162 Tab. u. 2 Abb., kt. *7289-2*
18. **Stefan Kroll:** Stadtgesellschaft und Krieg. Sozialstruktur, Bevölkerung und Wirtschaft in Stralsund und Stade 1700 bis 1715. 1997. 549 S. m. 20 Abb. u. 40 Tab., kt. *7273-1*

19/20. **Hans-Jürgen Gerhard / Karl Heinrich Kaufhold,** Hrsg.: Preise im vor- und frühindustriellen Deutschland. 2. Nahrungsmittel – Getränke – Gewürze. 3. Rohstoffe und Gewerbeprodukte (Abschlußbd. zu Bd. 15). 2001. 543 S., geb. *7291-5*

21. **Ulrich Brohm:** Die Handwerkspolitik Herzog August des Jüngeren von Braunschweig-Wolfenbüttel (1635–1666). Zur Rolle von Fürstenstaat und Zünften im Wiederaufbau nach dem Dreißigjährigen Krieg. 1999. 380 S. m. 5 Abb., 32 Tab., kt. *7368-4*

STUDIEN ZUR GEWERBE- UND HANDELSGESCHICHTE DER VORINDUSTRIELLEN ZEIT

Begründet von **Wilhelm Abel** und **Karl Heinrich Kaufhold.**
Herausgegeben von **Karl Heinrich Kaufhold** und **Markus A. Denzel**

22. **Karl Heinrich Kaufhold / Markus A. Denzel,** Hrsg.: Der Handel im Kurfürstentum / Königreich Hannover (1780–1850). Gegenstand und Methode. 2000. 266 S. m. 45 Tab., 35 Graf., 1 Kte., kt. *7630-2*
23. **Jörg Rode:** Der Handel im Königreich Bayern um 1810. 2001. 268 S., kt. *7882-5*
24. **Markus A. Denzel,** Hrsg.: **Wirtschaft – Politik – Geschichte.** Beiträge zum Gedenkkolloquium anläßlich des 100. Geburtstages von **Wilhelm Abel** am 16. Oktober 2004 in Leipzig. 2004. 160 S. m. 6 Abb, 9 Übers., 5 Graph. *8633-2*
25. **Gerhard Deter:** Handwerk vor dem Untergang? Das westfälische Kleingewerbe im Spiegel der preußischen Gewerbetabellen 1816–1861. 2005. 160 S., kt. *8791-9*
26. **Hans-Jürgen Gerhard / Alexander Engel:** Preisgeschichte der vorindustriellen Zeit.Ein Kompendium auf Basis ausgewählter Hamburger Materialien. 2006. 358 S., kt. *8961-6*
27. **Christian M. Zachlod: Die Staatsfinanzen des Fürstbistums Hildesheim vom Ende des Siebenjährigen Krieges bis zur Säkularisation (1763–1802/03).** 2007. 311 S., kt. *8978-4*
28. **Philipp Robinson Rössner: Scottish Trade with German Ports 1700–1770.** A Sketch of the North Sea Trades and the Atlantic Economy on Ground Level. 2008. 236 S. m. 1 Abb., kt. *9215-9*

FRANZ STEINER VERLAG STUTTGART